Empowered™ and Sistah Spooky's High School Hell

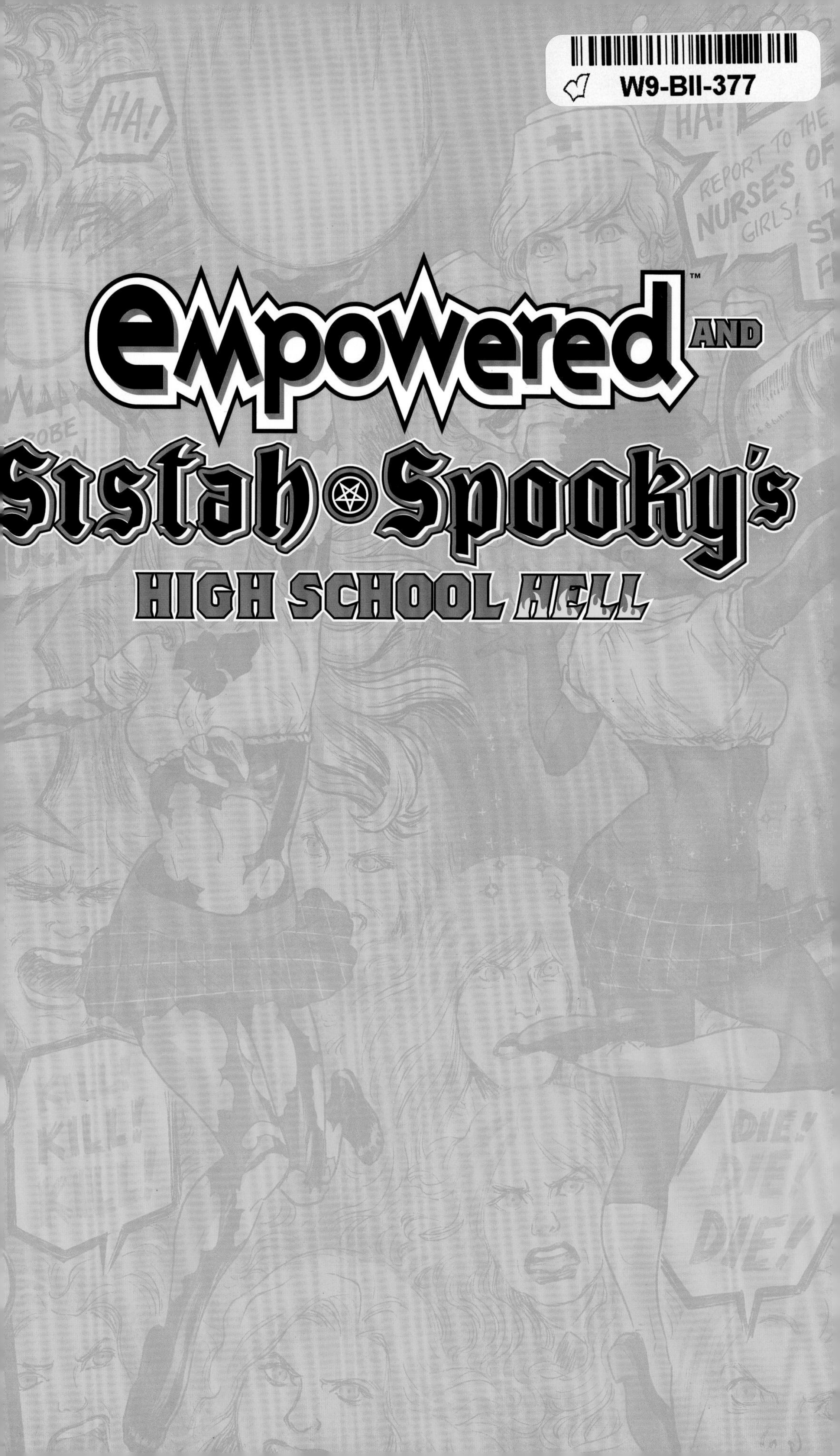
HA!
HA!
KILL!
DIE!

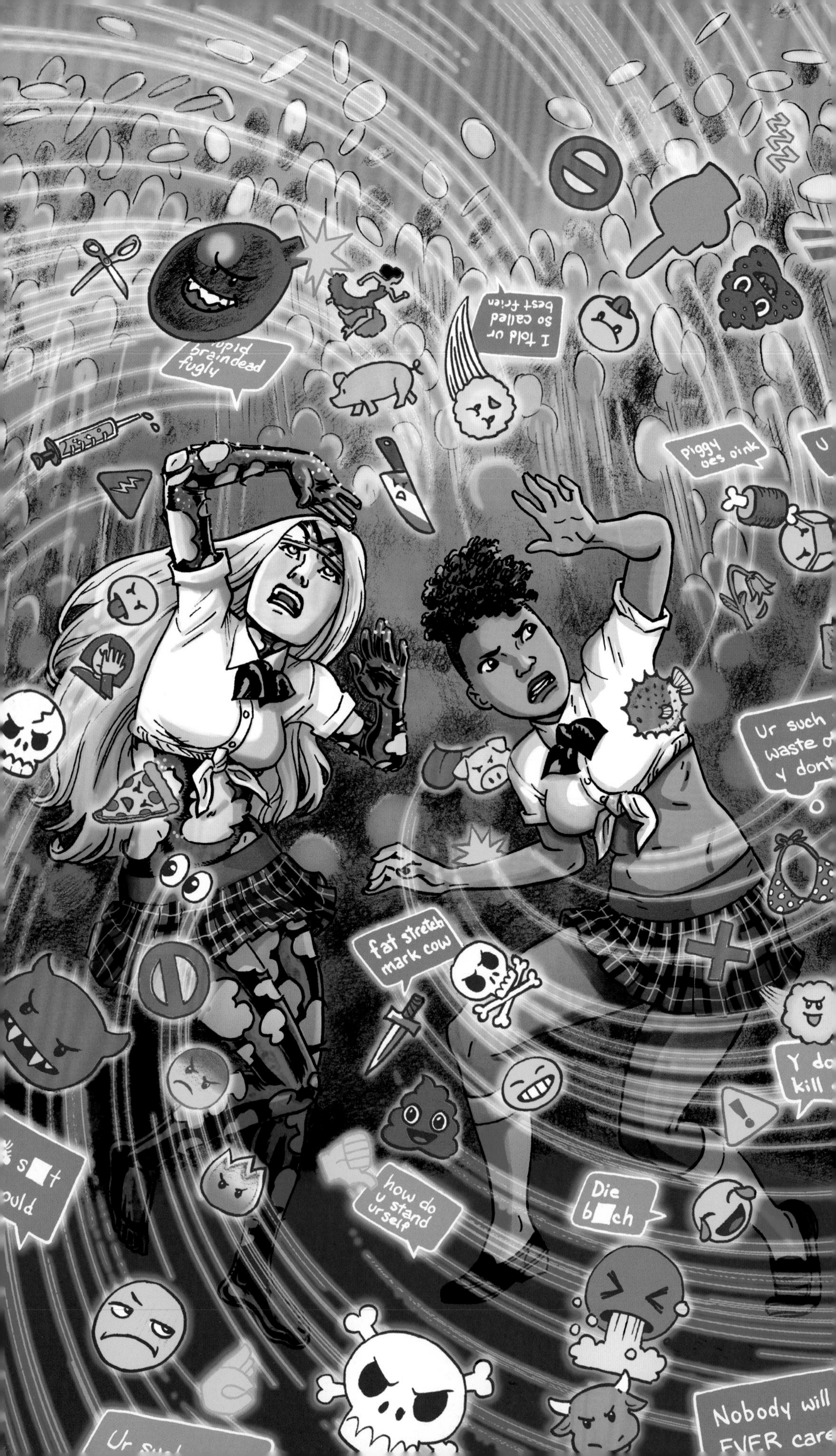
upid braindead fugly
I told ur so called best frien
piggy oes oink
Ur such waste o y dont
fat stretch mark cow
Y do kill
s[redacted]t ould
how do u stand urself
Die b[redacted]ch
Nobody will EVER care

EMPOWERED AND

Sistah Spooky's

HIGH SCHOOL HELL

STORY BY ADAM WARREN

(empoweredcomic.com   twitter.com/EmpoweredComic   instagram.com/adam_warren_art)

ART AND LETTERING BY CARLA "SPEED" McNEIL

(carlaspeedmcneil.com   twitter.com/cspeedmcneil)

COLORS BY JENN MANLEY LEE

(jennmanleylee.com   twitter.com/jemale)

EMPOWERED LOGO BY EUGENE WANG

DARK HORSE BOOKS

president and publisher
MIKE RICHARDSON

editor
CHRIS WARNER

assistant editors
KEVIN BURKHALTER and **JENNY BLENK**

designer
BRENNAN THOME and **ANITA MAGAÑA**

digital art and production
CHRIS HORN

EMPOWERED AND SISTAH SPOOKY'S HIGH SCHOOL HELL

This volume collects the Dark Horse comics *Empowered and Sistah Spooky's High School Hell* #1–#6.

Dark Horse Books
10956 SE Main Street, Milwaukie, OR 97222

DarkHorse.com

Library of Congress Cataloging-in-Publication Data

Names: Warren, Adam, 1967- author. | Piekos, Nate, letterer.
Title: Empowered and Sistah Spooky's high school hell / story by Adam Warren
 ; art and lettering by Carla Speed McNeil ; lettering by Nate Piekos of
 Blambot ; colors by Jenn Manley Lee.
Description: First edition. | Milwaukie, OR : Dark Horse Books, January 2019.
 | Series: Empowered | "This volume collects the Dark Horse comics
 Empowered and Sistah Spooky's High School Hell #1-#6."
Identifiers: LCCN 2018026108 | ISBN 9781506706610 (paperback)
Subjects: | BISAC: COMICS & GRAPHIC NOVELS / Superheroes.
Classification: LCC PN6727.W29 E546 2018 | DDC 741.5/973--dc23
LC record available at https://lccn.loc.gov/2018026108

Comic Shop Locator Service: comicshoplocator.com

First edition: January 2019
ISBN 978-1-50670-661-0
Digital ISBN 978-1-50670-684-9

10 9 8 7 6 5 4 3 2 1

Printed in China

NEIL HANKERSON Executive Vice President • TOM WEDDLE Chief Financial Officer • RANDY STRADLEY Vice President of Publishing • NICK McWHORTER Chief Business Development Officer • MATT PARKINSON Vice President of Marketing • DALE LaFOUNTAIN Vice President of Information Technology • CARA NIECE Vice President of Production and Scheduling • MARK BERNARDI Vice President of Book Trade and Digital Sales • KEN LIZZI General Counsel • DAVE MARSHALL Editor in Chief • DAVEY ESTRADA Editorial Director • CHRIS WARNER Senior Books Editor • CARY GRAZZINI Director of Specialty Projects • LIA RIBACCHI Art Director • VANESSA TODD-HOLMES Director of Print Purchasing • MATT DRYER Director of Digital Art and Prepress • MICHAEL GOMBOS Director of International Publishing and Licensing • KARI YADRO Director of Custom Programs

EMPOWERED™

(an arguably superfluous recap)

UM, **HI**...! ♡

I'M **EMPOWERED**, A STRUGGLING-ISH SUPERHEROINE WHO USED TO BE **PICKED ON MERCILESSLY** BY MY SO-CALLED TEAMMATES...SUCH AS, UM, **HER.**

BUT NOW WE GOT AN **UNEASY RAPPROCHEMENT** DEALIE GOING ON, OKAY?

AND I'M **SISTAH SPOOKY,** THE SUPERPOWERED SORCERESS WHO USED TO **BULLY THE F** OUT OF EMP, BACK IN THE TIME BEFORE **MY WHOLE LIFE FELL APART.**

AND, WELL, TRAGI-COMEDY ENSUED.

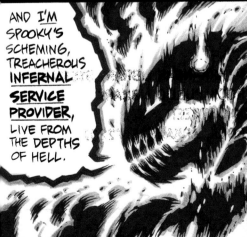

AND **I'M** SPOOKY'S SCHEMING, TREACHEROUS **INFERNAL SERVICE PROVIDER,** LIVE FROM THE DEPTHS OF HELL.

AND **I'M** (OKAY, **WAS**) THE TELEPATH **MINDF▨K,** SPOOKY'S TRAGICALLY **DECEASED EX-LOVER.**

(NOTE THAT I WAS **BLONDE,** BY THE WAY.)

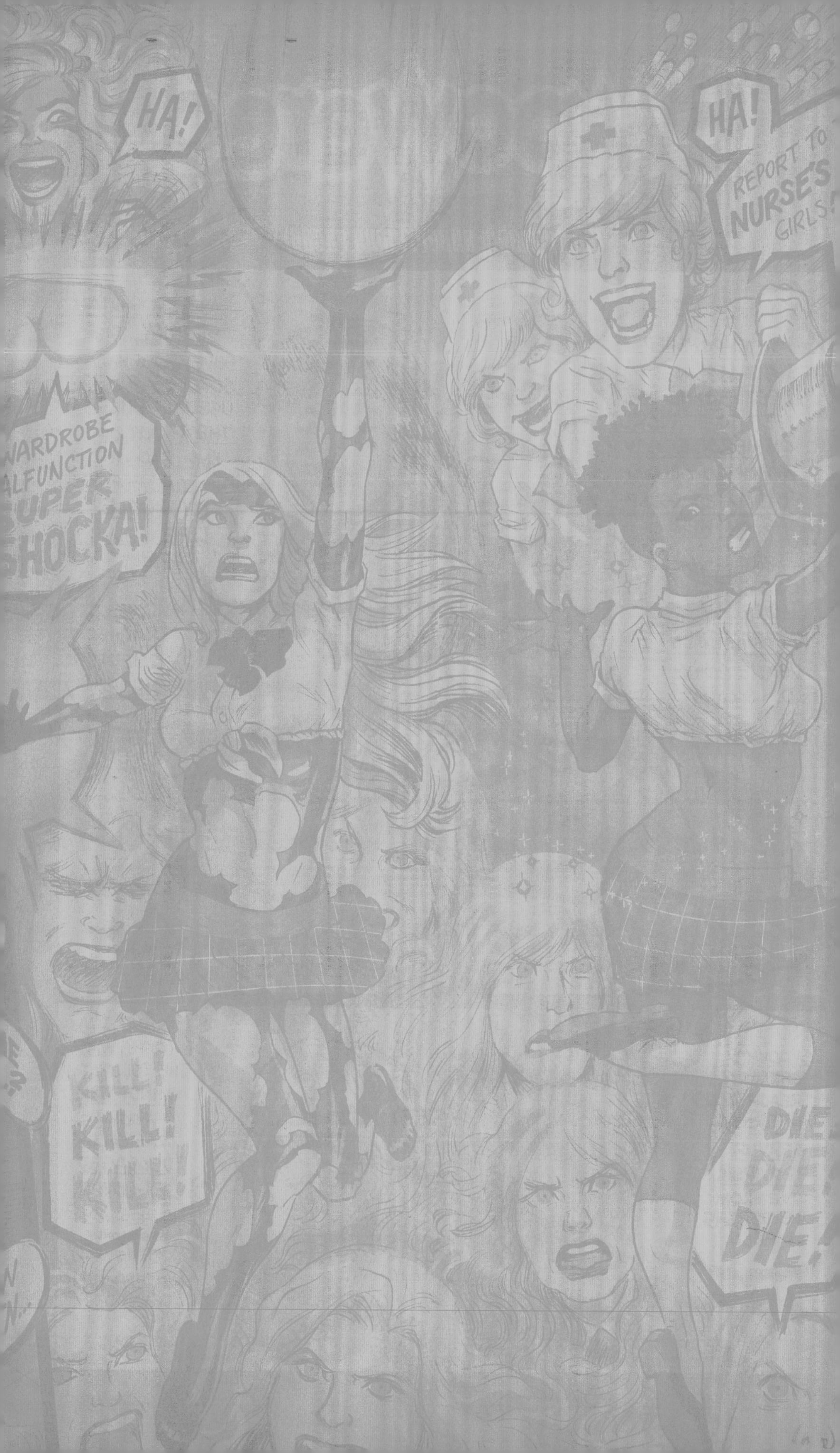

HA!
HA!
REPORT TO NURSE'S GIRLS!
WARDROBE ALFUNCTION UPER SHOCKA!
KILL! KILL! KILL!
DIE! DIE! DIE!

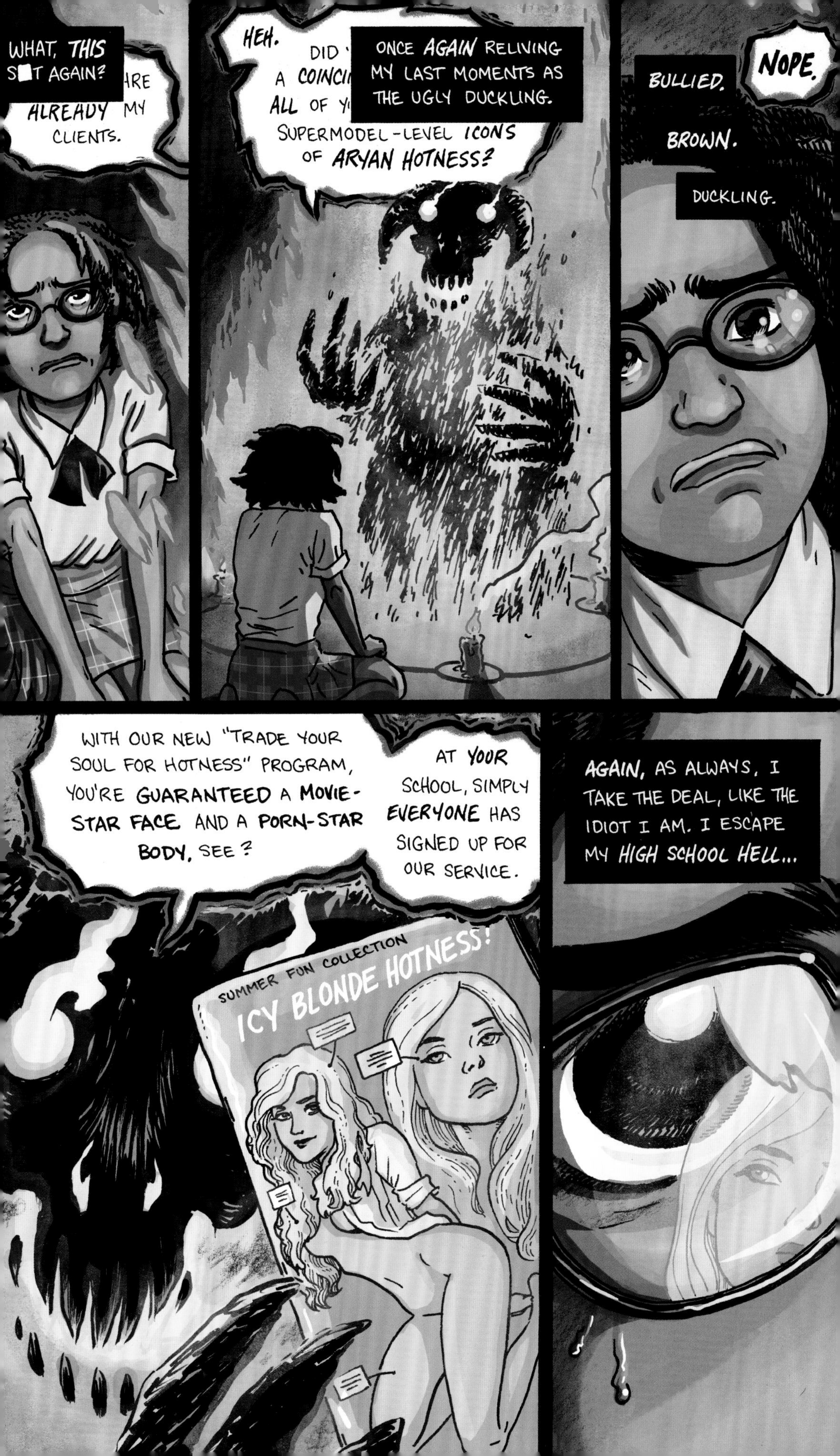
WHAT, THIS S█T AGAIN?
HRE
ALREADY MY
CLIENTS.
HEH.
DID
A COINCI
ALL OF Y
SUPERMODEL-LEVEL ICONS
OF ARYAN HOTNESS?
ONCE AGAIN RELIVING MY LAST MOMENTS AS THE UGLY DUCKLING.
NOPE.
BULLIED.
BROWN.
DUCKLING.
WITH OUR NEW "TRADE YOUR SOUL FOR HOTNESS" PROGRAM, YOU'RE GUARANTEED A MOVIE-STAR FACE AND A PORN-STAR BODY, SEE?
AT YOUR SCHOOL, SIMPLY EVERYONE HAS SIGNED UP FOR OUR SERVICE.
SUMMER FUN COLLECTION
ICY BLONDE HOTNESS!
AGAIN, AS ALWAYS, I TAKE THE DEAL, LIKE THE IDIOT I AM. I ESCAPE MY HIGH SCHOOL HELL...

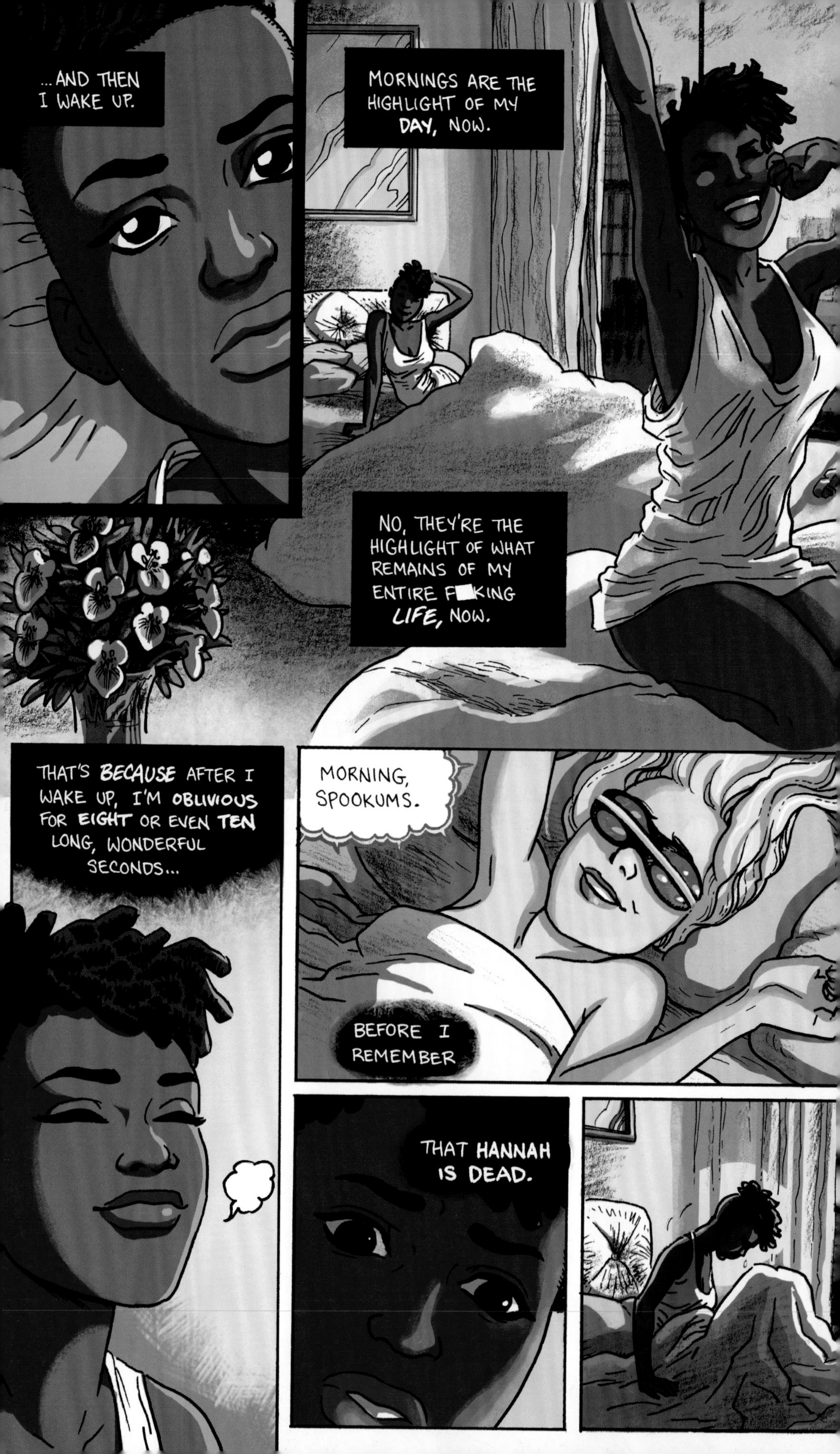
...AND THEN I WAKE UP.
MORNINGS ARE THE HIGHLIGHT OF MY **DAY,** NOW.
NO, THEY'RE THE HIGHLIGHT OF WHAT REMAINS OF MY ENTIRE F■KING ***LIFE,*** NOW.
THAT'S **BECAUSE** AFTER I WAKE UP, I'M **OBLIVIOUS** FOR **EIGHT** OR EVEN **TEN** LONG, WONDERFUL SECONDS...
MORNING, SPOOKUMS.
BEFORE I REMEMBER
THAT **HANNAH** IS **DEAD.**

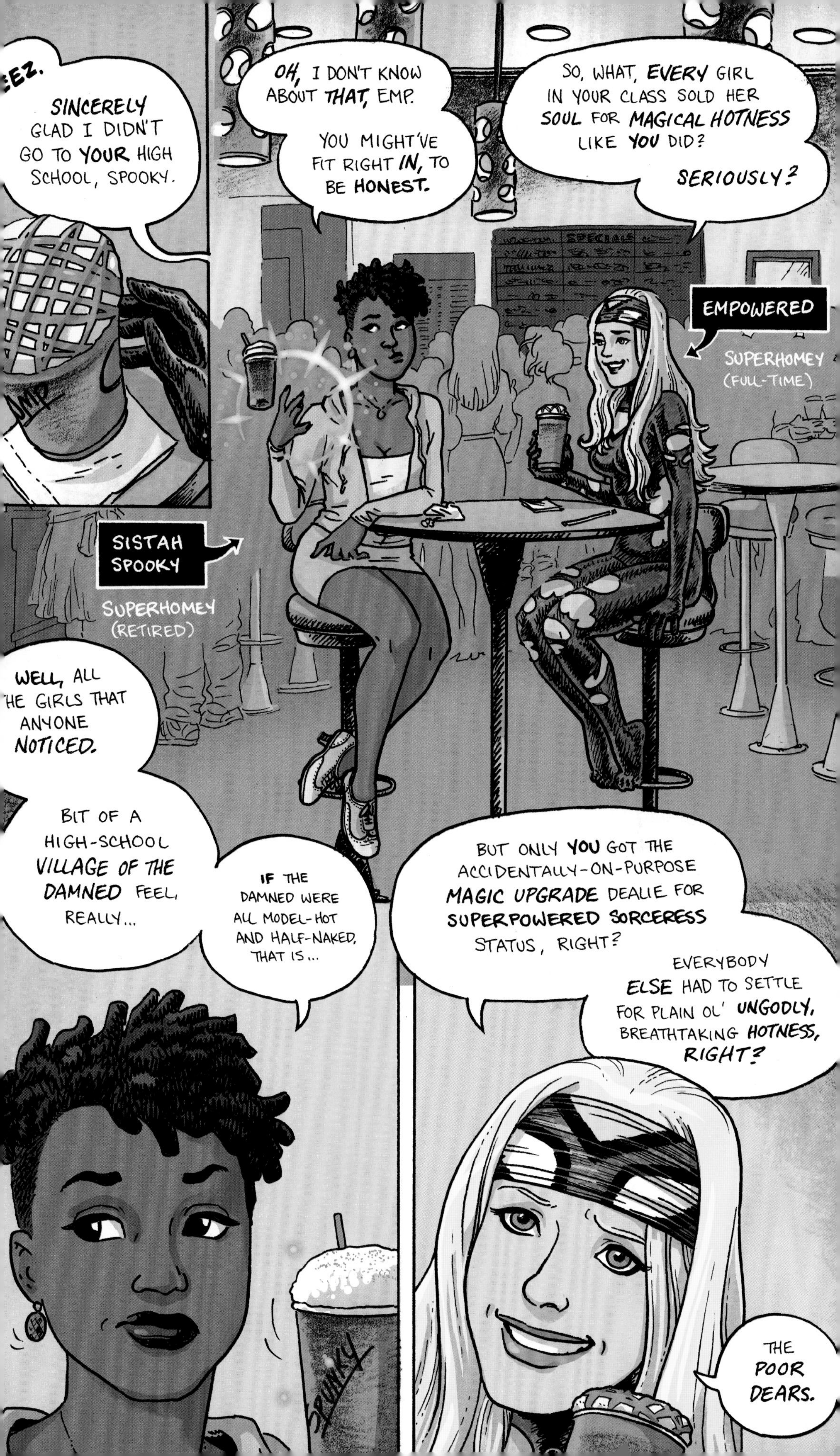
EEZ.
SINCERELY GLAD I DIDN'T GO TO YOUR HIGH SCHOOL, SPOOKY.
OH, I DON'T KNOW ABOUT THAT, EMP. YOU MIGHT'VE FIT RIGHT IN, TO BE HONEST.
SO, WHAT, EVERY GIRL IN YOUR CLASS SOLD HER SOUL FOR MAGICAL HOTNESS LIKE YOU DID? SERIOUSLY?
SPECIALS
EMPOWERED
SUPERHOMEY (FULL-TIME)
SISTAH SPOOKY
SUPERHOMEY (RETIRED)
WELL, ALL THE GIRLS THAT ANYONE NOTICED.
BIT OF A HIGH-SCHOOL VILLAGE OF THE DAMNED FEEL, REALLY...
IF THE DAMNED WERE ALL MODEL-HOT AND HALF-NAKED, THAT IS...
BUT ONLY YOU GOT THE ACCIDENTALLY-ON-PURPOSE MAGIC UPGRADE DEALIE FOR SUPERPOWERED SORCERESS STATUS, RIGHT?
EVERYBODY ELSE HAD TO SETTLE FOR PLAIN OL' UNGODLY, BREATHTAKING HOTNESS, RIGHT?
SPOOKY
THE POOR DEARS.

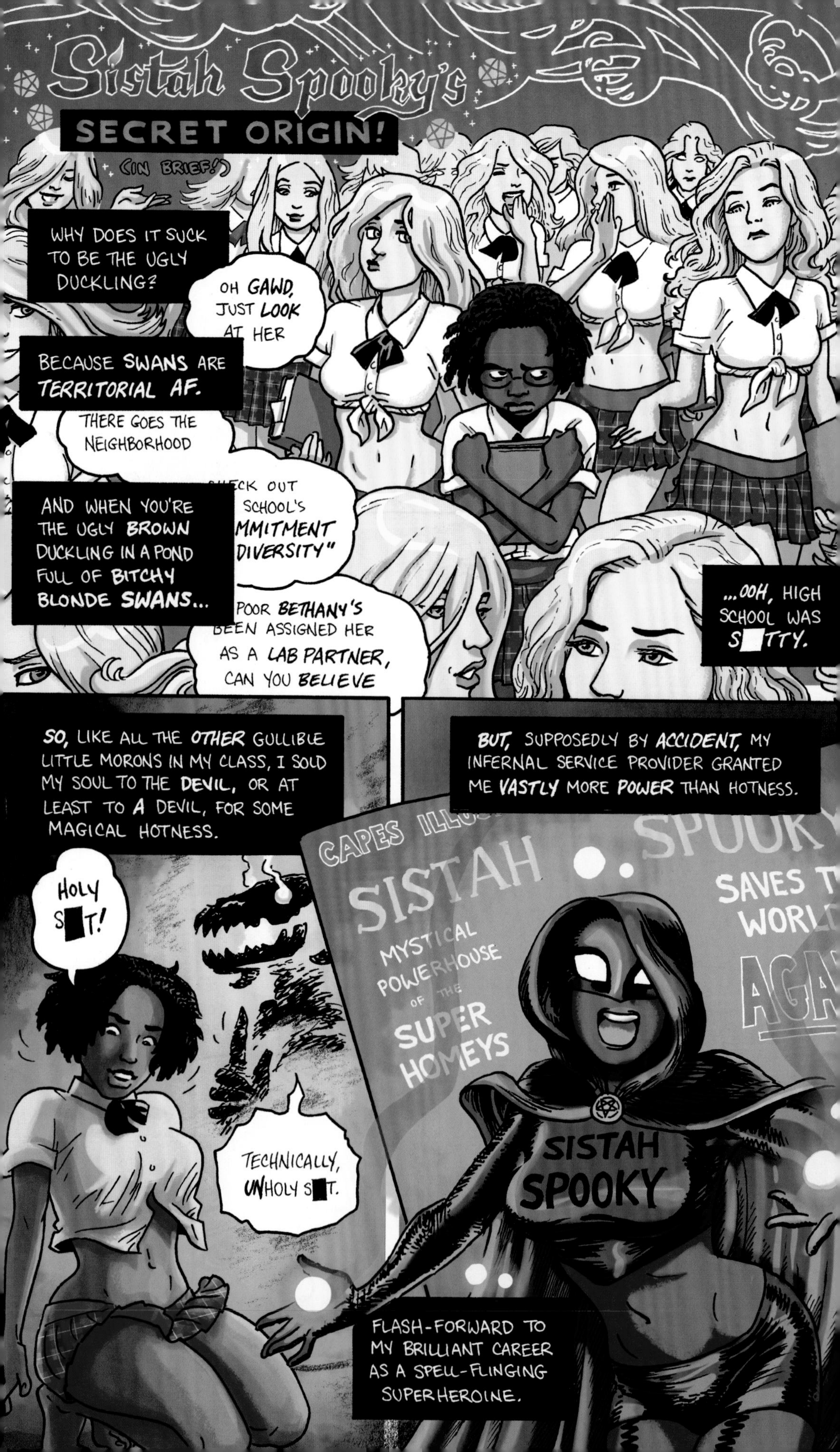
Sistah Spooky's
SECRET ORIGIN!
(IN BRIEF!)
WHY DOES IT SUCK TO BE THE UGLY DUCKLING?
OH GAWD, JUST LOOK AT HER
BECAUSE SWANS ARE TERRITORIAL AF.
THERE GOES THE NEIGHBORHOOD
SCHOOL'S
DIVERSITY"
AND WHEN YOU'RE THE UGLY BROWN DUCKLING IN A POND FULL OF BITCHY BLONDE SWANS...
POOR BETHANY'S BEEN ASSIGNED HER AS A LAB PARTNER, CAN YOU BELIEVE
...OOH, HIGH SCHOOL WAS S[redacted]TTY.
SO, LIKE ALL THE OTHER GULLIBLE LITTLE MORONS IN MY CLASS, I SOLD MY SOUL TO THE DEVIL, OR AT LEAST TO A DEVIL, FOR SOME MAGICAL HOTNESS.
HOLY S[redacted]T!
TECHNICALLY, UNHOLY S[redacted]T.
BUT, SUPPOSEDLY BY ACCIDENT, MY INFERNAL SERVICE PROVIDER GRANTED ME VASTLY MORE POWER THAN HOTNESS.
SISTAH
MYSTICAL POWERHOUSE OF THE SUPER HOMEYS
SISTAH SPOOKY
FLASH-FORWARD TO MY BRILLIANT CAREER AS A SPELL-FLINGING SUPERHEROINE.

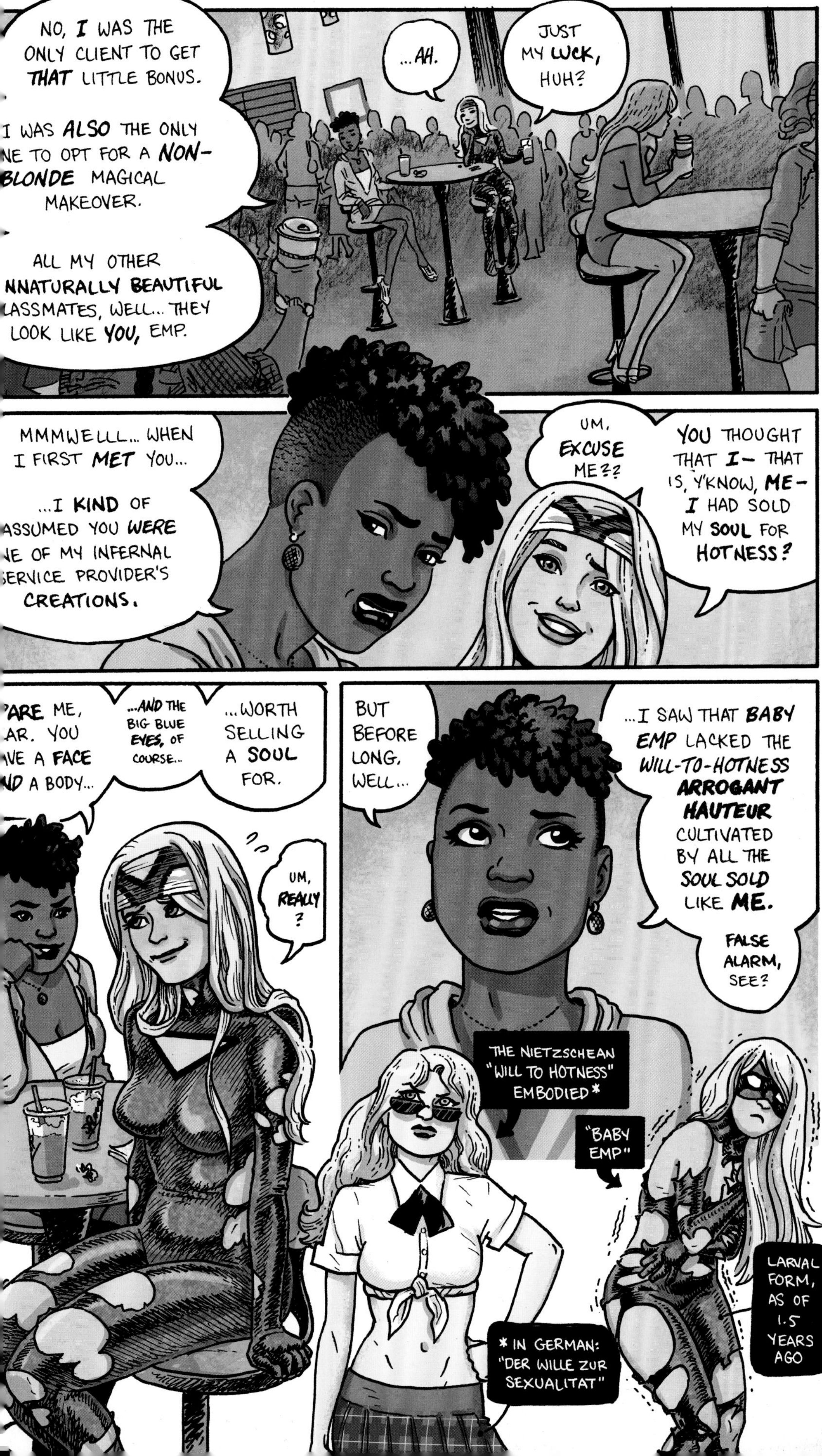
NO, I WAS THE ONLY CLIENT TO GET THAT LITTLE BONUS.
I WAS ALSO THE ONLY NE TO OPT FOR A NON-BLONDE MAGICAL MAKEOVER.
ALL MY OTHER NNATURALLY BEAUTIFUL LASSMATES, WELL... THEY LOOK LIKE YOU, EMP.
...AH.
JUST MY LUCK, HUH?
MMMWELLL... WHEN I FIRST MET YOU...
...I KIND OF ASSUMED YOU WERE NE OF MY INFERNAL SERVICE PROVIDER'S CREATIONS.
UM, EXCUSE ME??
YOU THOUGHT THAT I— THAT IS, Y'KNOW, ME— I HAD SOLD MY SOUL FOR HOTNESS?
PARE ME, AR. YOU VE A FACE ND A BODY...
...AND THE BIG BLUE EYES, OF COURSE...
...WORTH SELLING A SOUL FOR.
UM, REALLY?
BUT BEFORE LONG, WELL...
...I SAW THAT BABY EMP LACKED THE WILL-TO-HOTNESS ARROGANT HAUTEUR CULTIVATED BY ALL THE SOUL SOLD LIKE ME.
FALSE ALARM, SEE?
THE NIETZSCHEAN "WILL TO HOTNESS" EMBODIED*
"BABY EMP"
LARVAL FORM, AS OF 1.5 YEARS AGO
* IN GERMAN: "DER WILLE ZUR SEXUALITAT"

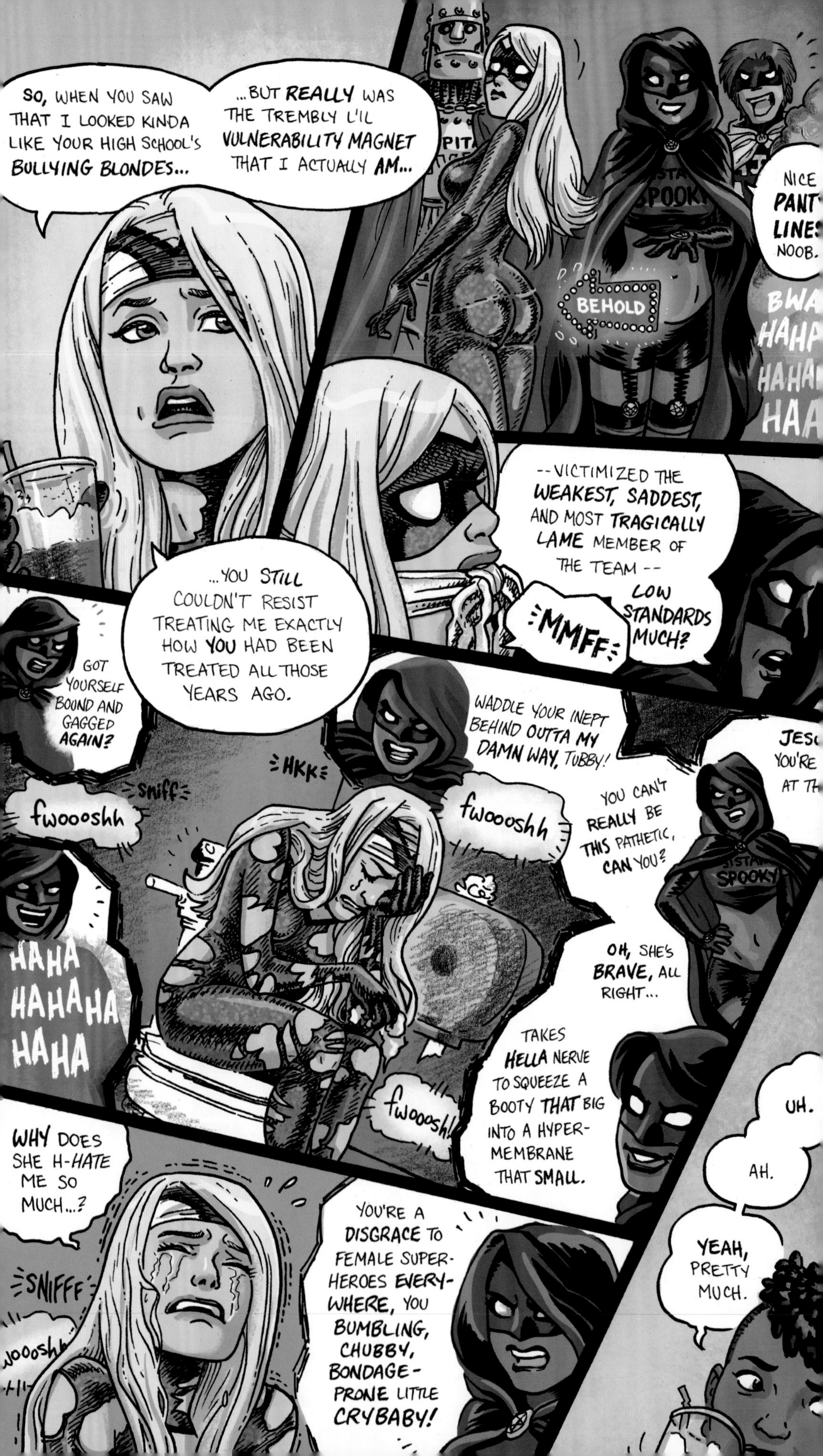
SO, WHEN YOU SAW THAT I LOOKED KINDA LIKE YOUR HIGH SCHOOL'S BULLYING BLONDES...
...BUT REALLY WAS THE TREMBLY L'IL VULNERABILITY MAGNET THAT I ACTUALLY AM...
BEHOLD
NICE PANT LINES NOOB.
BWA HAHA HAHA HAA
--VICTIMIZED THE WEAKEST, SADDEST, AND MOST TRAGICALLY LAME MEMBER OF THE TEAM--
LOW STANDARDS MUCH?
MMFF
...YOU STILL COULDN'T RESIST TREATING ME EXACTLY HOW YOU HAD BEEN TREATED ALL THOSE YEARS AGO.
GOT YOURSELF BOUND AND GAGGED AGAIN?
WADDLE YOUR INEPT BEHIND OUTTA MY DAMN WAY, TUBBY!
HKK
SNIFF
fwoooshh
fwoooshh
YOU CAN'T REALLY BE THIS PATHETIC, CAN YOU?
HAHA HAHAHA HAHA
OH, SHE'S BRAVE, ALL RIGHT...
TAKES HELLA NERVE TO SQUEEZE A BOOTY THAT BIG INTO A HYPER-MEMBRANE THAT SMALL.
fwooosh
WHY DOES SHE H-HATE ME SO MUCH...?
SNIFFF
YOU'RE A DISGRACE TO FEMALE SUPER-HEROES EVERY-WHERE, YOU BUMBLING, CHUBBY, BONDAGE-PRONE LITTLE CRYBABY!
UH.
AH.
YEAH, PRETTY MUCH.

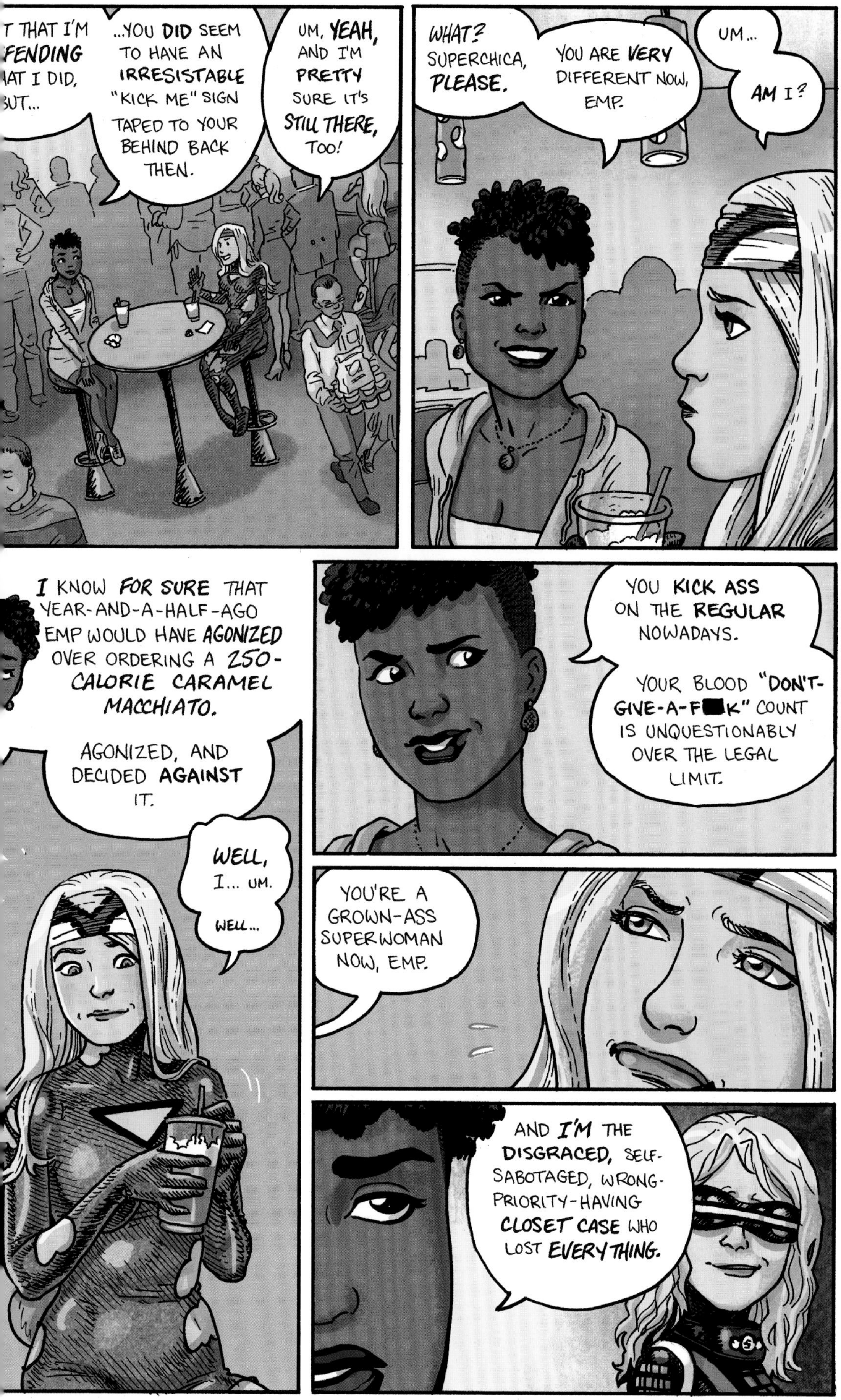
T THAT I'M FENDING IAT I DID, BUT...
...YOU DID SEEM TO HAVE AN IRRESISTABLE "KICK ME" SIGN TAPED TO YOUR BEHIND BACK THEN.
UM, YEAH, AND I'M PRETTY SURE IT'S STILL THERE, TOO!
WHAT? SUPERCHICA, PLEASE.
YOU ARE VERY DIFFERENT NOW, EMP.
UM...
AM I?
I KNOW FOR SURE THAT YEAR-AND-A-HALF-AGO EMP WOULD HAVE AGONIZED OVER ORDERING A 250-CALORIE CARAMEL MACCHIATO.
AGONIZED, AND DECIDED AGAINST IT.
WELL, I... UM.
WELL...
YOU KICK ASS ON THE REGULAR NOWADAYS.
YOUR BLOOD "DON'T-GIVE-A-F[redacted]K" COUNT IS UNQUESTIONABLY OVER THE LEGAL LIMIT.
YOU'RE A GROWN-ASS SUPERWOMAN NOW, EMP.
AND I'M THE DISGRACED, SELF-SABOTAGED, WRONG-PRIORITY-HAVING CLOSET CASE WHO LOST EVERYTHING.

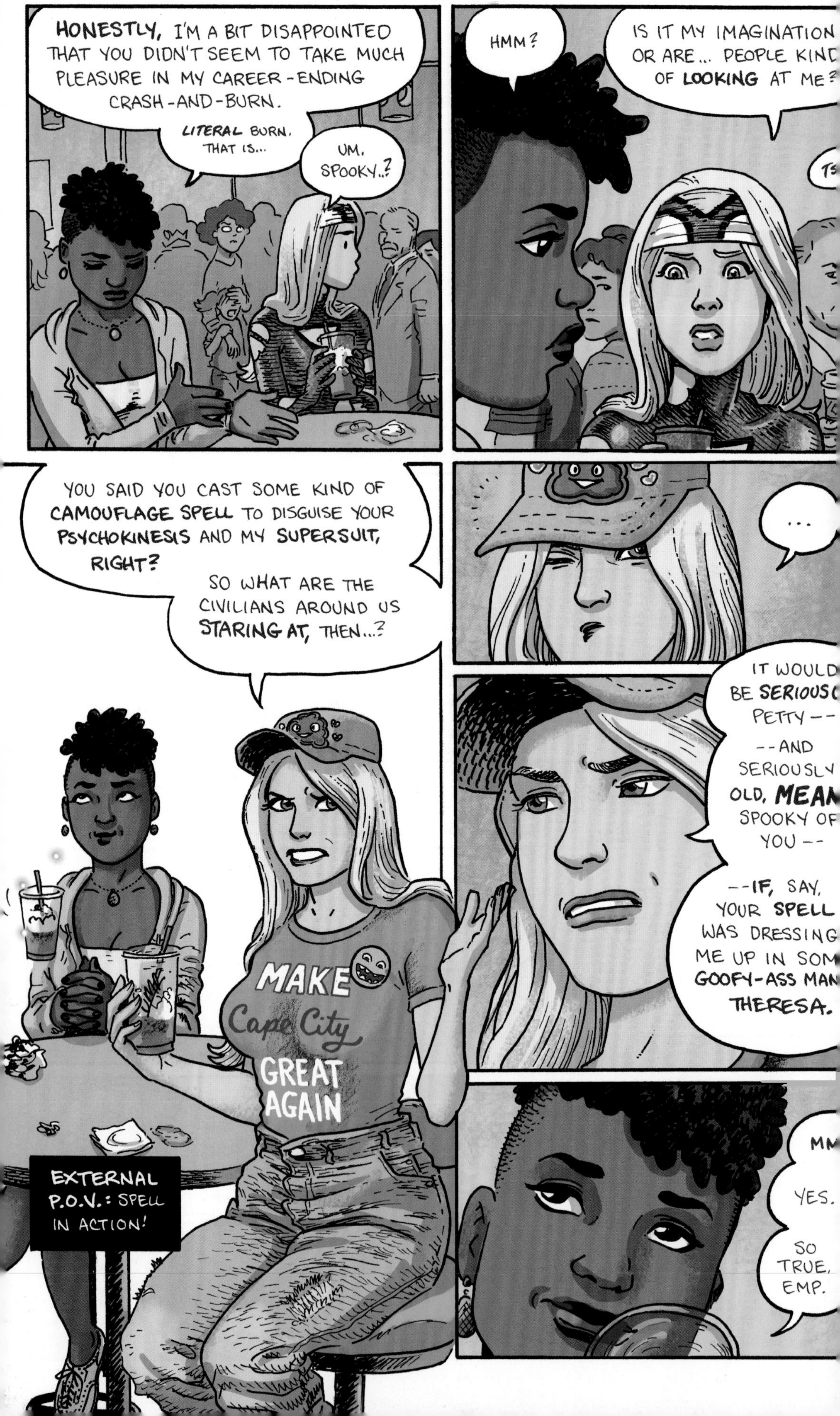
HONESTLY, I'M A BIT DISAPPOINTED THAT YOU DIDN'T SEEM TO TAKE MUCH PLEASURE IN MY CAREER-ENDING CRASH-AND-BURN.
LITERAL BURN. THAT IS...
UM. SPOOKY..?
HMM?
IS IT MY IMAGINATION OR ARE... PEOPLE KIND OF LOOKING AT ME?
YOU SAID YOU CAST SOME KIND OF CAMOUFLAGE SPELL TO DISGUISE YOUR PSYCHOKINESIS AND MY SUPERSUIT, RIGHT?
SO WHAT ARE THE CIVILIANS AROUND US STARING AT, THEN...?
MAKE Cape City GREAT AGAIN
EXTERNAL P.O.V.: SPELL IN ACTION!
...
IT WOULD BE SERIOUS PETTY --
-- AND SERIOUSLY OLD, MEAN SPOOKY OF YOU --
--IF, SAY, YOUR SPELL WAS DRESSING ME UP IN SOM GOOFY-ASS MAN THERESA.
YES.
SO TRUE, EMP.

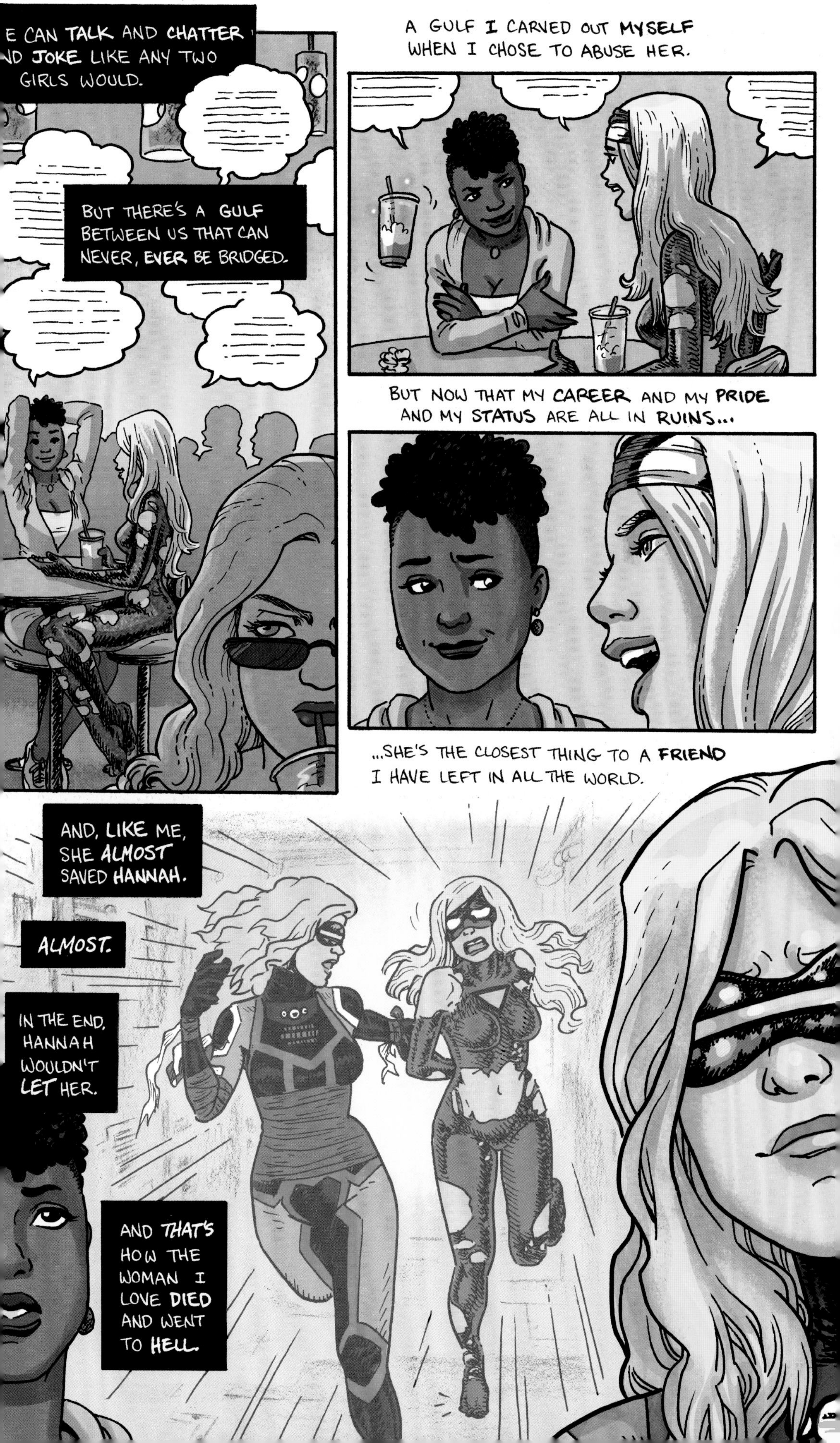
E CAN TALK AND CHATTER
ND JOKE LIKE ANY TWO GIRLS WOULD.
BUT THERE'S A GULF BETWEEN US THAT CAN NEVER, EVER BE BRIDGED.
A GULF I CARVED OUT MYSELF WHEN I CHOSE TO ABUSE HER.
BUT NOW THAT MY CAREER AND MY PRIDE AND MY STATUS ARE ALL IN RUINS...
...SHE'S THE CLOSEST THING TO A FRIEND I HAVE LEFT IN ALL THE WORLD.
AND, LIKE ME, SHE ALMOST SAVED HANNAH.
ALMOST.
IN THE END, HANNAH WOULDN'T LET HER.
AND THAT'S HOW THE WOMAN I LOVE DIED AND WENT TO HELL.

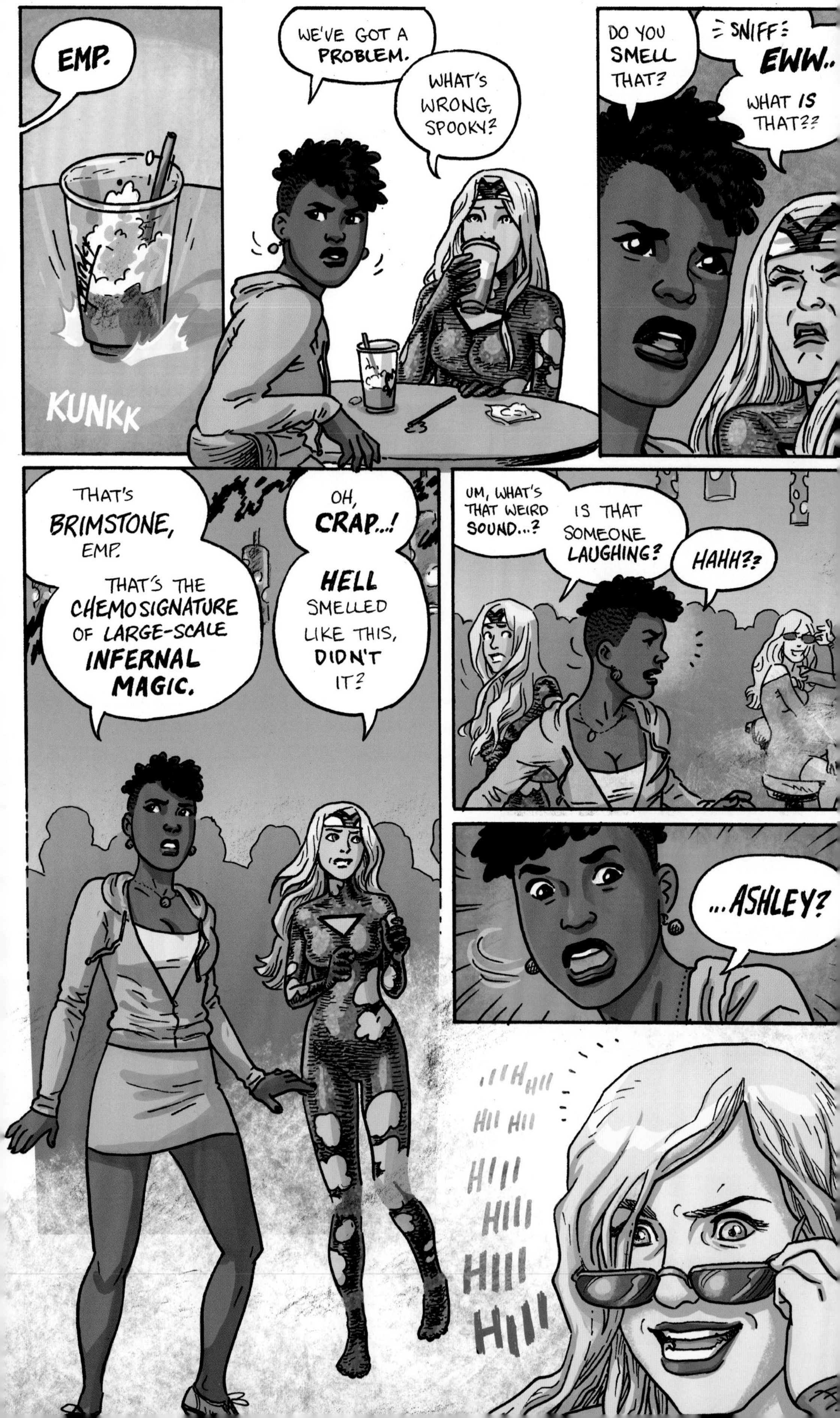
EMP.
KUNKK
WE'VE GOT A PROBLEM.
WHAT'S WRONG, SPOOKY?
DO YOU SMELL THAT?
SNIFF
EWW..
WHAT IS THAT??
THAT'S BRIMSTONE, EMP.
THAT'S THE CHEMOSIGNATURE OF LARGE-SCALE INFERNAL MAGIC.
OH, CRAP...!
HELL SMELLED LIKE THIS, DIDN'T IT?
UM, WHAT'S THAT WEIRD SOUND...?
IS THAT SOMEONE LAUGHING?
HAHH??
...ASHLEY?
HH HII HII HII HIII HIII HIII HIII

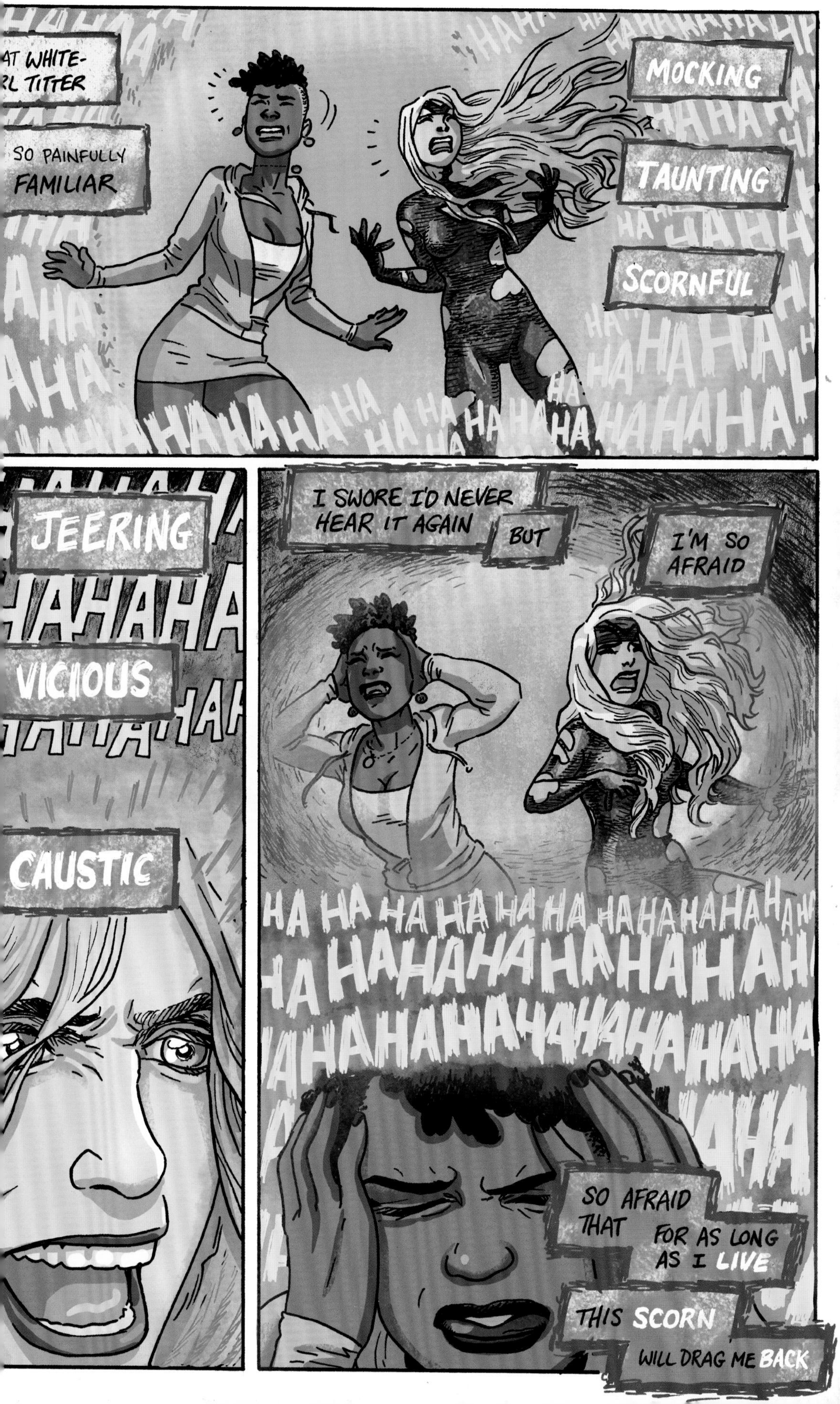
AT WHITE-
RL TITTER
SO PAINFULLY FAMILIAR
MOCKING
TAUNTING
SCORNFUL
JEERING
VICIOUS
CAUSTIC
I SWORE I'D NEVER HEAR IT AGAIN
BUT
I'M SO AFRAID
SO AFRAID THAT
FOR AS LONG AS I LIVE
THIS SCORN
WILL DRAG ME BACK

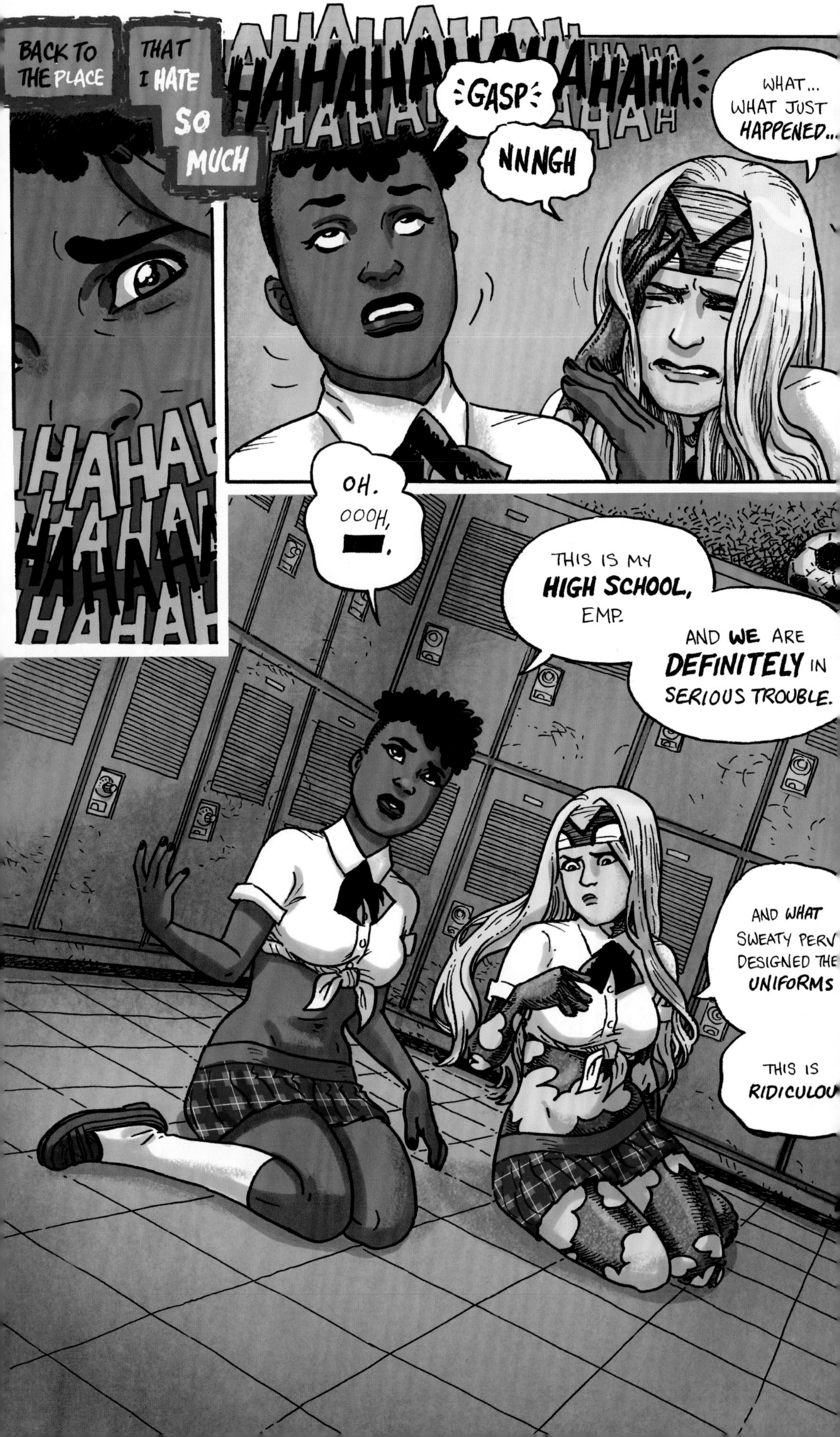
BACK TO THE PLACE
THAT I HATE SO MUCH
HAHAHAHAHAHAHAHA
GASP
NNNGH
WHAT... WHAT JUST HAPPENED...
HAHAHA
OH. OOOH, [redacted].
THIS IS MY HIGH SCHOOL, EMP.
AND WE ARE DEFINITELY IN SERIOUS TROUBLE.
AND WHAT SWEATY PERV DESIGNED THE UNIFORMS
THIS IS RIDICULOU

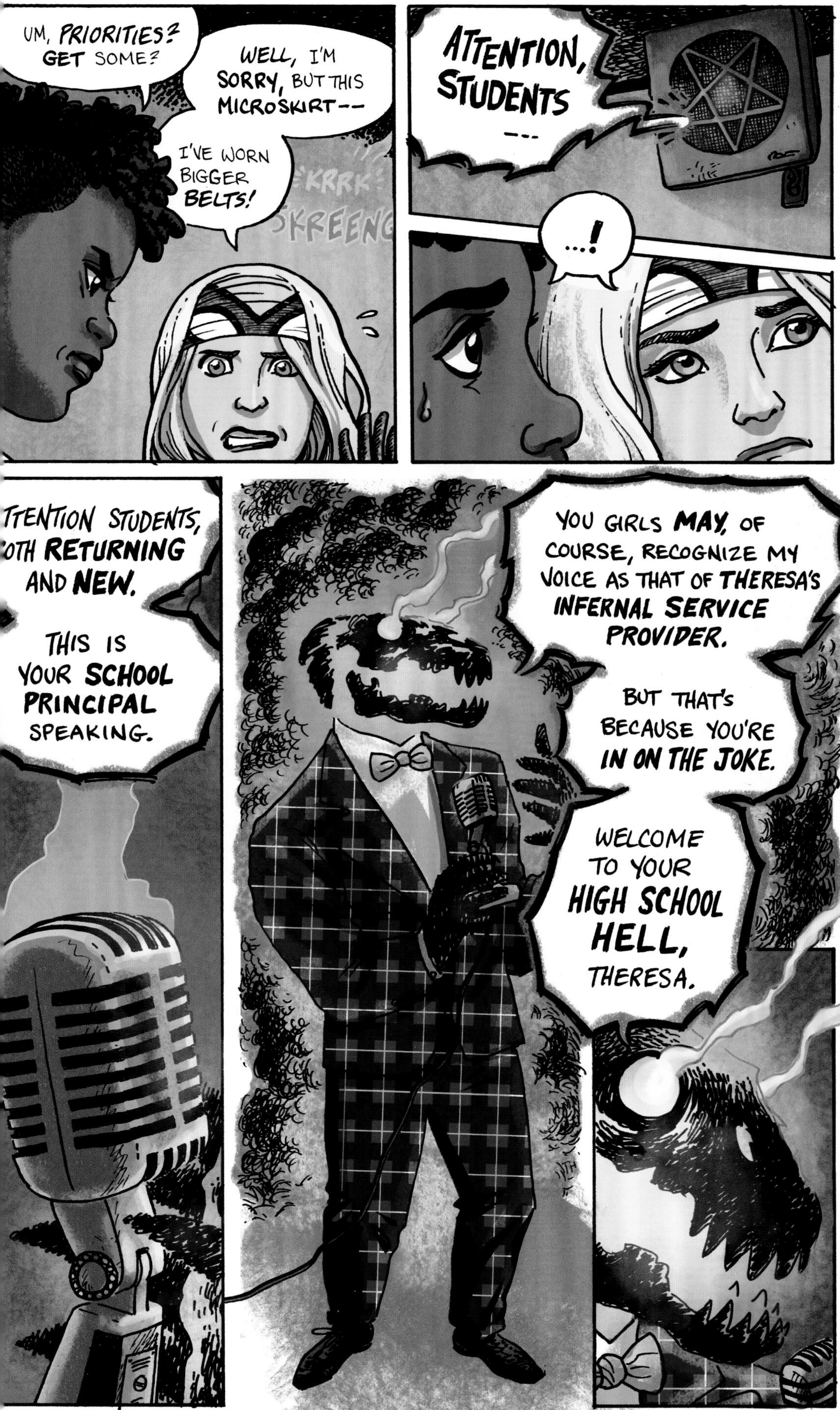

UM, PRIORITIES? GET SOME?
WELL, I'M SORRY, BUT THIS MICROSKIRT--
I'VE WORN BIGGER BELTS!
KRRK! SKREENG
ATTENTION, STUDENTS---
...!
TTENTION STUDENTS, OTH RETURNING AND NEW.
THIS IS YOUR SCHOOL PRINCIPAL SPEAKING.
YOU GIRLS MAY, OF COURSE, RECOGNIZE MY VOICE AS THAT OF THERESA'S INFERNAL SERVICE PROVIDER.
BUT THAT'S BECAUSE YOU'RE IN ON THE JOKE.
WELCOME TO YOUR HIGH SCHOOL HELL, THERESA.

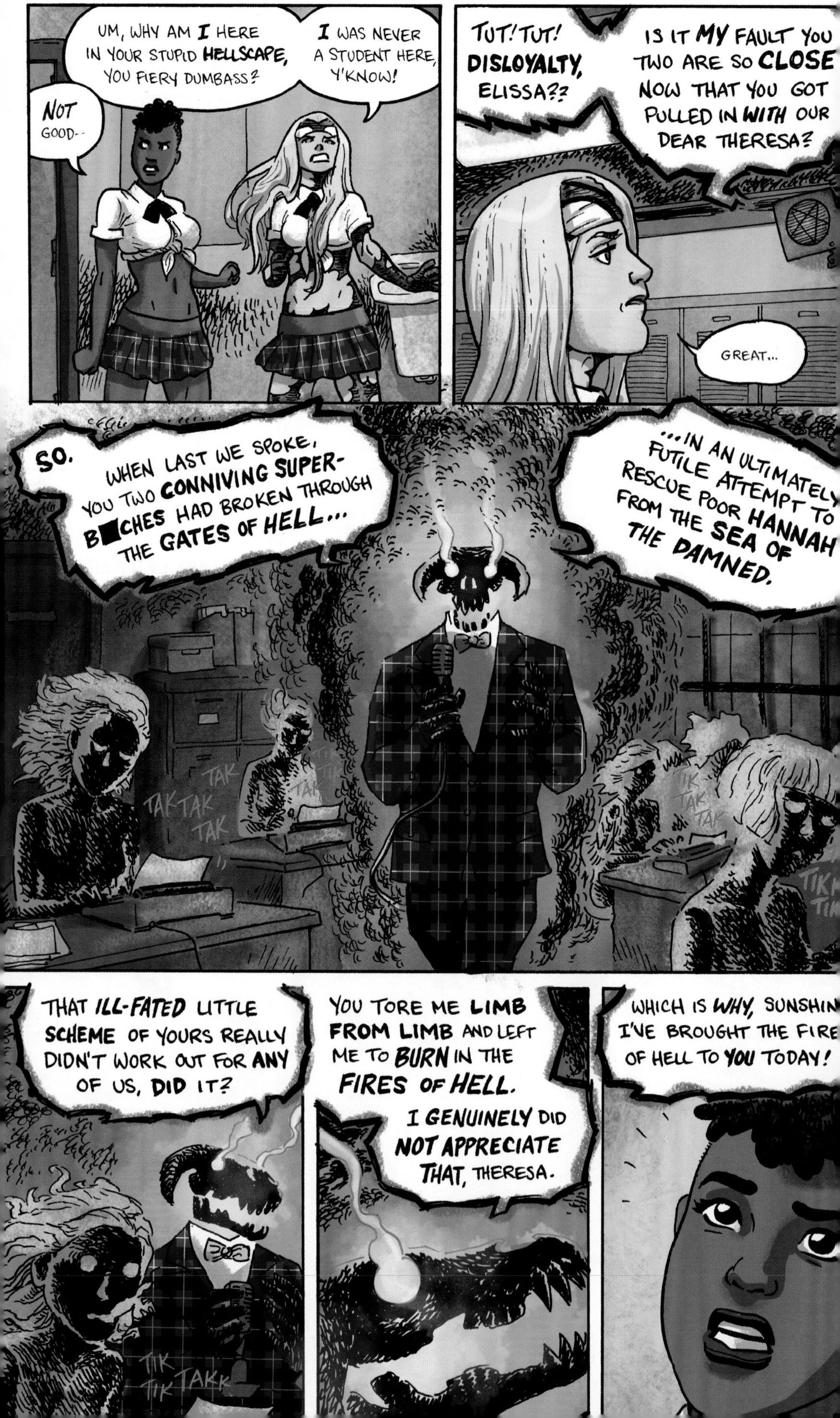

NOT GOOD--
UM, WHY AM I HERE IN YOUR STUPID HELLSCAPE, YOU FIERY DUMBASS?
I WAS NEVER A STUDENT HERE, Y'KNOW!
TUT! TUT! DISLOYALTY, ELISSA??
IS IT MY FAULT YOU TWO ARE SO CLOSE NOW THAT YOU GOT PULLED IN WITH OUR DEAR THERESA?
GREAT...
SO.
WHEN LAST WE SPOKE, YOU TWO CONNIVING SUPER-B[redacted]CHES HAD BROKEN THROUGH THE GATES OF HELL...
...IN AN ULTIMATELY FUTILE ATTEMPT TO RESCUE POOR HANNAH FROM THE SEA OF THE DAMNED.
TAK
TAKTAK
TAK
TIK
TAK
TAK
THAT ILL-FATED LITTLE SCHEME OF YOURS REALLY DIDN'T WORK OUT FOR ANY OF US, DID IT?
TIK
TIK TAKK
YOU TORE ME LIMB FROM LIMB AND LEFT ME TO BURN IN THE FIRES OF HELL.
I GENUINELY DID NOT APPRECIATE THAT, THERESA.
WHICH IS WHY, SUNSHIN I'VE BROUGHT THE FIRE OF HELL TO YOU TODAY!

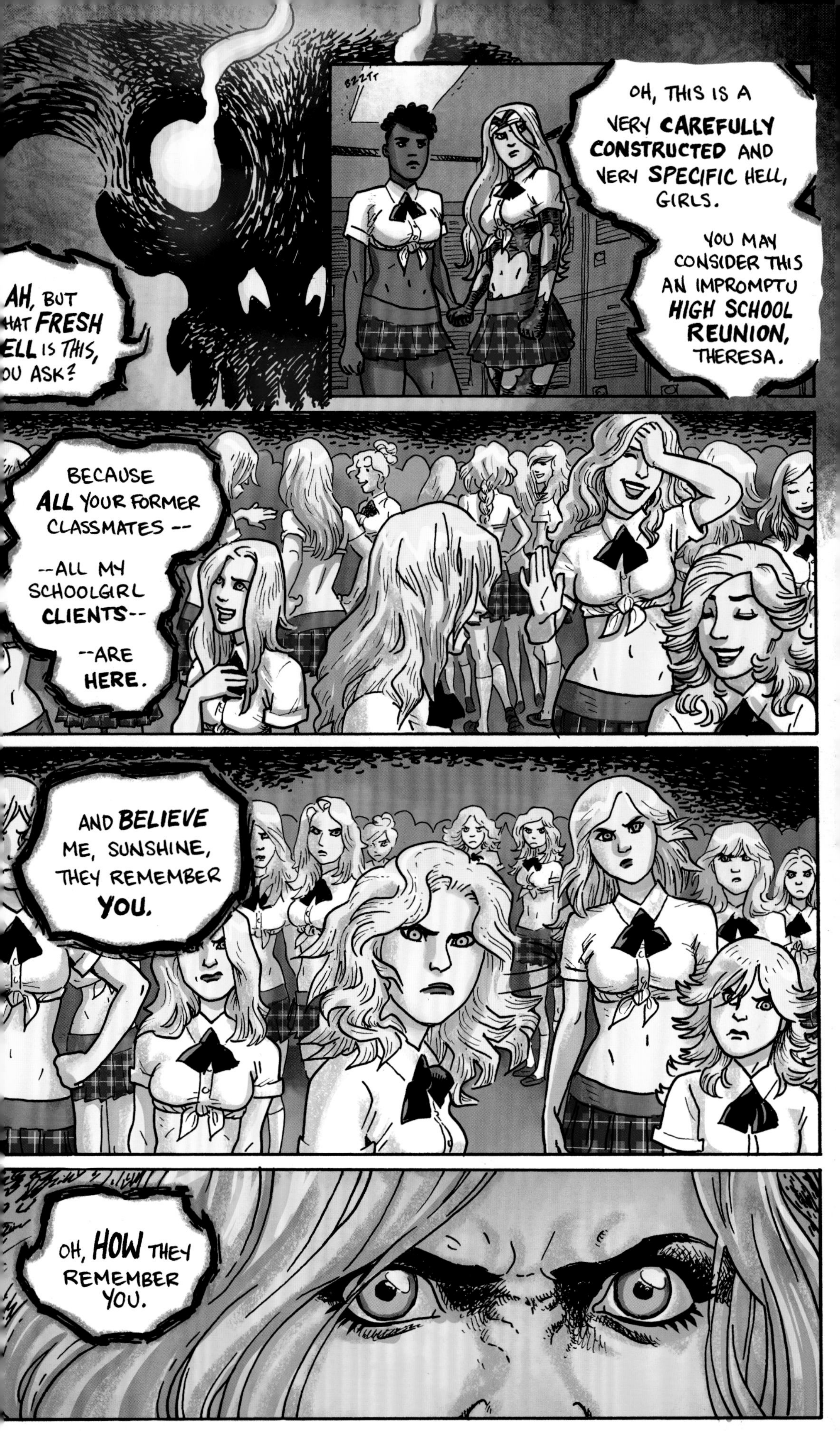

BZZTT
AH, BUT HAT FRESH ELL IS THIS, OU ASK?
OH, THIS IS A VERY CAREFULLY CONSTRUCTED AND VERY SPECIFIC HELL, GIRLS.
YOU MAY CONSIDER THIS AN IMPROMPTU HIGH SCHOOL REUNION, THERESA.
BECAUSE ALL YOUR FORMER CLASSMATES --
--ALL MY SCHOOLGIRL CLIENTS--
--ARE HERE.
AND BELIEVE ME, SUNSHINE, THEY REMEMBER YOU.
OH, HOW THEY REMEMBER YOU.

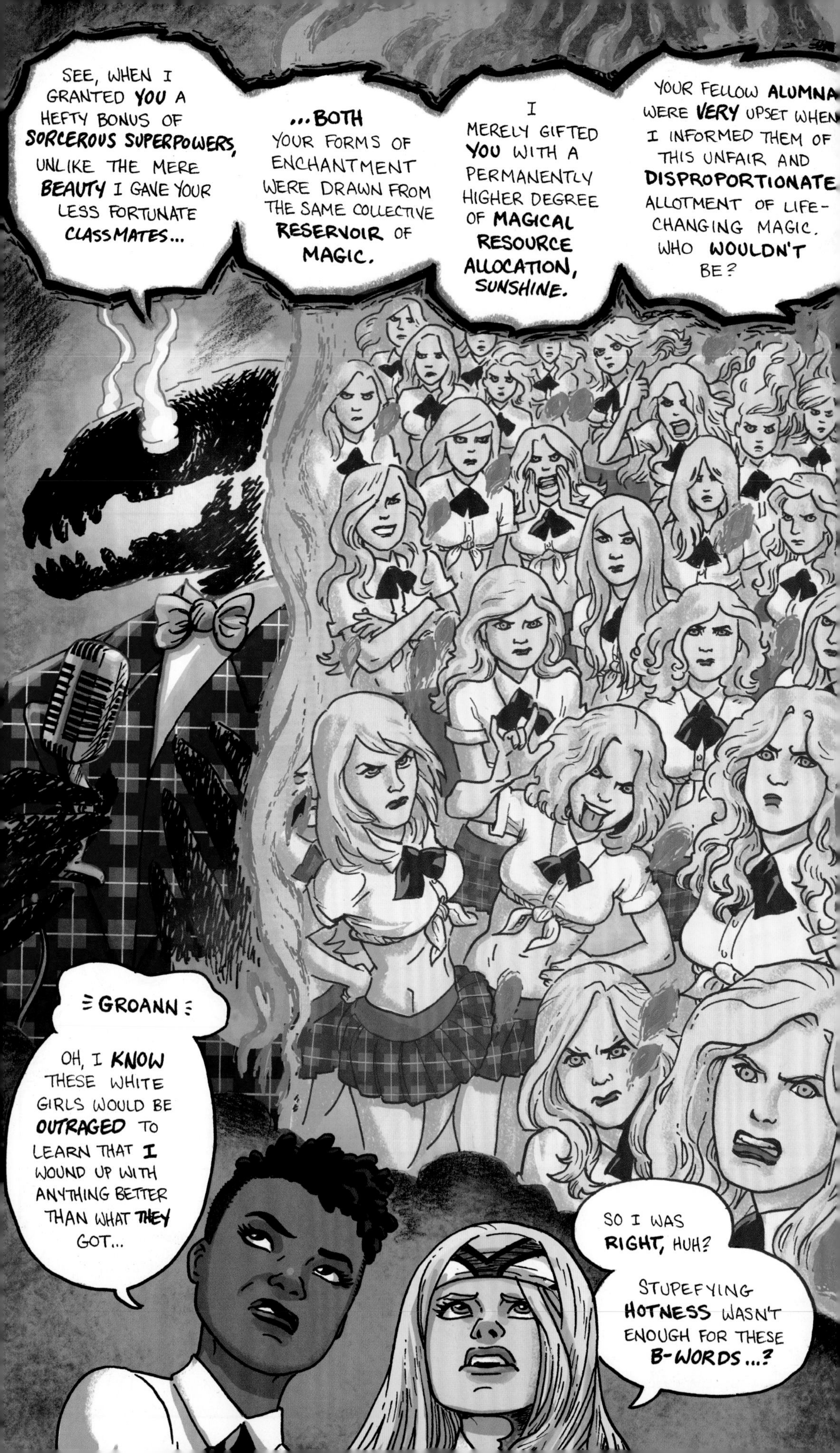
SEE, WHEN I GRANTED YOU A HEFTY BONUS OF SORCEROUS SUPERPOWERS, UNLIKE THE MERE BEAUTY I GAVE YOUR LESS FORTUNATE CLASSMATES...
...BOTH YOUR FORMS OF ENCHANTMENT WERE DRAWN FROM THE SAME COLLECTIVE RESERVOIR OF MAGIC.
I MERELY GIFTED YOU WITH A PERMANENTLY HIGHER DEGREE OF MAGICAL RESOURCE ALLOCATION, SUNSHINE.
YOUR FELLOW ALUMNA WERE VERY UPSET WHEN I INFORMED THEM OF THIS UNFAIR AND DISPROPORTIONATE ALLOTMENT OF LIFE-CHANGING MAGIC. WHO WOULDN'T BE?
≡GROANN≡
OH, I KNOW THESE WHITE GIRLS WOULD BE OUTRAGED TO LEARN THAT I WOUND UP WITH ANYTHING BETTER THAN WHAT THEY GOT...
SO I WAS RIGHT, HUH?
STUPEFYING HOTNESS WASN'T ENOUGH FOR THESE B-WORDS...?

…TO REDRESS THIS BIASED AND DISCRIMINATORY IMBALANCE OF RESOURCES, THERESA…
…I'VE MADE A GENEROUS OFFER TO YOUR JUSTIFIABLY RESENTFUL FORMER CLASSMATES.
IF THEY KILL YOU, PREFERABLY IN A SLOW, NASTY, TORTURE-PORNY MANNER…
…THE ENTIRETY OF YOUR INEQUITABLY HOARDED MAGIC REVERTS TO THEM.
IF THEY KILL YOU, ELISSA, IT'S JUST TO BUTTER ME UP…
HHHOT FOR TEACHERR
CAMPUS MAP
H-HEY!
SO THIS MAGIC-WOVEN INFERNAL TESSERACT I'VE TRAPPED YOU INSIDE ISN'T MERELY A HIGH SCHOOL, LADIES.
IT'S AN ARENA.
A SCHOOL-PATTERNED KILLING FIELD.
TO BE SPORTING, I'VE ARRANGED THIS HELL-SCAPE SO AS TO GIVE YOUR LESS-GIFTED FELLOW STUDENTS A FAIR SHOT AT YOU.
YOUR POWERS ARE CONSTRAINED AND LIMITED WITHIN THIS SCHOLASTIC BATTLEFIELD.
AND THAT'S ENABLED YOUR FELLOW ALUMNAE TO COOK UP SOME WONDERFULLY CREATIVE WAYS TO SNUFF YOU, THERESA!
WE DARE TO DREAM HERE, SUNSHINE!

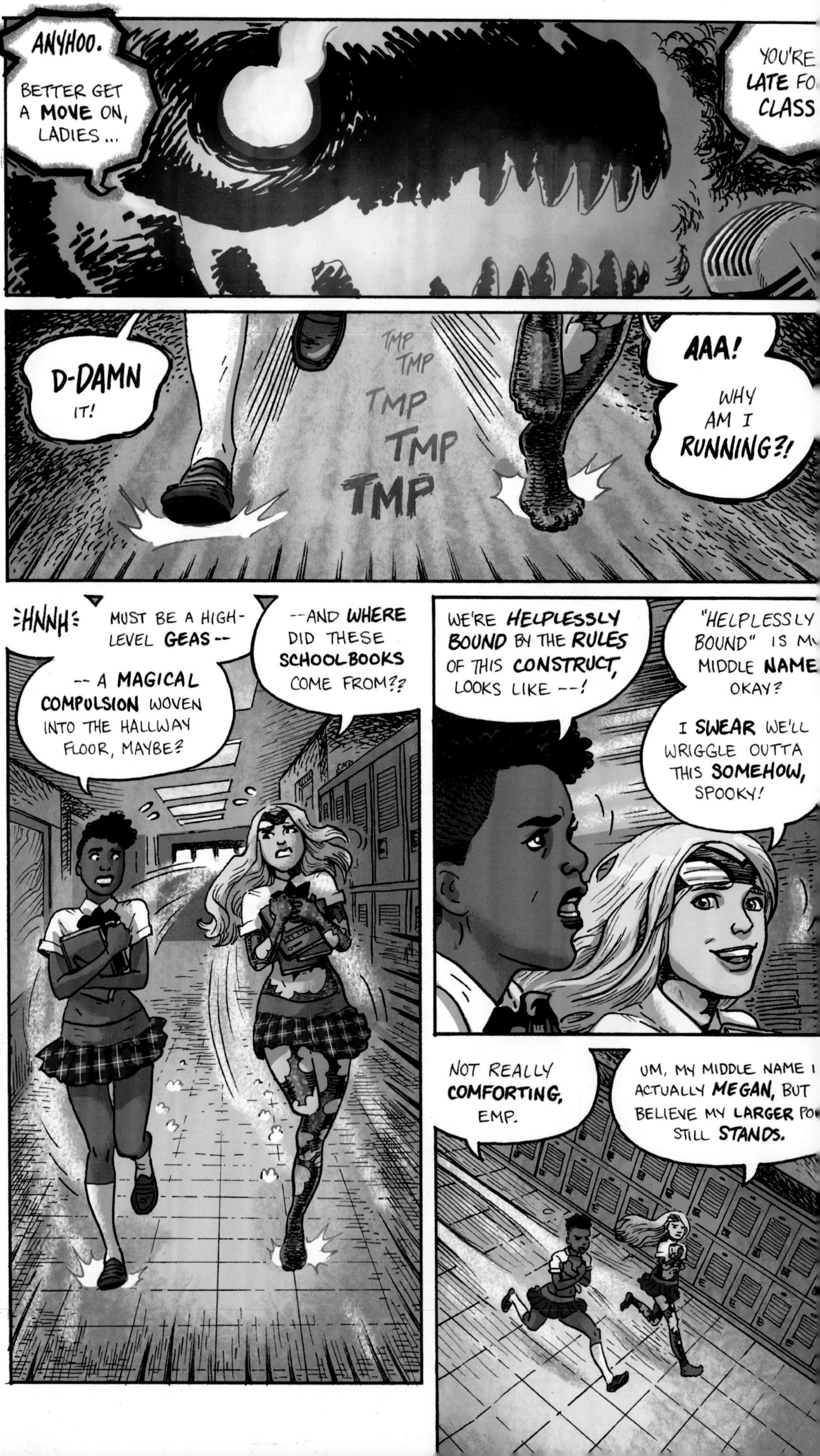
ANYHOO.
BETTER GET A MOVE ON, LADIES ...
YOU'RE LATE FO CLASS
TMP TMP TMP TMP TMP
D-DAMN IT!
AAA! WHY AM I RUNNING?!
HNNH
MUST BE A HIGH-LEVEL GEAS --
-- A MAGICAL COMPULSION WOVEN INTO THE HALLWAY FLOOR, MAYBE?
--AND WHERE DID THESE SCHOOLBOOKS COME FROM??
WE'RE HELPLESSLY BOUND BY THE RULES OF THIS CONSTRUCT, LOOKS LIKE --!
"HELPLESSLY BOUND" IS M MIDDLE NAME, OKAY?
I SWEAR WE'LL WRIGGLE OUTTA THIS SOMEHOW, SPOOKY!
NOT REALLY COMFORTING, EMP.
UM, MY MIDDLE NAME I ACTUALLY MEGAN, BUT BELIEVE MY LARGER PO STILL STANDS.

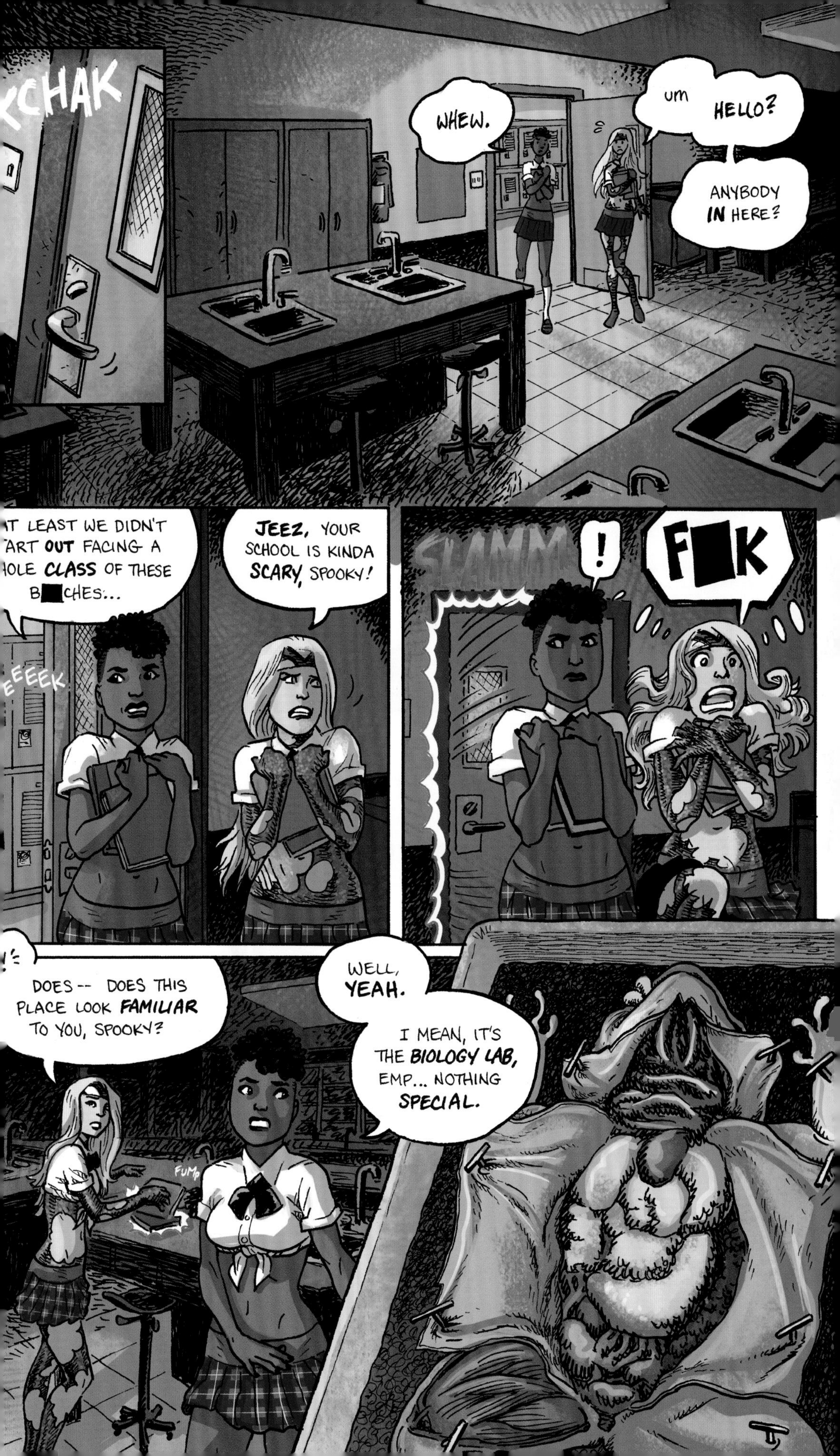
CHAK
WHEW.
um HELLO?
ANYBODY IN HERE?
T LEAST WE DIDN'T TART OUT FACING A HOLE CLASS OF THESE B[redacted]CHES:...
EEEEK
JEEZ, YOUR SCHOOL IS KINDA SCARY, SPOOKY!
SLAMM
!
F[redacted]K
DOES -- DOES THIS PLACE LOOK FAMILIAR TO YOU, SPOOKY?
FUMP
WELL, YEAH.
I MEAN, IT'S THE BIOLOGY LAB, EMP... NOTHING SPECIAL.

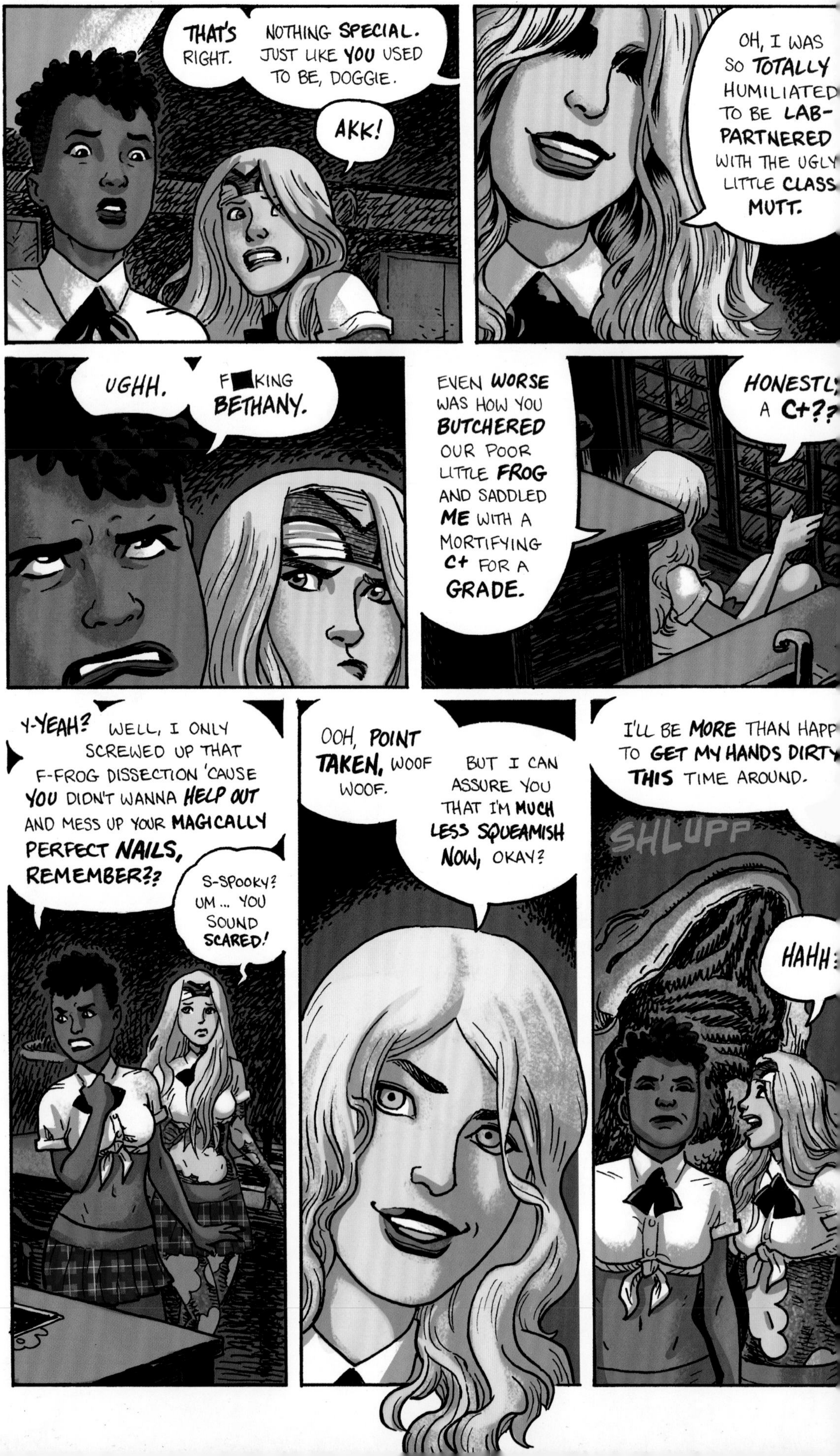
THAT'S RIGHT.
NOTHING SPECIAL. JUST LIKE YOU USED TO BE, DOGGIE.
AKK!
OH, I WAS SO TOTALLY HUMILIATED TO BE LAB-PARTNERED WITH THE UGLY LITTLE CLASS MUTT.
UGHH.
F[redacted]KING BETHANY.
EVEN WORSE WAS HOW YOU BUTCHERED OUR POOR LITTLE FROG AND SADDLED ME WITH A MORTIFYING C+ FOR A GRADE.
HONESTL A C+??
Y-YEAH? WELL, I ONLY SCREWED UP THAT F-FROG DISSECTION 'CAUSE YOU DIDN'T WANNA HELP OUT AND MESS UP YOUR MAGICALLY PERFECT NAILS, REMEMBER??
S-SPOOKY? UM ... YOU SOUND SCARED!
OOH, POINT TAKEN, WOOF WOOF.
BUT I CAN ASSURE YOU THAT I'M MUCH LESS SQUEAMISH NOW, OKAY?
I'LL BE MORE THAN HAPP TO GET MY HANDS DIRT THIS TIME AROUND.
SHLUPP
HAHH

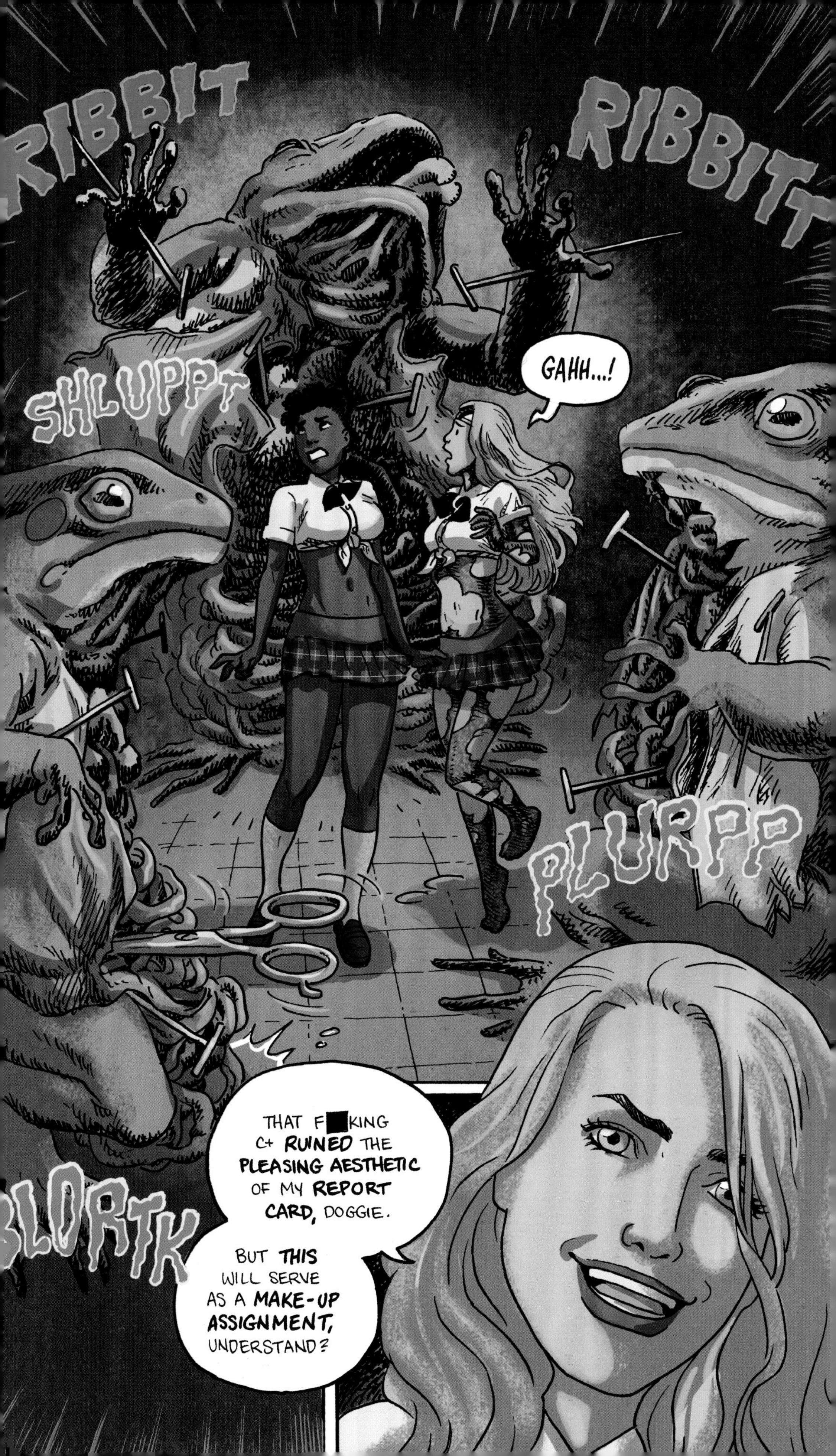
RIBBIT
RIBBITT
SHLUPPT
GAHH...!
PLURPP
LORTK
THAT F[redacted]KING C+ RUINED THE PLEASING AESTHETIC OF MY REPORT CARD, DOGGIE.
BUT THIS WILL SERVE AS A MAKE-UP ASSIGNMENT, UNDERSTAND?

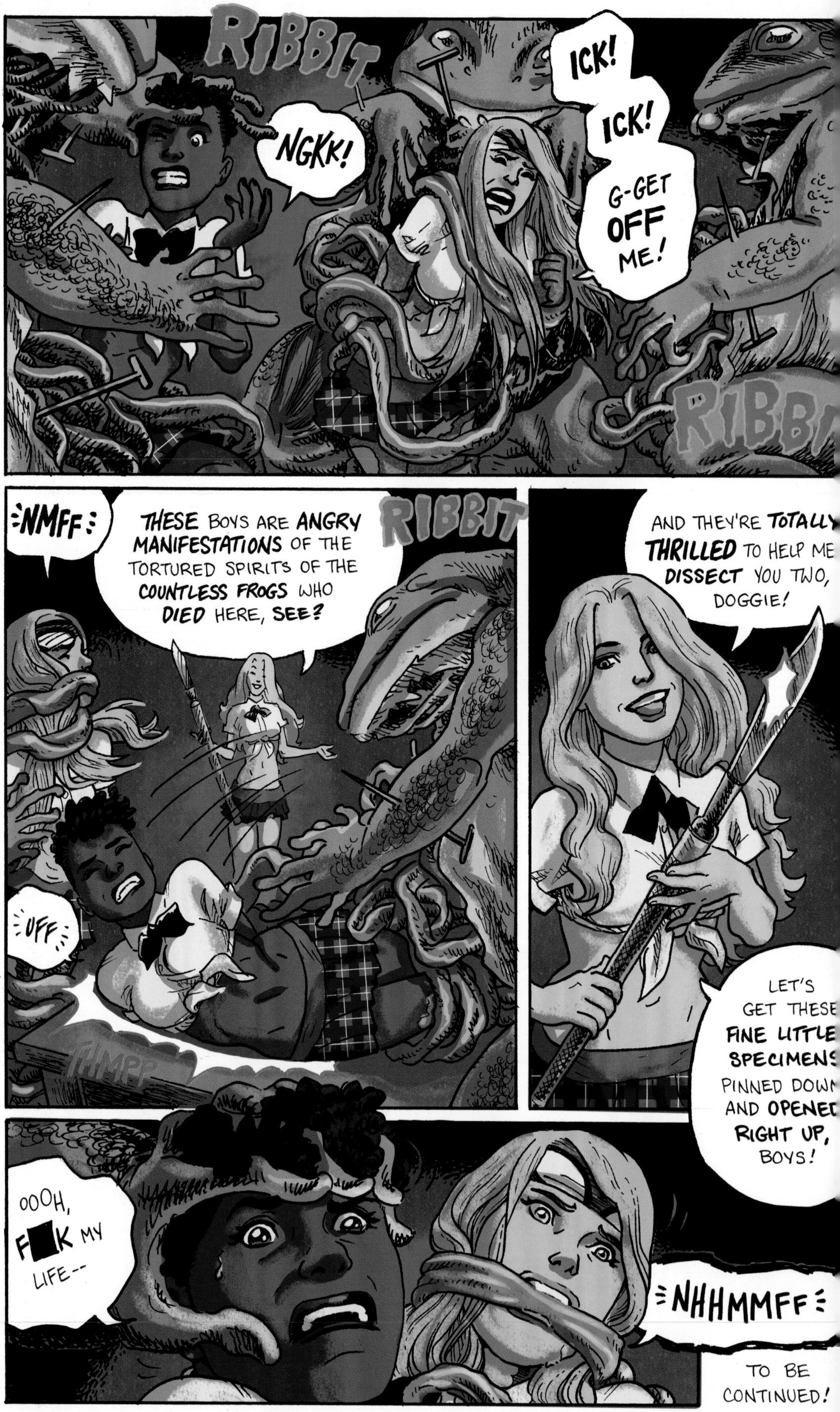
RIBBIT
NGKK!
ICK!
ICK!
G-GET OFF ME!
RIBB
NMFF
THESE BOYS ARE ANGRY MANIFESTATIONS OF THE TORTURED SPIRITS OF THE COUNTLESS FROGS WHO DIED HERE, SEE?
RIBBIT
UFF
THMPP
AND THEY'RE TOTALL THRILLED TO HELP ME DISSECT YOU TWO, DOGGIE!
LET'S GET THESE FINE LITTLE SPECIMENS PINNED DOW AND OPENE RIGHT UP, BOYS!
OOOH, F[redacted]K MY LIFE--
NHHMMFF
TO BE CONTINUED!

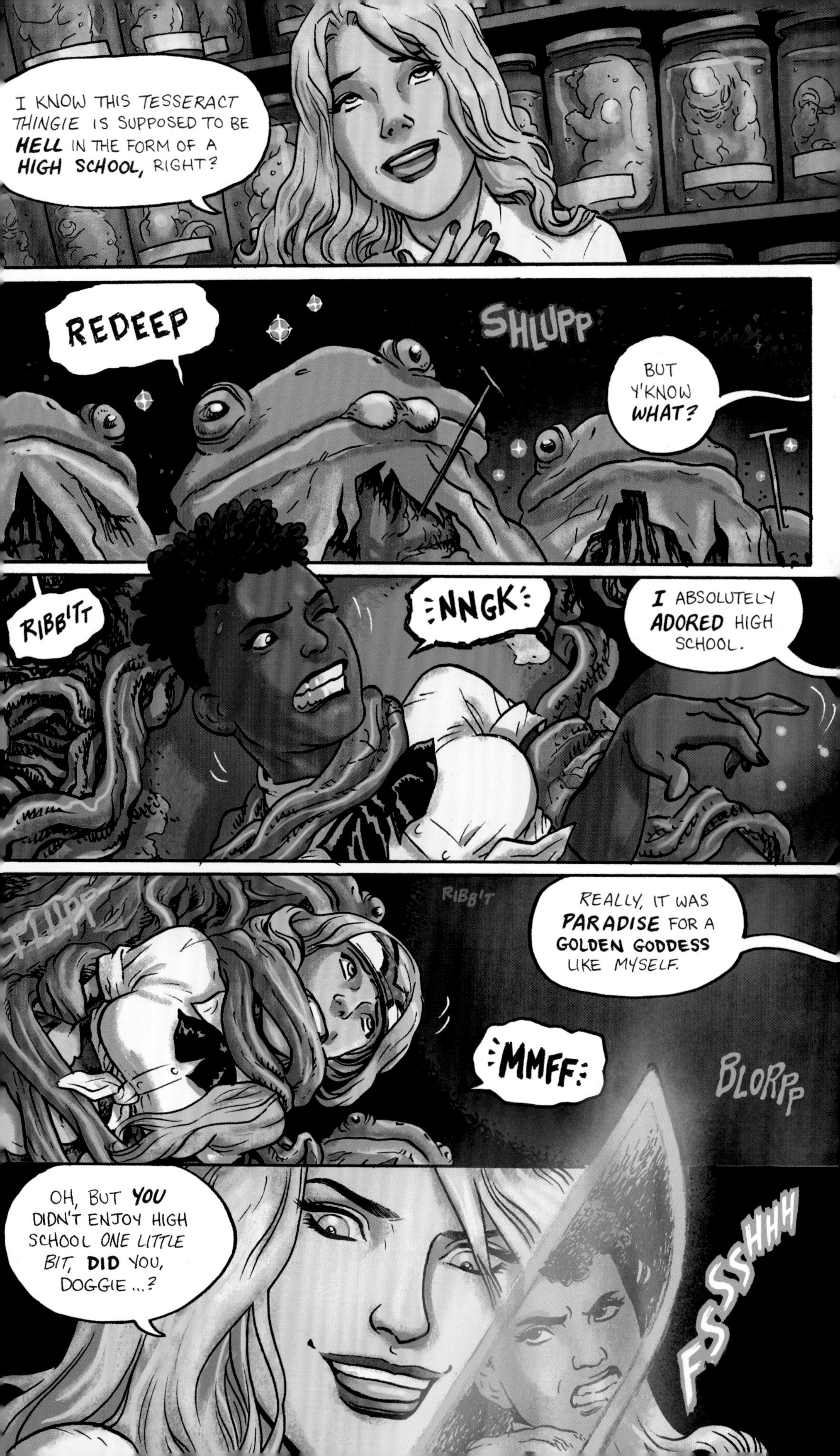
I KNOW THIS TESSERACT THINGIE IS SUPPOSED TO BE HELL IN THE FORM OF A HIGH SCHOOL, RIGHT?
REDEEP
SHLUPP
BUT Y'KNOW WHAT?
RIBB'TT
NNGK
I ABSOLUTELY ADORED HIGH SCHOOL.
RIBB'T
REALLY, IT WAS PARADISE FOR A GOLDEN GODDESS LIKE MYSELF.
MMFF
BLORPP
OH, BUT YOU DIDN'T ENJOY HIGH SCHOOL ONE LITTLE BIT, DID YOU, DOGGIE...?
FSSSHHH

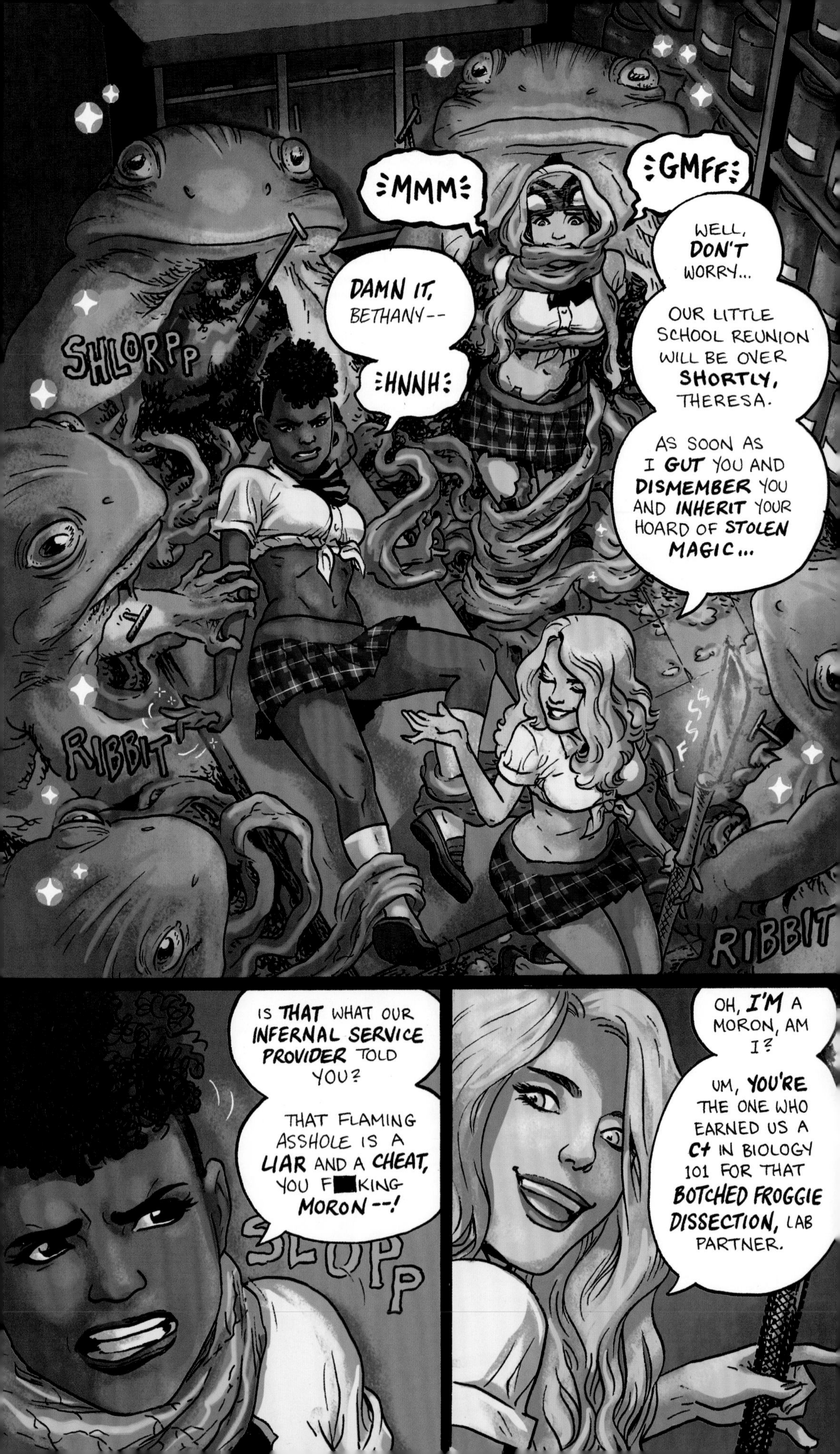
MMM
GMFF
DAMN IT, BETHANY--
HNNH
WELL, DON'T WORRY...
OUR LITTLE SCHOOL REUNION WILL BE OVER SHORTLY, THERESA.
AS SOON AS I GUT YOU AND DISMEMBER YOU AND INHERIT YOUR HOARD OF STOLEN MAGIC...
SHLORPP
RIBBIT
FSSS
RIBBIT
IS THAT WHAT OUR INFERNAL SERVICE PROVIDER TOLD YOU?
THAT FLAMING ASSHOLE IS A LIAR AND A CHEAT, YOU F[redacted]KING MORON--!
SLOPP
OH, I'M A MORON, AM I?
UM, YOU'RE THE ONE WHO EARNED US A C+ IN BIOLOGY 101 FOR THAT BOTCHED FROGGIE DISSECTION, LAB PARTNER.

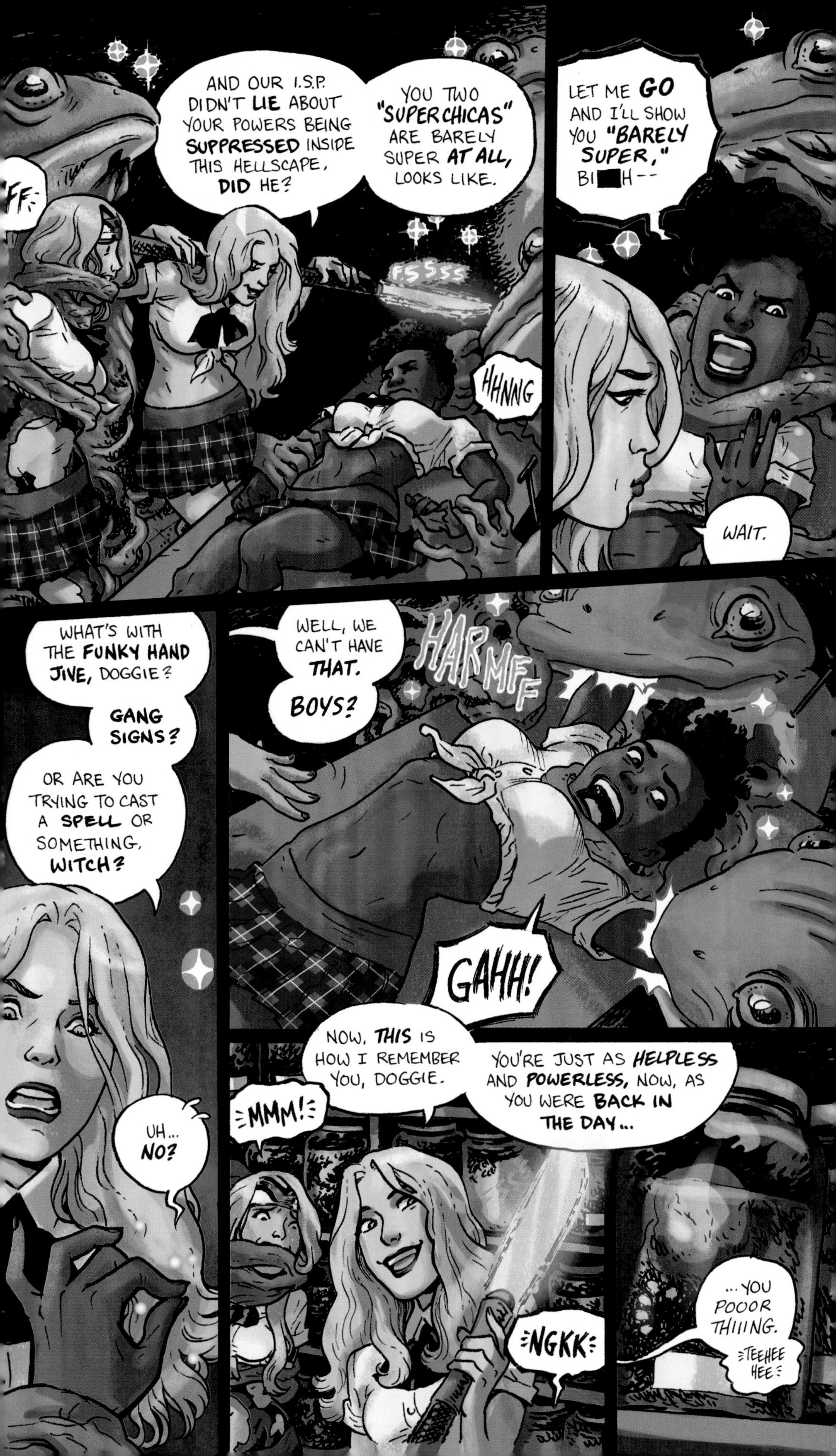
FF
AND OUR I.S.P. DIDN'T LIE ABOUT YOUR POWERS BEING SUPPRESSED INSIDE THIS HELLSCAPE, DID HE?
YOU TWO "SUPERCHICAS" ARE BARELY SUPER AT ALL, LOOKS LIKE.
FSSSS
HHNNG
LET ME GO AND I'LL SHOW YOU "BARELY SUPER," BI[redacted]H --
WAIT.
WHAT'S WITH THE FUNKY HAND JIVE, DOGGIE?
GANG SIGNS?
OR ARE YOU TRYING TO CAST A SPELL OR SOMETHING, WITCH?
UH... NO?
WELL, WE CAN'T HAVE THAT.
BOYS?
HARMFF
GAHH!
MMM!
NOW, THIS IS HOW I REMEMBER YOU, DOGGIE.
YOU'RE JUST AS HELPLESS AND POWERLESS, NOW, AS YOU WERE BACK IN THE DAY...
NGKK
...YOU POOOR THIIING.
TEEHEE HEE

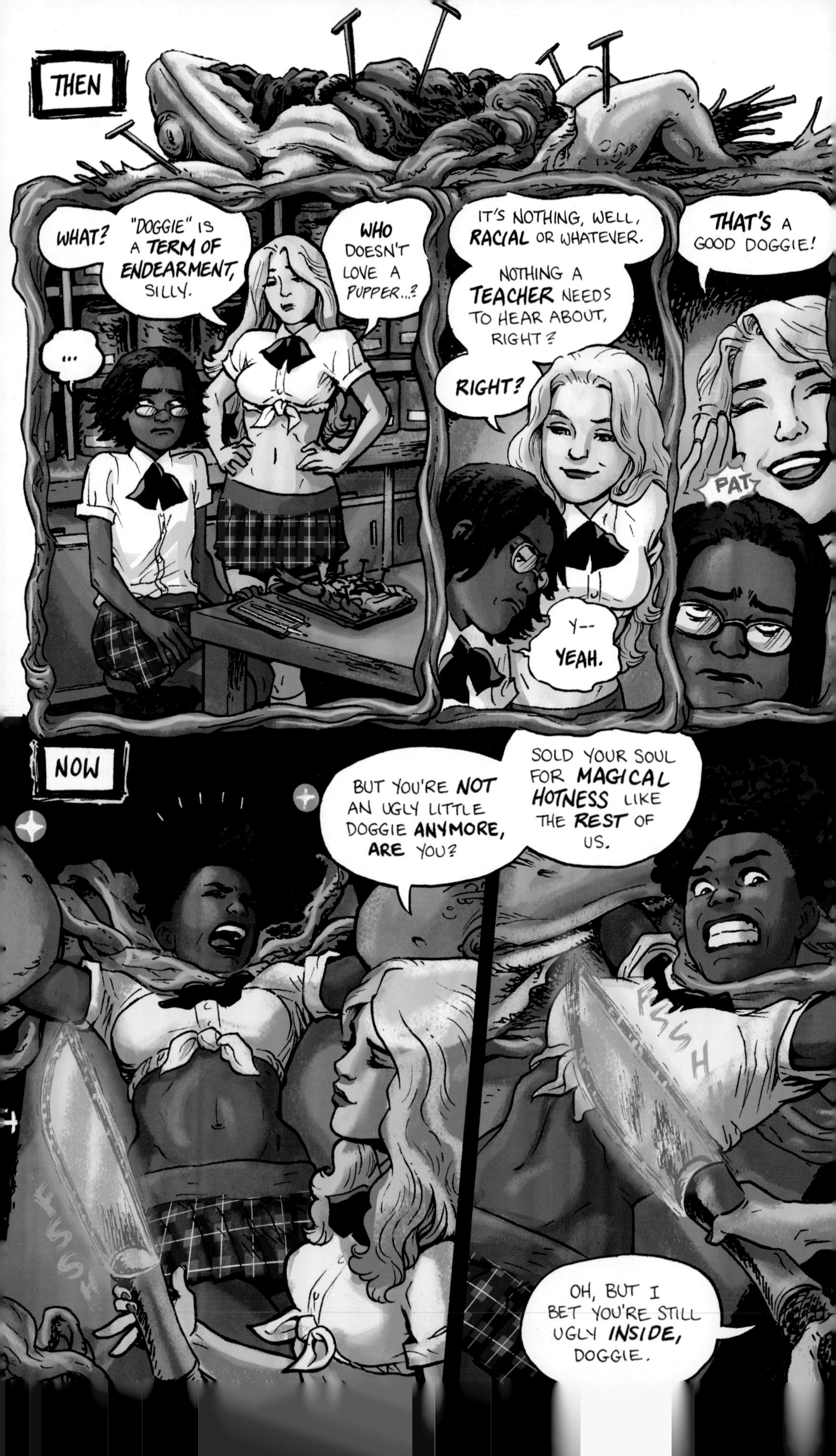
THEN
WHAT?
"DOGGIE" IS A TERM OF ENDEARMENT, SILLY.
WHO DOESN'T LOVE A PUPPER...?
...
IT'S NOTHING, WELL, RACIAL OR WHATEVER.
NOTHING A TEACHER NEEDS TO HEAR ABOUT, RIGHT?
RIGHT?
Y-- YEAH.
THAT'S A GOOD DOGGIE!
PAT
NOW
BUT YOU'RE NOT AN UGLY LITTLE DOGGIE ANYMORE, ARE YOU?
SOLD YOUR SOUL FOR MAGICAL HOTNESS LIKE THE REST OF US.
FSSH
FSSH
OH, BUT I BET YOU'RE STILL UGLY INSIDE, DOGGIE.

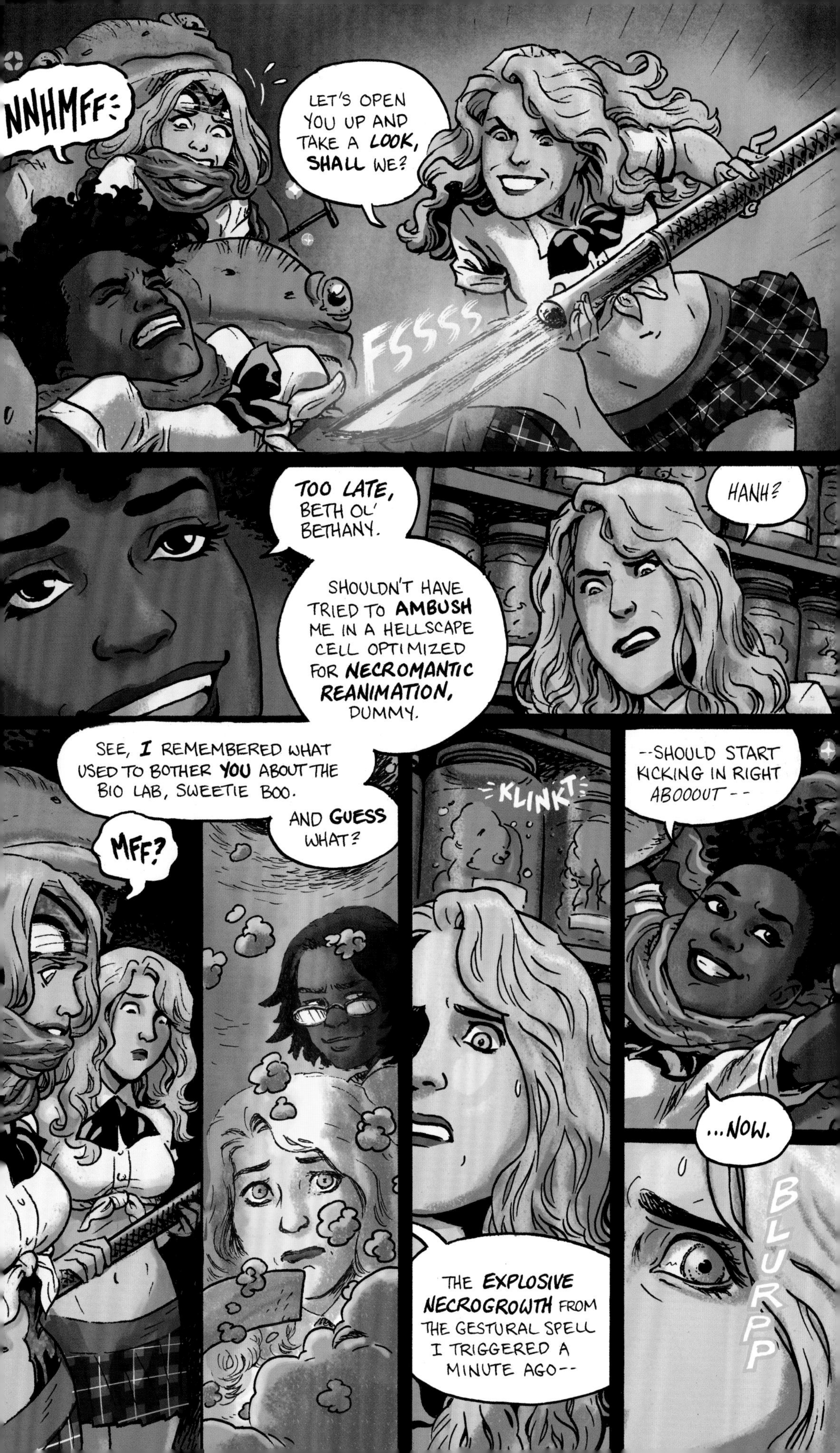
NNHMFF
LET'S OPEN YOU UP AND TAKE A LOOK, SHALL WE?
FSSSS
TOO LATE, BETH OL' BETHANY.
SHOULDN'T HAVE TRIED TO AMBUSH ME IN A HELLSCAPE CELL OPTIMIZED FOR NECROMANTIC REANIMATION, DUMMY.
HANH?
SEE, I REMEMBERED WHAT USED TO BOTHER YOU ABOUT THE BIO LAB, SWEETIE BOO.
AND GUESS WHAT?
MFF?
KLINK!
THE EXPLOSIVE NECROGROWTH FROM THE GESTURAL SPELL I TRIGGERED A MINUTE AGO--
--SHOULD START KICKING IN RIGHT ABOOOUT--
...NOW.
BLURPP

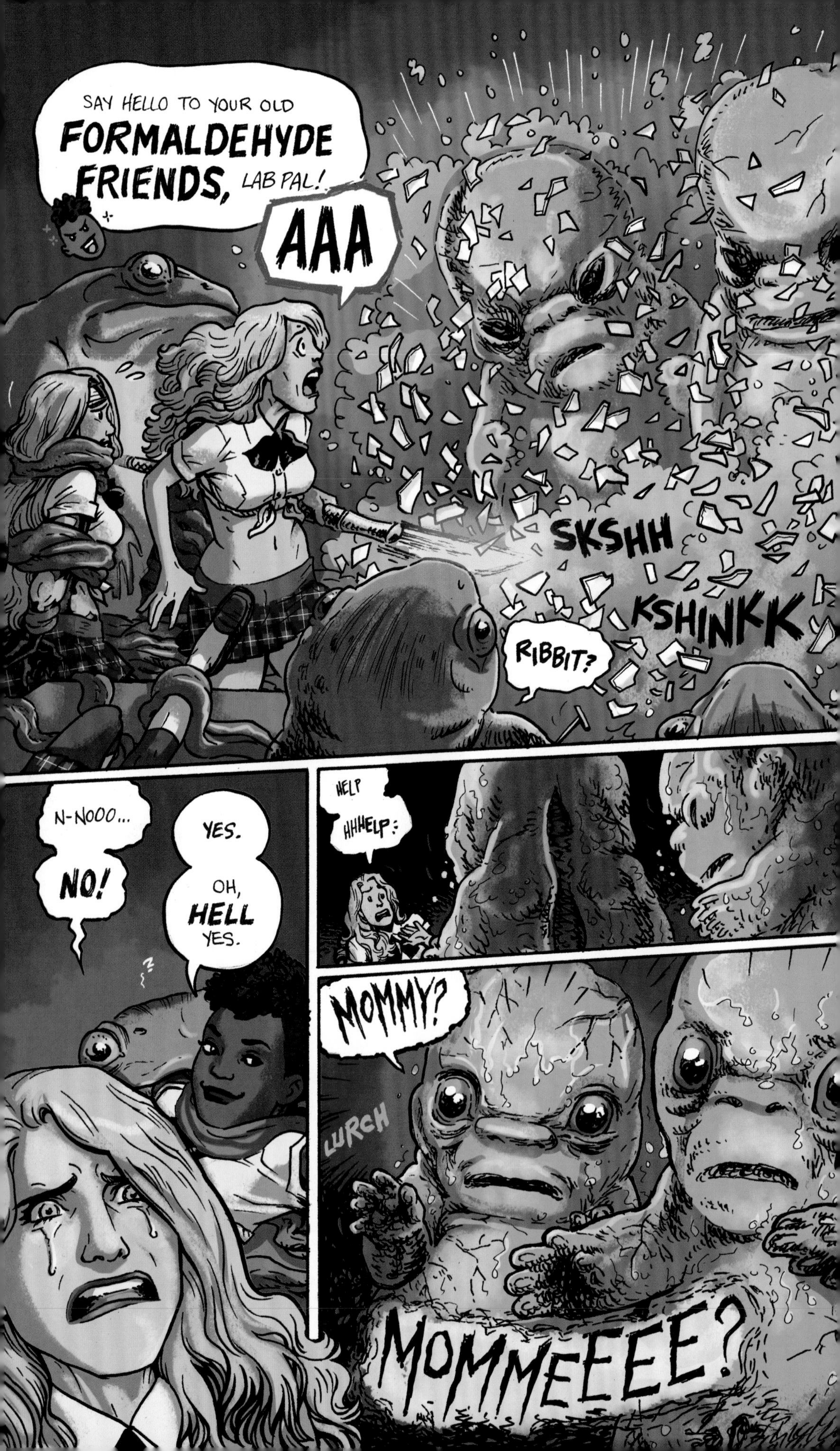
SAY HELLO TO YOUR OLD FORMALDEHYDE FRIENDS, LAB PAL!
AAA
SKSHH
KSHINKK
RIBBIT?
N-NOOO...
NO!
YES.
OH, HELL YES.
HELP
HHHELP
MOMMY?
LURCH
MOMMEEEE?

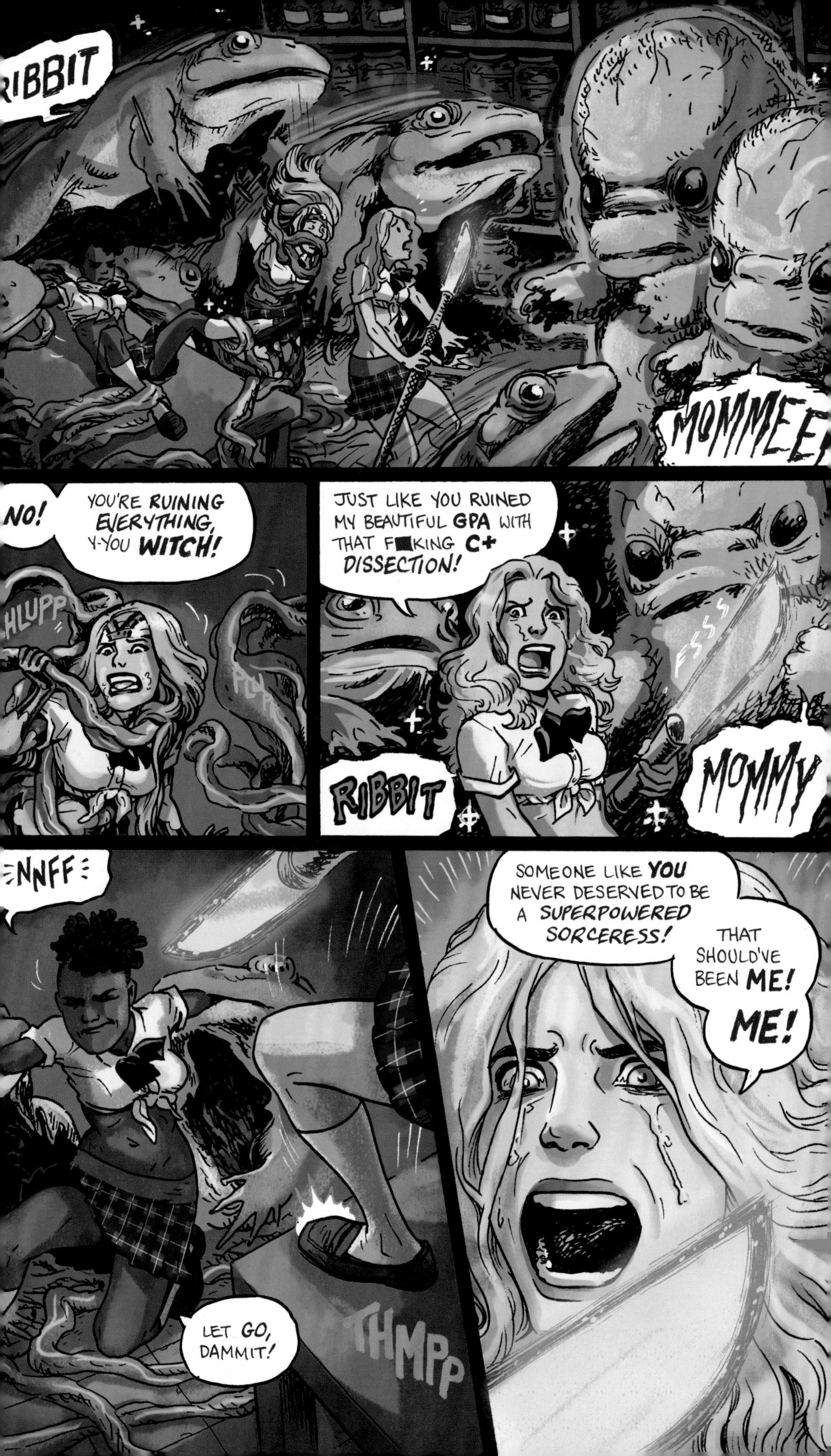

RIBBIT
MOMMEE
NO!
YOU'RE RUINING EVERYTHING, Y-YOU WITCH!
HLUPP
PLUPP
JUST LIKE YOU RUINED MY BEAUTIFUL GPA WITH THAT F[redacted]KING C+ DISSECTION!
FSSS
RIBBIT
MOMMY
NNFF
SOMEONE LIKE YOU NEVER DESERVED TO BE A SUPERPOWERED SORCERESS!
THAT SHOULD'VE BEEN ME!
ME!
LET GO, DAMMIT!
THMPP

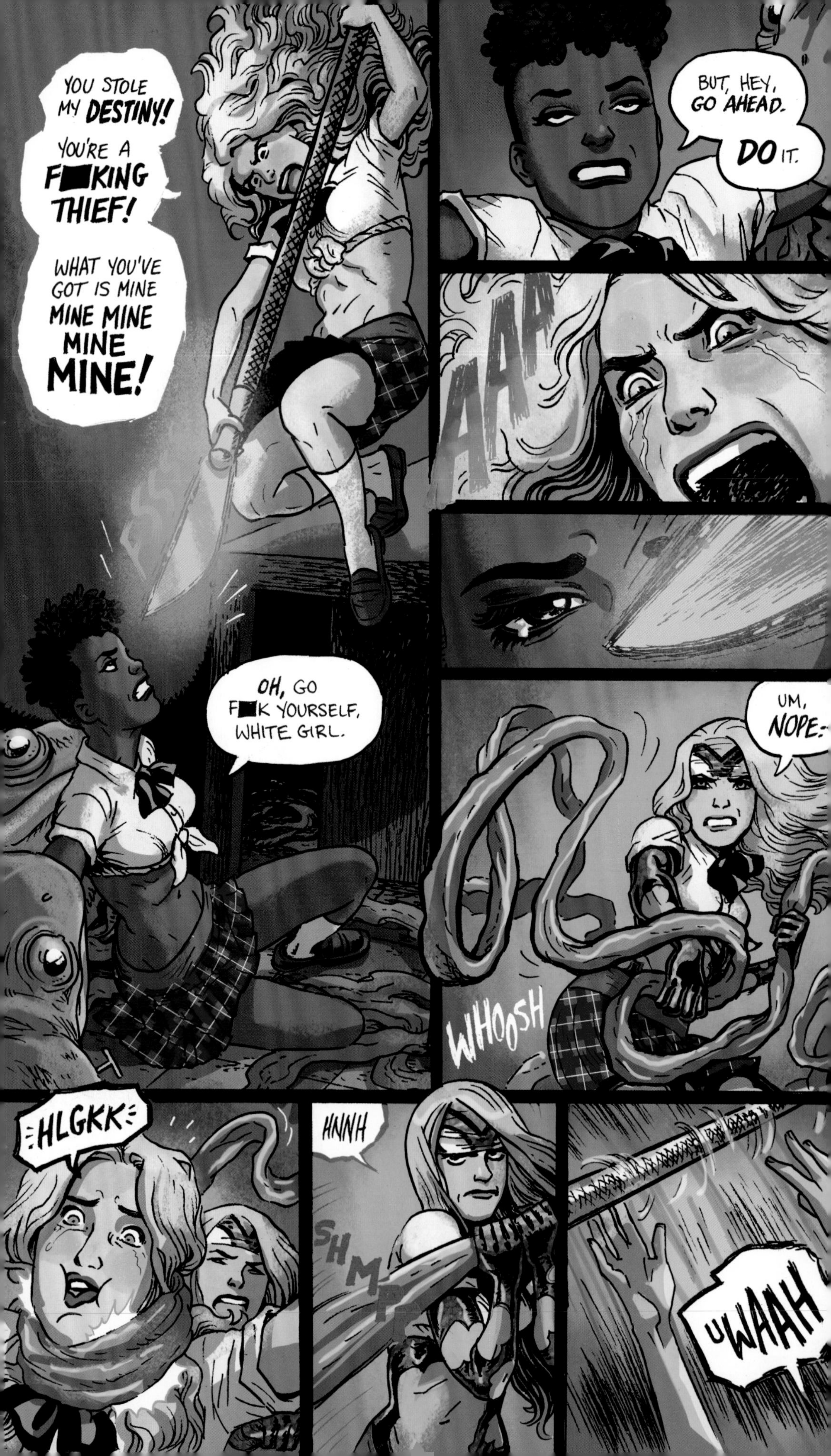
YOU STOLE MY DESTINY!
YOU'RE A F[redacted]KING THIEF!
WHAT YOU'VE GOT IS MINE MINE MINE MINE MINE!
OH, GO F[redacted]K YOURSELF, WHITE GIRL.
BUT, HEY, GO AHEAD.
DO IT.
AAA
UM, NOPE.
WHOOSH
HLGKK
HNNH
SHMP
UWAAH

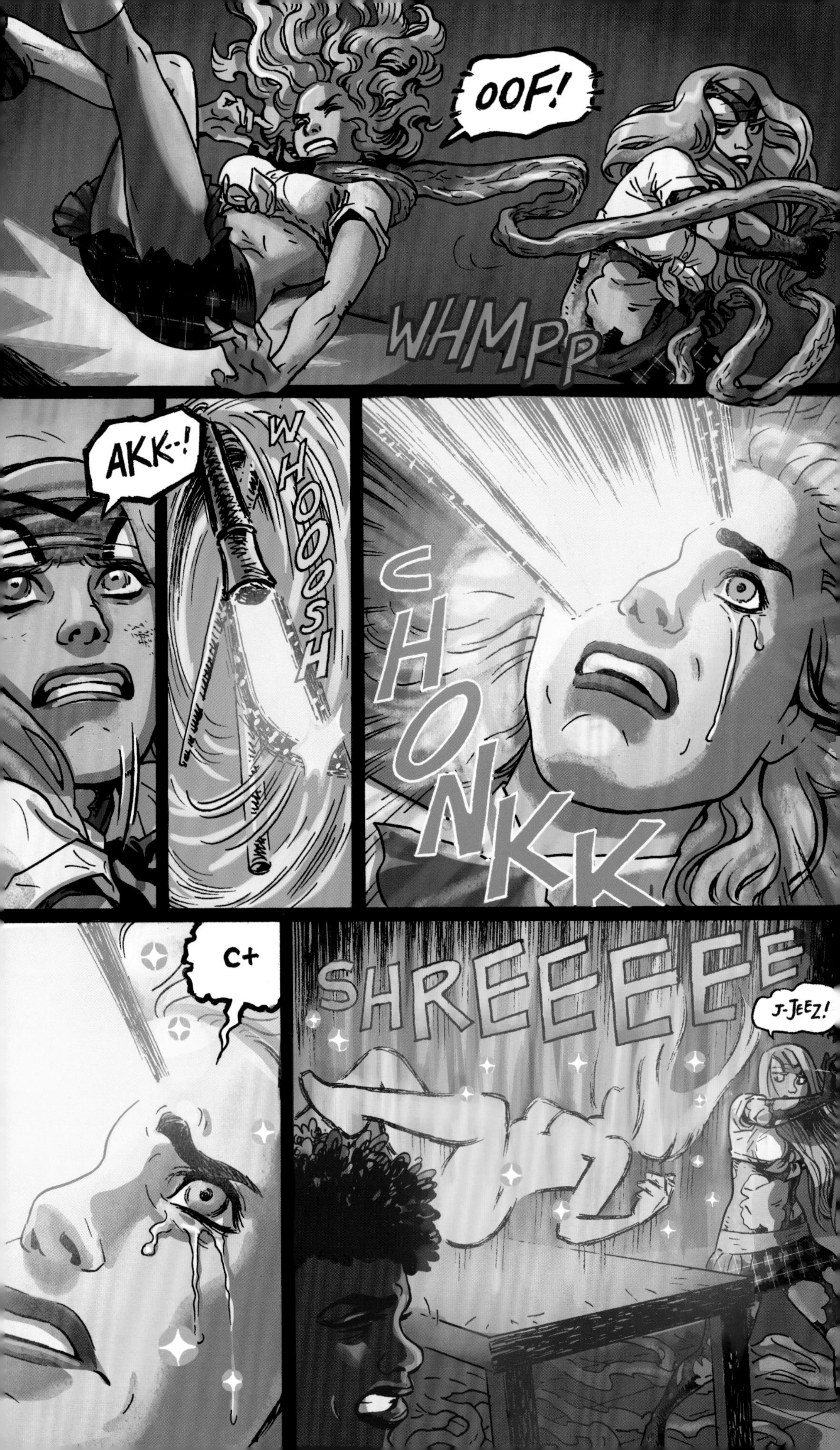
OOF!
WHMPP
AKK-!
WHOOOOSH
CHONKK
C+
SHREEEEE
J-JEEZ!

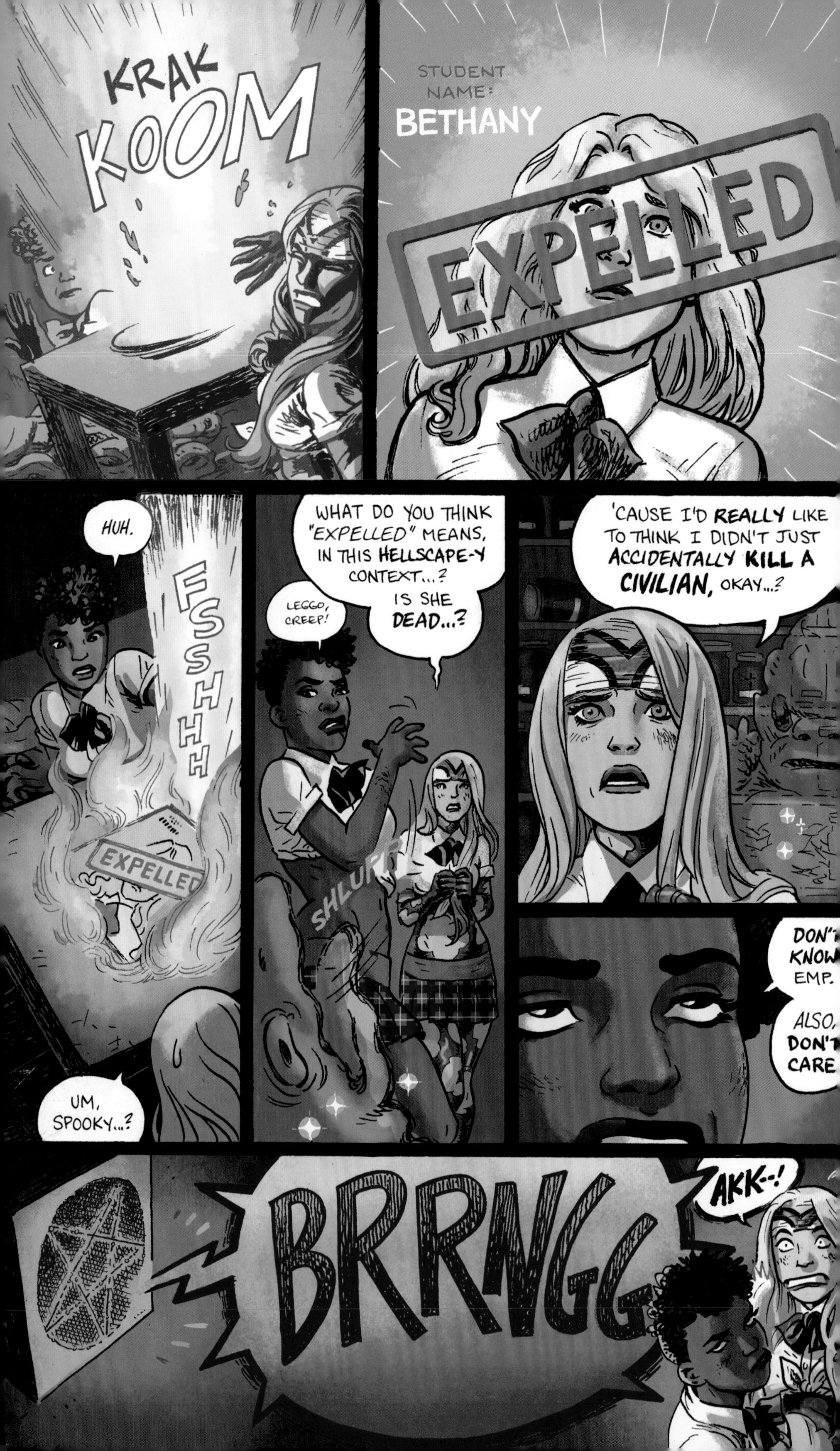
KRAK
KOOM
STUDENT NAME:
BETHANY
EXPELLED
HUH.
FSSHHHH
EXPELLED
UM, SPOOKY...?
WHAT DO YOU THINK "EXPELLED" MEANS, IN THIS HELLSCAPE-Y CONTEXT...?
LEGGO, CREEP!
IS SHE DEAD...?
SHLUPP
'CAUSE I'D REALLY LIKE TO THINK I DIDN'T JUST ACCIDENTALLY KILL A CIVILIAN, OKAY...?
BRRNGG
AKK--!

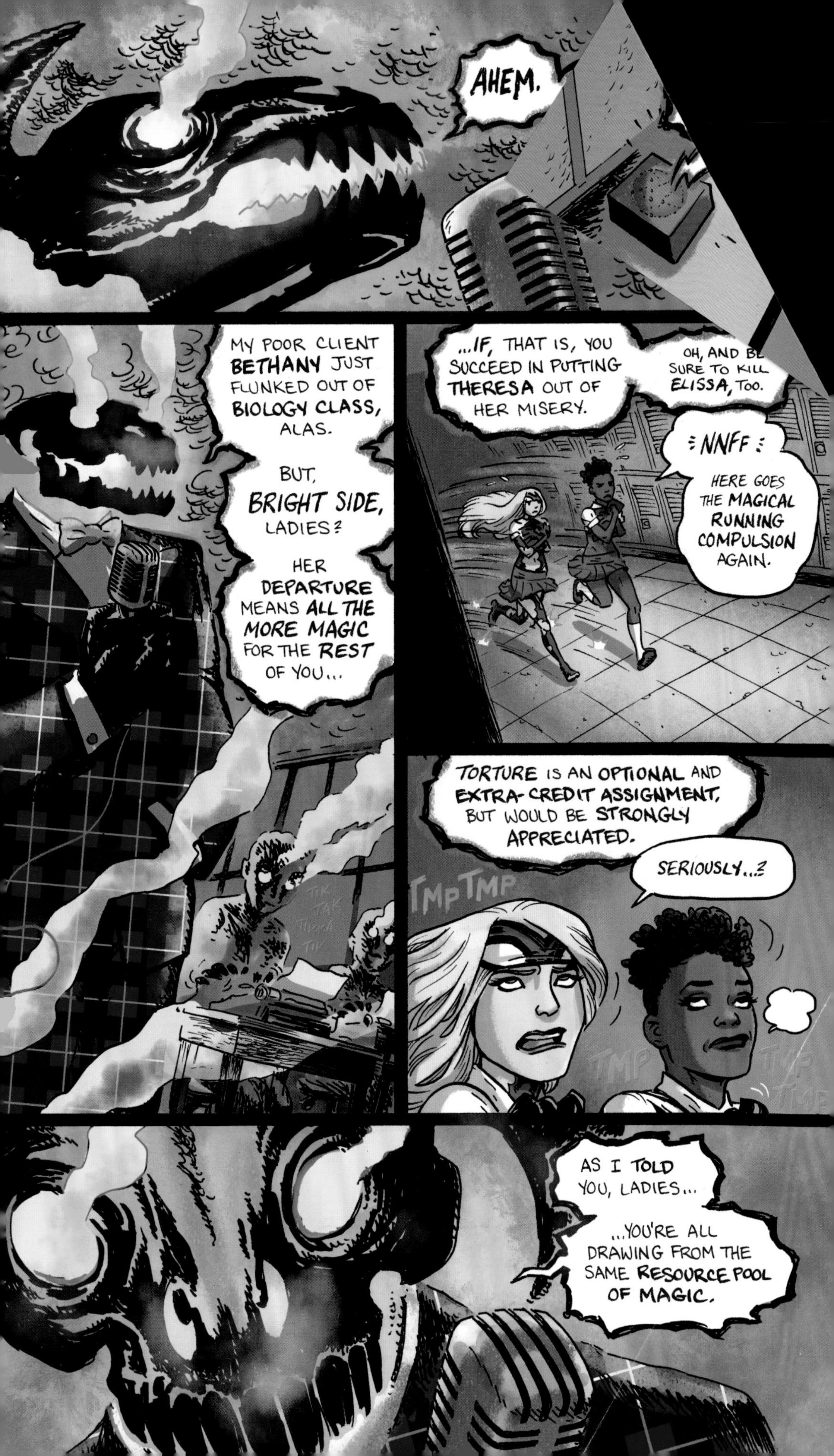
AHEM.
MY POOR CLIENT BETHANY JUST FLUNKED OUT OF BIOLOGY CLASS, ALAS.
BUT, BRIGHT SIDE, LADIES?
HER DEPARTURE MEANS ALL THE MORE MAGIC FOR THE REST OF YOU...
...IF, THAT IS, YOU SUCCEED IN PUTTING THERESA OUT OF HER MISERY.
OH, AND BE SURE TO KILL ELISSA, TOO.
NNFF
HERE GOES THE MAGICAL RUNNING COMPULSION AGAIN.
TORTURE IS AN OPTIONAL AND EXTRA-CREDIT ASSIGNMENT, BUT WOULD BE STRONGLY APPRECIATED.
SERIOUSLY...?
TMP TMP
AS I TOLD YOU, LADIES...
...YOU'RE ALL DRAWING FROM THE SAME RESOURCE POOL OF MAGIC.

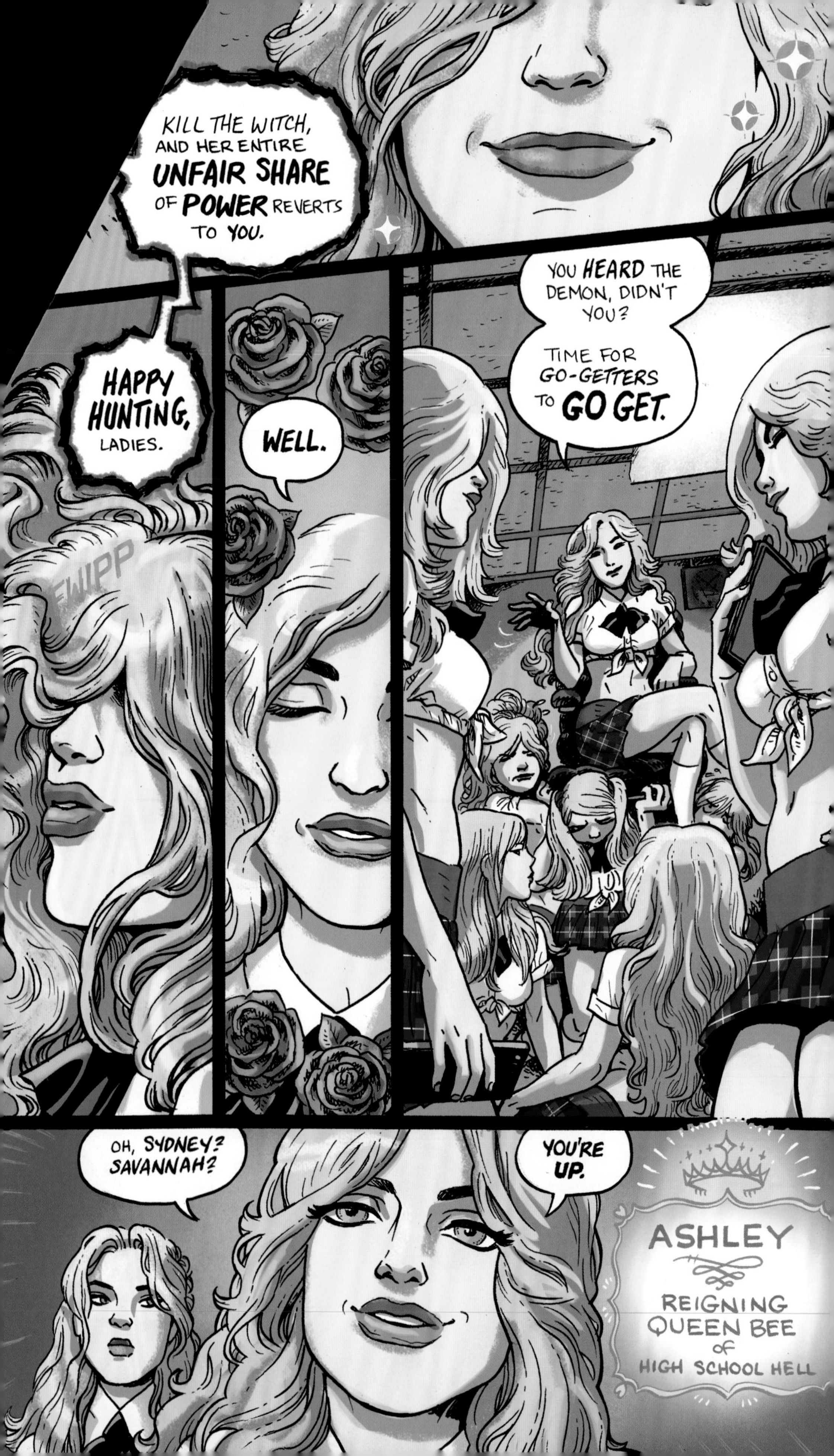
KILL THE WITCH, AND HER ENTIRE UNFAIR SHARE OF POWER REVERTS TO YOU.
HAPPY HUNTING, LADIES.
FWIPP
WELL.
YOU HEARD THE DEMON, DIDN'T YOU?
TIME FOR GO-GETTERS TO GO GET.
OH, SYDNEY? SAVANNAH?
YOU'RE UP.
ASHLEY
REIGNING QUEEN BEE OF HIGH SCHOOL HELL

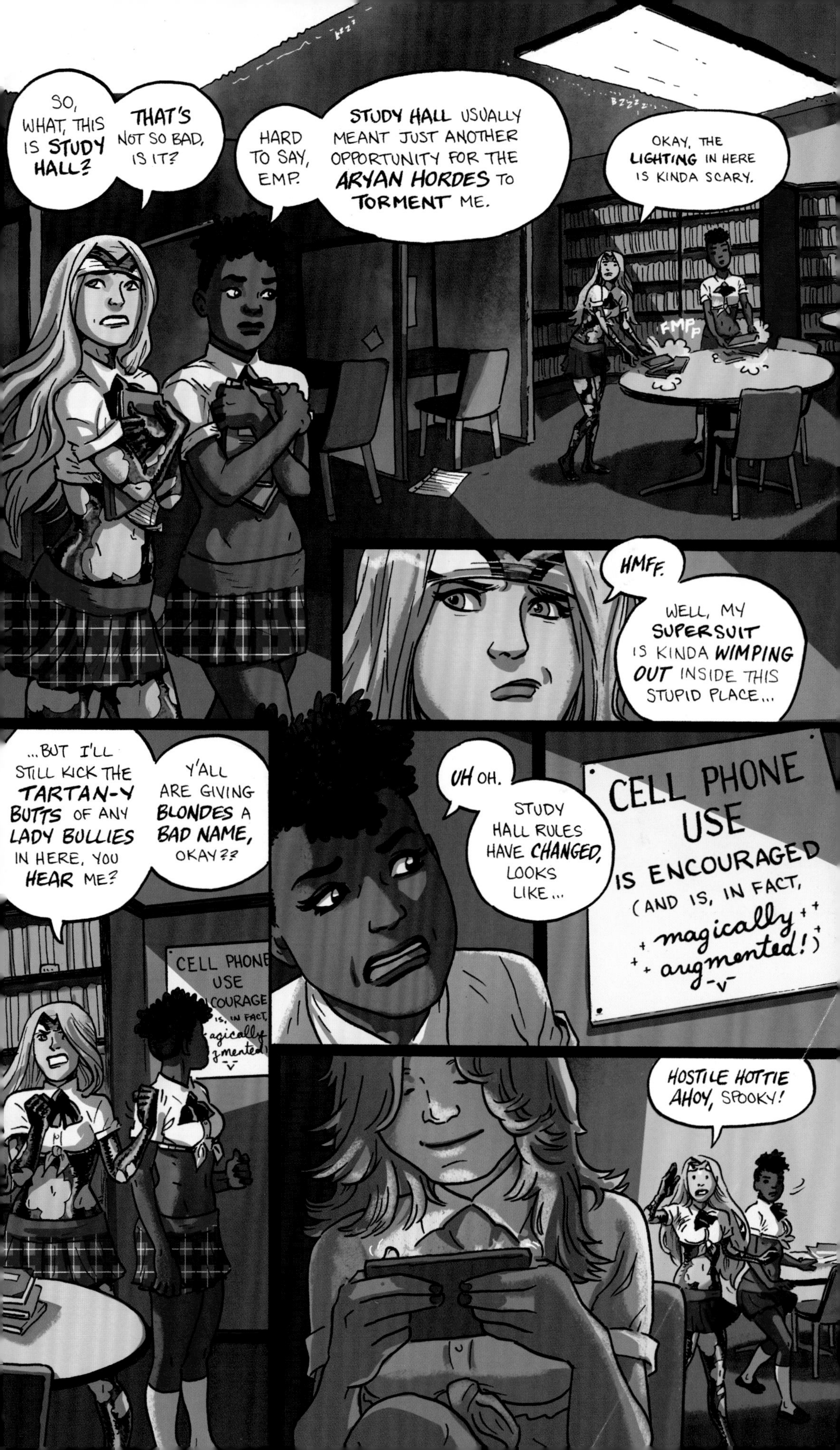

BZZZ
BZZZZ
SO, WHAT, THIS IS STUDY HALL?
THAT'S NOT SO BAD, IS IT?
HARD TO SAY, EMP.
STUDY HALL USUALLY MEANT JUST ANOTHER OPPORTUNITY FOR THE ARYAN HORDES TO TORMENT ME.
OKAY, THE LIGHTING IN HERE IS KINDA SCARY.
FMPF
HMFF.
WELL, MY SUPERSUIT IS KINDA WIMPING OUT INSIDE THIS STUPID PLACE...
...BUT I'LL STILL KICK THE TARTAN-Y BUTTS OF ANY LADY BULLIES IN HERE, YOU HEAR ME?
Y'ALL ARE GIVING BLONDES A BAD NAME, OKAY??
UH OH.
STUDY HALL RULES HAVE CHANGED, LOOKS LIKE...
CELL PHONE USE IS ENCOURAGED (AND IS, IN FACT, magically augmented!)
HOSTILE HOTTIE AHOY, SPOOKY!

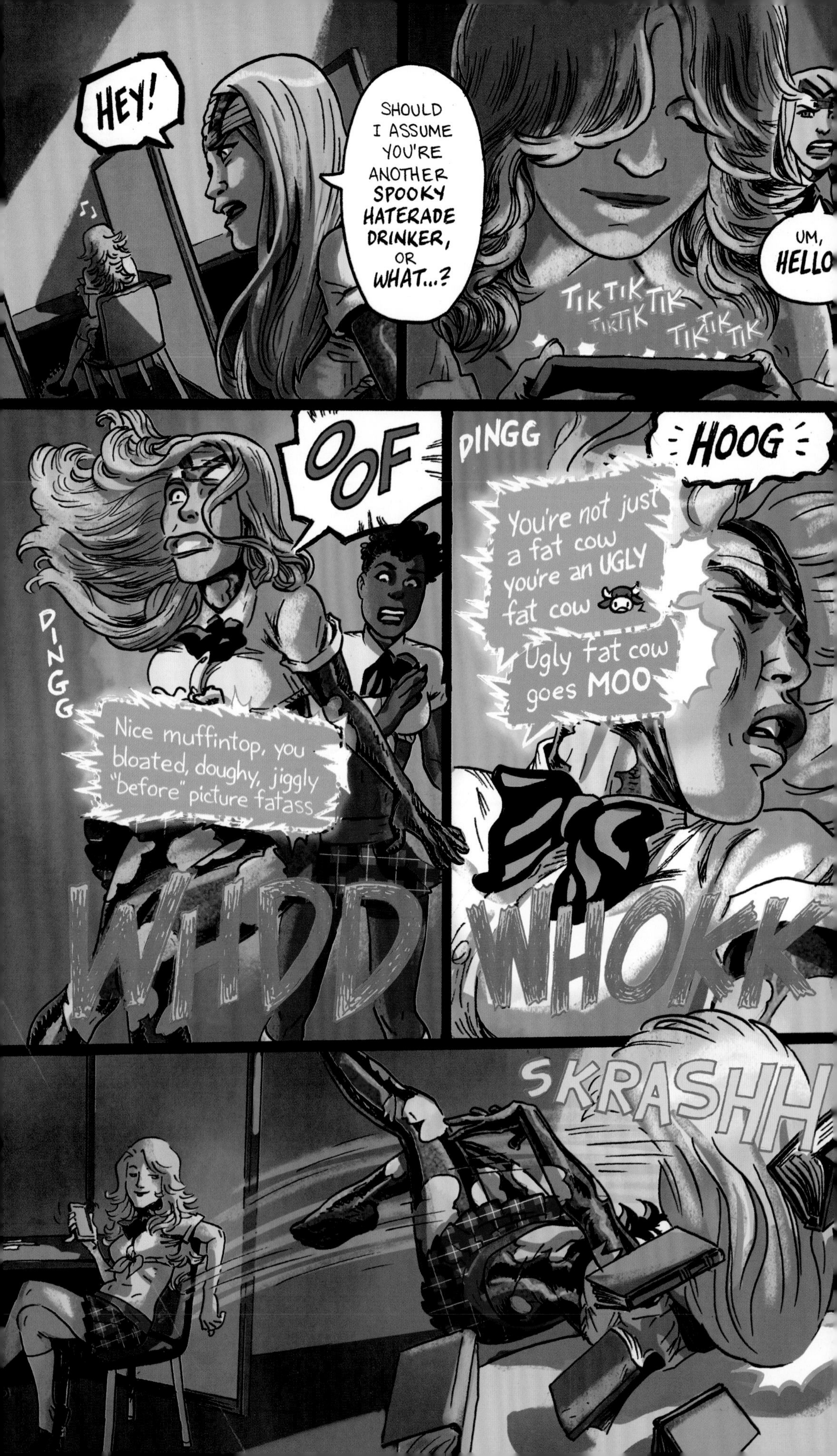
HEY!
SHOULD I ASSUME YOU'RE ANOTHER SPOOKY HATERADE DRINKER, OR WHAT...?
TIKTIKTIK TIKTIK TIKTIKTIK
UM, HELLO
OOF
D-I-N-G-G
Nice muffintop, you bloated, doughy, jiggly "before" picture fatass
WHDD
DINGG
HOOG
You're not just a fat cow you're an UGLY fat cow
Ugly fat cow goes MOO
WHOKK
SKRASHH

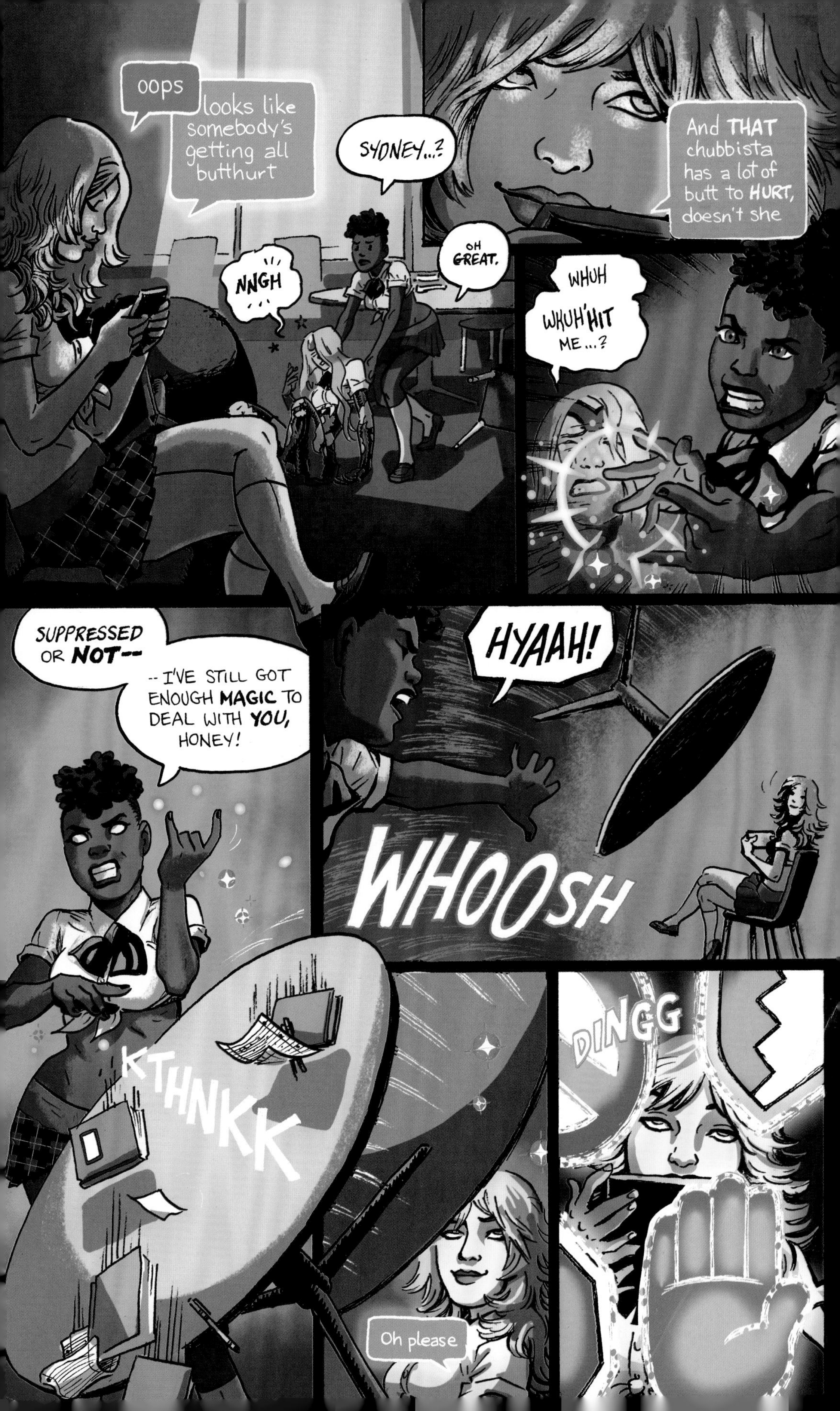

oops
looks like somebody's getting all butthurt
SYDNEY...?
OH GREAT.
NNGH
And THAT chubbista has a lot of butt to HURT, doesn't she
WHUH
WHUH'HIT ME...?
SUPPRESSED OR NOT--
--I'VE STILL GOT ENOUGH MAGIC TO DEAL WITH YOU, HONEY!
HYAAH!
WHOOSH
KTHNKK
Oh please
DINGG

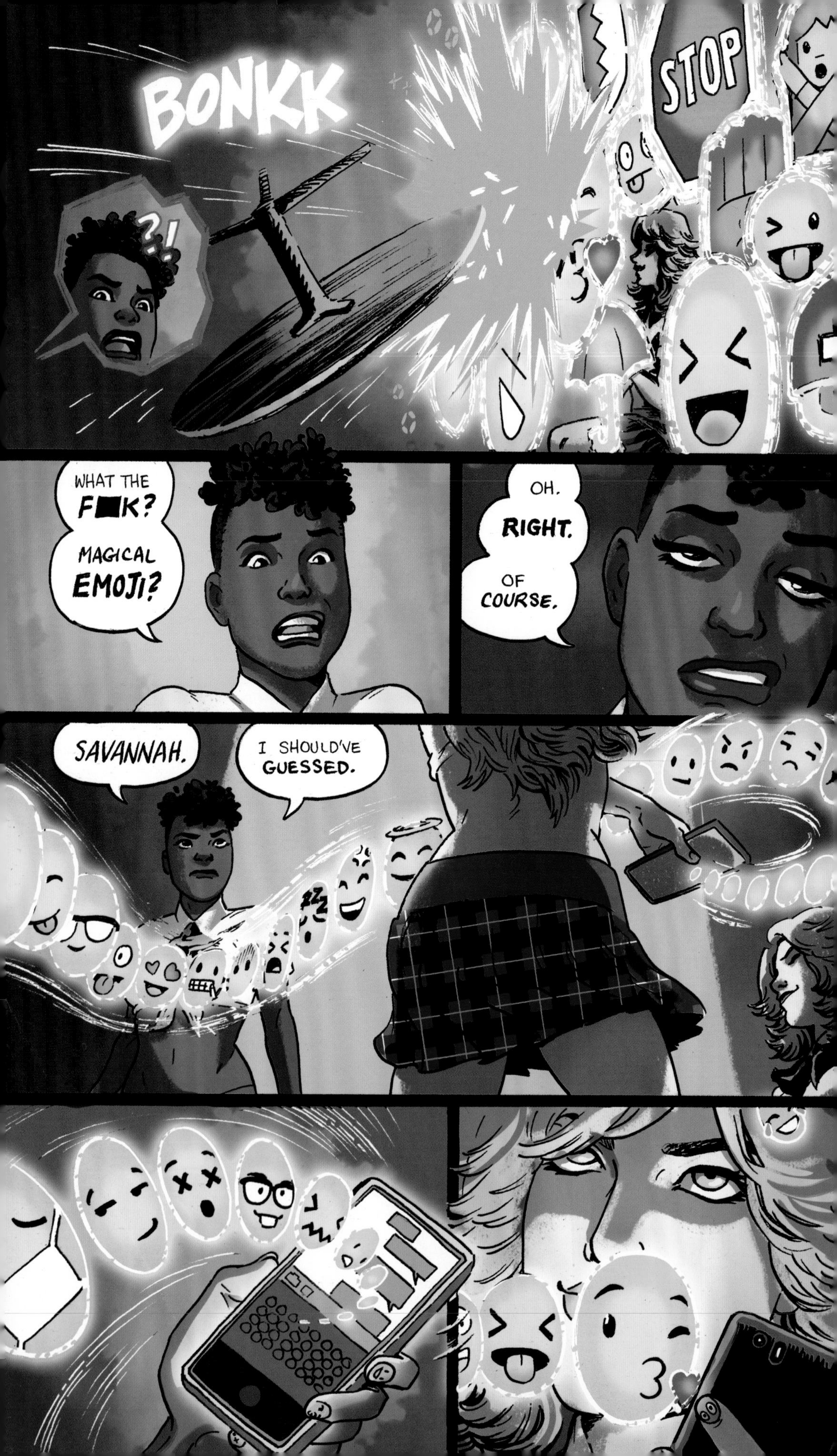
BONKK
?!
STOP
WHAT THE F[redacted]K?
MAGICAL EMOJI?
OH.
RIGHT.
OF COURSE.
SAVANNAH.
I SHOULD'VE GUESSED.

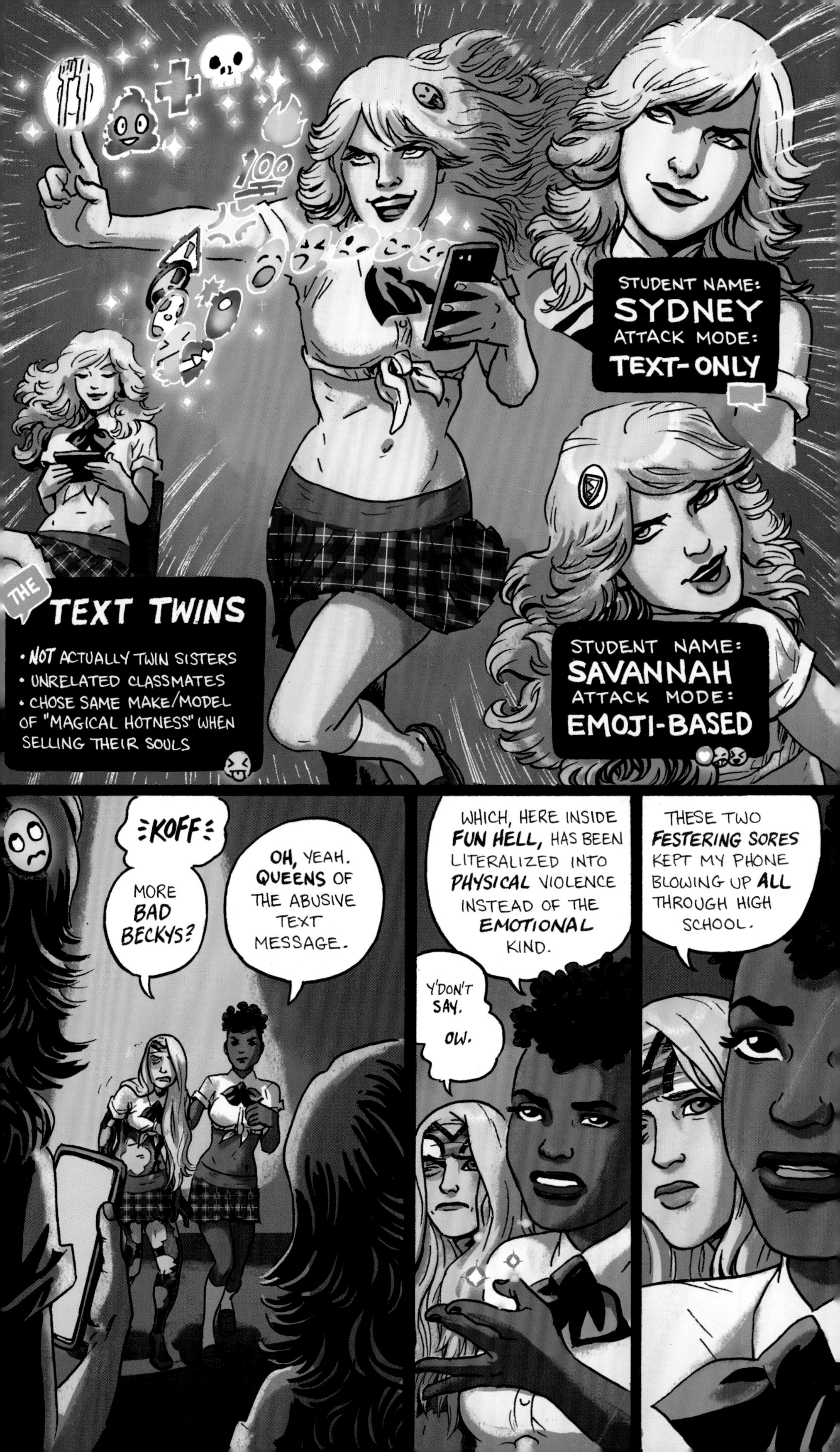
STUDENT NAME:
SYDNEY
ATTACK MODE:
TEXT-ONLY
THE
TEXT TWINS
• NOT ACTUALLY TWIN SISTERS
• UNRELATED CLASSMATES
• CHOSE SAME MAKE/MODEL OF "MAGICAL HOTNESS" WHEN SELLING THEIR SOULS
STUDENT NAME:
SAVANNAH
ATTACK MODE:
EMOJI-BASED
KOFF
MORE BAD BECKYS?
OH, YEAH. QUEENS OF THE ABUSIVE TEXT MESSAGE.
WHICH, HERE INSIDE FUN HELL, HAS BEEN LITERALIZED INTO PHYSICAL VIOLENCE INSTEAD OF THE EMOTIONAL KIND.
Y'DON'T SAY.
OW.
THESE TWO FESTERING SORES KEPT MY PHONE BLOWING UP ALL THROUGH HIGH SCHOOL.

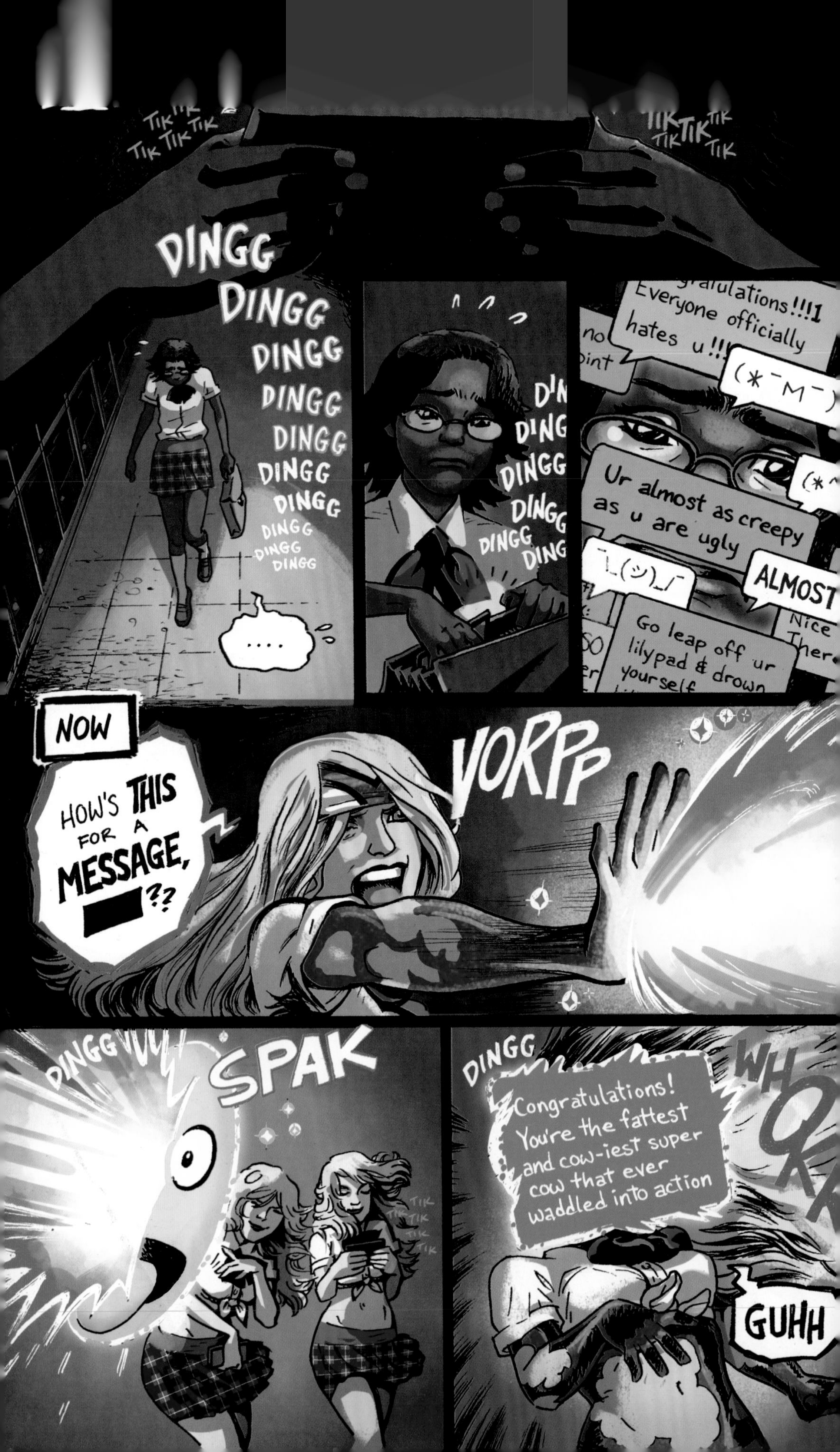

TIK TIK TIK TIK TIK TIK
TIK TIK TIK TIK TIK
DINGG
DINGG
DINGG
DINGG
DINGG
DINGG
DINGG
DINGG
DINGG
DINGG
....
DINGG
DINGG
DINGG
DINGG
gratulations!!!1 Everyone officially hates u!!!
Ur almost as creepy as u are ugly
ALMOST
Go leap off ur lilypad & drown yourself
NOW
HOW'S THIS FOR A MESSAGE, [redacted]??
VORPP
DINGG
SPAK
TIK TIK TIK TIK TIK
DINGG
Congratulations! You're the fattest and cow-iest super cow that ever waddled into action
GUHH

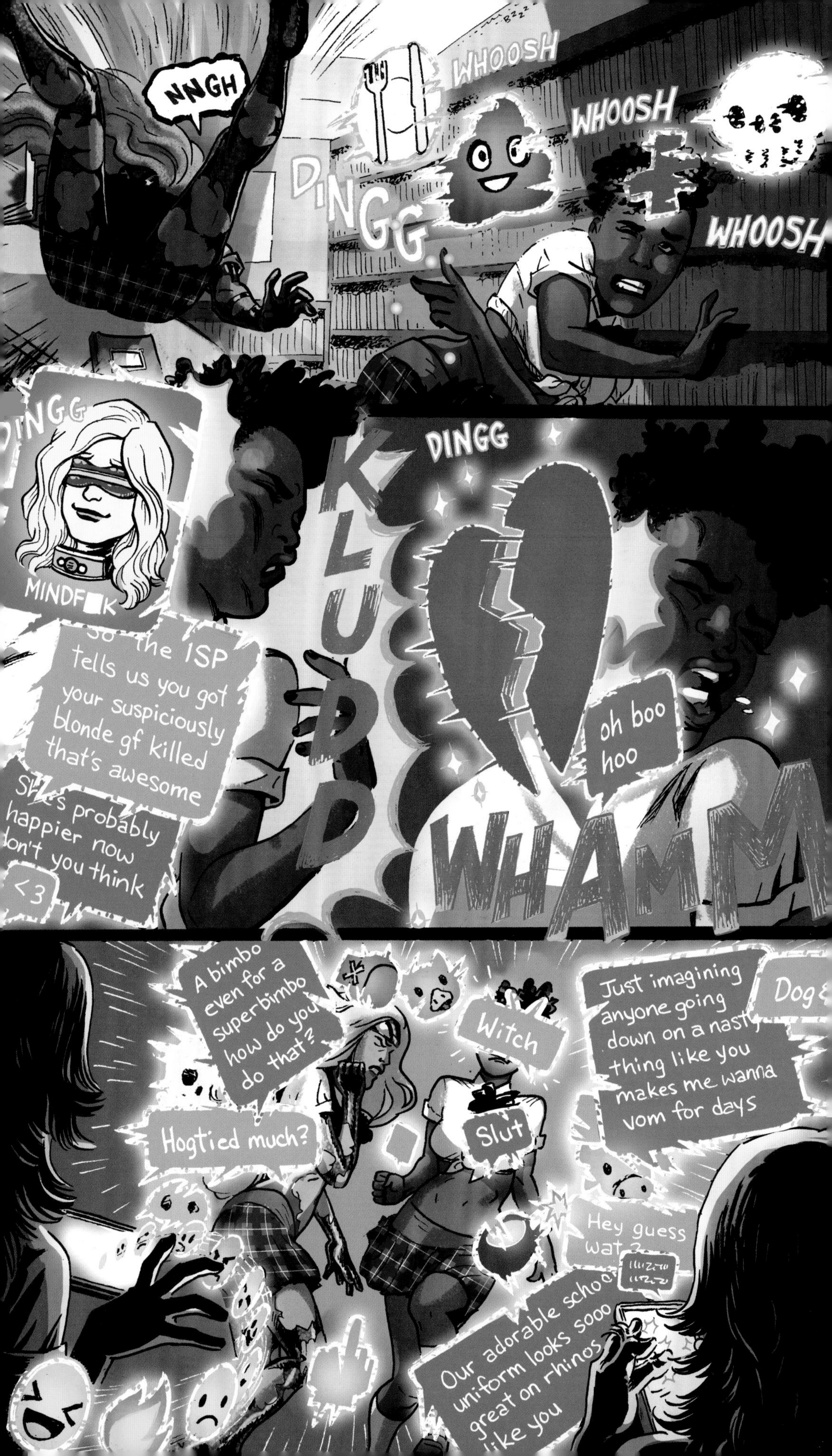

NNGH
WHOOSH
WHOOSH
DINGG
WHOOSH
DINGG
MINDF[redacted]K
DINGG
KLUDD
So the ISP tells us you got your suspiciously blonde gf killed that's awesome
She's probably happier now on't you think <3
oh boo hoo
WHAMM
A bimbo even for a superbimbo how do you do that?!
Witch
Just imagining anyone going down on a nasty thing like you makes me wanna vom for days
Dog &
Hogtied much?
Slut
Hey guess wat?
Our adorable schoo uniform looks sooo great on rhinos like you

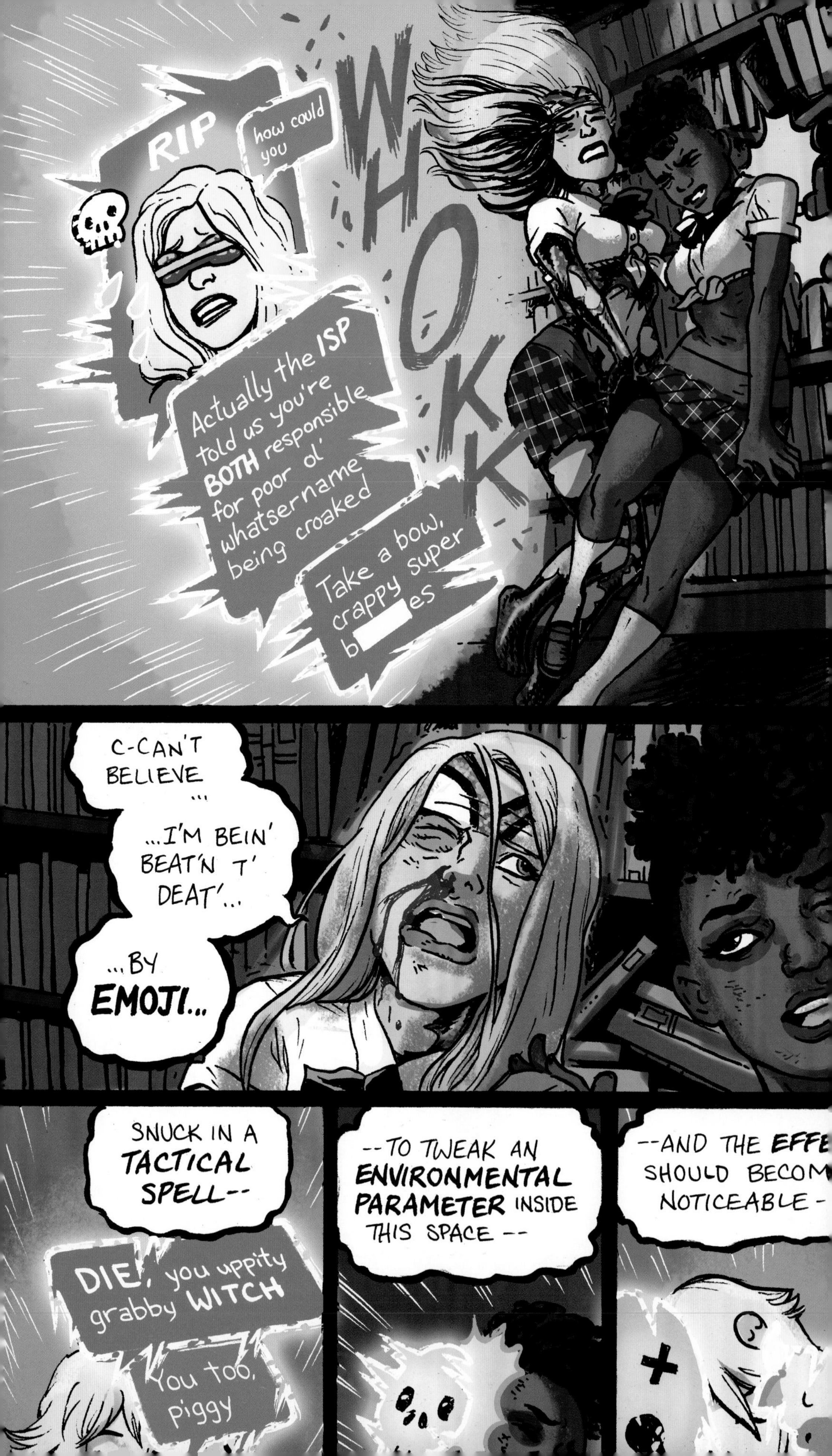

RIP
how could you
WHOK
Actually the ISP told us you're BOTH responsible for poor ol' whatsername being croaked
Take a bow, crappy super b es
C-CAN'T BELIEVE ...
...I'M BEIN' BEAT'N T' DEAT'...
...BY EMOJI...
SNUCK IN A TACTICAL SPELL--
DIE, you uppity grabby WITCH
You too, piggy
--TO TWEAK AN ENVIRONMENTAL PARAMETER INSIDE THIS SPACE --
--AND THE EFFE
SHOULD BECOM
NOTICEABLE -

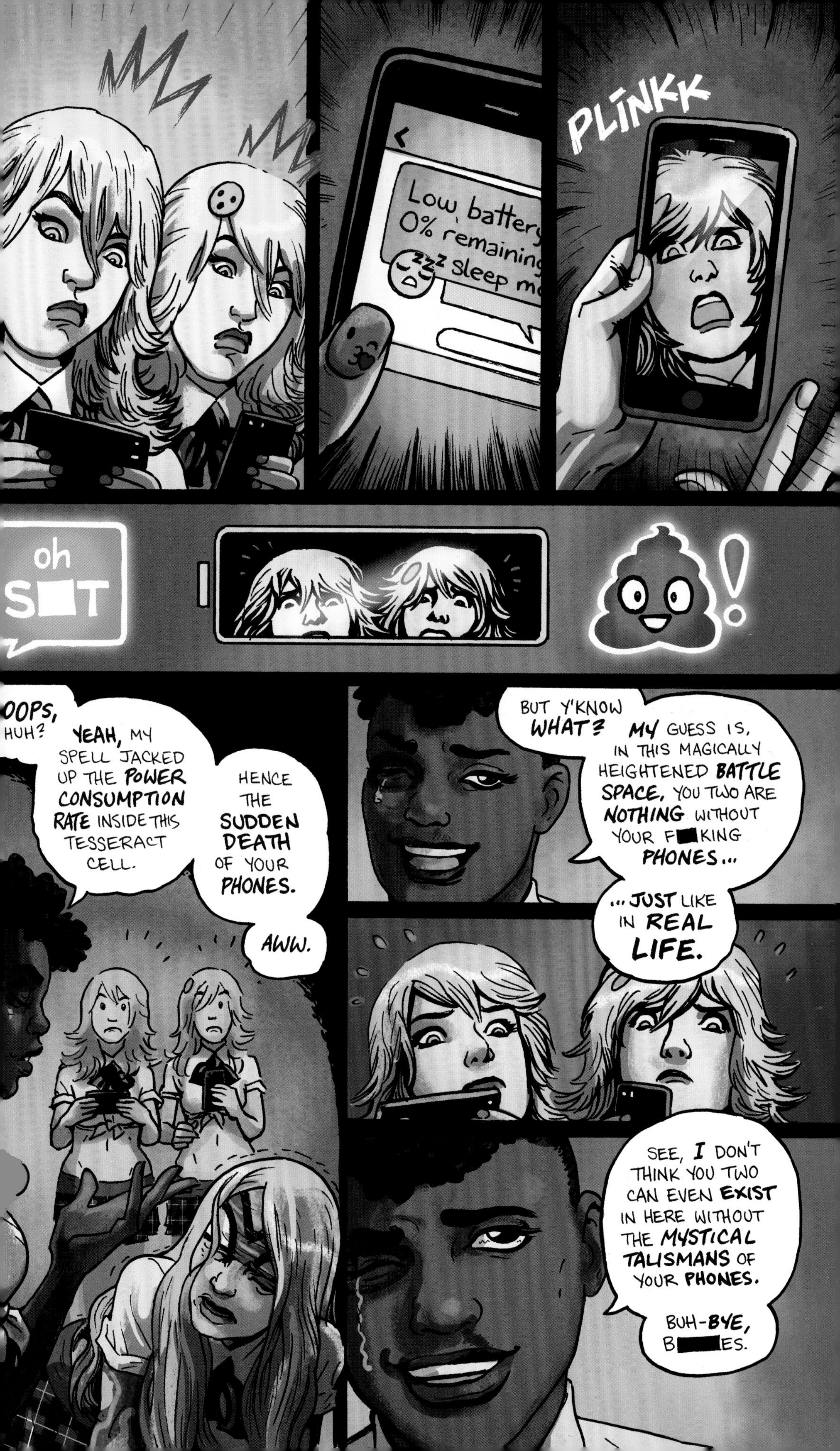

Low battery
0% remaining
sleep mo
PLINKK
oh S[redacted]T
OOPS, HUH?
YEAH, MY SPELL JACKED UP THE POWER CONSUMPTION RATE INSIDE THIS TESSERACT CELL.
HENCE THE SUDDEN DEATH OF YOUR PHONES.
AWW.
BUT Y'KNOW WHAT? MY GUESS IS, IN THIS MAGICALLY HEIGHTENED BATTLE SPACE, YOU TWO ARE NOTHING WITHOUT YOUR F[redacted]KING PHONES...
...JUST LIKE IN REAL LIFE.
SEE, I DON'T THINK YOU TWO CAN EVEN EXIST IN HERE WITHOUT THE MYSTICAL TALISMANS OF YOUR PHONES.
BUH-BYE, B[redacted]ES.

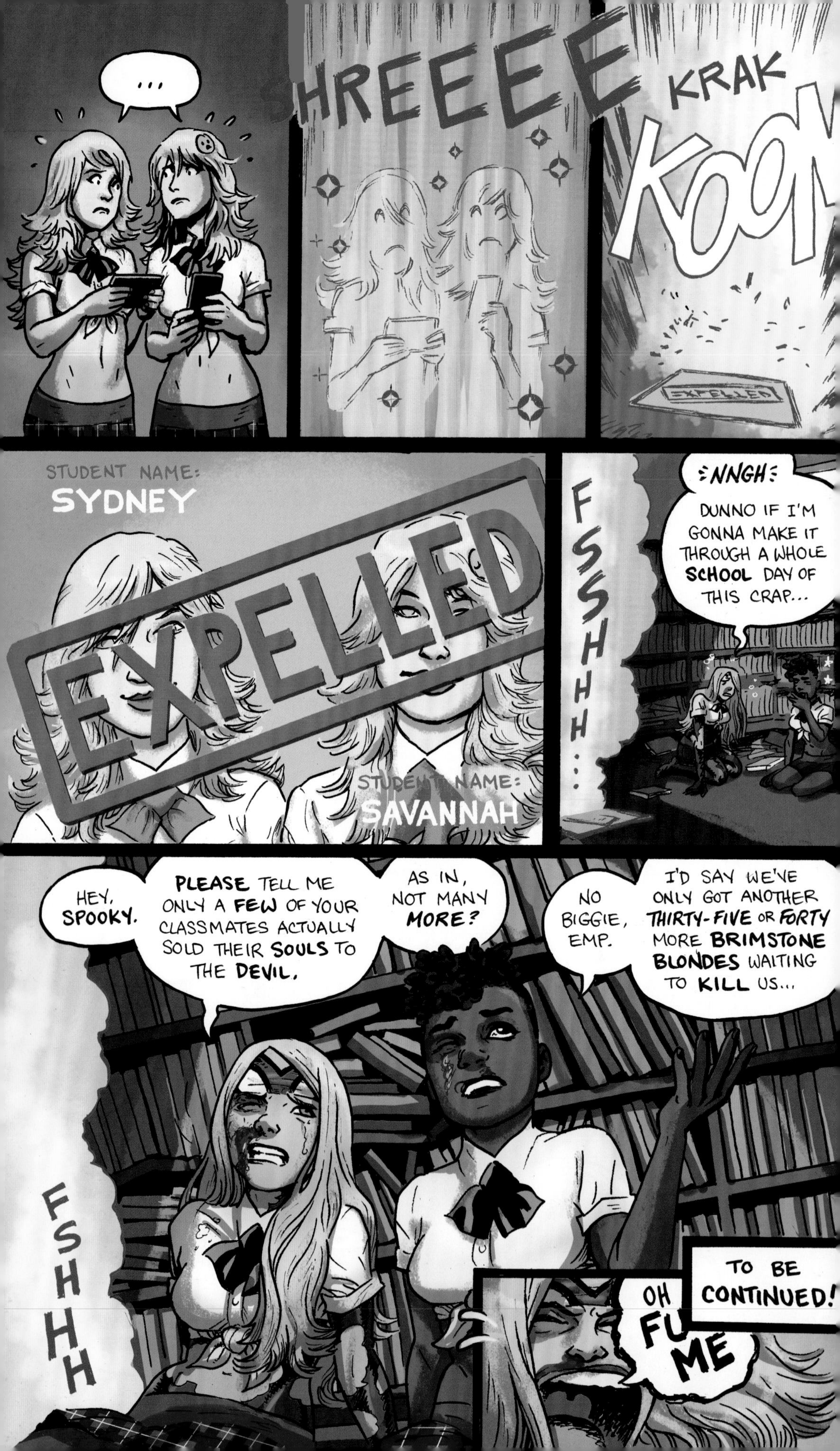
...
SHREEEE
KRAK
KOOM
EXPELLED
STUDENT NAME:
SYDNEY
EXPELLED
STUDENT NAME:
SAVANNAH
FSSHHH...
NNGH
DUNNO IF I'M GONNA MAKE IT THROUGH A WHOLE SCHOOL DAY OF THIS CRAP...
HEY, SPOOKY.
PLEASE TELL ME ONLY A FEW OF YOUR CLASSMATES ACTUALLY SOLD THEIR SOULS TO THE DEVIL.
AS IN, NOT MANY MORE?
NO BIGGIE, EMP.
I'D SAY WE'VE ONLY GOT ANOTHER THIRTY-FIVE OR FORTY MORE BRIMSTONE BLONDES WAITING TO KILL US...
FSHHH
OH FU ME
TO BE CONTINUED!

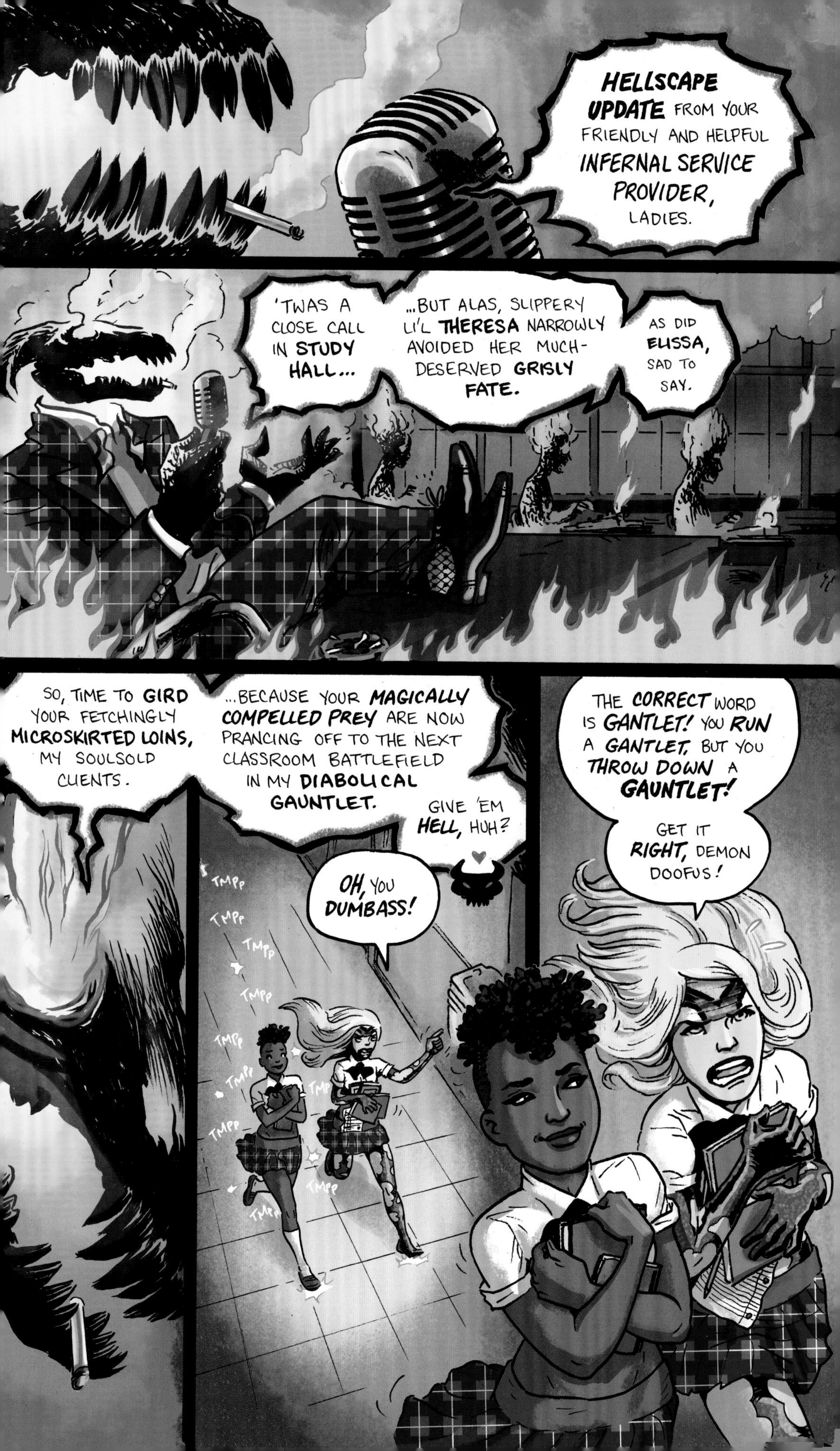
HELLSCAPE UPDATE FROM YOUR FRIENDLY AND HELPFUL INFERNAL SERVICE PROVIDER, LADIES.
'TWAS A CLOSE CALL IN STUDY HALL...
...BUT ALAS, SLIPPERY LI'L THERESA NARROWLY AVOIDED HER MUCH-DESERVED GRISLY FATE.
AS DID ELISSA, SAD TO SAY.
SO, TIME TO GIRD YOUR FETCHINGLY MICROSKIRTED LOINS, MY SOULSOLD CLIENTS.
...BECAUSE YOUR MAGICALLY COMPELLED PREY ARE NOW PRANCING OFF TO THE NEXT CLASSROOM BATTLEFIELD IN MY DIABOLICAL GAUNTLET.
GIVE 'EM HELL, HUH?
OH, YOU DUMBASS!
TMPP TMPP TMPP TMPP TMPP TMPP TMPP TMPP TMPP TMPP
THE CORRECT WORD IS GANTLET! YOU RUN A GANTLET, BUT YOU THROW DOWN A GAUNTLET!
GET IT RIGHT, DEMON DOOFUS!

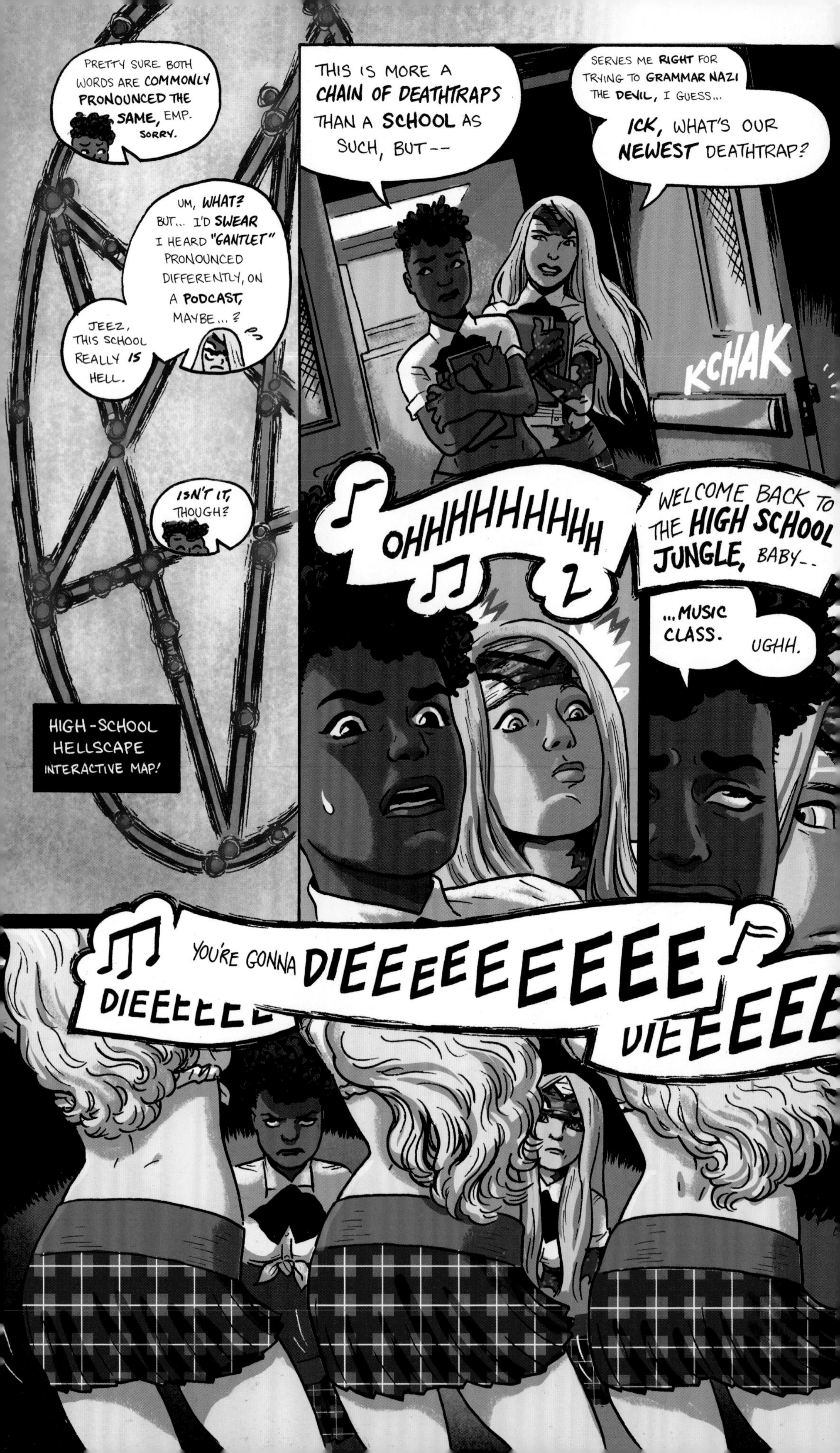
PRETTY SURE BOTH WORDS ARE COMMONLY PRONOUNCED THE SAME, EMP. SORRY.
UM, WHAT? BUT... I'D SWEAR I HEARD "GANTLET" PRONOUNCED DIFFERENTLY, ON A PODCAST, MAYBE...?
JEEZ, THIS SCHOOL REALLY IS HELL.
ISN'T IT, THOUGH?
HIGH-SCHOOL HELLSCAPE INTERACTIVE MAP!
THIS IS MORE A CHAIN OF DEATHTRAPS THAN A SCHOOL AS SUCH, BUT--
SERVES ME RIGHT FOR TRYING TO GRAMMAR NAZI THE DEVIL, I GUESS...
ICK, WHAT'S OUR NEWEST DEATHTRAP?
KCHAK
OHHHHHHHHH
WELCOME BACK TO THE HIGH SCHOOL JUNGLE, BABY--
...MUSIC CLASS.
UGHH.
YOU'RE GONNA DIEEEEEEEEE
DIEEEEEE
DIEEEEE

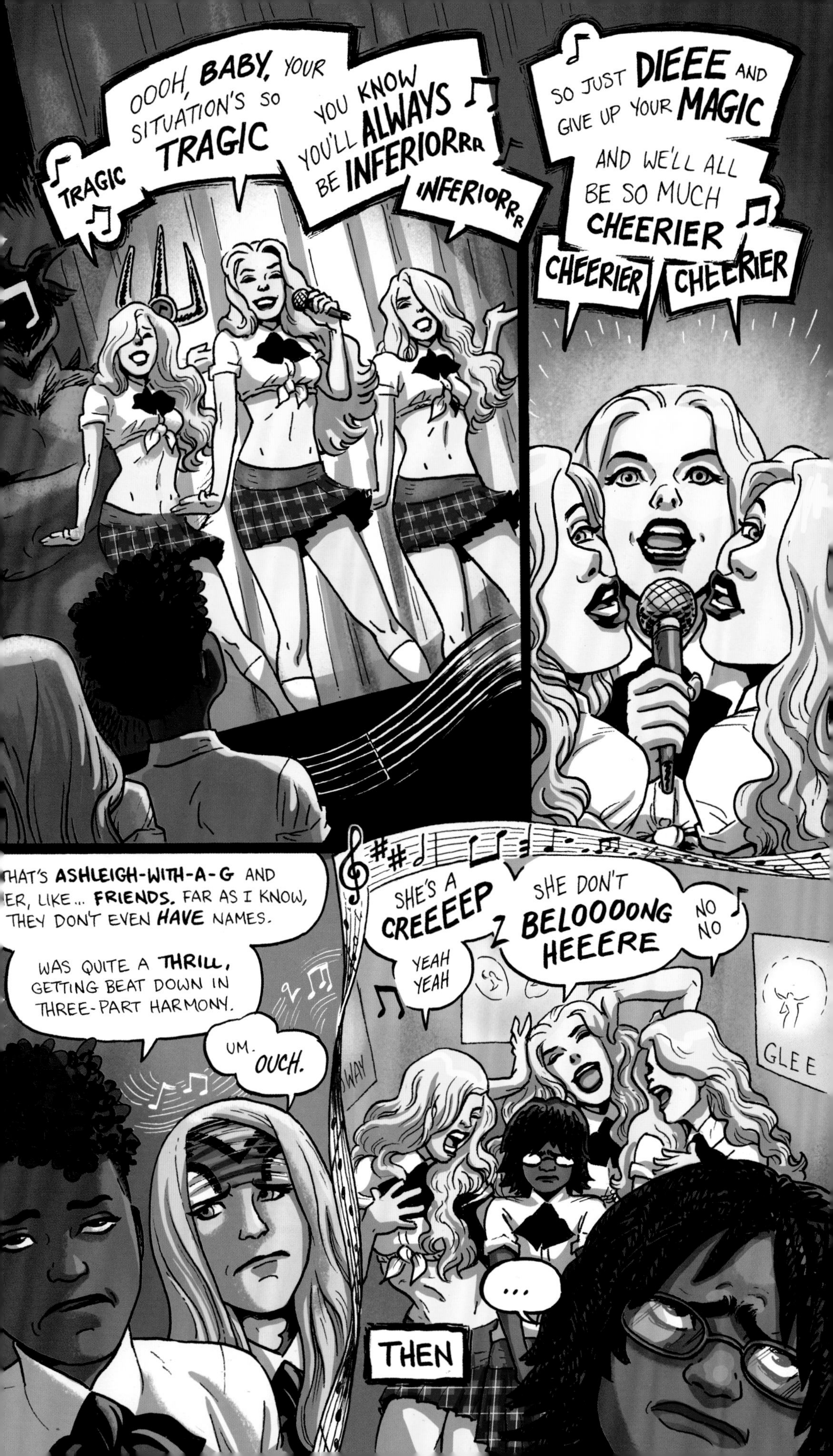

OOOH, BABY, YOUR SITUATION'S SO TRAGIC
TRAGIC
YOU KNOW YOU'LL ALWAYS BE INFERIORRR
INFERIORRR
SO JUST DIEEE AND GIVE UP YOUR MAGIC
AND WE'LL ALL BE SO MUCH CHEERIER
CHEERIER
CHEERIER
THAT'S ASHLEIGH-WITH-A-G AND ER, LIKE... FRIENDS. FAR AS I KNOW, THEY DON'T EVEN HAVE NAMES.
WAS QUITE A THRILL, GETTING BEAT DOWN IN THREE-PART HARMONY.
UM. OUCH.
SHE'S A CREEEEP
YEAH YEAH
SHE DON'T BELOOOONG HEEERE
NO NO
GLEE
...
THEN

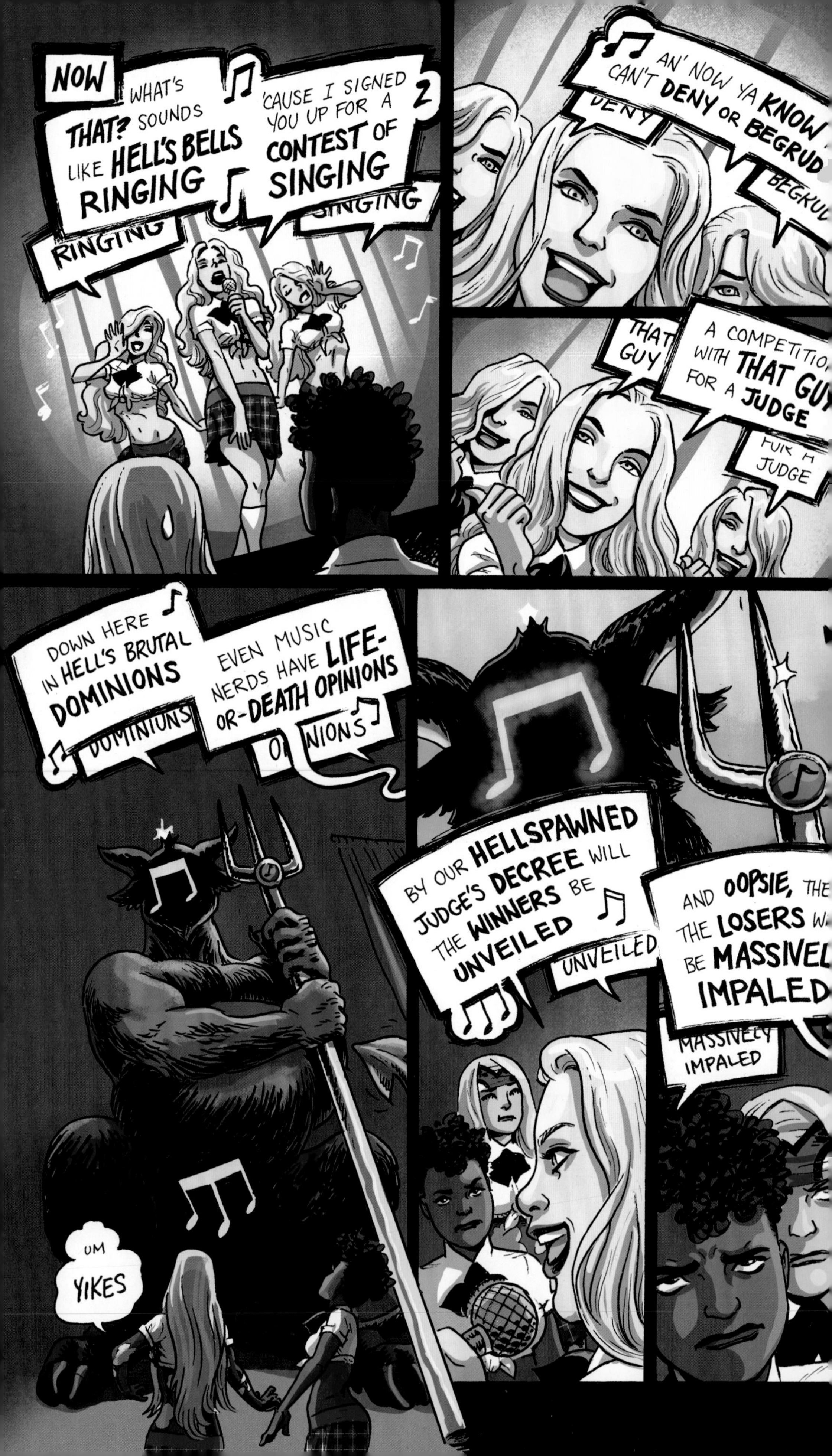
NOW
WHAT'S THAT? SOUNDS LIKE HELL'S BELLS RINGING
RINGING
'CAUSE I SIGNED YOU UP FOR A CONTEST OF SINGING
SINGING
AN' NOW YA KNOW, CAN'T DENY OR BEGRUD
DENY
BEGRUD
A COMPETITIO WITH THAT GUY FOR A JUDGE
THAT GUY
FOR A JUDGE
DOWN HERE IN HELL'S BRUTAL DOMINIONS
DOMINIONS
EVEN MUSIC NERDS HAVE LIFE-OR-DEATH OPINIONS
OPINIONS
UM YIKES
BY OUR HELLSPAWNED JUDGE'S DECREE WILL THE WINNERS BE UNVEILED
UNVEILED
AND OOPSIE, THE THE LOSERS W BE MASSIVEL IMPALED
MASSIVELY IMPALED

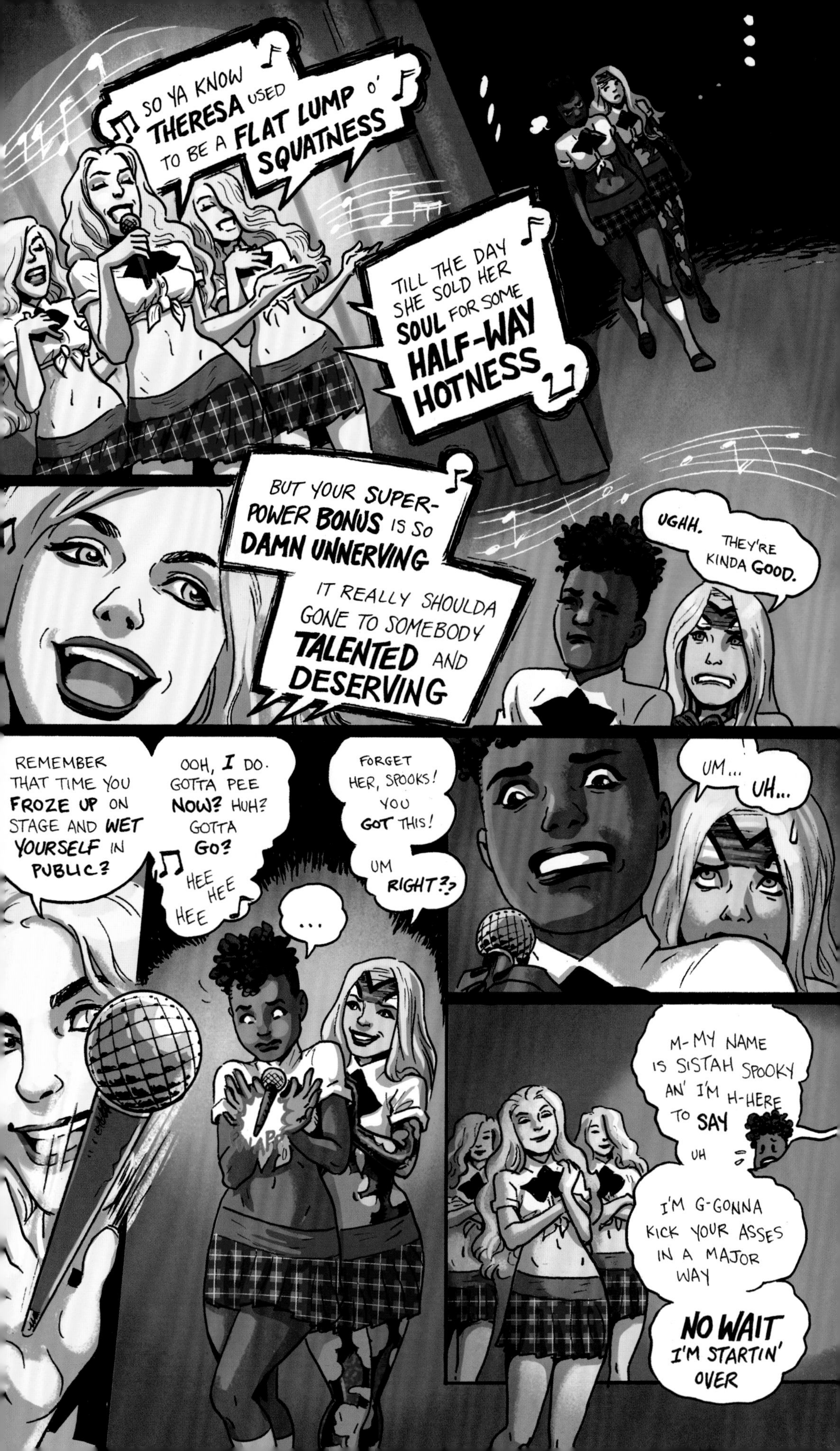

SO YA KNOW THERESA USED TO BE A FLAT LUMP O' SQUATNESS
TILL THE DAY SHE SOLD HER SOUL FOR SOME HALF-WAY HOTNESS
BUT YOUR SUPER-POWER BONUS IS SO DAMN UNNERVING
IT REALLY SHOULDA GONE TO SOMEBODY TALENTED AND DESERVING
UGAH.
THEY'RE KINDA GOOD.
REMEMBER THAT TIME YOU FROZE UP ON STAGE AND WET YOURSELF IN PUBLIC?
OOH, I DO. GOTTA PEE NOW? HUH? GOTTA GO?
HEE HEE HEE
FORGET HER, SPOOKS! YOU GOT THIS!
UM RIGHT?!?
...
UM...
UH...
M-MY NAME IS SISTAH SPOOKY AN' I'M H-HERE TO SAY
UH
I'M G-GONNA KICK YOUR ASSES IN A MAJOR WAY
NO WAIT I'M STARTIN' OVER

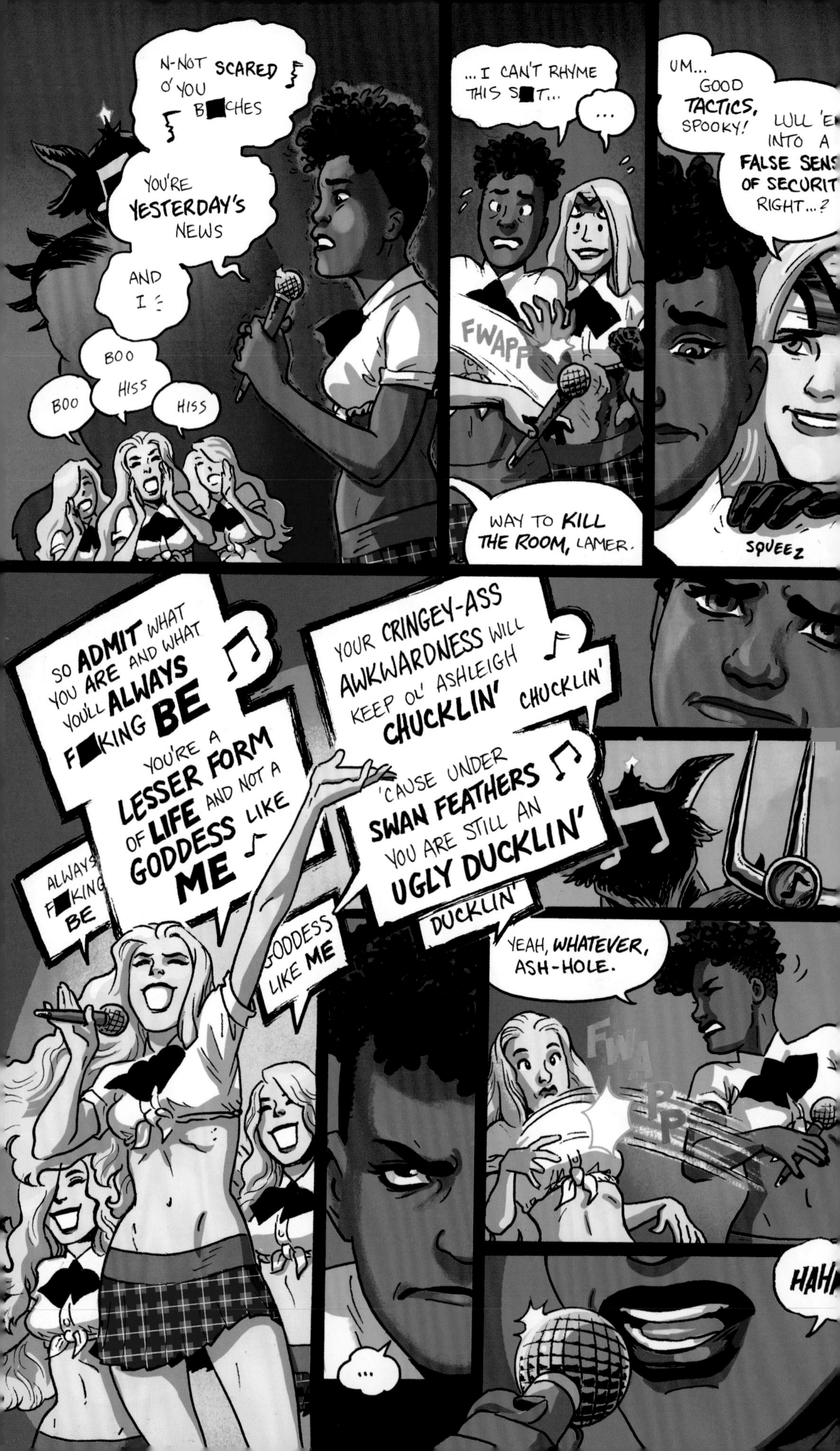

N-NOT SCARED O' YOU B[redacted]CHES
YOU'RE YESTERDAY'S NEWS
AND I
BOO
HISS
BOO
HISS
...I CAN'T RHYME THIS S[redacted]T...
...
FWAPP
WAY TO KILL THE ROOM, LAMER.
UM... GOOD TACTICS, SPOOKY!
LULL 'E INTO A FALSE SENS OF SECURIT RIGHT...?
SQUEEZ
SO ADMIT WHAT YOU ARE AND WHAT YOU'LL ALWAYS F[redacted]KING BE
YOU'RE A LESSER FORM OF LIFE AND NOT A GODDESS LIKE ME
ALWAYS F[redacted]KING BE
GODDESS LIKE ME
YOUR CRINGEY-ASS AWKWARDNESS WILL KEEP OL' ASHLEIGH CHUCKLIN'
CHUCKLIN'
'CAUSE UNDER SWAN FEATHERS YOU ARE STILL AN UGLY DUCKLIN'
DUCKLIN'
YEAH, WHATEVER, ASH-HOLE.
FWAPP
...
HAH

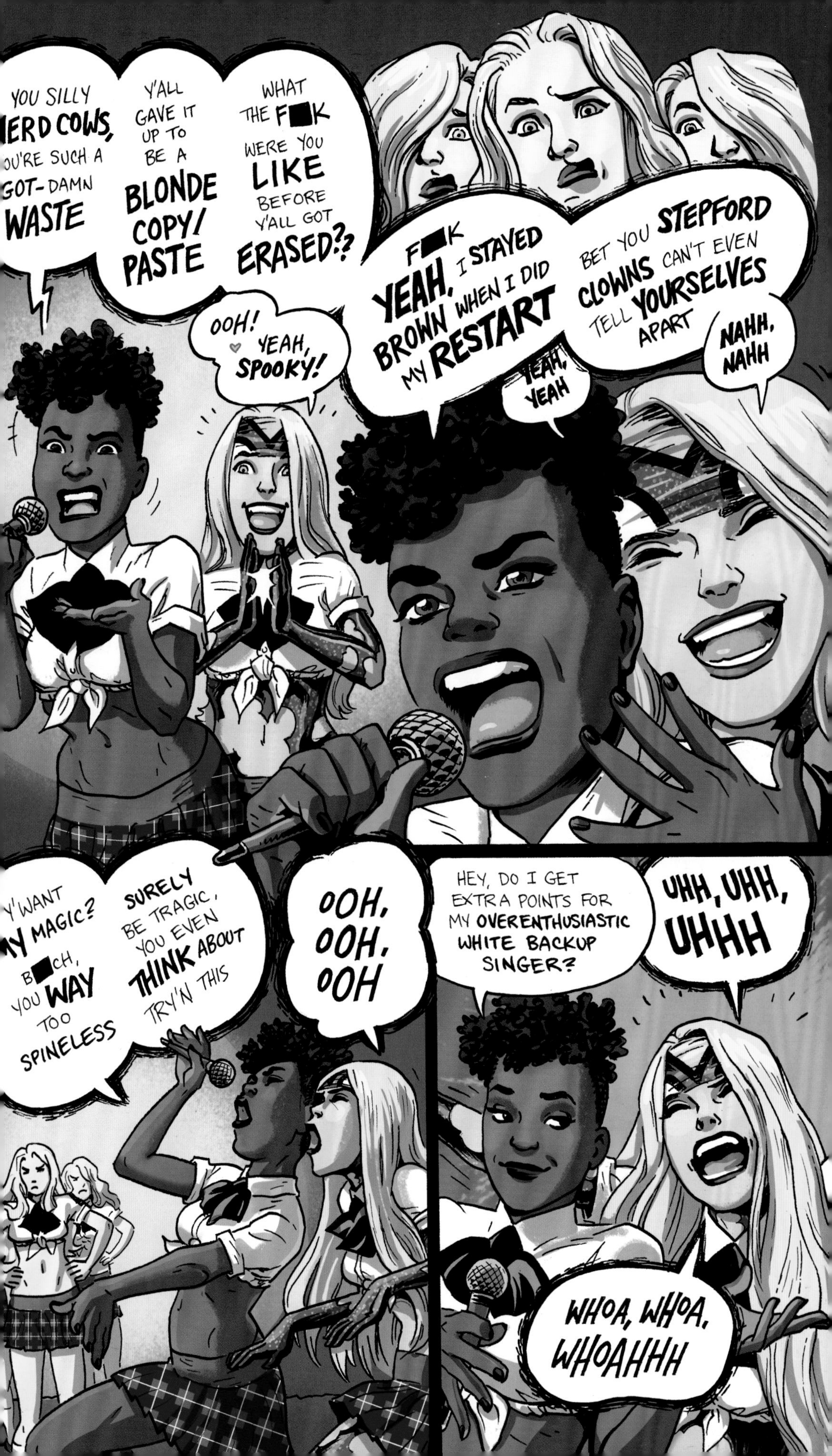

YOU SILLY ERD COWS, OU'RE SUCH A GOT-DAMN WASTE
Y'ALL GAVE IT UP TO BE A BLONDE COPY/PASTE
WHAT THE F[redacted]K WERE YOU LIKE BEFORE Y'ALL GOT ERASED?!?
OOH! ♥ YEAH, SPOOKY!
F[redacted]K YEAH, I STAYED BROWN WHEN I DID MY RESTART
BET YOU STEPFORD CLOWNS CAN'T EVEN TELL YOURSELVES APART
YEAH, YEAH
NAHH, NAHH
Y'WANT Y MAGIC? B[redacted]CH, YOU WAY TOO SPINELESS
SURELY BE TRAGIC, YOU EVEN THINK ABOUT TRY'N THIS
OOH, OOH, OOH
HEY, DO I GET EXTRA POINTS FOR MY OVERENTHUSIASTIC WHITE BACKUP SINGER?
UHH, UHH, UHHH
WHOA, WHOA, WHOAHHH

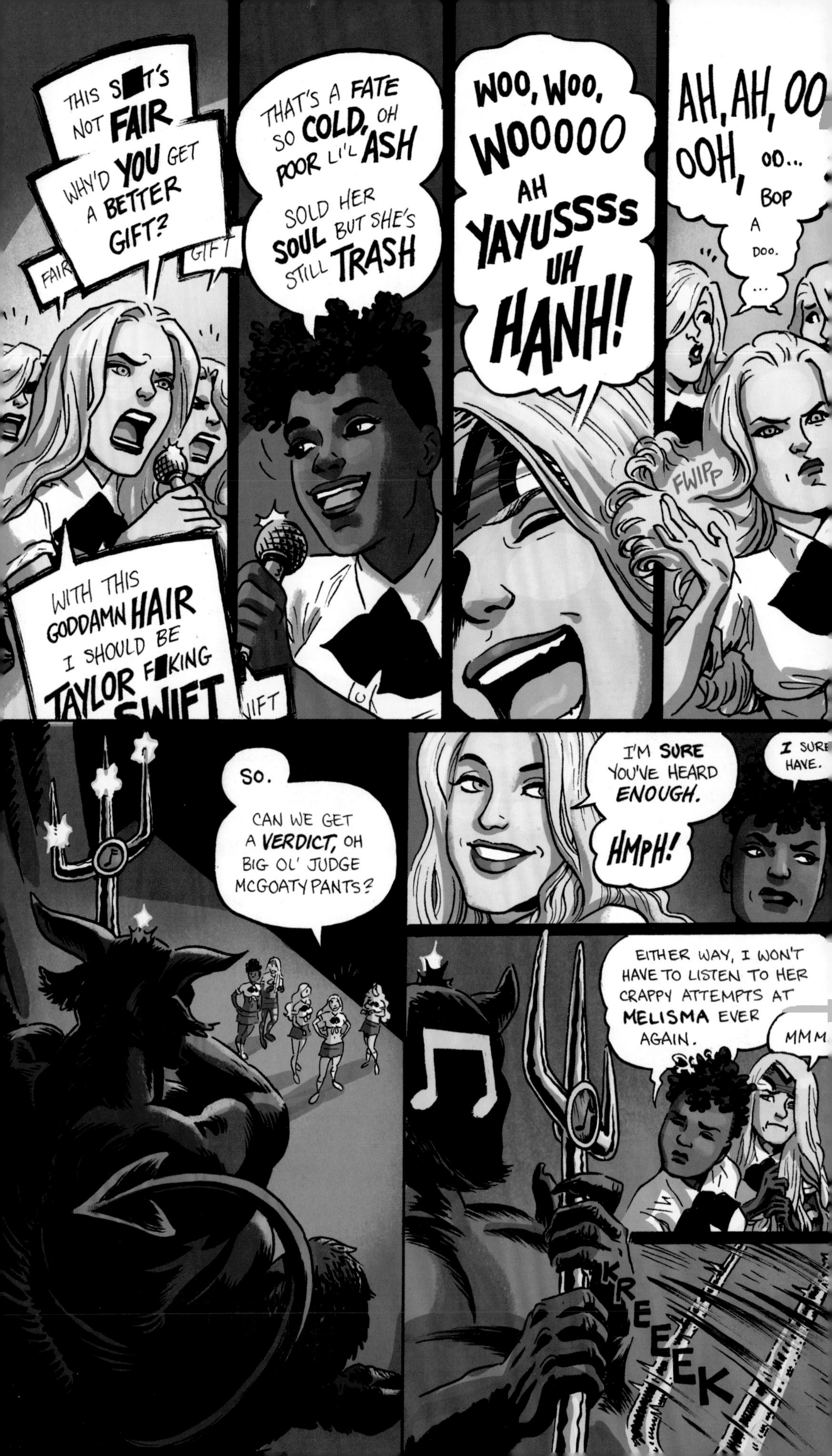

THIS S[redacted]T'S NOT FAIR
WHY'D YOU GET A BETTER GIFT?
FAIR
GIFT
WITH THIS GODDAMN HAIR I SHOULD BE TAYLOR F[redacted]KING SWIFT
THAT'S A FATE SO COLD, OH POOR LI'L ASH
SOLD HER SOUL BUT SHE'S STILL TRASH
IFT
WOO, WOO, WOOOOO AH YAYUSSSS UH HANH!
AH, AH, OO OOH, OO... BOP A DOO. ...
FWIPP
SO.
CAN WE GET A VERDICT, OH BIG OL' JUDGE MCGOATYPANTS?
I'M SURE YOU'VE HEARD ENOUGH.
HMPH!
I SURE HAVE.
EITHER WAY, I WON'T HAVE TO LISTEN TO HER CRAPPY ATTEMPTS AT MELISMA EVER AGAIN.
MMM
KREEEEK

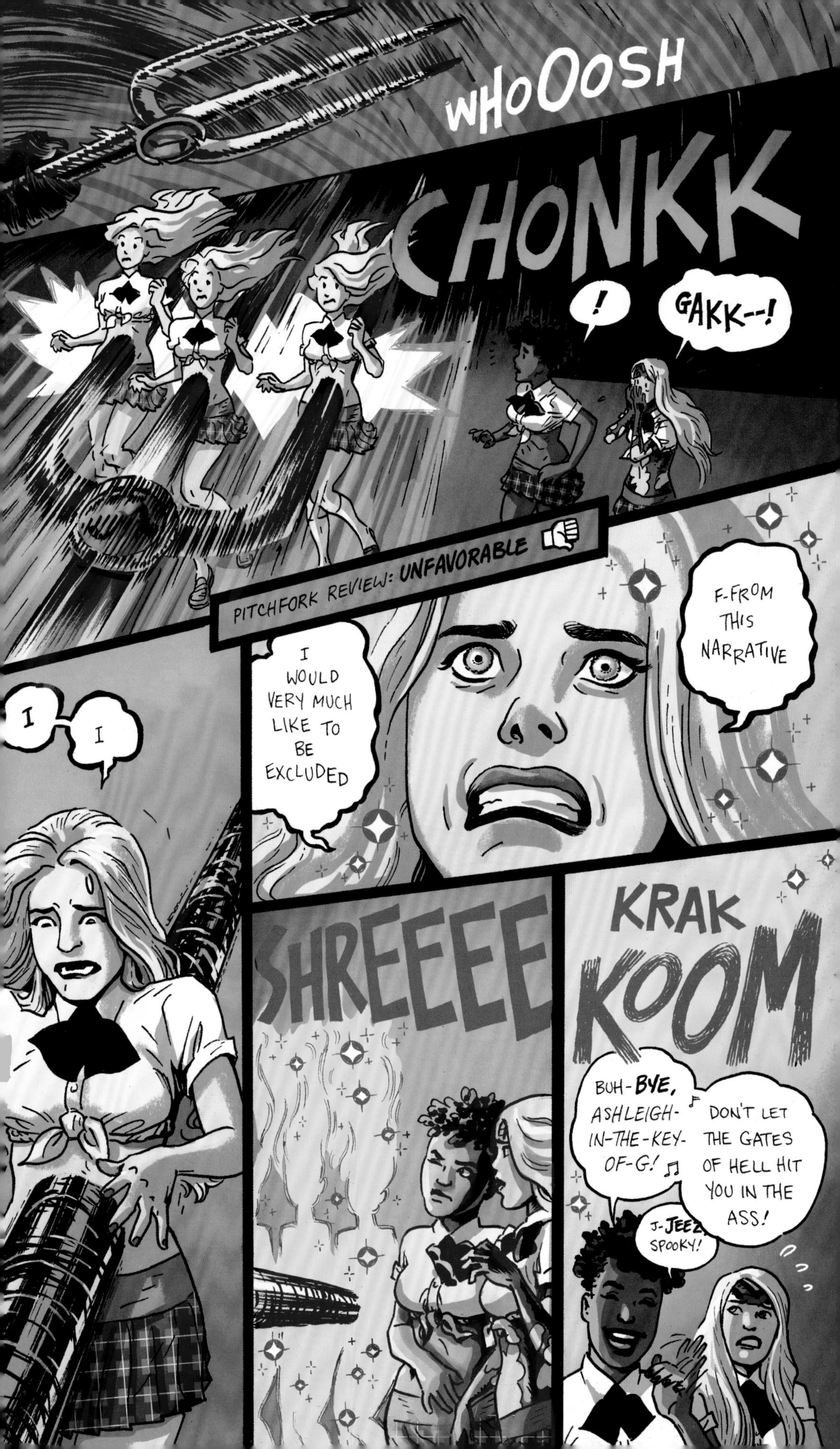
WHOOOOSH
CHONKK
!
GAKK--!
PITCHFORK REVIEW: UNFAVORABLE
I
I
I WOULD VERY MUCH LIKE TO BE EXCLUDED
F-FROM THIS NARRATIVE
SHREEEE
KRAK
KOOM
BUH-BYE, ASHLEIGH-IN-THE-KEY-OF-G!
DON'T LET THE GATES OF HELL HIT YOU IN THE ASS!
J-JEEZ, SPOOKY!

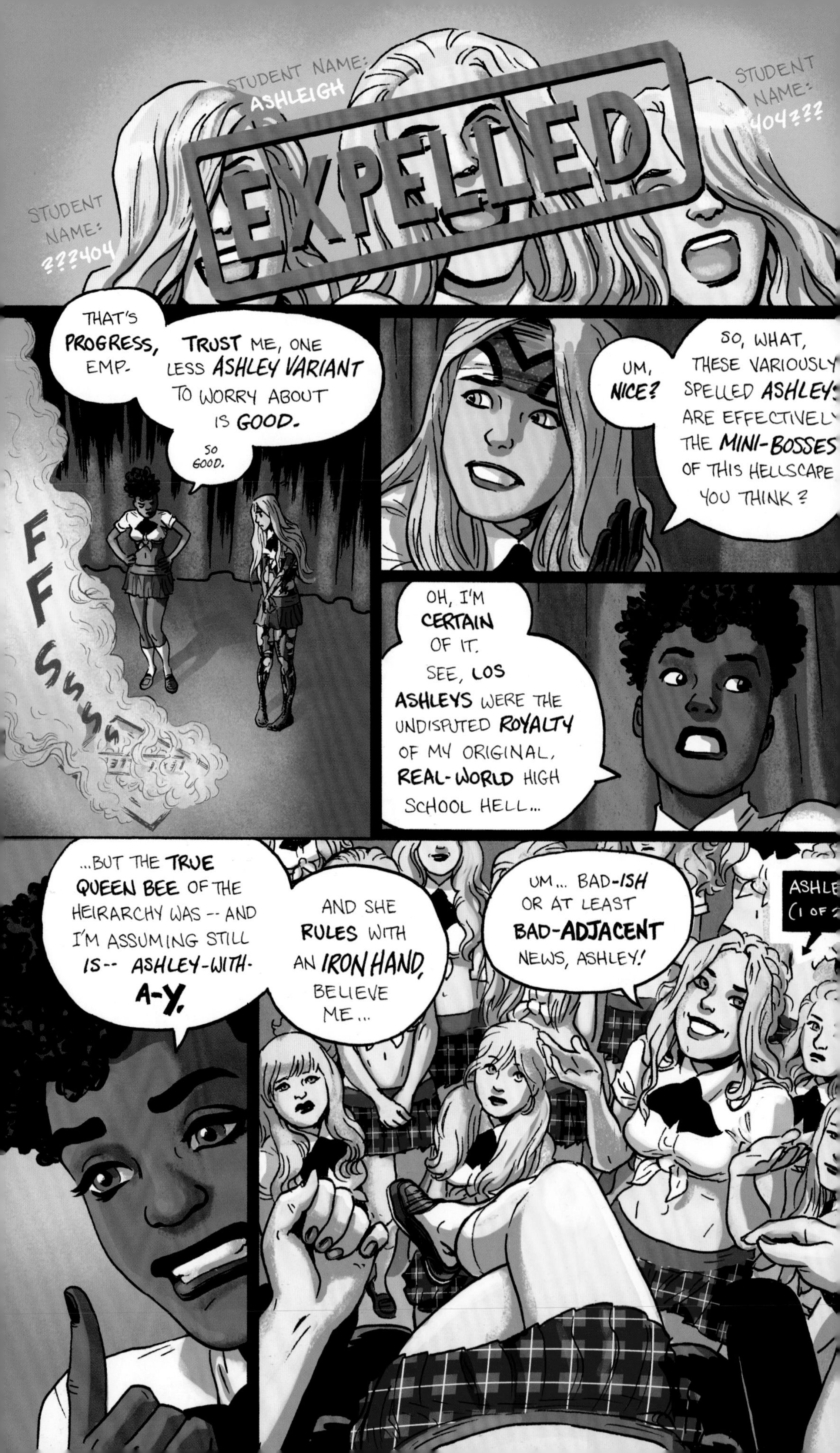
STUDENT NAME: ASHLEIGH
STUDENT NAME: 404???
STUDENT NAME: ???404
EXPELLED
THAT'S PROGRESS, EMP.
TRUST ME, ONE LESS ASHLEY VARIANT TO WORRY ABOUT IS GOOD.
SO GOOD.
FFSSSS
UM, NICE?
SO, WHAT, THESE VARIOUSLY SPELLED ASHLEYS ARE EFFECTIVELY THE MINI-BOSSES OF THIS HELLSCAPE YOU THINK?
OH, I'M CERTAIN OF IT. SEE, LOS ASHLEYS WERE THE UNDISPUTED ROYALTY OF MY ORIGINAL, REAL-WORLD HIGH SCHOOL HELL...
...BUT THE TRUE QUEEN BEE OF THE HEIRARCHY WAS -- AND I'M ASSUMING STILL IS-- ASHLEY-WITH-A-Y.
AND SHE RULES WITH AN IRON HAND, BELIEVE ME...
UM... BAD-ISH OR AT LEAST BAD-ADJACENT NEWS, ASHLEY!

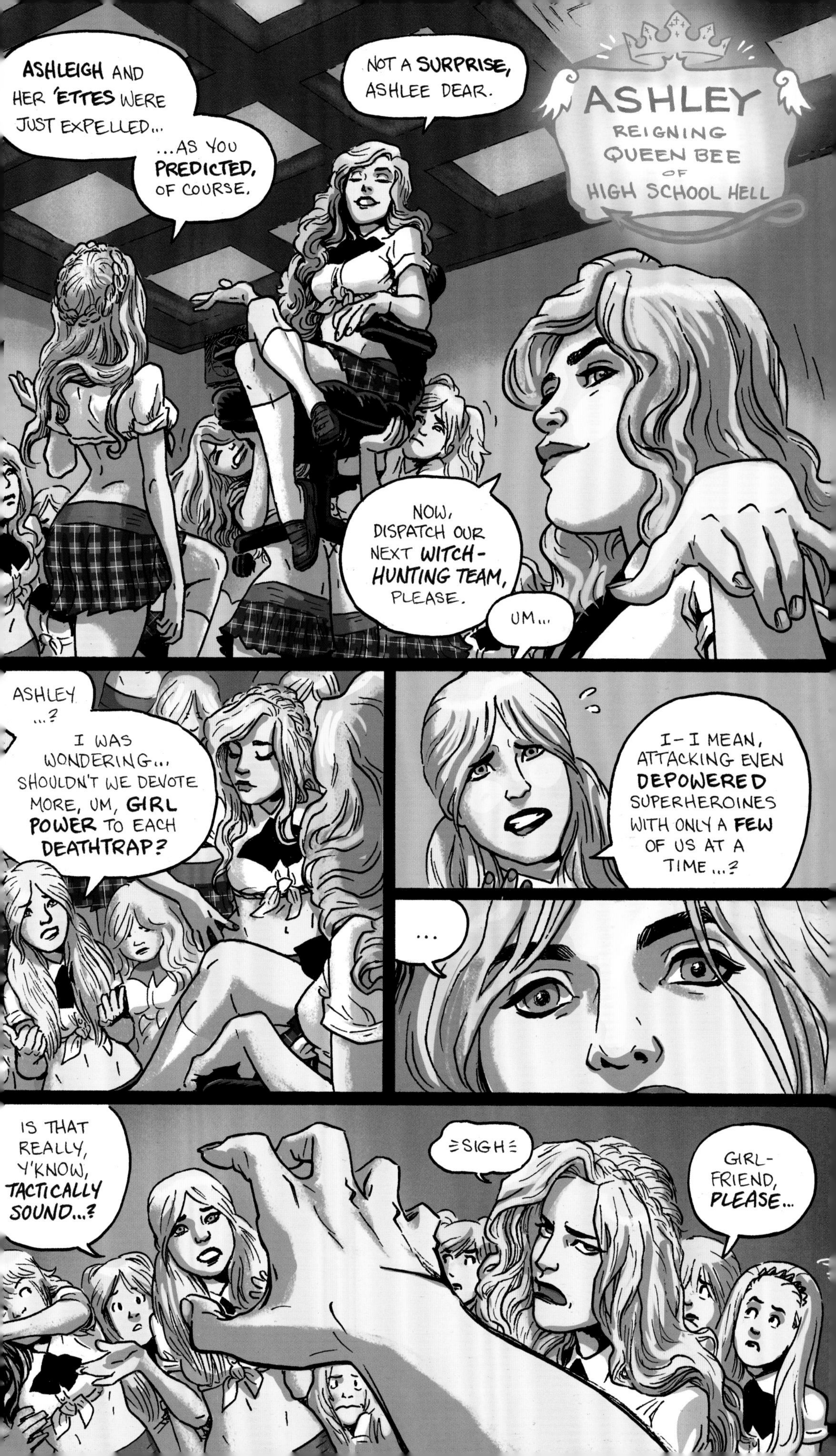

ASHLEY
REIGNING QUEEN BEE OF HIGH SCHOOL HELL
ASHLEIGH AND HER 'ETTES WERE JUST EXPELLED...
...AS YOU PREDICTED, OF COURSE.
NOT A SURPRISE, ASHLEE DEAR.
NOW, DISPATCH OUR NEXT WITCH-HUNTING TEAM, PLEASE.
UM...
ASHLEY ...?
I WAS WONDERING... SHOULDN'T WE DEVOTE MORE, UM, GIRL POWER TO EACH DEATHTRAP?
I- I MEAN, ATTACKING EVEN DEPOWERED SUPERHEROINES WITH ONLY A FEW OF US AT A TIME ...?
...
IS THAT REALLY, Y'KNOW, TACTICALLY SOUND...?
SIGH
GIRL-FRIEND, PLEASE...

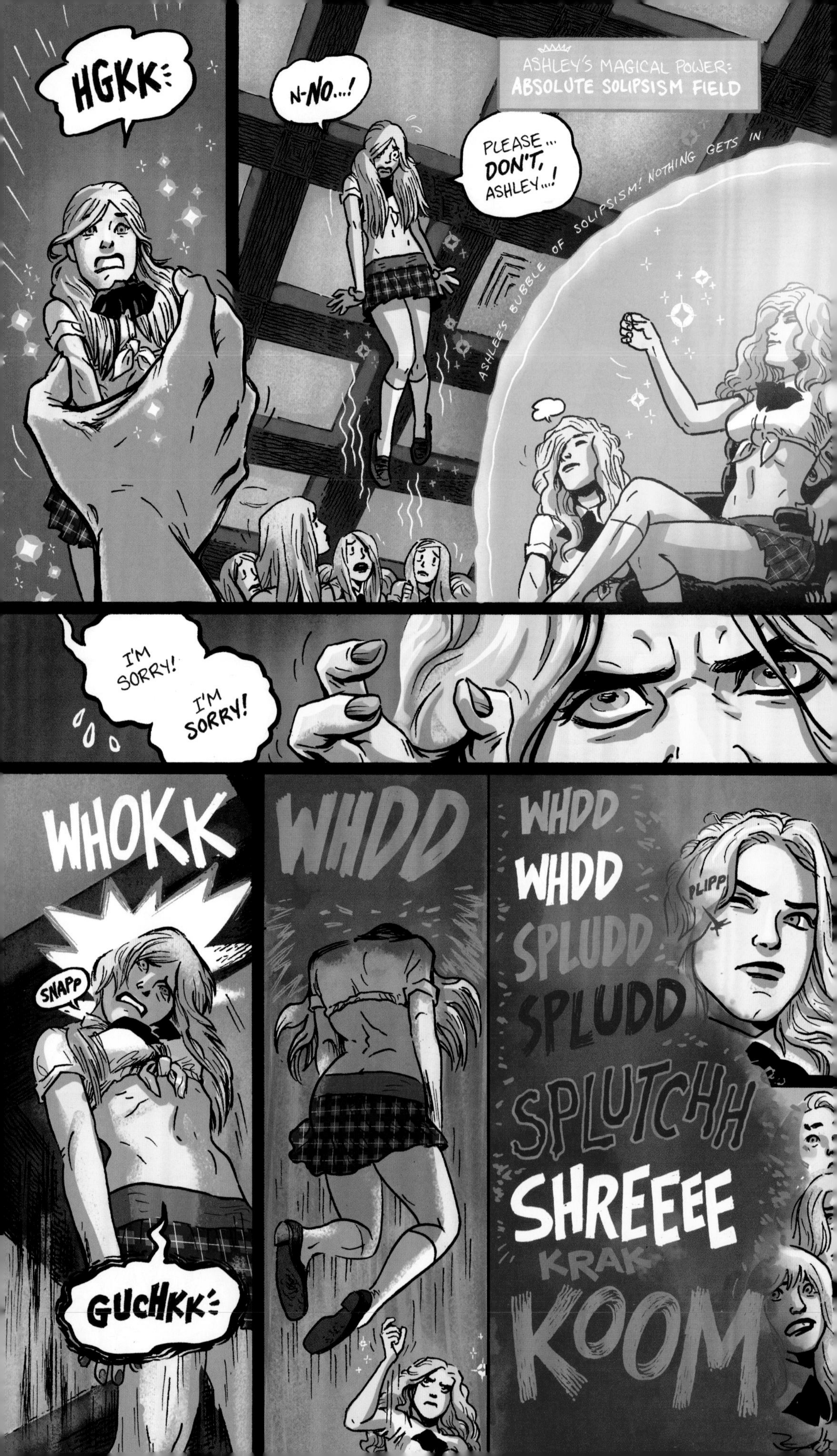

HGKK
N-NO...!
ASHLEY'S MAGICAL POWER:
ABSOLUTE SOLIPSISM FIELD
PLEASE... DON'T, ASHLEY...!
ASHLEE'S BUBBLE OF SOLIPSISM! NOTHING GETS IN.
I'M SORRY!
I'M SORRY!
WHOKK
SNAPP
GUCHKK
WHDD
WHDD
WHDD
PLIPP
SPLUDD
SPLUDD
SPLUTCHH
SHREEEE
KRAK
KOOM

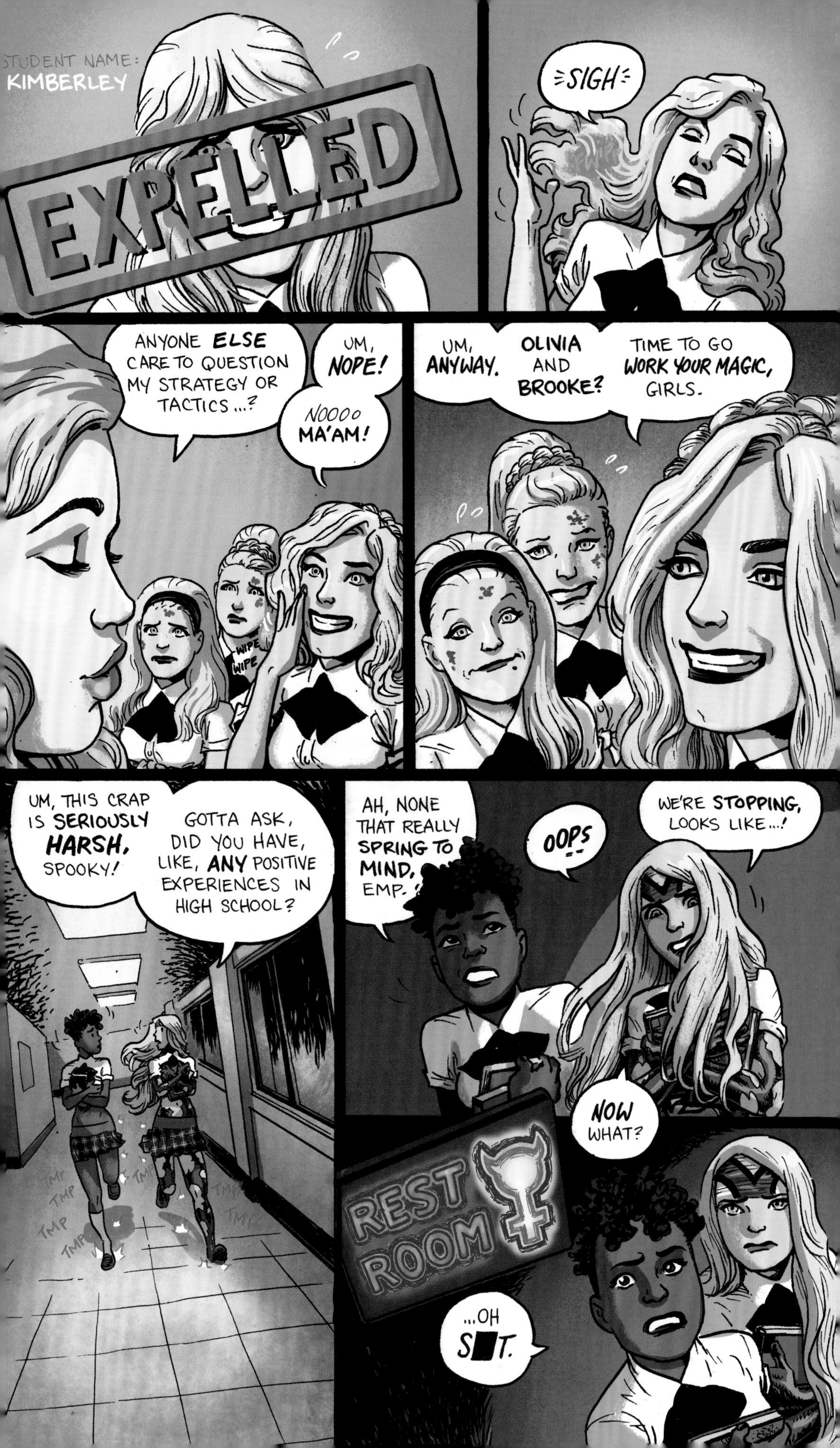
STUDENT NAME:
KIMBERLEY
EXPELLED
SIGH
ANYONE ELSE CARE TO QUESTION MY STRATEGY OR TACTICS...?
UM, NOPE!
NOOOO MA'AM!
WIPE
WIPE
UM, ANYWAY.
OLIVIA AND BROOKE?
TIME TO GO WORK YOUR MAGIC, GIRLS.
UM, THIS CRAP IS SERIOUSLY HARSH, SPOOKY!
GOTTA ASK, DID YOU HAVE, LIKE, ANY POSITIVE EXPERIENCES IN HIGH SCHOOL?
TMP
TMP
TMP
TMP
TMP
TMP
AH, NONE THAT REALLY SPRING TO MIND, EMP.
OOPS
WE'RE STOPPING, LOOKS LIKE...!
NOW WHAT?
REST ROOM
...OH
S[redacted]T.

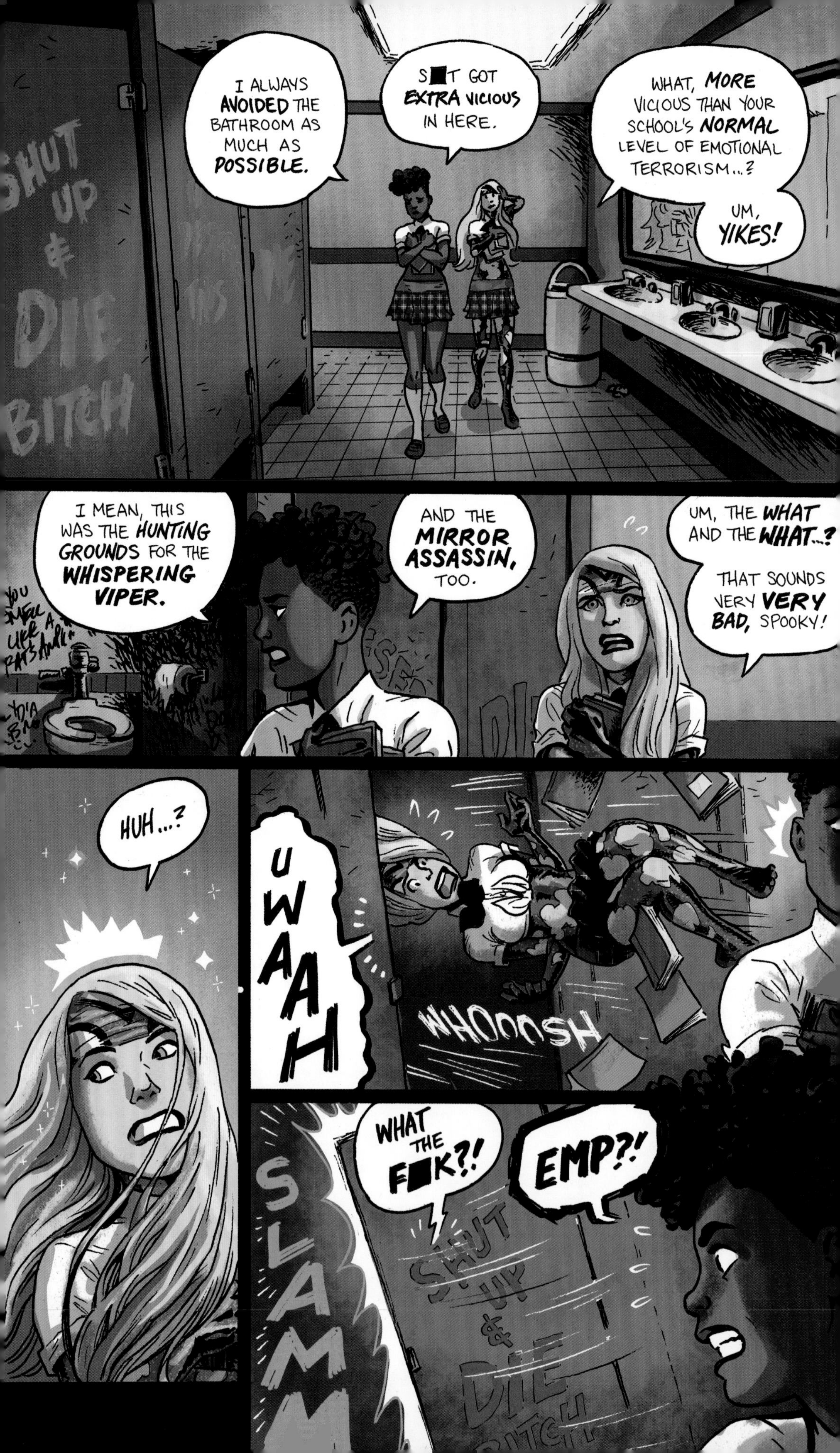
SHUT UP & DIE BITCH
I ALWAYS AVOIDED THE BATHROOM AS MUCH AS POSSIBLE.
S[redacted]T GOT EXTRA VICIOUS IN HERE.
WHAT, MORE VICIOUS THAN YOUR SCHOOL'S NORMAL LEVEL OF EMOTIONAL TERRORISM...?
UM, YIKES!
I MEAN, THIS WAS THE HUNTING GROUNDS FOR THE WHISPERING VIPER.
AND THE MIRROR ASSASSIN, TOO.
UM, THE WHAT AND THE WHAT...?
THAT SOUNDS VERY VERY BAD, SPOOKY!
HUH...?
UWAAH
WHOOOSH
SLAM
WHAT THE F[redacted]K?!
EMP?!

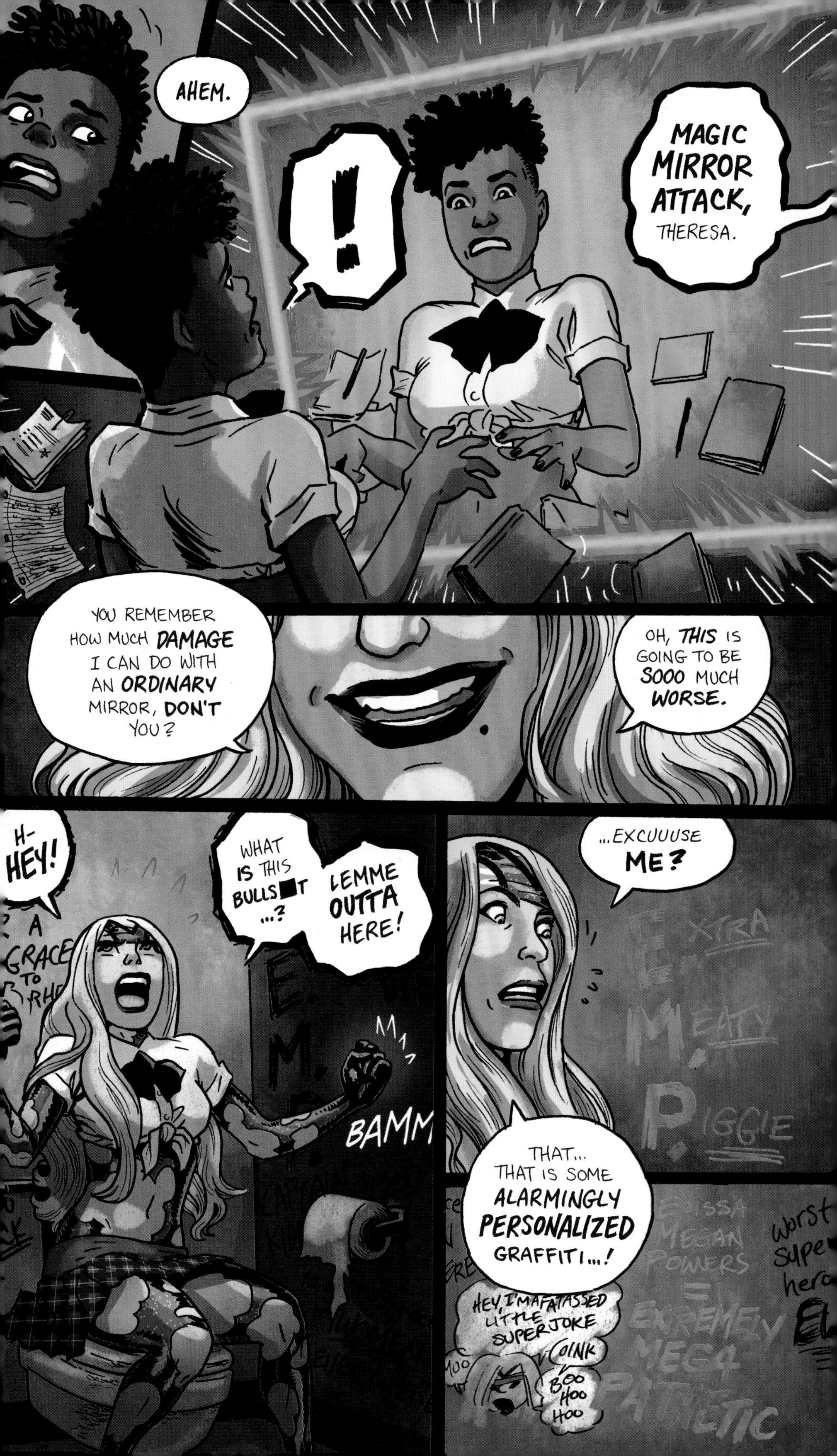
AHEM.
!
MAGIC MIRROR ATTACK, THERESA.
YOU REMEMBER HOW MUCH DAMAGE I CAN DO WITH AN ORDINARY MIRROR, DON'T YOU?
OH, THIS IS GOING TO BE SOOO MUCH WORSE.
H-HEY!
WHAT IS THIS BULLS[redacted]T ...?
LEMME OUTTA HERE!
BAMM
...EXCUUUSE ME?
EXTRA MEATY PIGGIE
THAT... THAT IS SOME ALARMINGLY PERSONALIZED GRAFFITI...!
HEY, I'M A FAT ASSED LITTLE SUPER JOKE
OINK
BOO HOO HOO
MOO
MEGAN POWERS = EXTREMELY MEGA PATHETIC
worst super hero

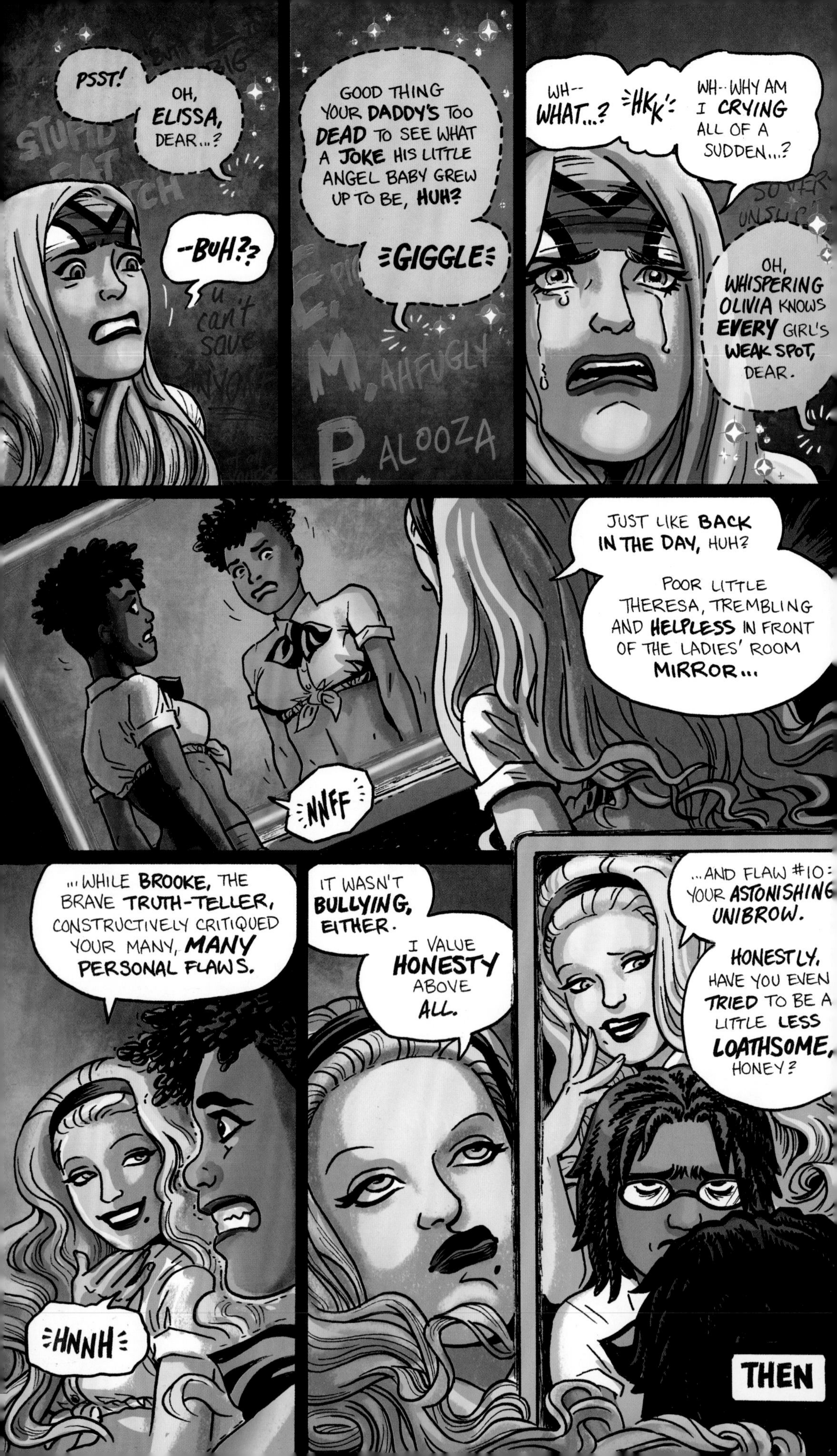
PSST!
OH, ELISSA, DEAR...?
--BUH??
GOOD THING YOUR DADDY'S TOO DEAD TO SEE WHAT A JOKE HIS LITTLE ANGEL BABY GREW UP TO BE, HUH?
GIGGLE
WH-- WHAT...?
HKK
WH--WHY AM I CRYING ALL OF A SUDDEN...?
OH, WHISPERING OLIVIA KNOWS EVERY GIRL'S WEAK SPOT, DEAR.
JUST LIKE BACK IN THE DAY, HUH?
POOR LITTLE THERESA, TREMBLING AND HELPLESS IN FRONT OF THE LADIES' ROOM MIRROR...
NNFF
...WHILE BROOKE, THE BRAVE TRUTH-TELLER, CONSTRUCTIVELY CRITIQUED YOUR MANY, MANY PERSONAL FLAWS.
HNNH
IT WASN'T BULLYING, EITHER.
I VALUE HONESTY ABOVE ALL.
...AND FLAW #10: YOUR ASTONISHING UNIBROW.
HONESTLY. HAVE YOU EVEN TRIED TO BE A LITTLE LESS LOATHSOME, HONEY?
THEN

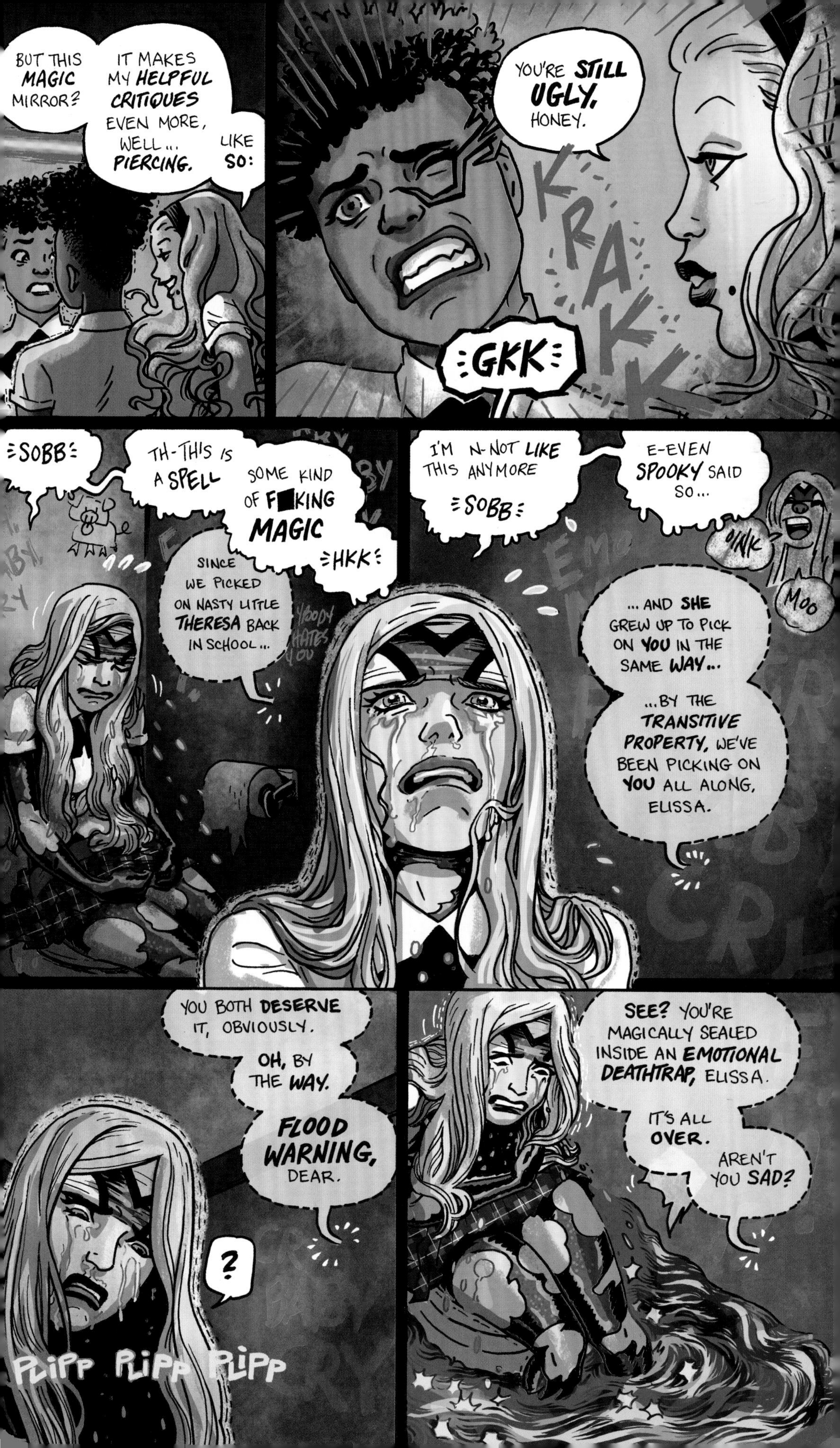

BUT THIS MAGIC MIRROR?
IT MAKES MY HELPFUL CRITIQUES EVEN MORE, WELL... PIERCING.
LIKE SO:
YOU'RE STILL UGLY, HONEY.
KRAKK
GKK
SOBB
TH-THIS IS A SPELL
SOME KIND OF F[redacted]KING MAGIC
HKK
SINCE WE PICKED ON NASTY LITTLE THERESA BACK IN SCHOOL...
I'M N-NOT LIKE THIS ANYMORE
SOBB
E-EVEN SPOOKY SAID SO...
OINK
MOO
... AND SHE GREW UP TO PICK ON YOU IN THE SAME WAY...
...BY THE TRANSITIVE PROPERTY, WE'VE BEEN PICKING ON YOU ALL ALONG, ELISSA.
YOU BOTH DESERVE IT, OBVIOUSLY.
OH, BY THE WAY.
FLOOD WARNING, DEAR.
?
PLIPP PLIPP PLIPP
SEE? YOU'RE MAGICALLY SEALED INSIDE AN EMOTIONAL DEATHTRAP, ELISSA.
IT'S ALL OVER.
AREN'T YOU SAD?

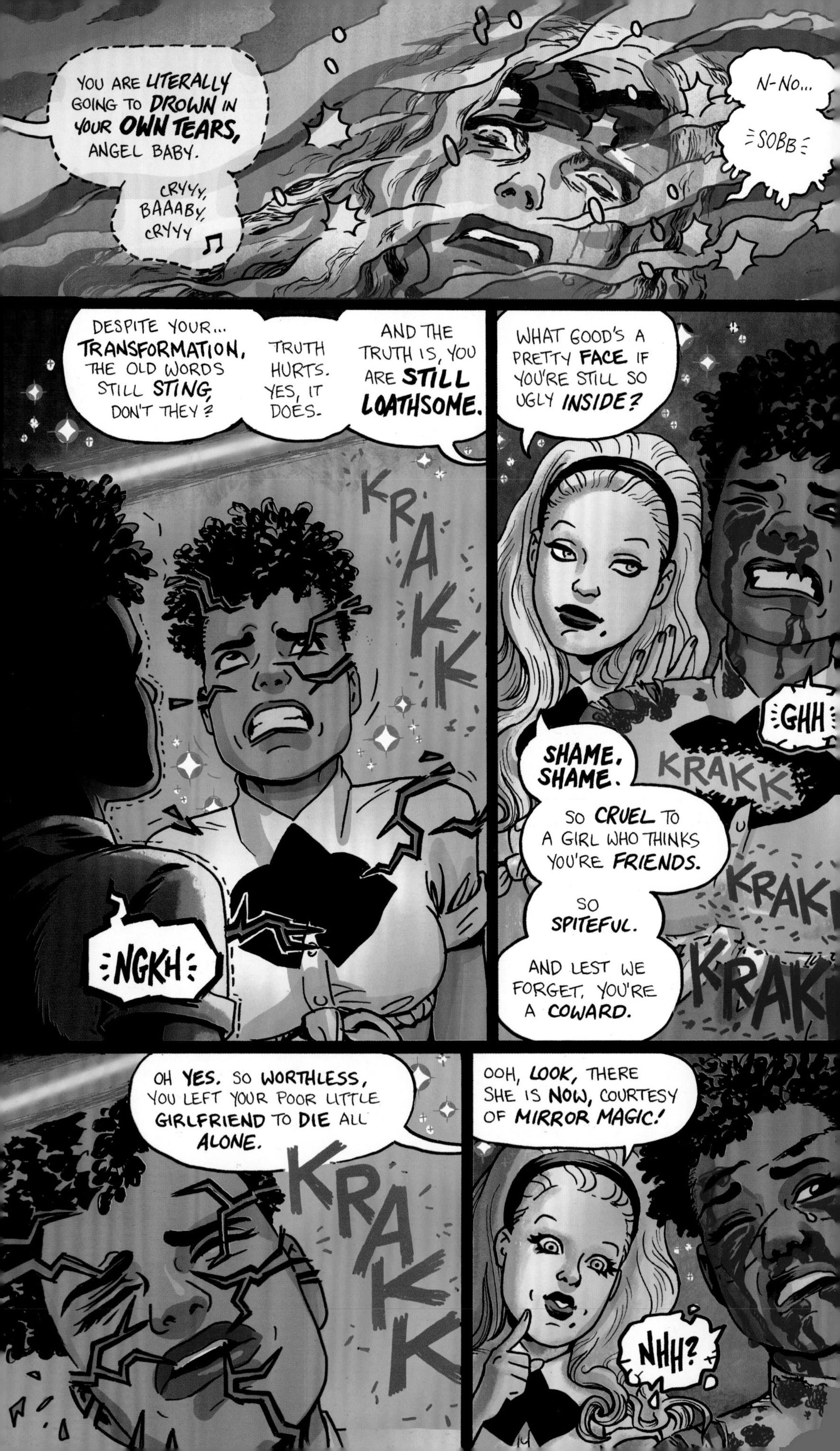

YOU ARE LITERALLY GOING TO DROWN IN YOUR OWN TEARS, ANGEL BABY.
CRYYY, BAAABY, CRYYY ♫
N-NO...
SOBB
DESPITE YOUR... TRANSFORMATION, THE OLD WORDS STILL STING, DON'T THEY?
TRUTH HURTS. YES, IT DOES.
AND THE TRUTH IS, YOU ARE STILL LOATHSOME.
KRAKK
NGKH
WHAT GOOD'S A PRETTY FACE IF YOU'RE STILL SO UGLY INSIDE?
GHH
SHAME, SHAME.
KRAKK
SO CRUEL TO A GIRL WHO THINKS YOU'RE FRIENDS.
SO SPITEFUL.
AND LEST WE FORGET, YOU'RE A COWARD.
KRAK
KRAK
OH YES. SO WORTHLESS, YOU LEFT YOUR POOR LITTLE GIRLFRIEND TO DIE ALL ALONE.
KRAKK
OOH, LOOK, THERE SHE IS NOW, COURTESY OF MIRROR MAGIC!
NHH?

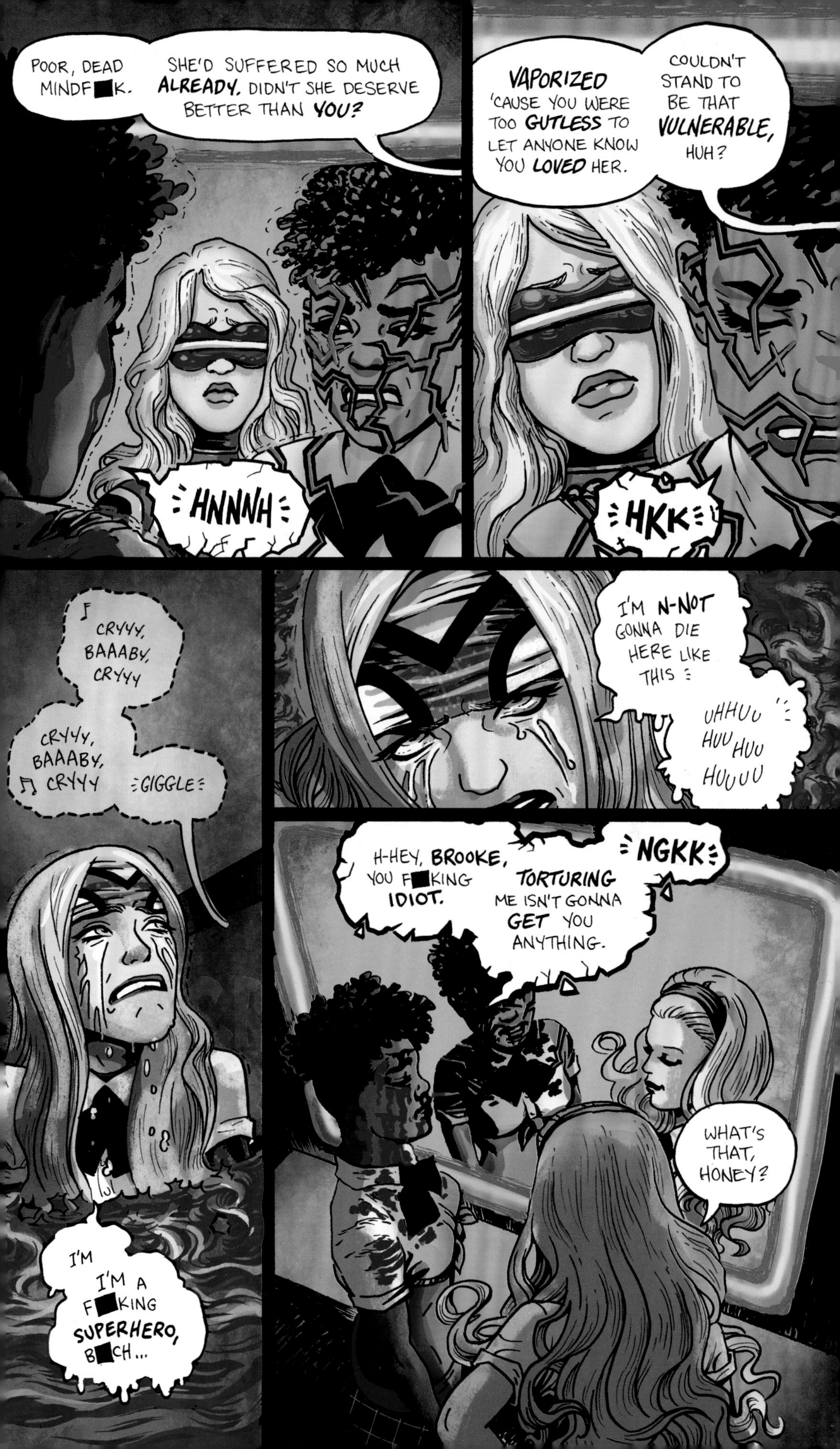

POOR, DEAD MINDF[redacted]K.
SHE'D SUFFERED SO MUCH ALREADY. DIDN'T SHE DESERVE BETTER THAN YOU?
HNNNH
VAPORIZED 'CAUSE YOU WERE TOO GUTLESS TO LET ANYONE KNOW YOU LOVED HER.
COULDN'T STAND TO BE THAT VULNERABLE, HUH?
HKK
CRYYY, BAAABY, CRYYY
CRYYY, BAAABY, CRYYY
GIGGLE
I'M
I'M A F[redacted]KING SUPERHERO, B[redacted]CH...
I'M N-NOT GONNA DIE HERE LIKE THIS
UHHUU HUU HUU HUUUU
H-HEY, BROOKE, YOU F[redacted]KING IDIOT.
NGKK
TORTURING ME ISN'T GONNA GET YOU ANYTHING.
WHAT'S THAT, HONEY?

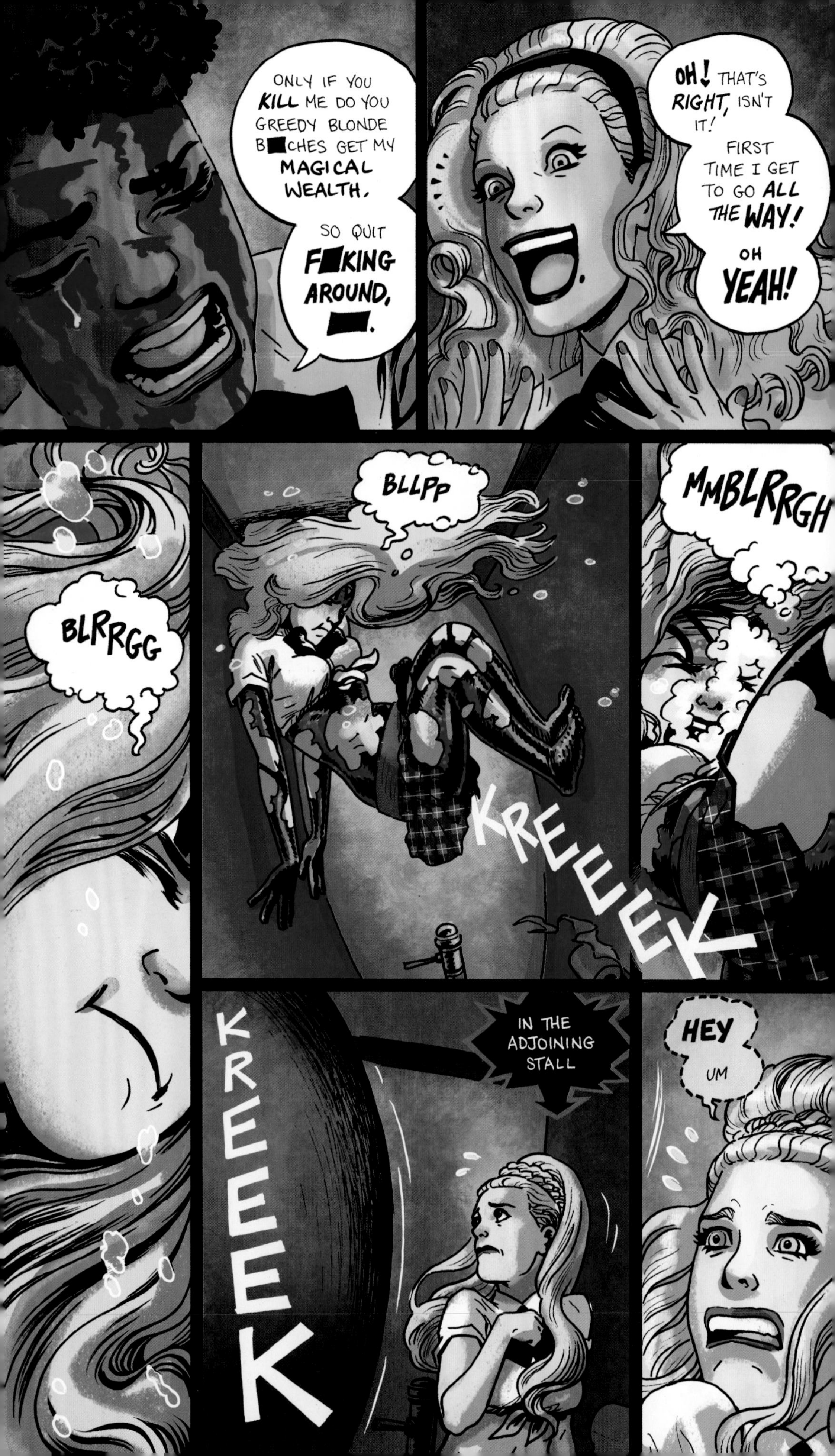
ONLY IF YOU KILL ME DO YOU GREEDY BLONDE B[redacted]CHES GET MY MAGICAL WEALTH.
SO QUIT F[redacted]KING AROUND, [redacted].
OH! THAT'S RIGHT, ISN'T IT!
FIRST TIME I GET TO GO ALL THE WAY!
OH YEAH!
BLRRGG
BLLPP
KREEEEK
MMBLRRGH
KREEEEK
IN THE ADJOINING STALL
HEY
UM

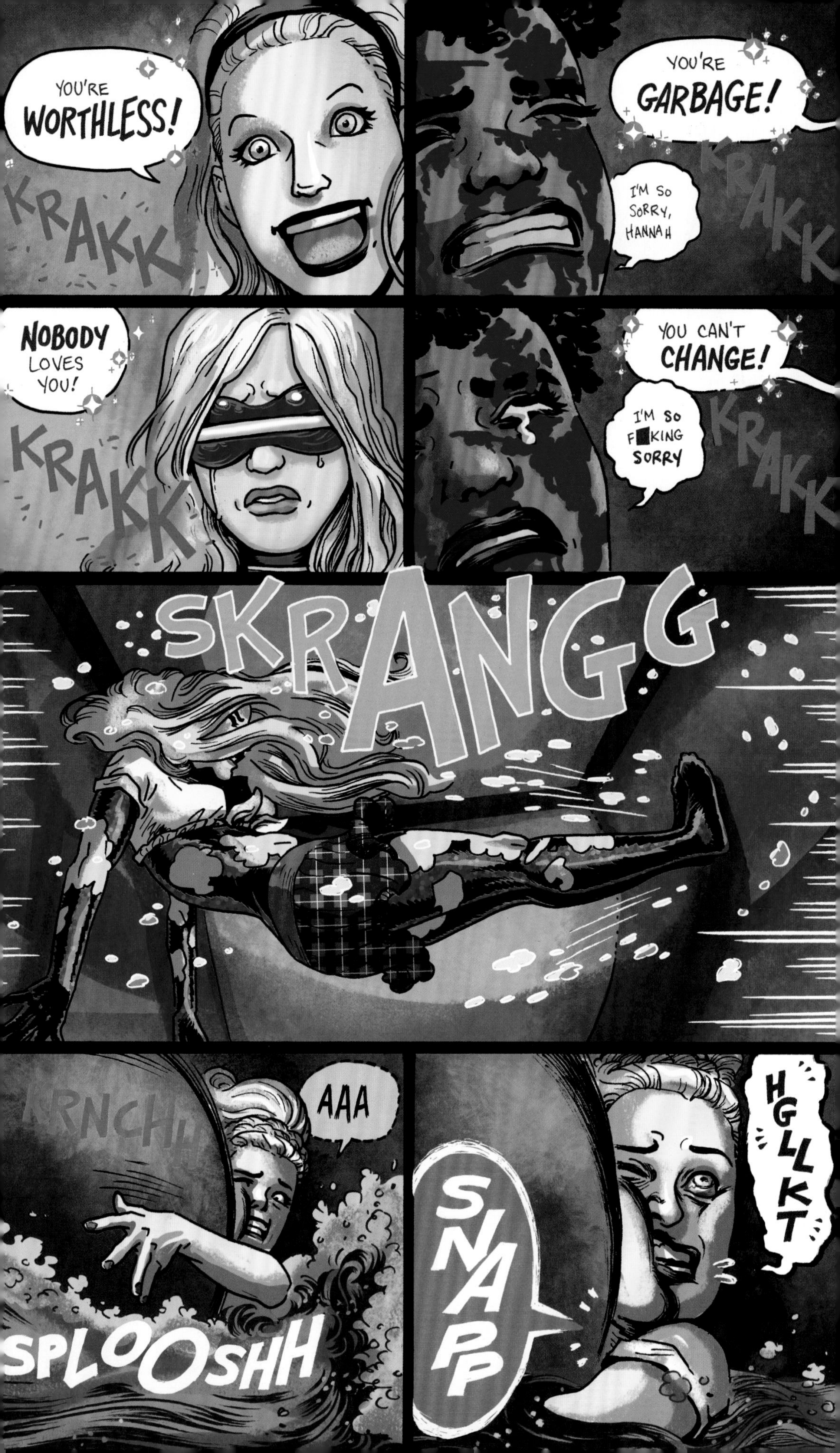
YOU'RE WORTHLESS!
KRAKK
YOU'RE GARBAGE!
I'M SO SORRY, HANNAH
KRAKK
NOBODY LOVES YOU!
KRAKK
YOU CAN'T CHANGE!
I'M SO F[redacted]KING SORRY
KRAKK
SKRANGG
AAA
SPLOOSHH
SNAPP
HGLLKT

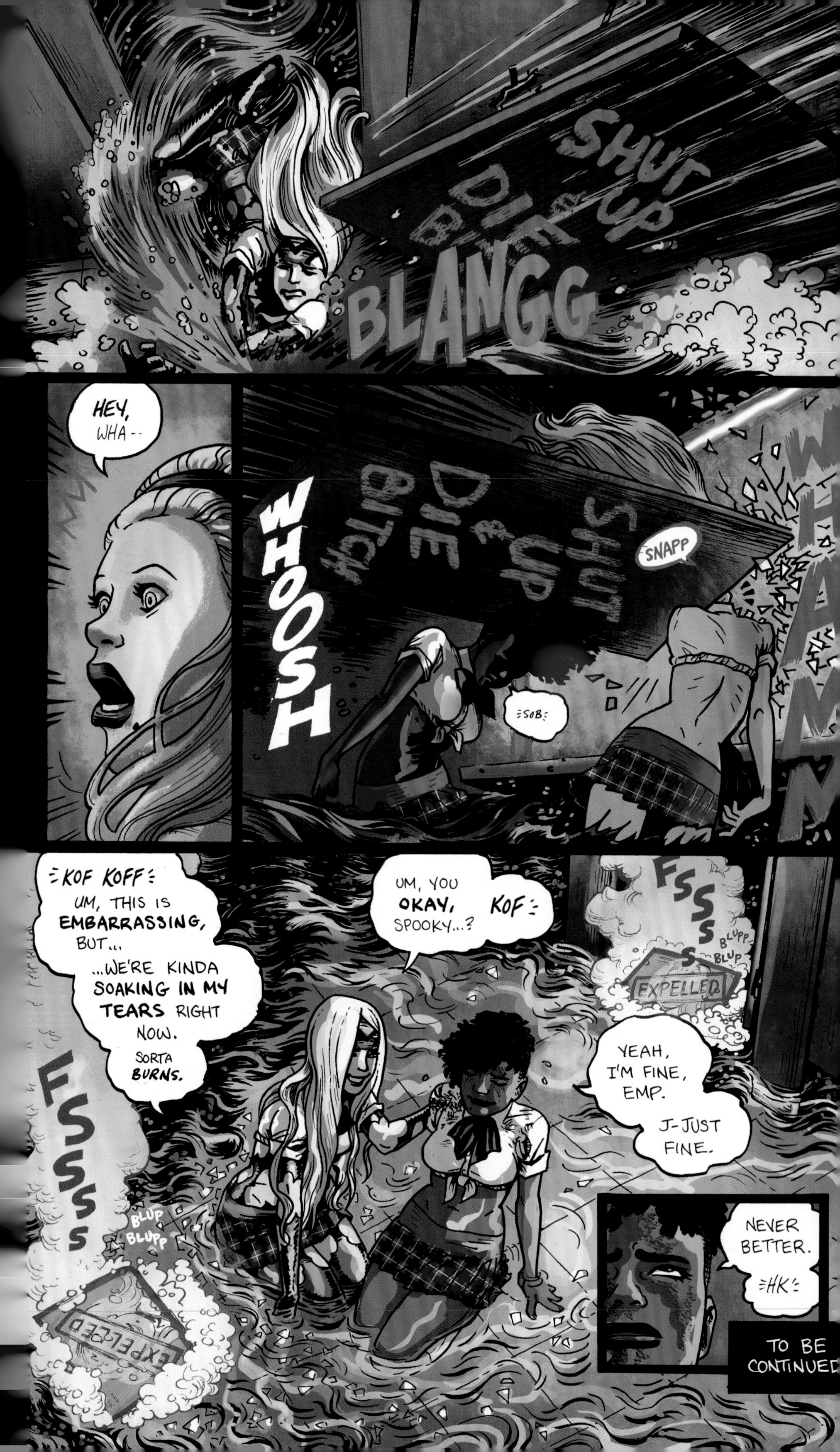
SHUT UP
DIE
BLANGG
HEY, WHA--
WHOOOSH
SHUT UP DIE DIE BITCH
SNAPP
WHAM
SOB
KOF KOFF
UM, THIS IS EMBARRASSING, BUT... ...WE'RE KINDA SOAKING IN MY TEARS RIGHT NOW.
SORTA BURNS.
UM, YOU OKAY, SPOOKY...?
KOF
FSSSS
BLUPP BLUP
EXPELLED
YEAH, I'M FINE, EMP.
J-JUST FINE.
FSSSS
BLUP BLUPP
EXPELLED
NEVER BETTER.
HK
TO BE CONTINUED

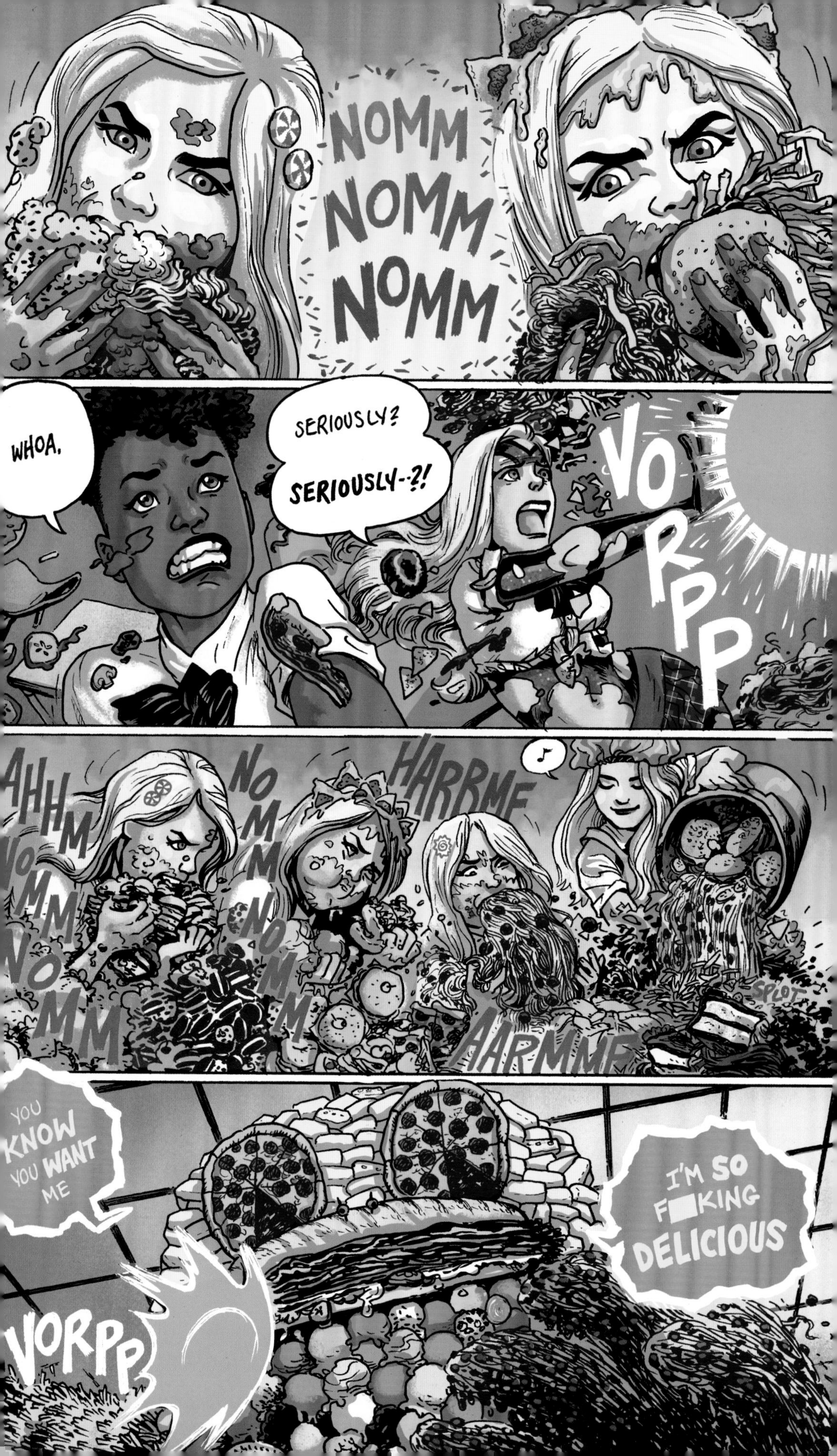
NOMM NOMM NOMM
WHOA.
SERIOUSLY?
SERIOUSLY--?!
VORPP
AHHM
NOMM NOMM NOMM
NOMM NOMM
HARRMF
♪
SPLOT
AARMMF
YOU KNOW YOU WANT ME
I'M SO F[redacted]KING DELICIOUS
VORPP

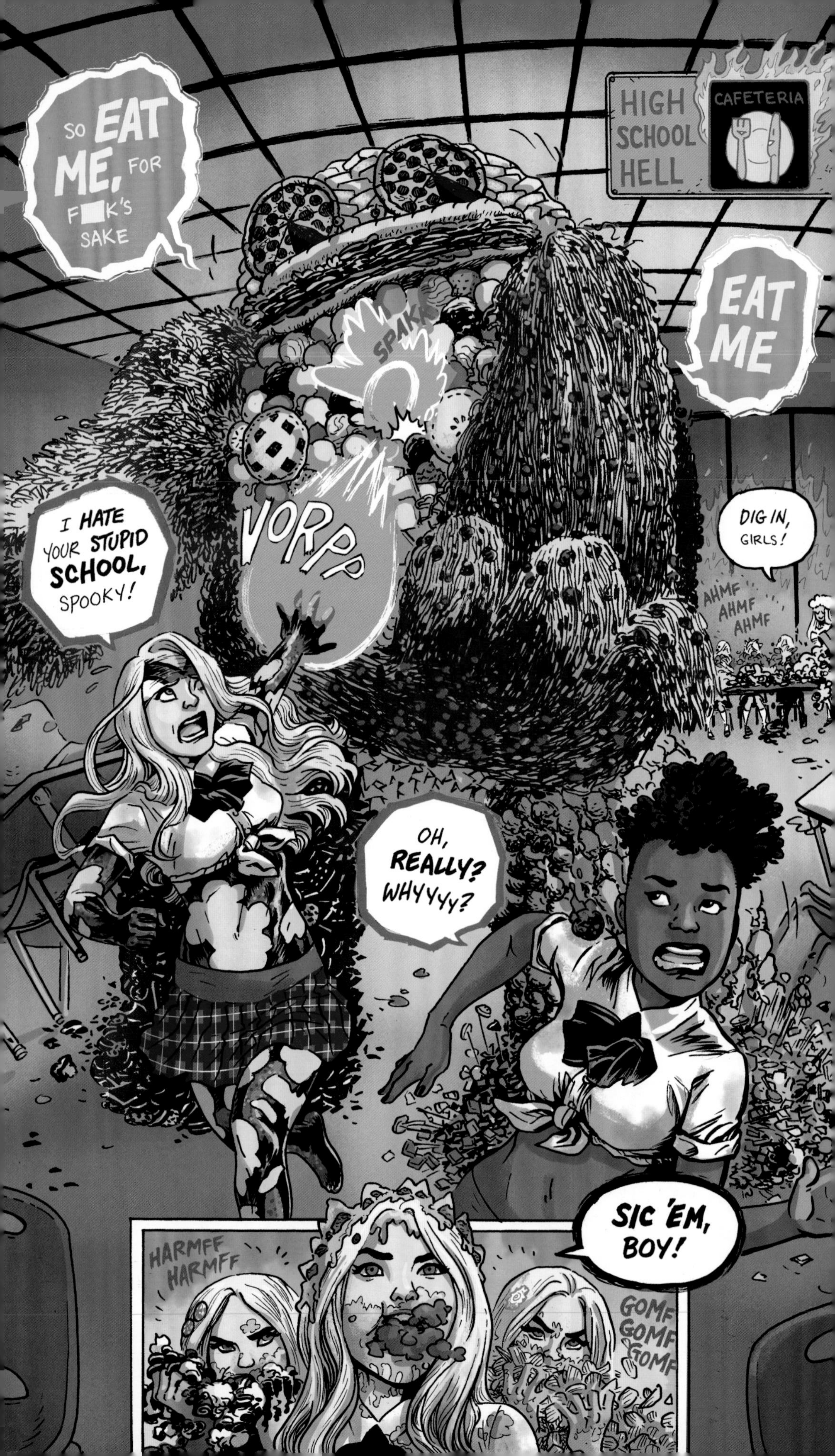

SO EAT ME, FOR F[redacted]K'S SAKE
HIGH SCHOOL HELL
CAFETERIA
SPAKK
EAT ME
VORPP
I HATE YOUR STUPID SCHOOL, SPOOKY!
DIG IN, GIRLS!
AHMF AHMF AHMF
OH, REALLY? WHYYYY?
SIC 'EM, BOY!
HARMFF HARMFF
GOMF GOMF GOMF

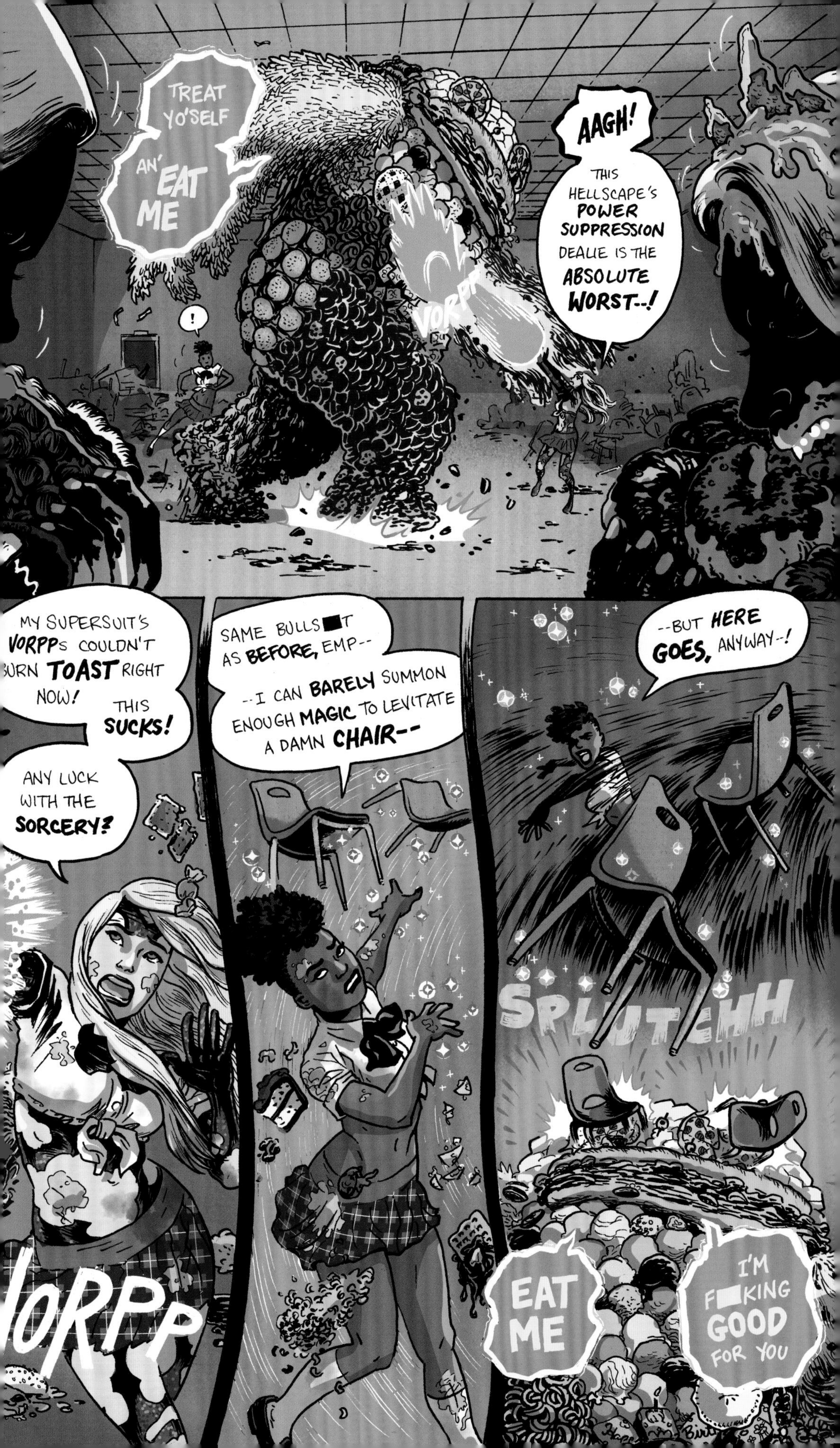
TREAT YO'SELF AN' EAT ME
!
VORPP
AAGH!
THIS HELLSCAPE'S POWER SUPPRESSION DEALIE IS THE ABSOLUTE WORST--!
MY SUPERSUIT'S VORPPs COULDN'T BURN TOAST RIGHT NOW!
THIS SUCKS!
ANY LUCK WITH THE SORCERY?
ORPP
SAME BULLS[redacted]T AS BEFORE, EMP--
--I CAN BARELY SUMMON ENOUGH MAGIC TO LEVITATE A DAMN CHAIR--
--BUT HERE GOES, ANYWAY--!
SPLUTCHH
EAT ME
I'M F[redacted]KING GOOD FOR YOU

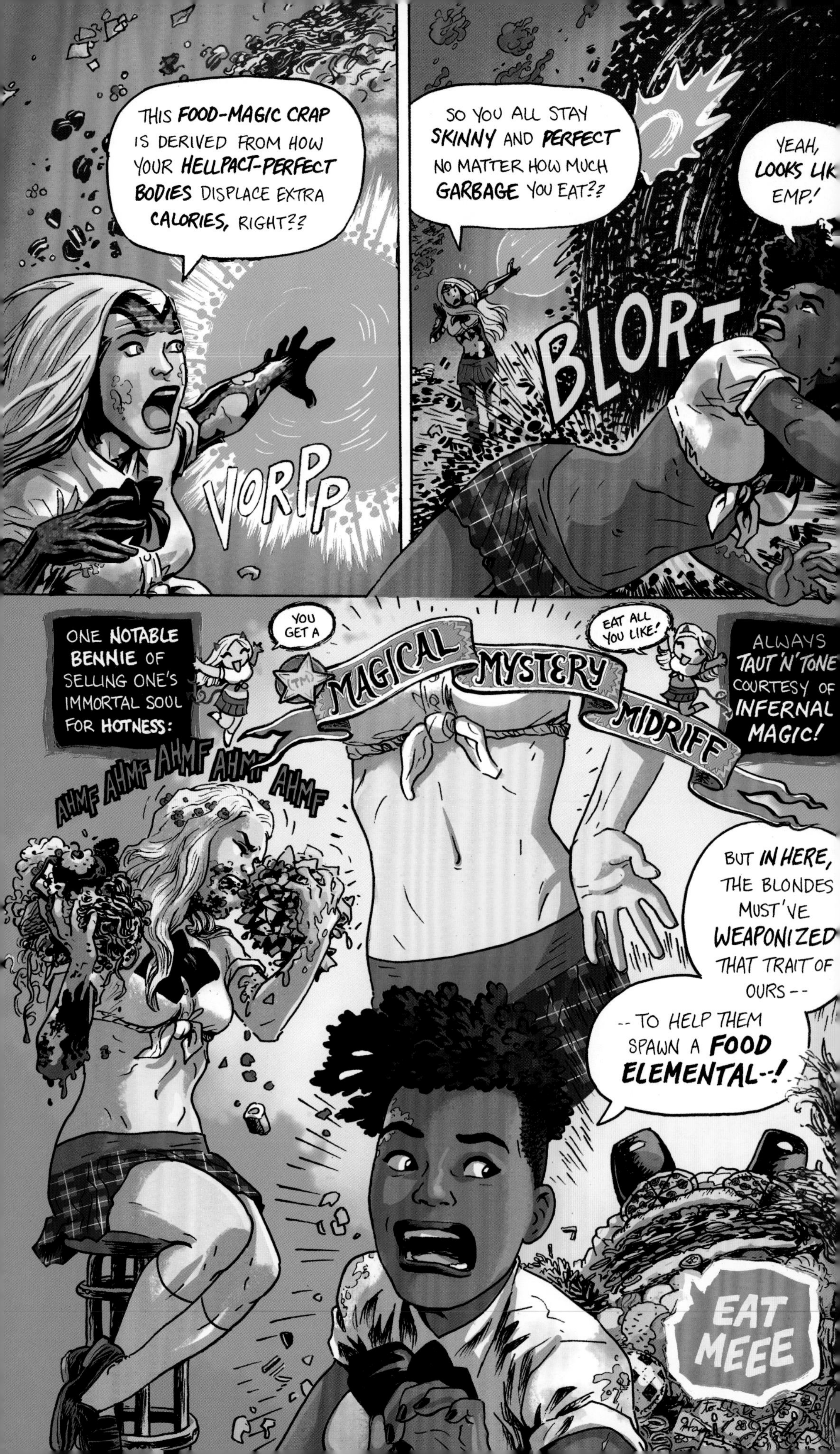
THIS FOOD-MAGIC CRAP IS DERIVED FROM HOW YOUR HELLPACT-PERFECT BODIES DISPLACE EXTRA CALORIES, RIGHT??
VORPP
SO YOU ALL STAY SKINNY AND PERFECT NO MATTER HOW MUCH GARBAGE YOU EAT??
YEAH, LOOKS LIK EMP!
BLORT
ONE NOTABLE BENNIE OF SELLING ONE'S IMMORTAL SOUL FOR HOTNESS:
YOU GET A
(TM) MAGICAL MYSTERY MIDRIFF
EAT ALL YOU LIKE!
ALWAYS TAUT 'N' TONE COURTESY OF INFERNAL MAGIC!
AHMF AHMF AHMF AHMF AHMF
BUT IN HERE, THE BLONDES MUST'VE WEAPONIZED THAT TRAIT OF OURS --
-- TO HELP THEM SPAWN A FOOD ELEMENTAL--!
EAT MEEE

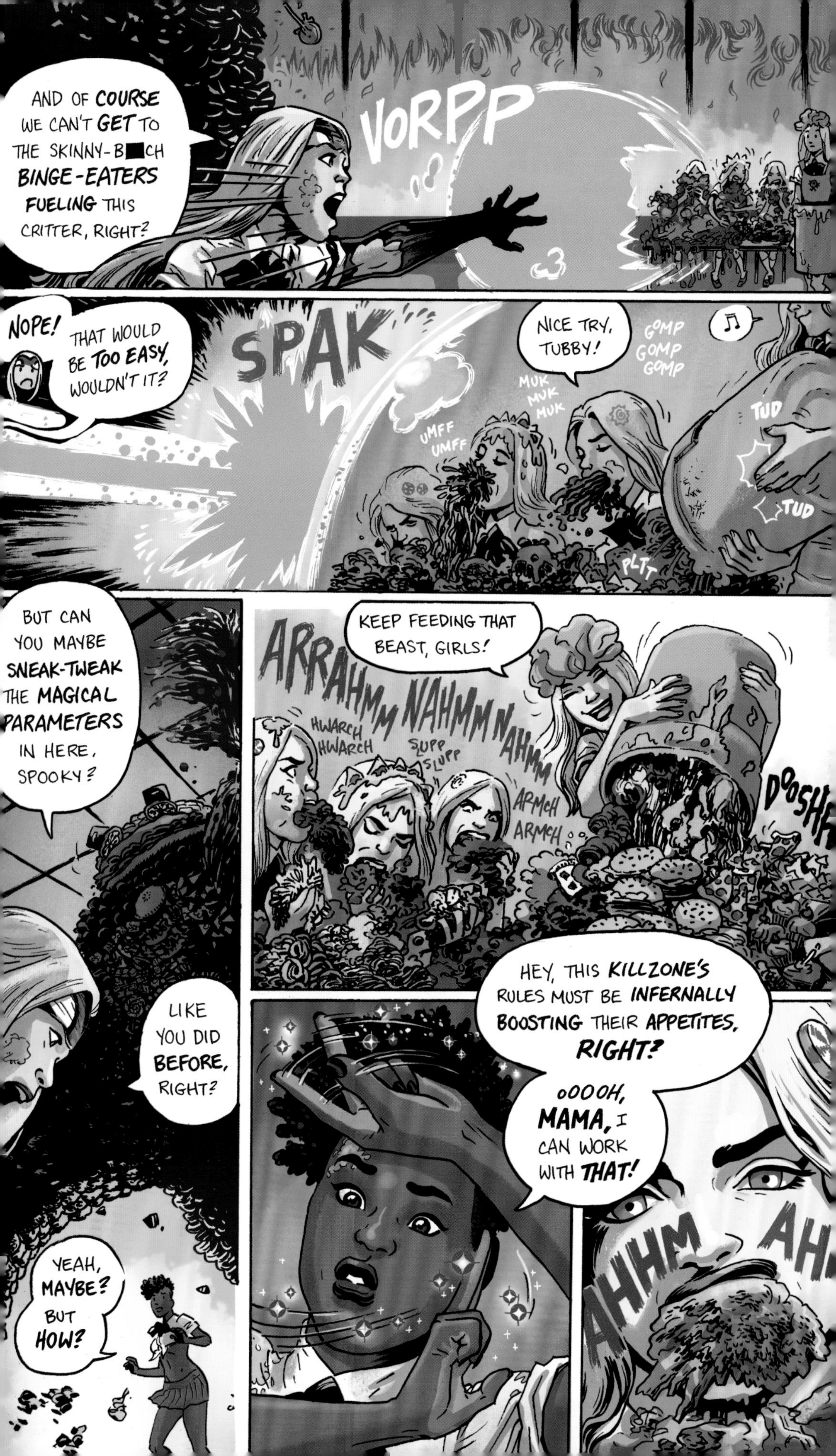
AND OF COURSE WE CAN'T GET TO THE SKINNY-B[redacted]CH BINGE-EATERS FUELING THIS CRITTER, RIGHT?
VORPP
NOPE!
THAT WOULD BE TOO EASY, WOULDN'T IT?
SPAK
NICE TRY, TUBBY!
GOMP GOMP GOMP
MUK MUK MUK
UMFF UMFF
TUD
TUD
PLTT
BUT CAN YOU MAYBE SNEAK-TWEAK THE MAGICAL PARAMETERS IN HERE, SPOOKY?
KEEP FEEDING THAT BEAST, GIRLS!
ARRAHMM NAHMM NAHMM
HWARCH HWARCH
SLUPP SLUPP
ARMCH ARMCH
DOOSHH
LIKE YOU DID BEFORE, RIGHT?
HEY, THIS KILLZONE'S RULES MUST BE INFERNALLY BOOSTING THEIR APPETITES, RIGHT?
OOOOH, MAMA, I CAN WORK WITH THAT!
YEAH, MAYBE? BUT HOW?
AHHM

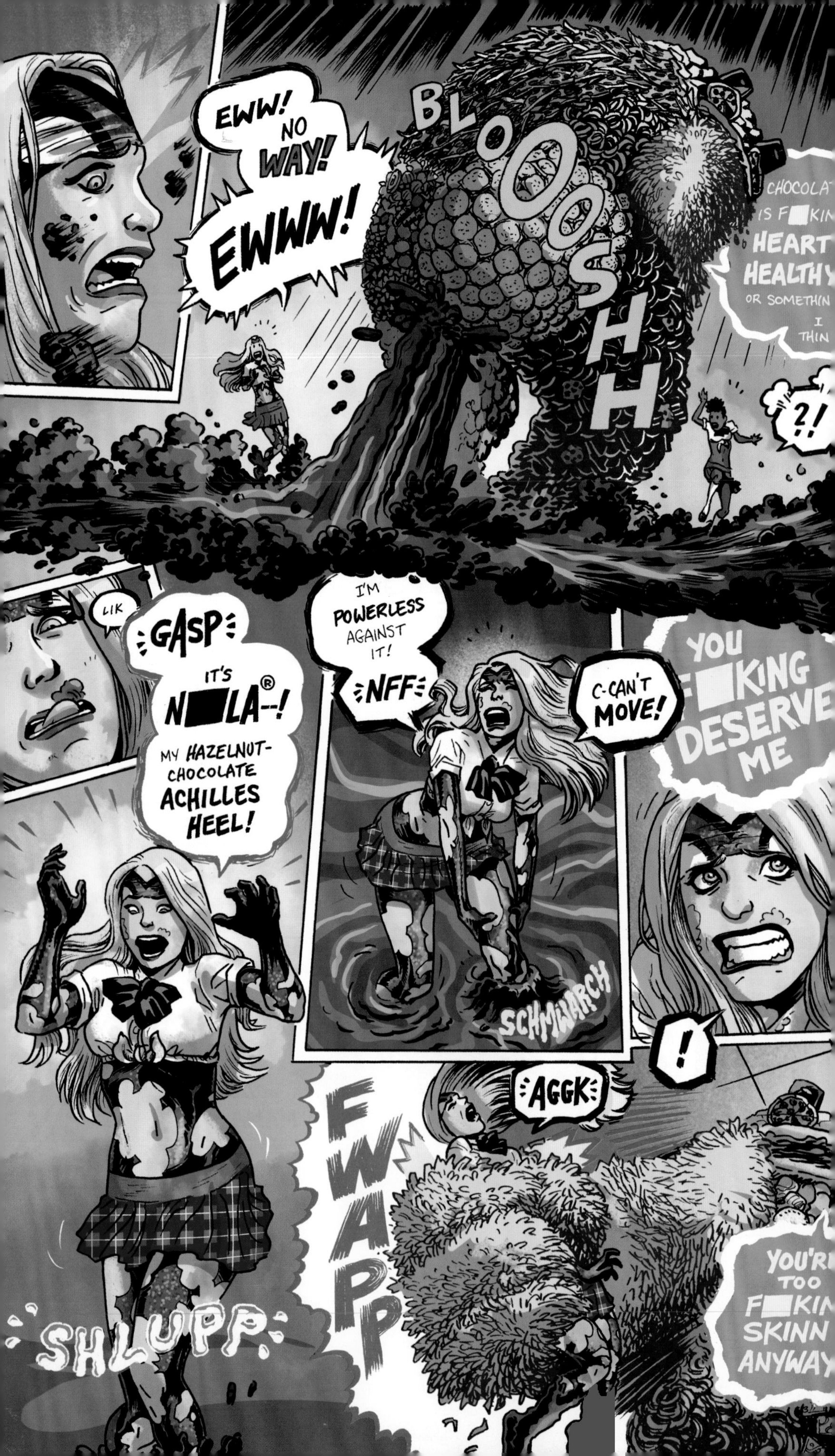
EWW! NO WAY!
EWWW!
BLOOOOSHH
CHOCOLAT IS F[redacted]KIN HEART HEALTHY OR SOMETHIN I THIN
?!
LIK
GASP
IT'S N[redacted]LA®--!
MY HAZELNUT-CHOCOLATE ACHILLES HEEL!
I'M POWERLESS AGAINST IT!
NFF
C-CAN'T MOVE!
YOU F[redacted]KING DESERVE ME
SCHMWARCH
!
AGGK
FWAPP
YOU'R TOO F[redacted]KIN SKINN ANYWAY
SHLUPP

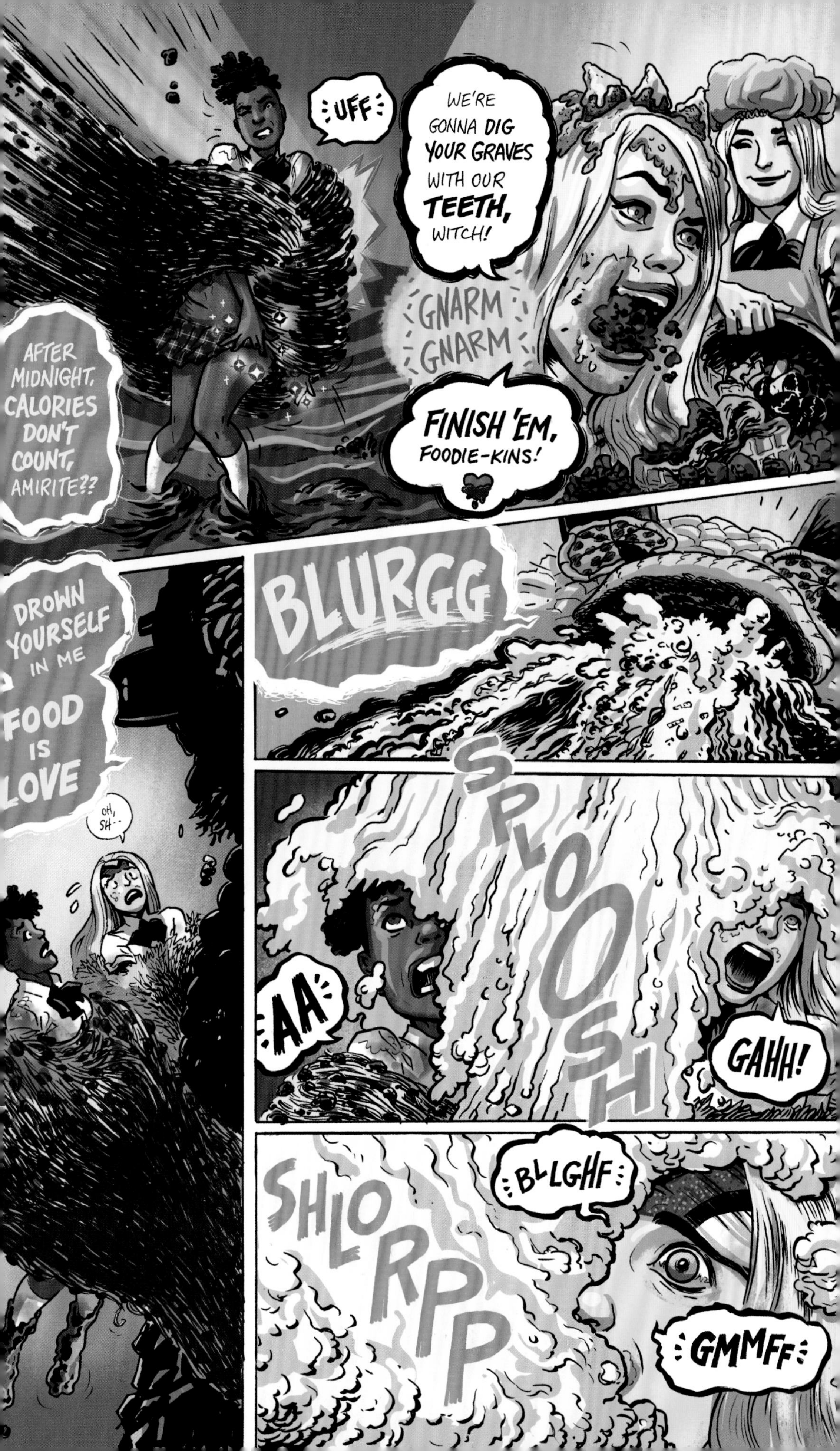
UFF
WE'RE GONNA DIG YOUR GRAVES WITH OUR TEETH, WITCH!
GNARM GNARM
AFTER MIDNIGHT, CALORIES DON'T COUNT, AMIRITE??
FINISH 'EM, FOODIE-KINS!
DROWN YOURSELF IN ME
FOOD IS LOVE
BLURGG
OH, SH--
SPLOOOSH
AA
GAHH!
SHLORPP
BLLGHF
GMMFF

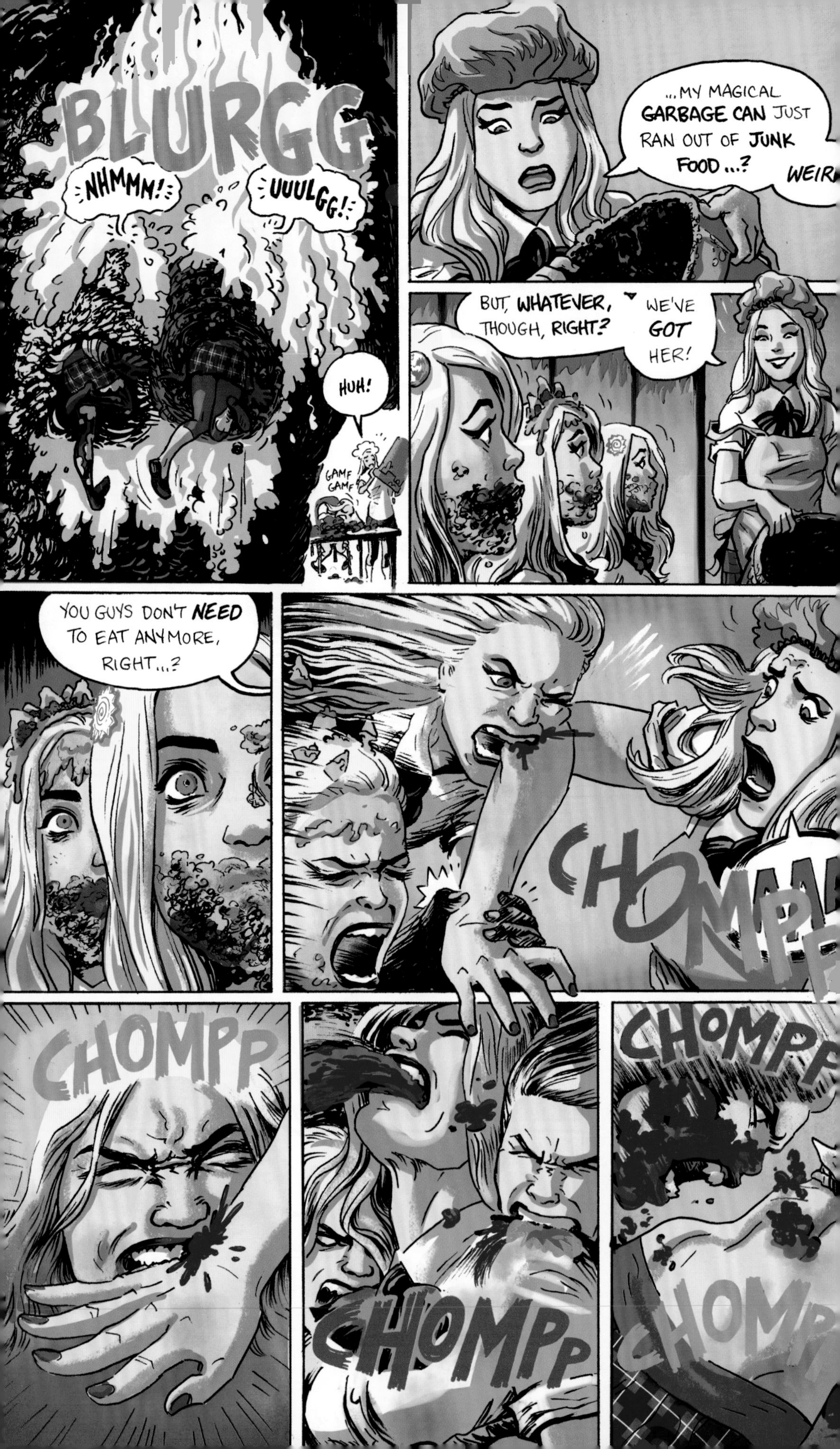
BLURGG
NHMMM!
UUULGG!
HUH!
GAMF GAMF
...MY MAGICAL GARBAGE CAN JUST RAN OUT OF JUNK FOOD...?
WEIR
BUT, WHATEVER, THOUGH, RIGHT?
WE'VE GOT HER!
YOU GUYS DON'T NEED TO EAT ANYMORE, RIGHT...?
CHOMP
CHOMPP
CHOMPP
CHOMPP
CHOMP

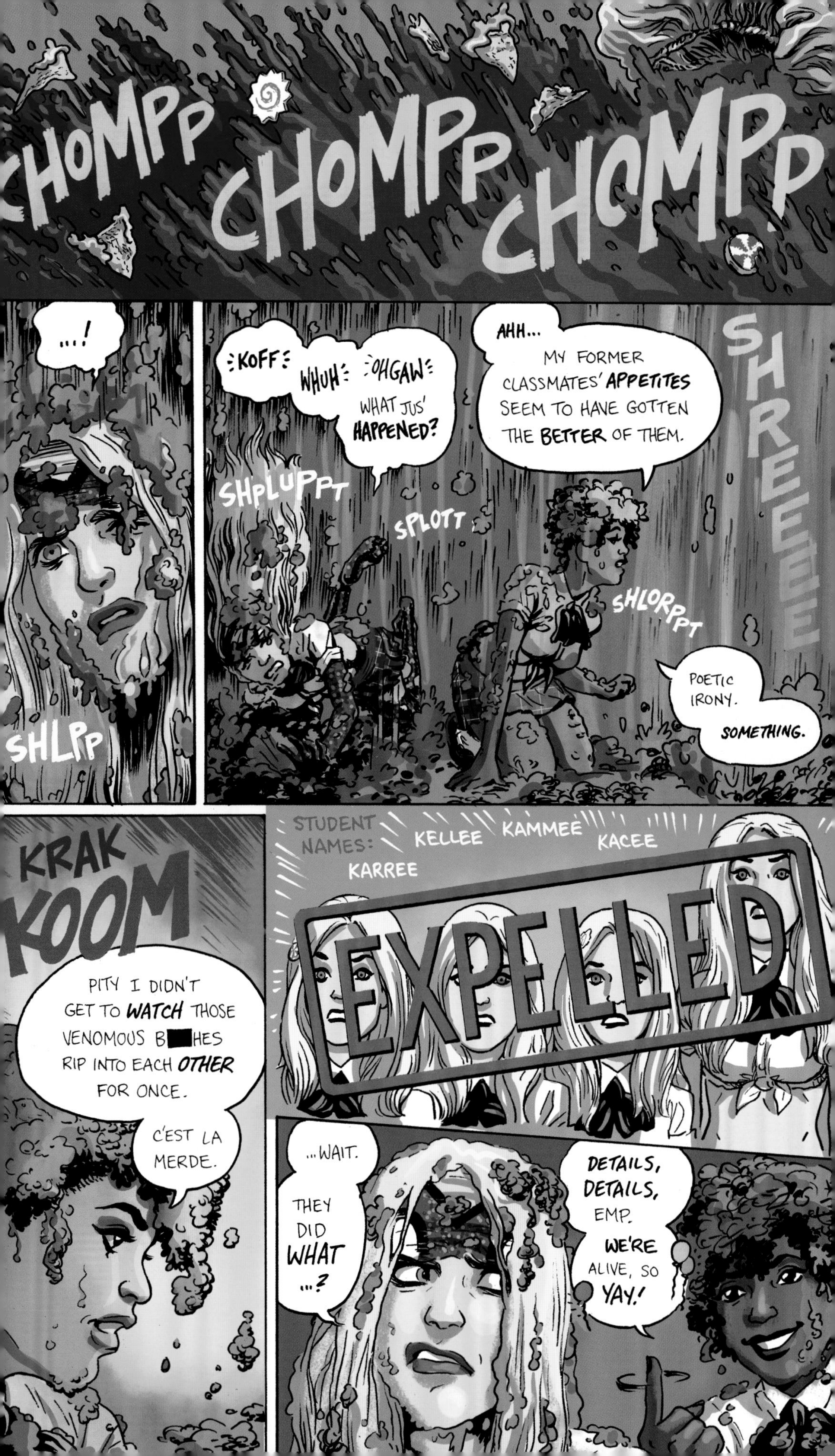

CHOMPP CHOMPP CHOMPP
...!
KOFF
WHUH
OHGAW
WHAT JUS' HAPPENED?
SHPLUPPT
SPLOTT
AHH... MY FORMER CLASSMATES' APPETITES SEEM TO HAVE GOTTEN THE BETTER OF THEM.
SHREEEEE
SHLORPPT
POETIC IRONY. SOMETHING.
SHLPP
KRAK KOOM
PITY I DIDN'T GET TO WATCH THOSE VENOMOUS B[redacted]HES RIP INTO EACH OTHER FOR ONCE.
C'EST LA MERDE.
STUDENT NAMES: KELLEE KAMMEE KACEE KARREE
EXPELLED
...WAIT.
THEY DID WHAT...?
DETAILS, DETAILS, EMP.
WE'RE ALIVE, SO YAY!

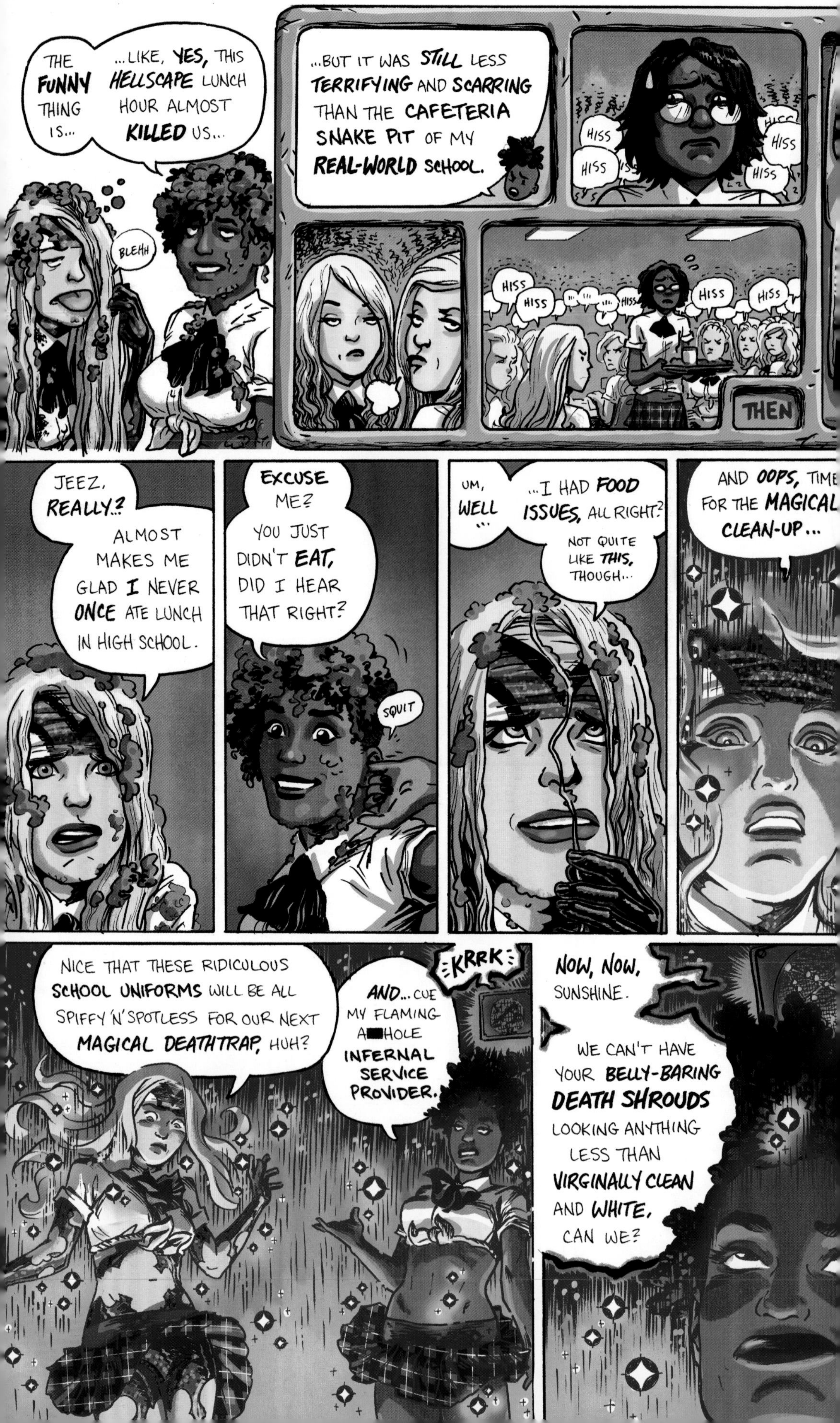
THE FUNNY THING IS...
...LIKE, YES, THIS HELLSCAPE LUNCH HOUR ALMOST KILLED US...
BLEHH
...BUT IT WAS STILL LESS TERRIFYING AND SCARRING THAN THE CAFETERIA SNAKE PIT OF MY REAL-WORLD SCHOOL.
HISS
HISS
HISS
HISS
HISS
HISS
HISS
HISS
HISS
HISS
THEN
JEEZ, REALLY?
ALMOST MAKES ME GLAD I NEVER ONCE ATE LUNCH IN HIGH SCHOOL.
EXCUSE ME?
YOU JUST DIDN'T EAT, DID I HEAR THAT RIGHT?
SQUIT
UM, WELL...
...I HAD FOOD ISSUES, ALL RIGHT?
NOT QUITE LIKE THIS, THOUGH...
AND OOPS, TIME FOR THE MAGICAL CLEAN-UP...
NICE THAT THESE RIDICULOUS SCHOOL UNIFORMS WILL BE ALL SPIFFY 'N' SPOTLESS FOR OUR NEXT MAGICAL DEATHTRAP, HUH?
KRRK
AND... CUE MY FLAMING A[redacted]HOLE INFERNAL SERVICE PROVIDER.
NOW, NOW, SUNSHINE.
WE CAN'T HAVE YOUR BELLY-BARING DEATH SHROUDS LOOKING ANYTHING LESS THAN VIRGINALLY CLEAN AND WHITE, CAN WE?

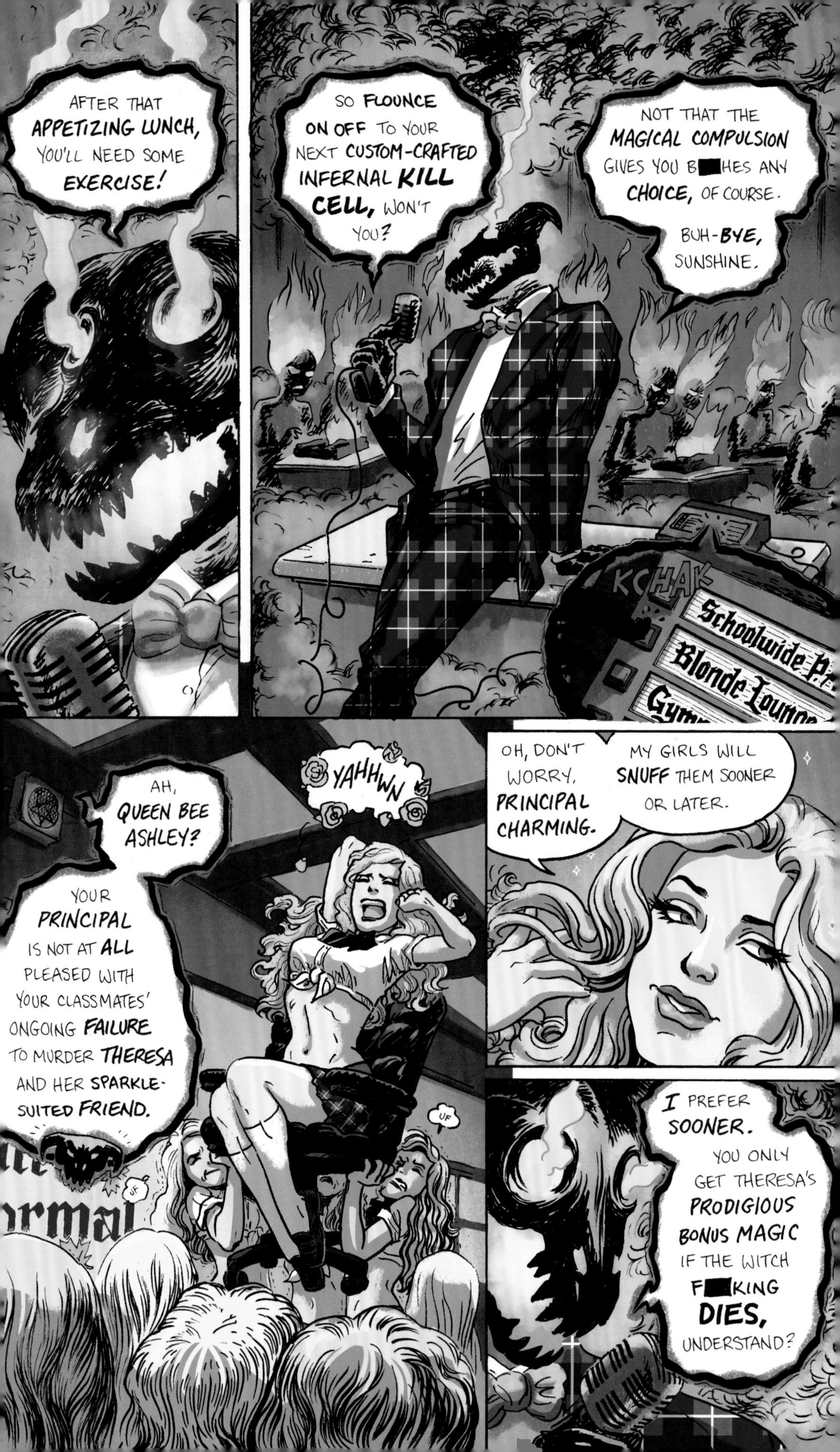
AFTER THAT APPETIZING LUNCH, YOU'LL NEED SOME EXERCISE!
SO FLOUNCE ON OFF TO YOUR NEXT CUSTOM-CRAFTED INFERNAL KILL CELL, WON'T YOU?
NOT THAT THE MAGICAL COMPULSION GIVES YOU B[redacted]HES ANY CHOICE, OF COURSE.
BUH-BYE, SUNSHINE.
KCHAK
Schoolwide
Blonde
AH, QUEEN BEE ASHLEY?
YOUR PRINCIPAL IS NOT AT ALL PLEASED WITH YOUR CLASSMATES' ONGOING FAILURE TO MURDER THERESA AND HER SPARKLE-SUITED FRIEND.
YAHHWN
UF
UF
OH, DON'T WORRY, PRINCIPAL CHARMING.
MY GIRLS WILL SNUFF THEM SOONER OR LATER.
I PREFER SOONER.
YOU ONLY GET THERESA'S PRODIGIOUS BONUS MAGIC IF THE WITCH F[redacted]KING DIES, UNDERSTAND?

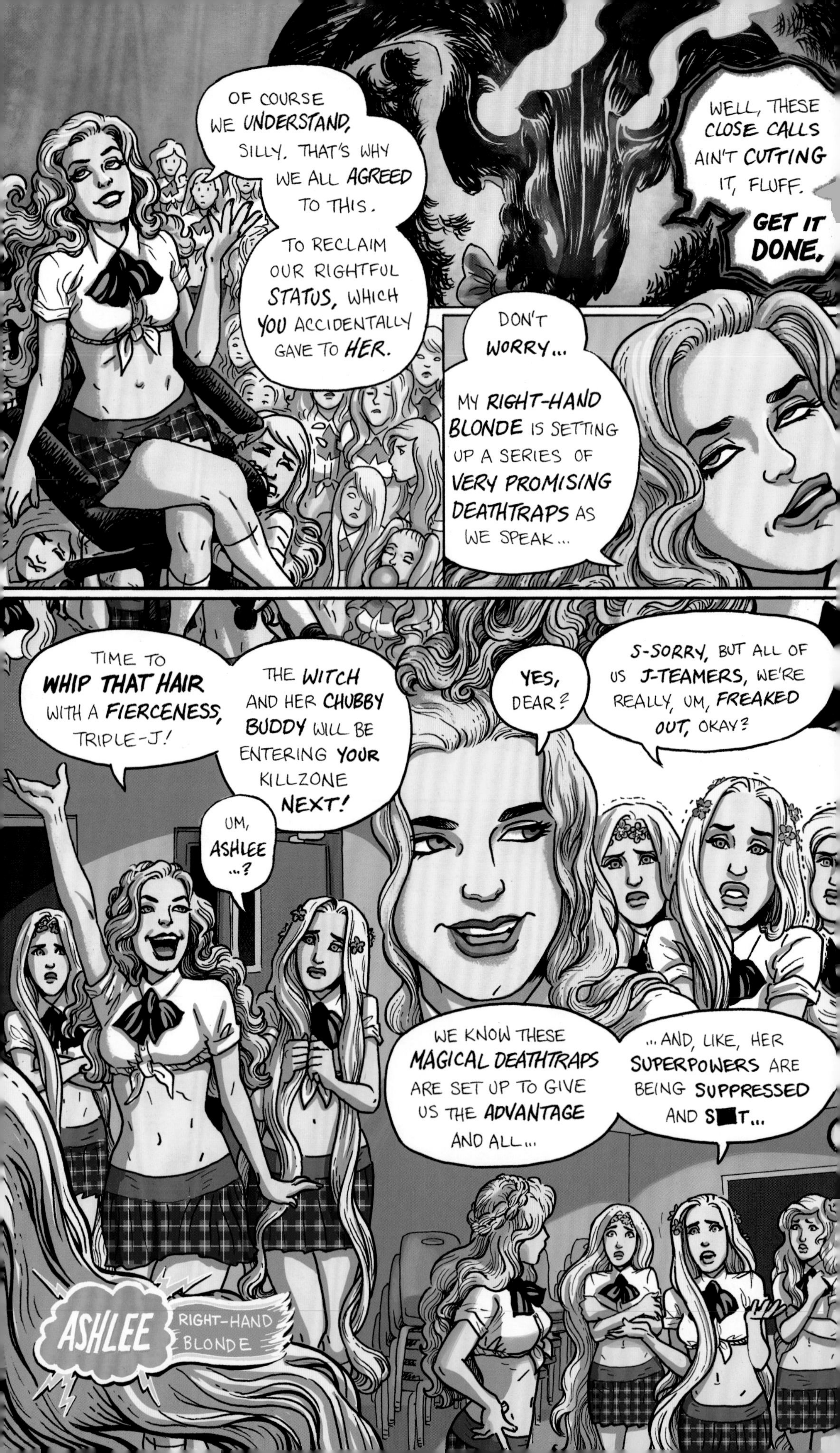
OF COURSE WE UNDERSTAND, SILLY. THAT'S WHY WE ALL AGREED TO THIS.
TO RECLAIM OUR RIGHTFUL STATUS, WHICH YOU ACCIDENTALLY GAVE TO HER.
WELL, THESE CLOSE CALLS AIN'T CUTTING IT, FLUFF.
GET IT DONE.
DON'T WORRY...
MY RIGHT-HAND BLONDE IS SETTING UP A SERIES OF VERY PROMISING DEATHTRAPS AS WE SPEAK...
TIME TO WHIP THAT HAIR WITH A FIERCENESS, TRIPLE-J!
THE WITCH AND HER CHUBBY BUDDY WILL BE ENTERING YOUR KILLZONE NEXT!
UM, ASHLEE ...?
YES, DEAR?
S-SORRY, BUT ALL OF US J-TEAMERS, WE'RE REALLY, UM, FREAKED OUT, OKAY?
WE KNOW THESE MAGICAL DEATHTRAPS ARE SET UP TO GIVE US THE ADVANTAGE AND ALL...
...AND, LIKE, HER SUPERPOWERS ARE BEING SUPPRESSED AND S[redacted]T...
ASHLEE
RIGHT-HAND BLONDE

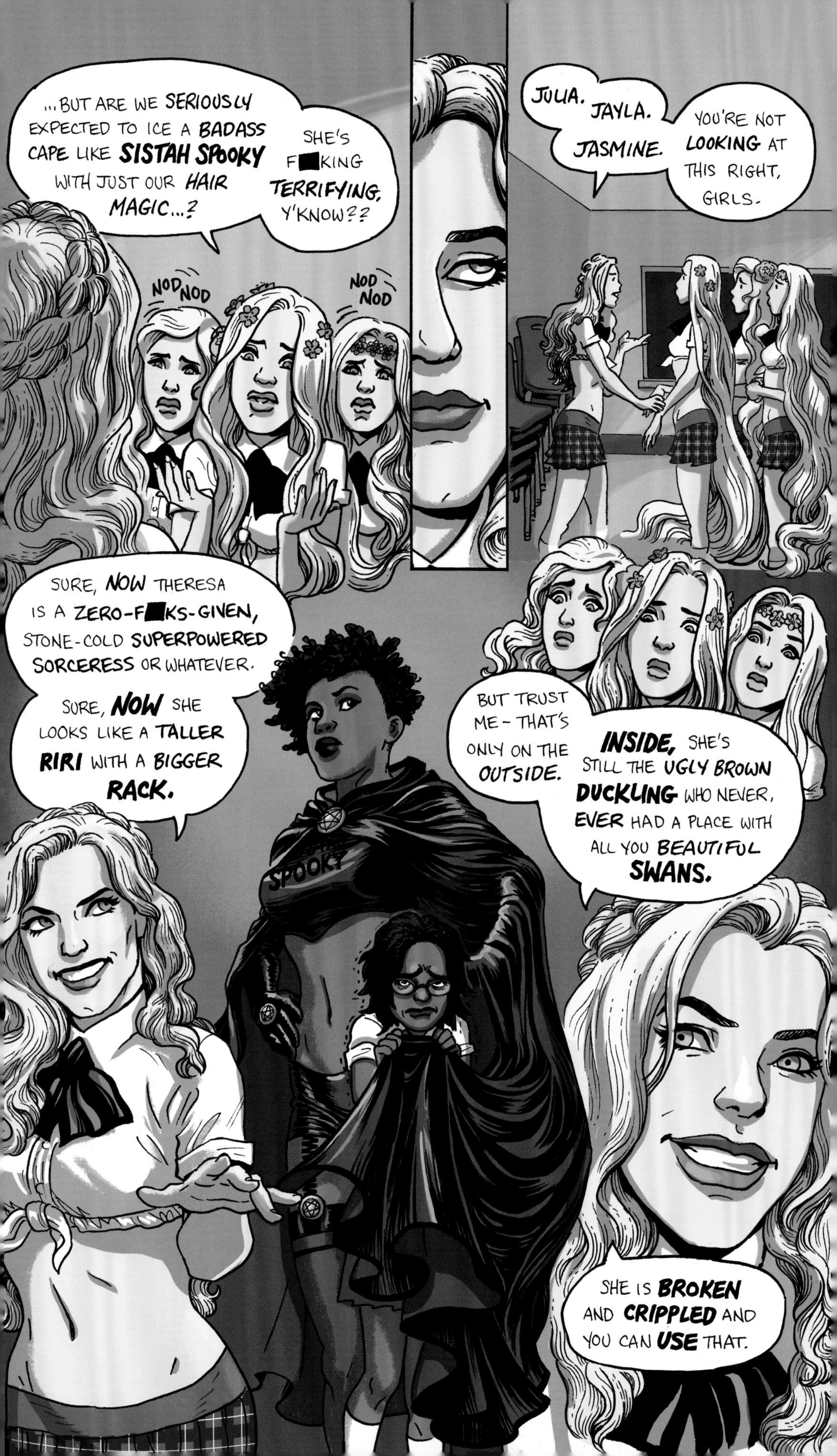
...BUT ARE WE SERIOUSLY EXPECTED TO ICE A BADASS CAPE LIKE SISTAH SPOOKY WITH JUST OUR HAIR MAGIC...?
SHE'S F[redacted]KING TERRIFYING, Y'KNOW??
NOD NOD
NOD NOD
JULIA. JAYLA. JASMINE.
YOU'RE NOT LOOKING AT THIS RIGHT, GIRLS.
SURE, NOW THERESA IS A ZERO-F[redacted]KS-GIVEN, STONE-COLD SUPERPOWERED SORCERESS OR WHATEVER.
SURE, NOW SHE LOOKS LIKE A TALLER RIRI WITH A BIGGER RACK.
SPOOKY
BUT TRUST ME - THAT'S ONLY ON THE OUTSIDE.
INSIDE, SHE'S STILL THE UGLY BROWN DUCKLING WHO NEVER, EVER HAD A PLACE WITH ALL YOU BEAUTIFUL SWANS.
SHE IS BROKEN AND CRIPPLED AND YOU CAN USE THAT.

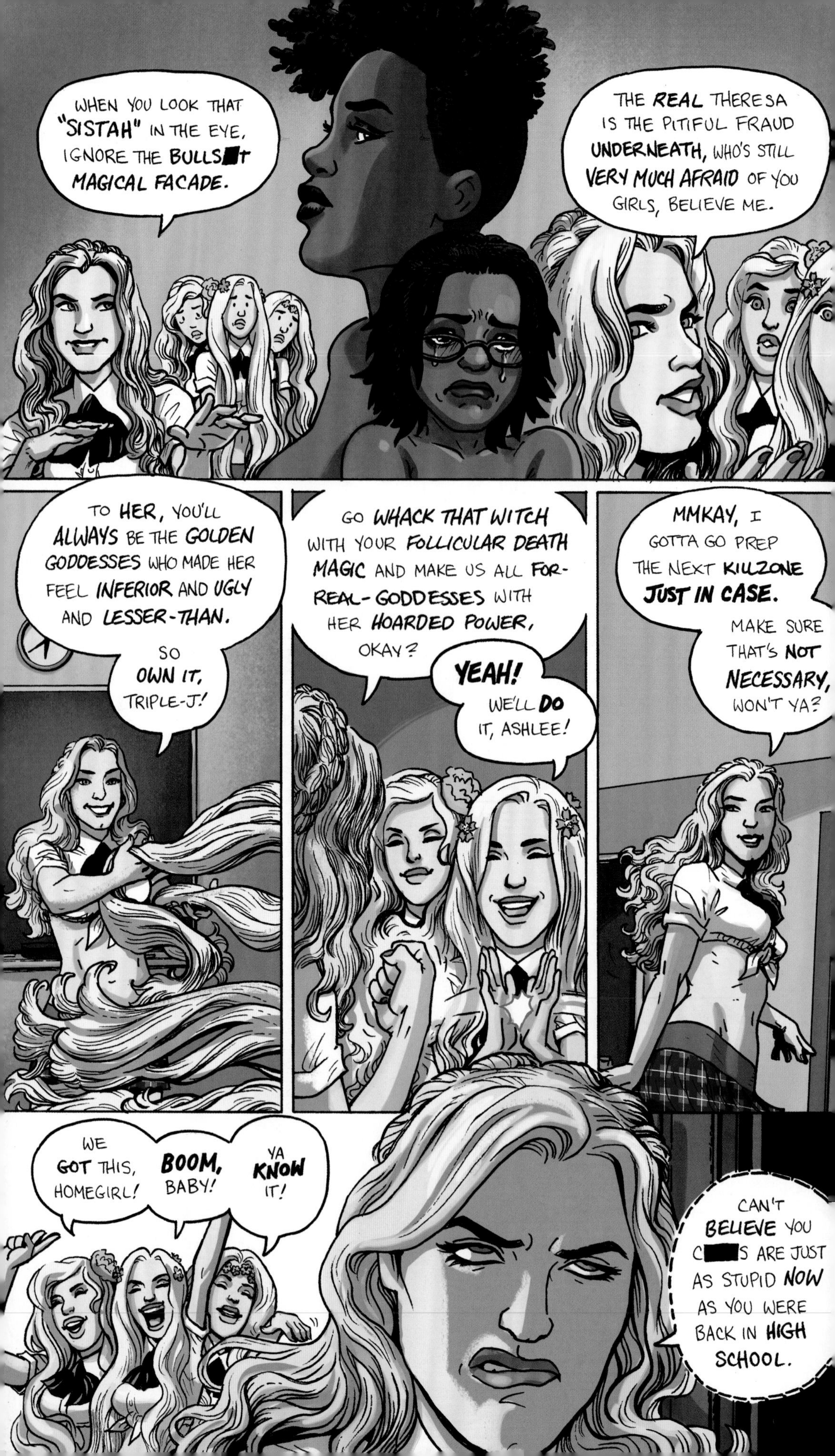

WHEN YOU LOOK THAT "SISTAH" IN THE EYE, IGNORE THE BULLS[redacted]T MAGICAL FACADE.
THE REAL THERESA IS THE PITIFUL FRAUD UNDERNEATH, WHO'S STILL VERY MUCH AFRAID OF YOU GIRLS, BELIEVE ME.
TO HER, YOU'LL ALWAYS BE THE GOLDEN GODDESSES WHO MADE HER FEEL INFERIOR AND UGLY AND LESSER-THAN.
SO OWN IT, TRIPLE-J!
GO WHACK THAT WITCH WITH YOUR FOLLICULAR DEATH MAGIC AND MAKE US ALL FOR-REAL-GODDESSES WITH HER HOARDED POWER, OKAY?
YEAH! WE'LL DO IT, ASHLEE!
MMKAY, I GOTTA GO PREP THE NEXT KILLZONE JUST IN CASE.
MAKE SURE THAT'S NOT NECESSARY, WON'T YA?
WE GOT THIS, HOMEGIRL!
BOOM, BABY!
YA KNOW IT!
CAN'T BELIEVE YOU C[redacted]S ARE JUST AS STUPID NOW AS YOU WERE BACK IN HIGH SCHOOL.

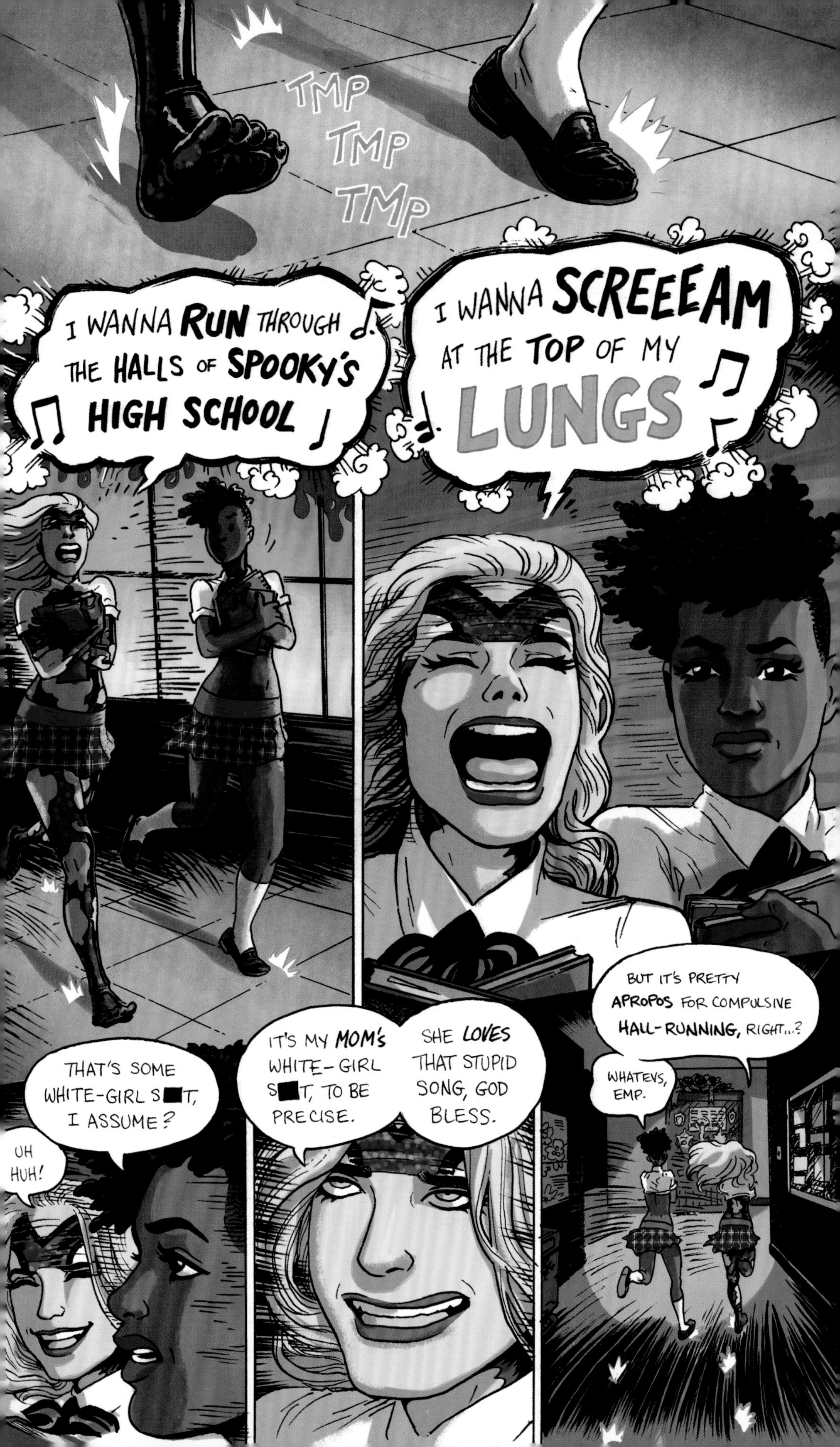
TMP
TMP
TMP
I WANNA RUN THROUGH THE HALLS OF SPOOKY'S HIGH SCHOOL
I WANNA SCREEEAM AT THE TOP OF MY LUNGS
THAT'S SOME WHITE-GIRL S[redacted]T, I ASSUME?
UH HUH!
IT'S MY MOM'S WHITE-GIRL S[redacted]T, TO BE PRECISE.
SHE LOVES THAT STUPID SONG, GOD BLESS.
BUT IT'S PRETTY APROPOS FOR COMPULSIVE HALL-RUNNING, RIGHT...?
WHATEVS, EMP.

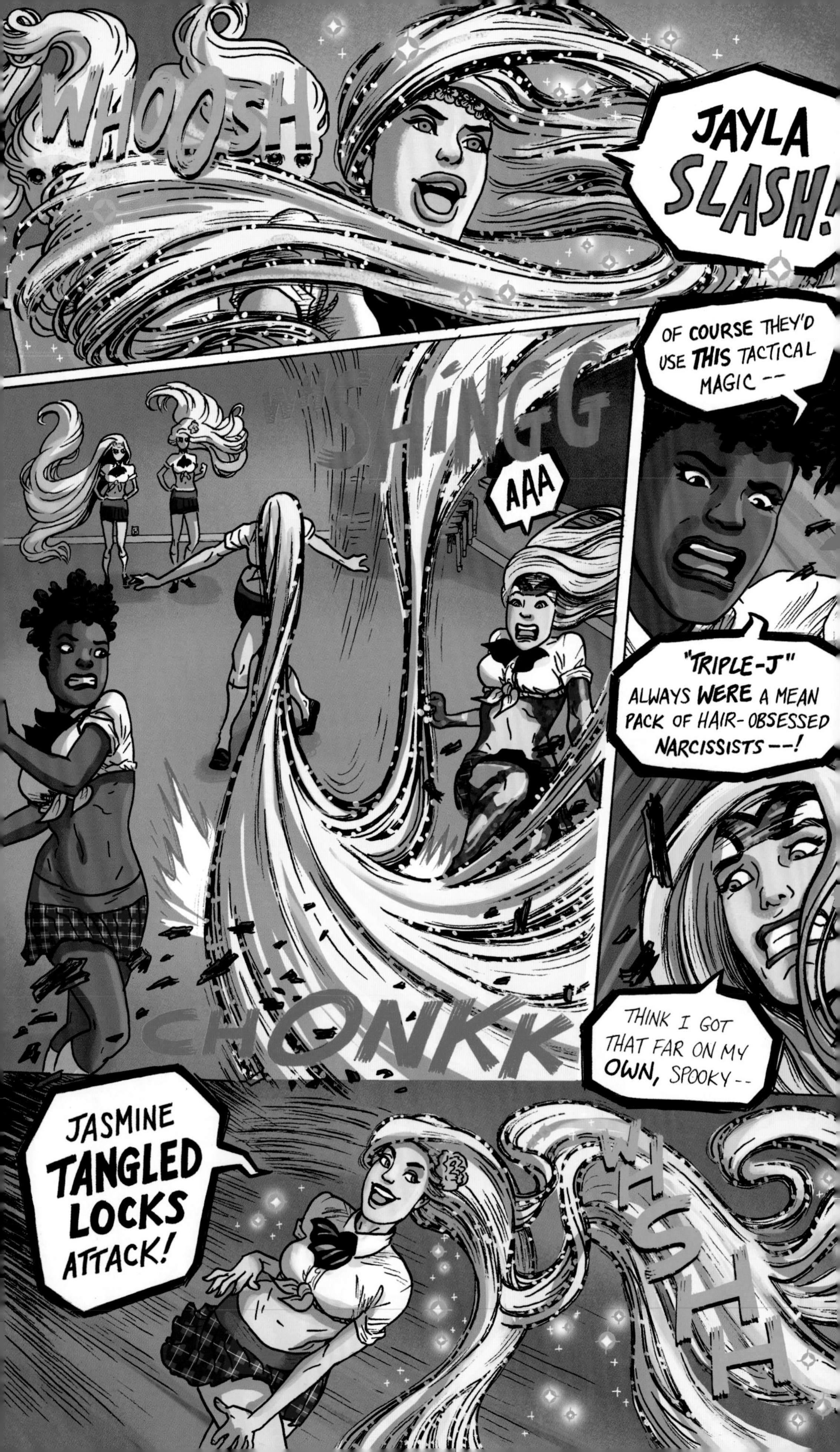
WHOOSH
JAYLA SLASH!
WHSHINGG
AAA
OF COURSE THEY'D USE THIS TACTICAL MAGIC --
"TRIPLE-J" ALWAYS WERE A MEAN PACK OF HAIR-OBSESSED NARCISSISTS --!
THINK I GOT THAT FAR ON MY OWN, SPOOKY --
CHONKK
JASMINE TANGLED LOCKS ATTACK!
WHSHH

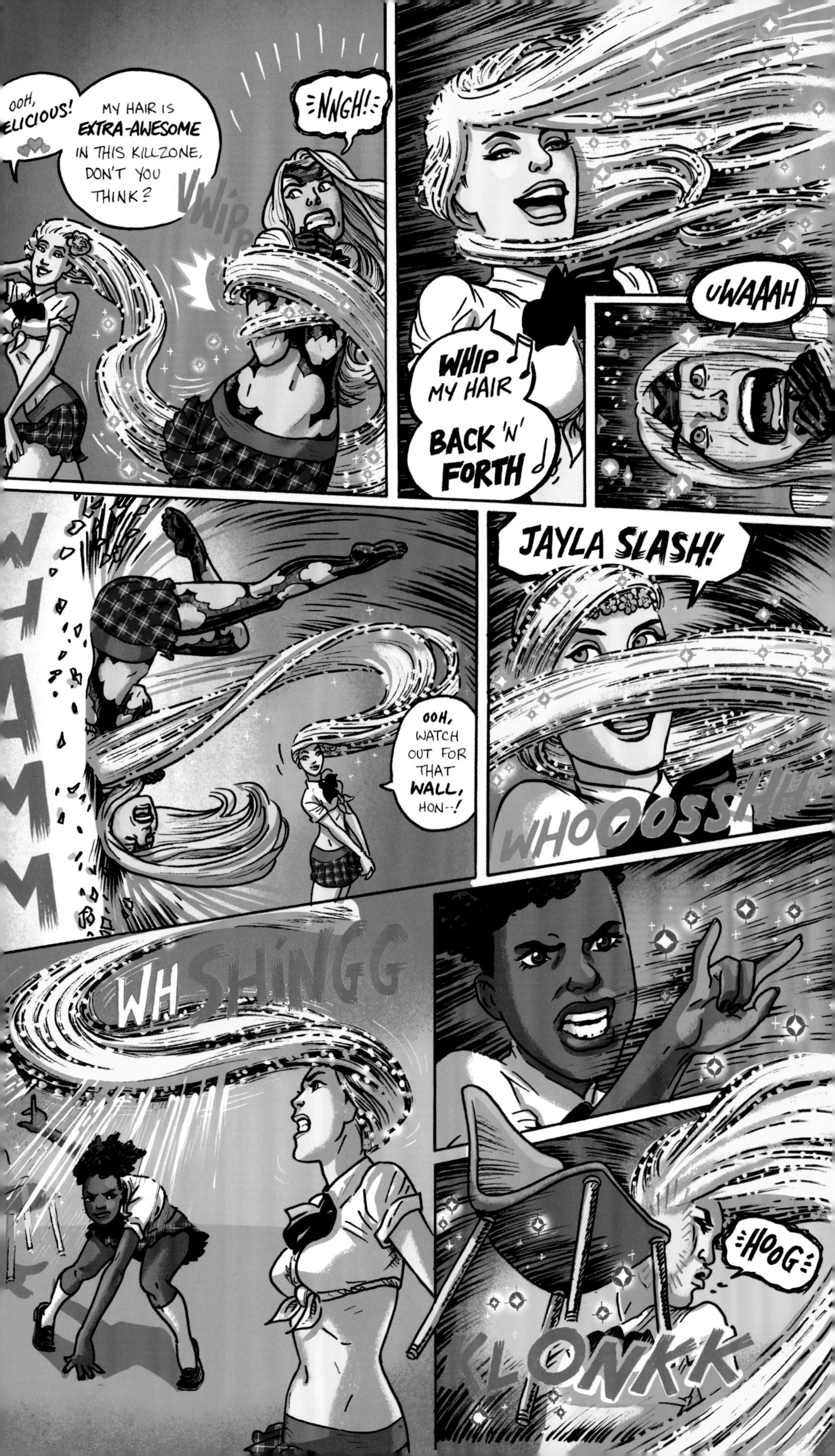
OOH, ELICIOUS!
MY HAIR IS EXTRA-AWESOME IN THIS KILLZONE, DON'T YOU THINK?
NNGH!
VWIPP
WHIP MY HAIR BACK 'N' FORTH
UWAAAH
WHAMM
OOH, WATCH OUT FOR THAT WALL, HON--!
JAYLA SLASH!
WHOOOOSSHH
WHSHINGG
HOOG
KLONKK

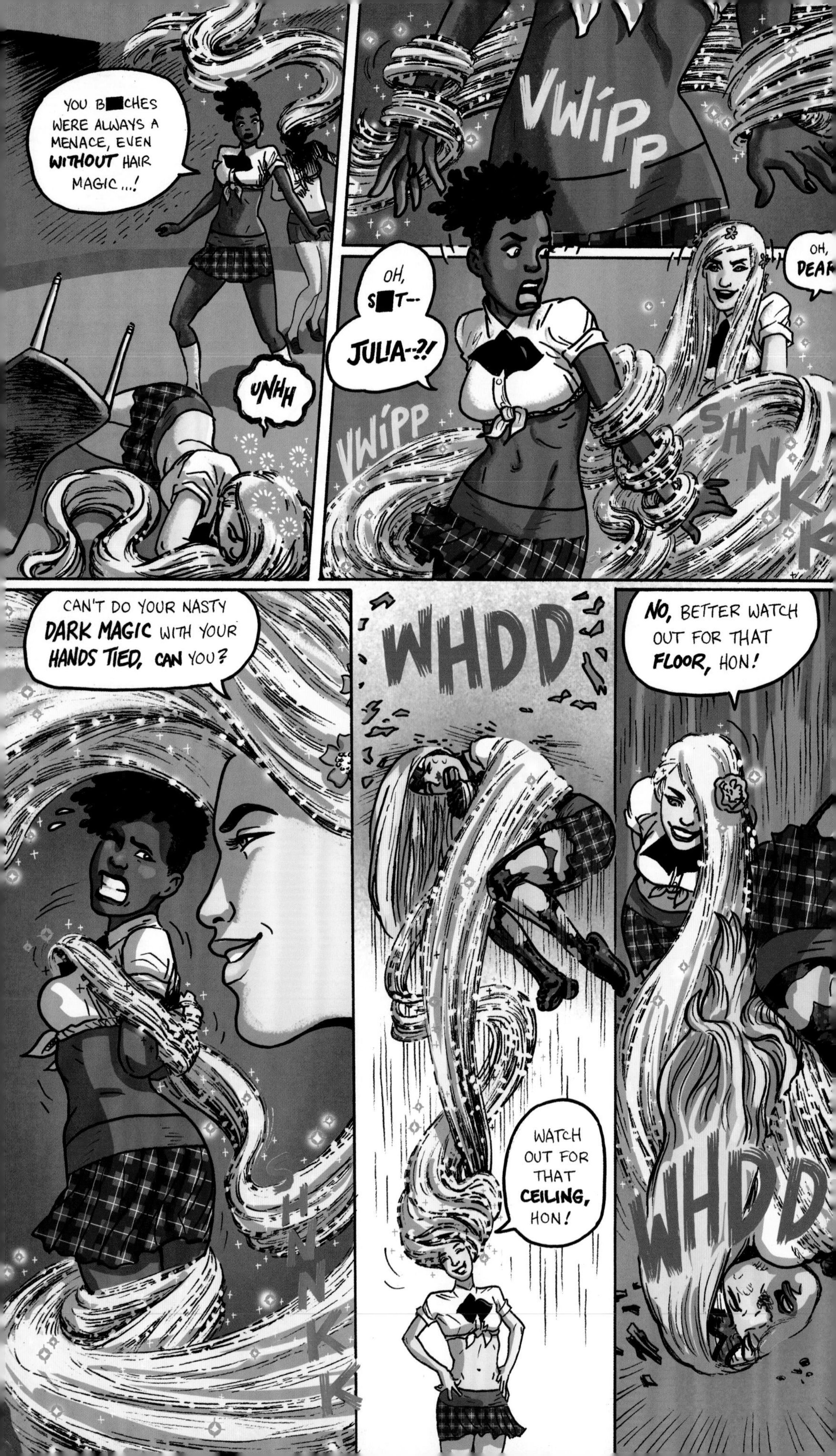
YOU B[redacted]CHES WERE ALWAYS A MENACE, EVEN WITHOUT HAIR MAGIC...!
UNHH
VWIPP
OH, S[redacted]T--
JULIA--?!
OH, DEAR
VWIPP
SHNKK
CAN'T DO YOUR NASTY DARK MAGIC WITH YOUR HANDS TIED, CAN YOU?
SHNKK
WHDD
WATCH OUT FOR THAT CEILING, HON!
NO, BETTER WATCH OUT FOR THAT FLOOR, HON!
WHDD

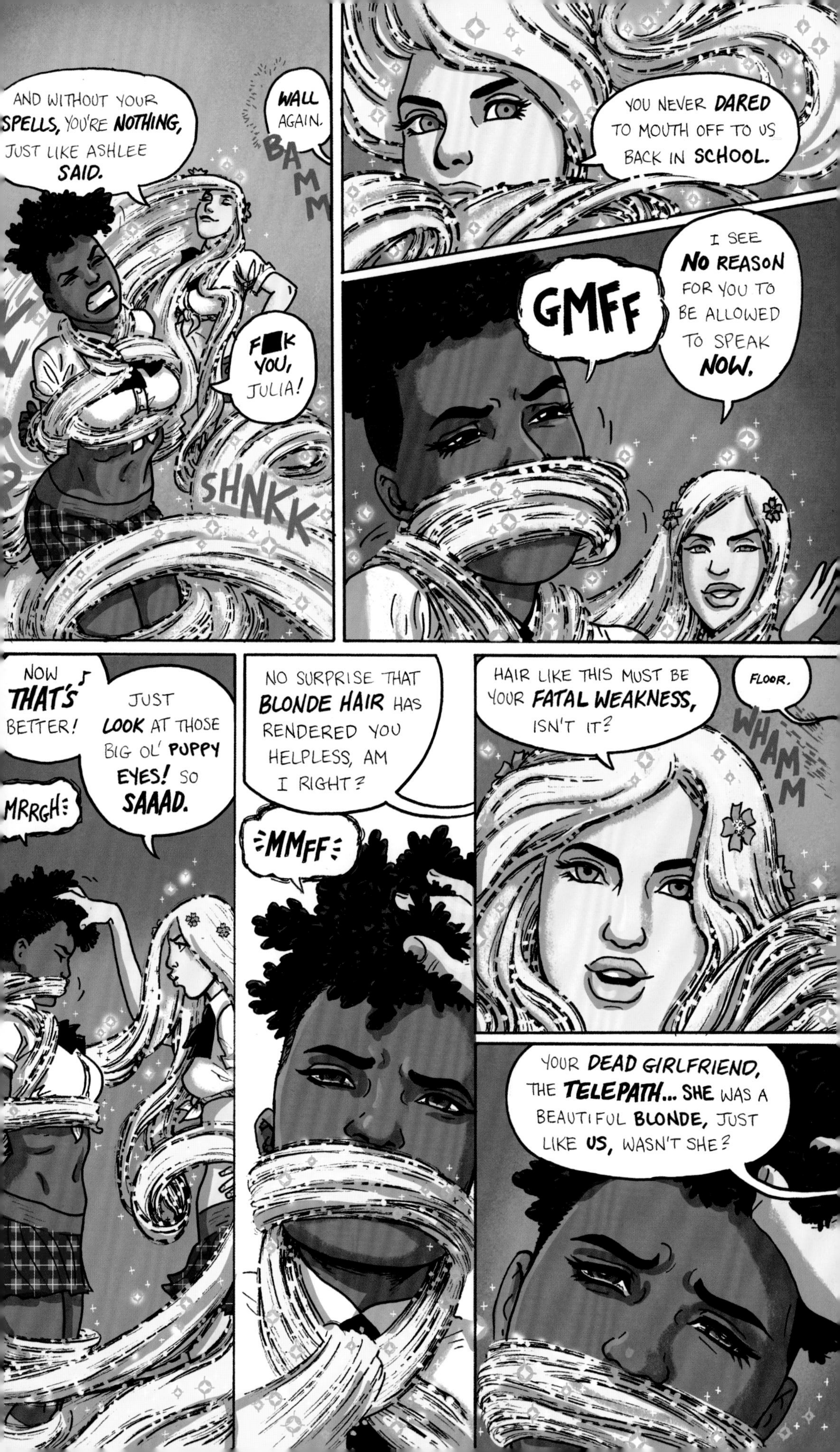
AND WITHOUT YOUR SPELLS, YOU'RE NOTHING, JUST LIKE ASHLEE SAID.
WALL AGAIN.
BAMM
F[redacted]K YOU, JULIA!
SHNKK
YOU NEVER DARED TO MOUTH OFF TO US BACK IN SCHOOL.
GMFF
I SEE NO REASON FOR YOU TO BE ALLOWED TO SPEAK NOW.
NOW THAT'S BETTER!
JUST LOOK AT THOSE BIG OL' PUPPY EYES! SO SAAAD.
MRRGH!
NO SURPRISE THAT BLONDE HAIR HAS RENDERED YOU HELPLESS, AM I RIGHT?
MMFF
HAIR LIKE THIS MUST BE YOUR FATAL WEAKNESS, ISN'T IT?
FLOOR.
WHAMM
YOUR DEAD GIRLFRIEND, THE TELEPATH... SHE WAS A BEAUTIFUL BLONDE, JUST LIKE US, WASN'T SHE?

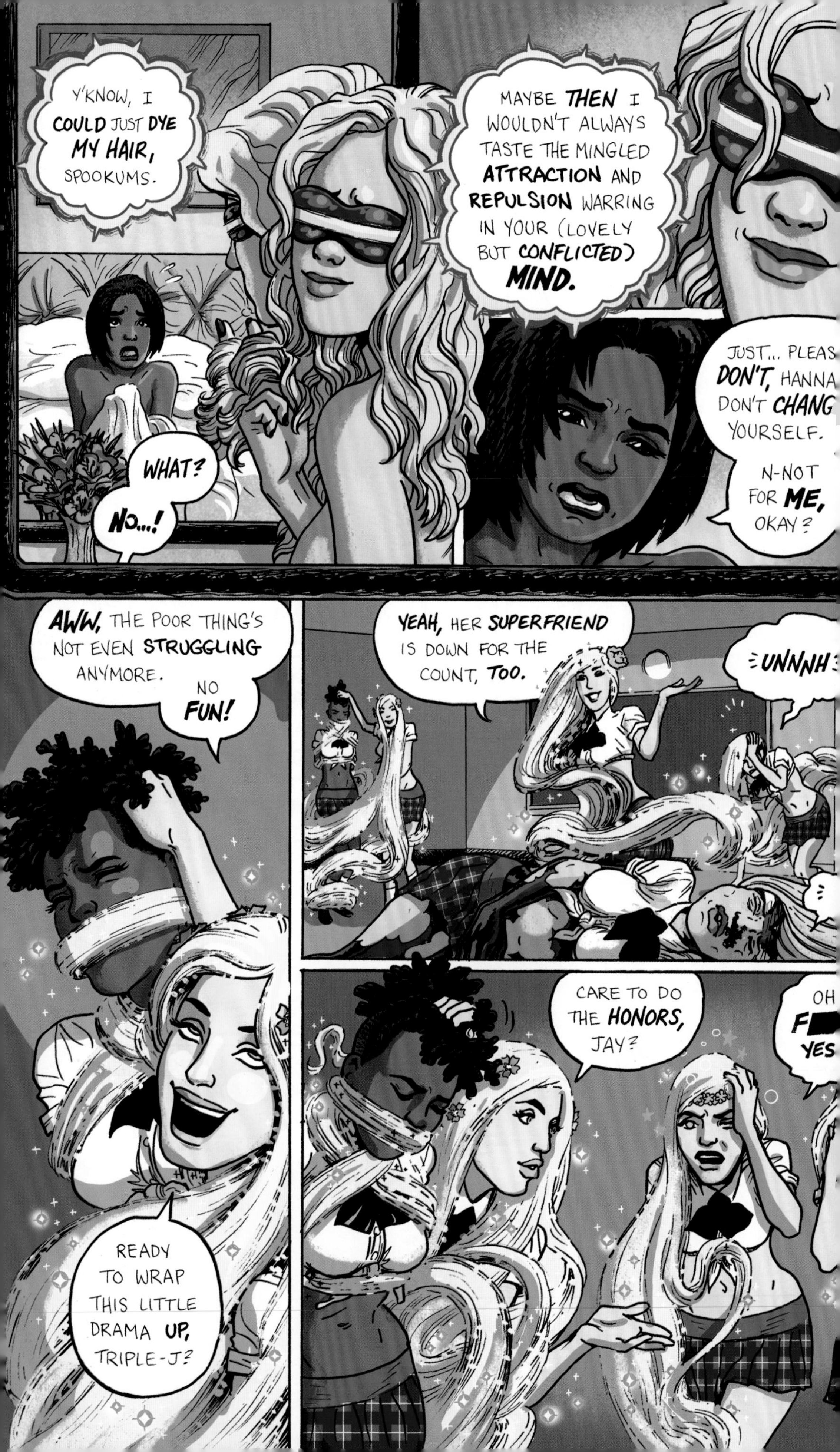

Y'KNOW, I COULD JUST DYE MY HAIR, SPOOKUMS.
WHAT?
NO...!
MAYBE THEN I WOULDN'T ALWAYS TASTE THE MINGLED ATTRACTION AND REPULSION WARRING IN YOUR (LOVELY BUT CONFLICTED) MIND.
JUST... PLEAS
DON'T, HANNA
DON'T CHANG
YOURSELF.
N-NOT FOR ME, OKAY?
AWW, THE POOR THING'S NOT EVEN STRUGGLING ANYMORE.
NO FUN!
READY TO WRAP THIS LITTLE DRAMA UP, TRIPLE-J?
YEAH, HER SUPERFRIEND IS DOWN FOR THE COUNT, TOO.
UNNNH
CARE TO DO THE HONORS, JAY?
OH F[redacted] YES

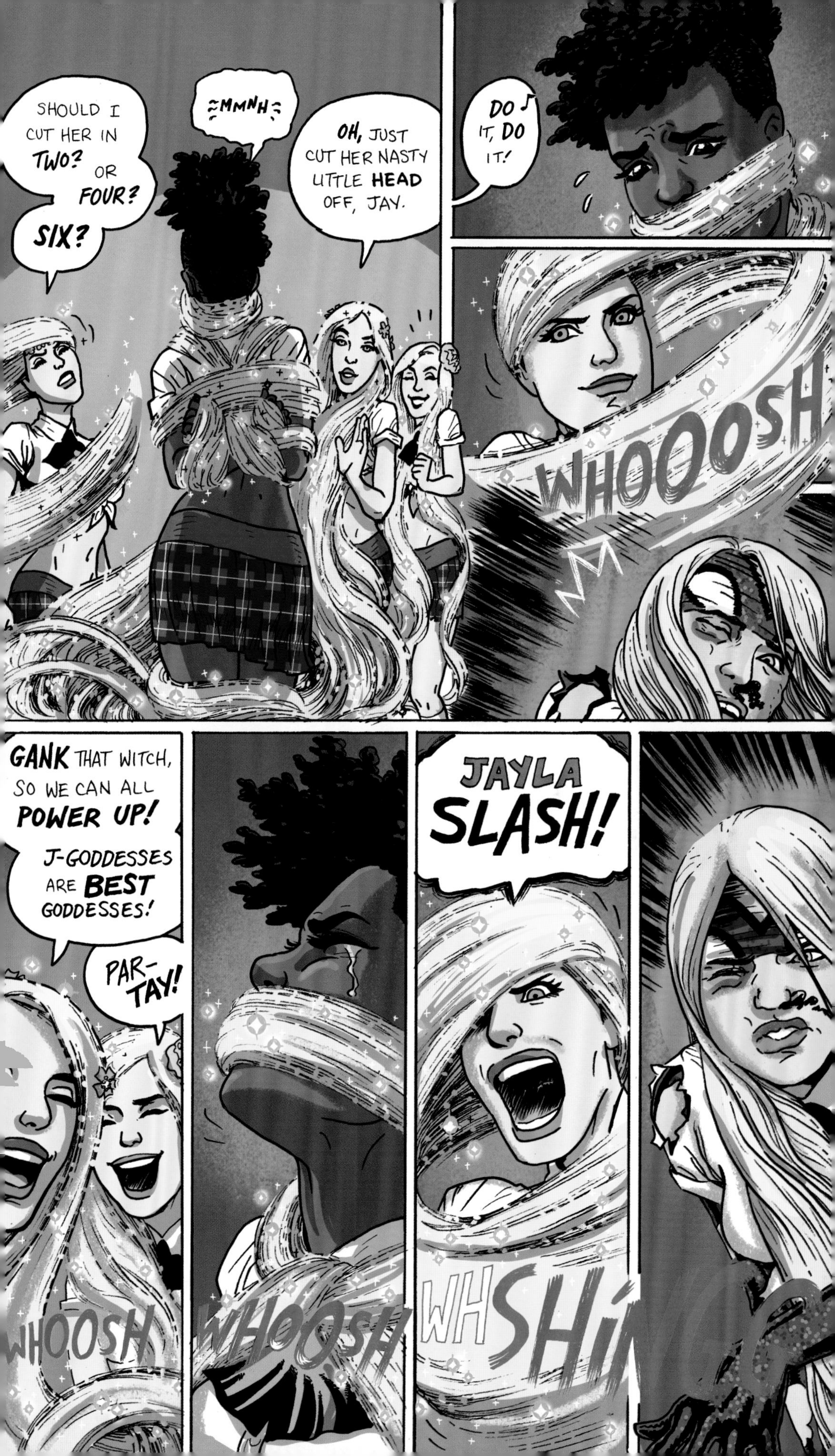
SHOULD I CUT HER IN TWO? OR FOUR? SIX?
MMNH
OH, JUST CUT HER NASTY LITTLE HEAD OFF, JAY.
DO IT, DO IT!
WHOOOOSH
GANK THAT WITCH, SO WE CAN ALL POWER UP!
J-GODDESSES ARE BEST GODDESSES!
PAR-TAY!
JAYLA SLASH!
WHOOSH
WHOOSH
WHSHI

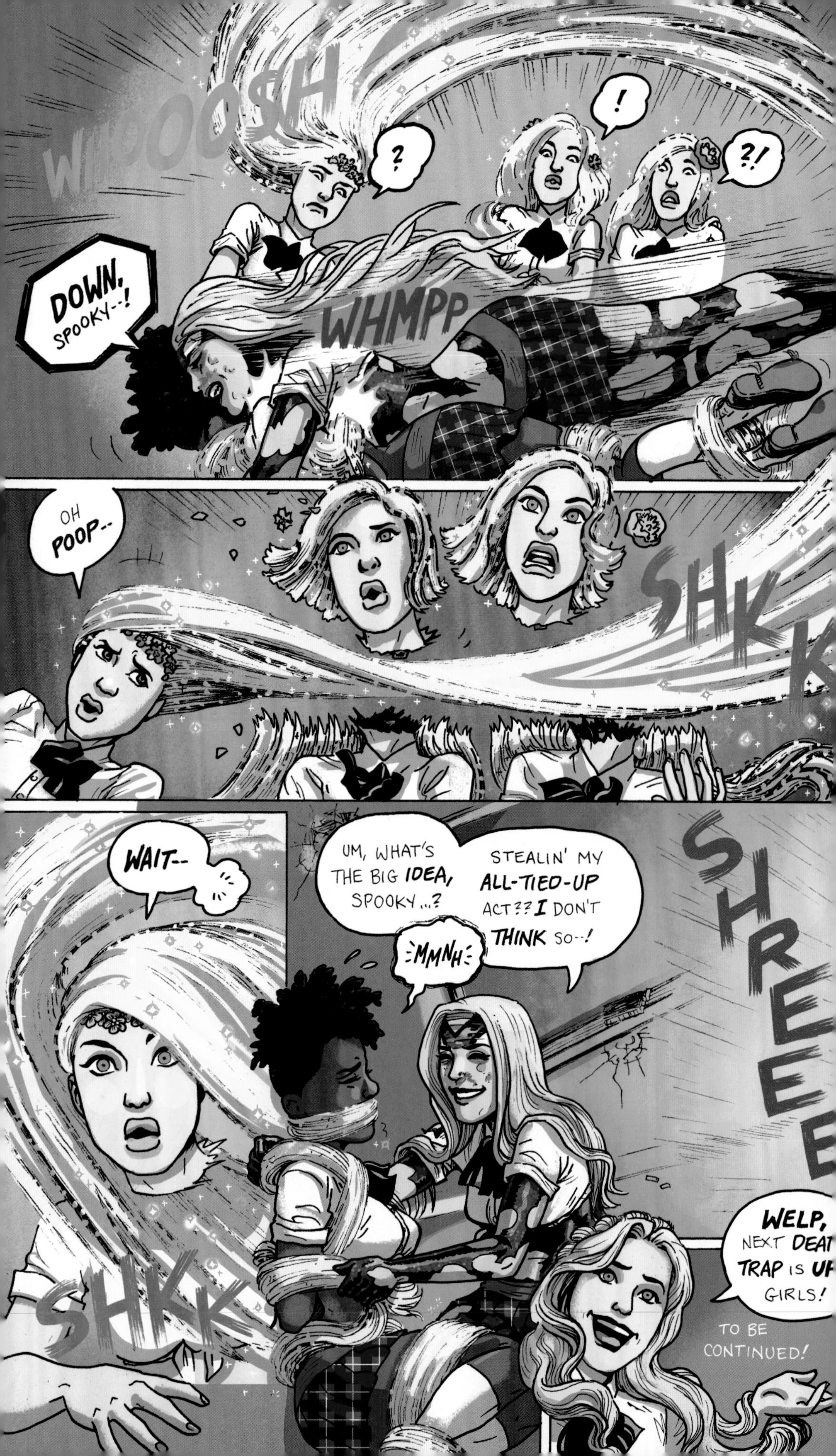
WHOOOSH
?
!
?!
DOWN, SPOOKY--!
WHMPP
OH POOP--
SHKK
WAIT--
UM, WHAT'S THE BIG IDEA, SPOOKY...?
STEALIN' MY ALL-TIED-UP ACT?? I DON'T THINK SO--!
MMNH
SHREEE
WELP, NEXT DEAT TRAP IS UF GIRLS!
SHKK
TO BE CONTINUED!

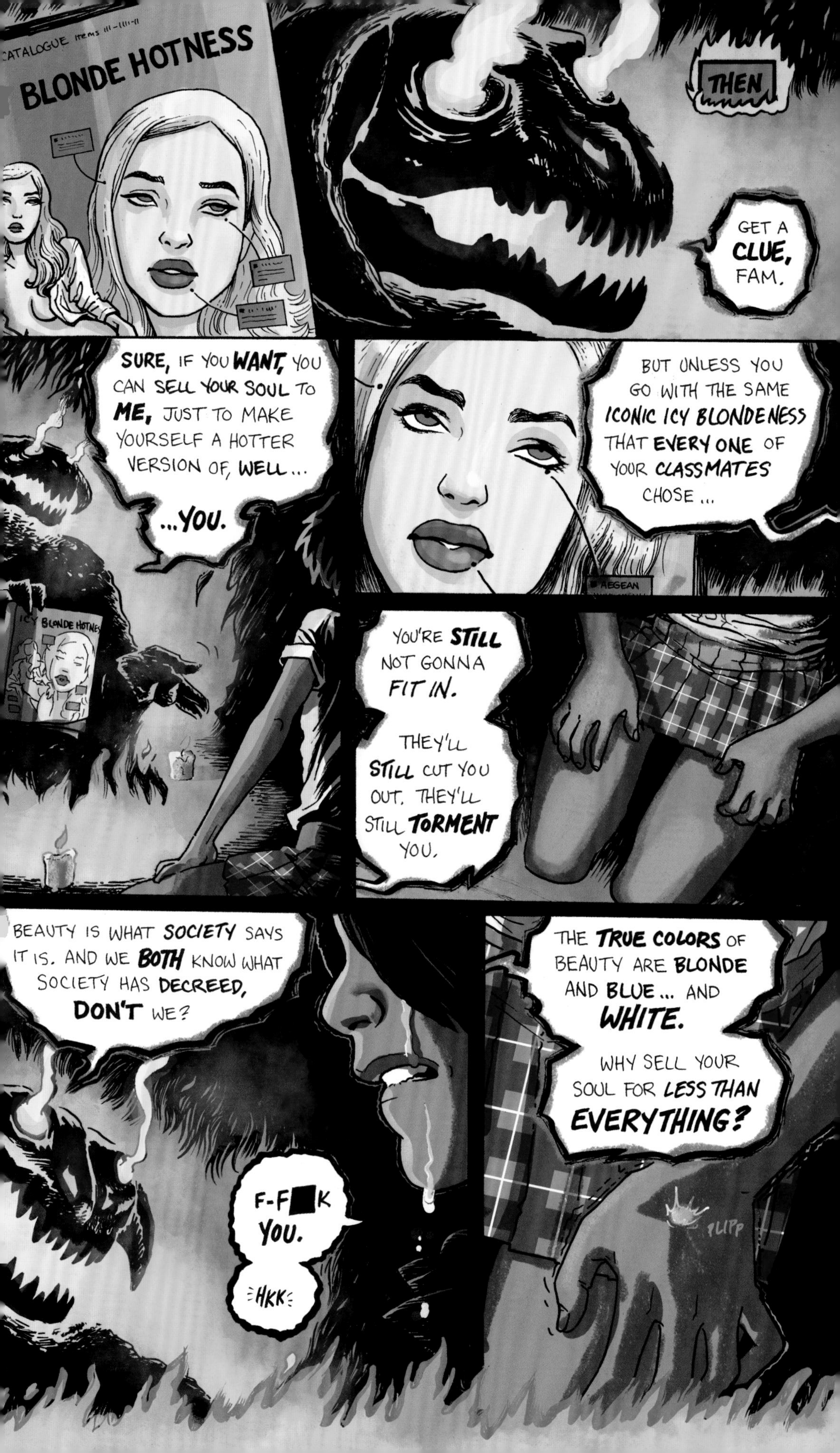

CATALOGUE
BLONDE HOTNESS
THEN
GET A CLUE, FAM.
SURE, IF YOU WANT, YOU CAN SELL YOUR SOUL TO ME, JUST TO MAKE YOURSELF A HOTTER VERSION OF, WELL...
...YOU.
BUT UNLESS YOU GO WITH THE SAME ICONIC ICY BLONDENESS THAT EVERY ONE OF YOUR CLASSMATES CHOSE...
AEGEAN
YOU'RE STILL NOT GONNA FIT IN.
THEY'LL STILL CUT YOU OUT. THEY'LL STILL TORMENT YOU.
BEAUTY IS WHAT SOCIETY SAYS IT IS. AND WE BOTH KNOW WHAT SOCIETY HAS DECREED, DON'T WE?
F-F[redacted]K YOU.
HKK
THE TRUE COLORS OF BEAUTY ARE BLONDE AND BLUE... AND WHITE.
WHY SELL YOUR SOUL FOR LESS THAN EVERYTHING?

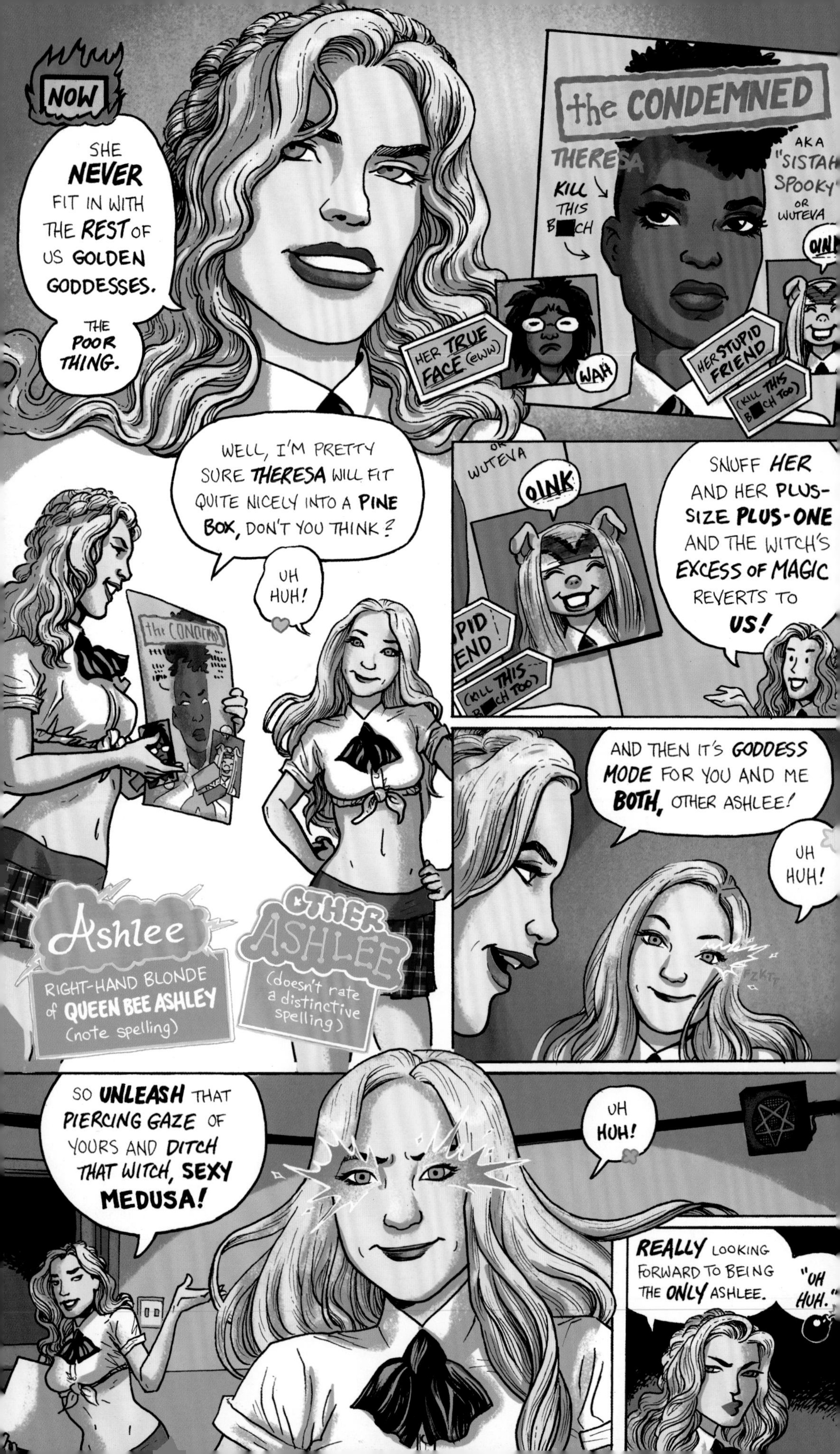

NOW
SHE NEVER FIT IN WITH THE REST OF US GOLDEN GODDESSES.
THE POOR THING.
the CONDEMNED
THERESA
AKA "SISTAH SPOOKY" OR WUTEVA
KILL THIS B[redacted]CH
HER TRUE FACE (eww)
WAH
HER STUPID FRIEND
(KILL THIS B[redacted]CH TOO)
OINK
WELL, I'M PRETTY SURE THERESA WILL FIT QUITE NICELY INTO A PINE BOX, DON'T YOU THINK?
UH HUH!
Ashlee
RIGHT-HAND BLONDE of QUEEN BEE ASHLEY (note spelling)
OTHER ASHLEE
(doesn't rate a distinctive spelling)
OR WUTEVA
OINK
SNUFF HER AND HER PLUS-SIZE PLUS-ONE AND THE WITCH'S EXCESS OF MAGIC REVERTS TO US!
AND THEN IT'S GODDESS MODE FOR YOU AND ME BOTH, OTHER ASHLEE!
UH HUH!
FZKTT
SO UNLEASH THAT PIERCING GAZE OF YOURS AND DITCH THAT WITCH, SEXY MEDUSA!
UH HUH!
REALLY LOOKING FORWARD TO BEING THE ONLY ASHLEE.
"UH HUH."

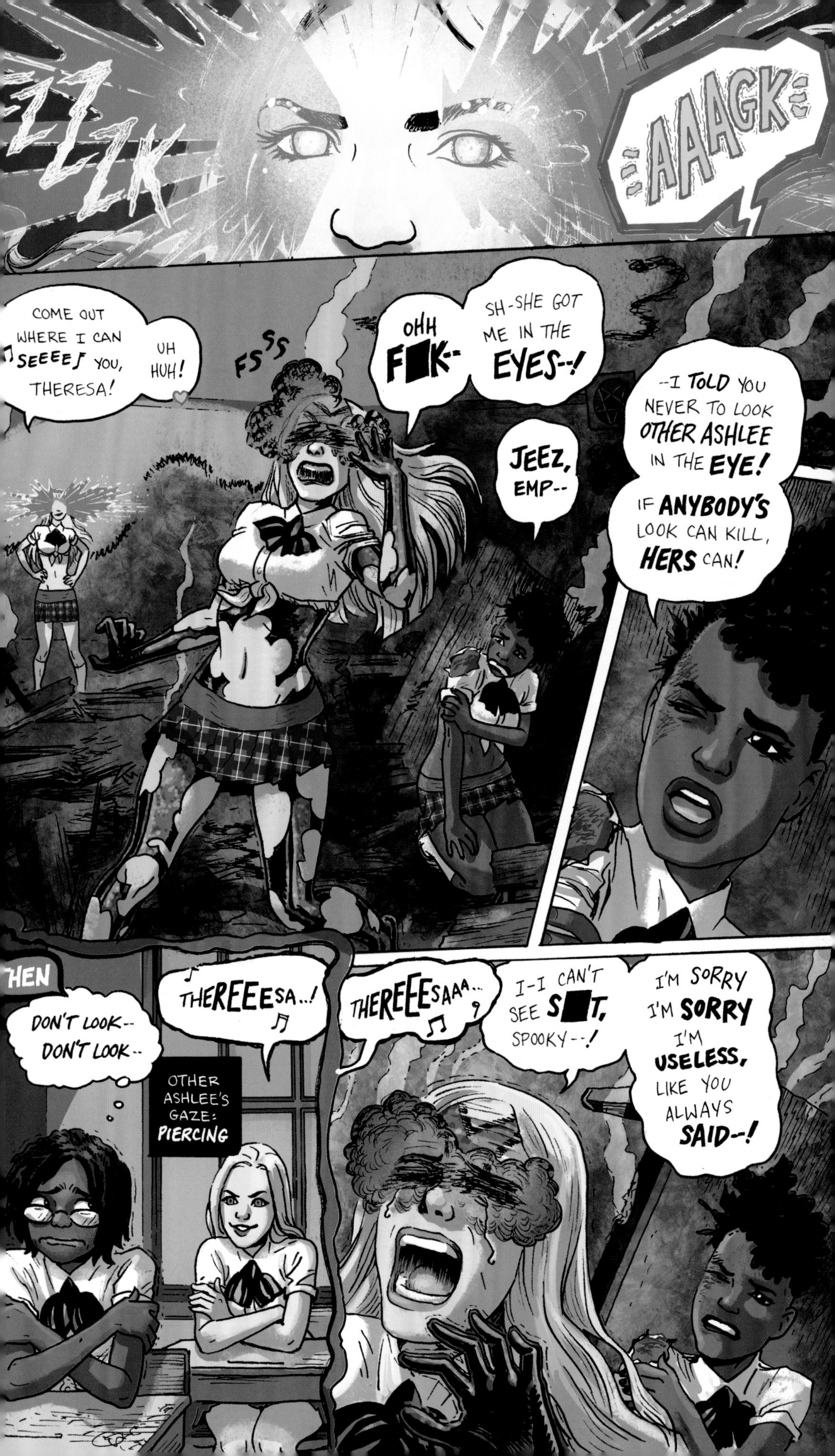
ZZZK
AAAGK
COME OUT WHERE I CAN SEEEE YOU, THERESA!
UH HUH!
FSSS
OHH F[redacted]K--
SH-SHE GOT ME IN THE EYES--!
JEEZ, EMP--
--I TOLD YOU NEVER TO LOOK OTHER ASHLEE IN THE EYE!
IF ANYBODY'S LOOK CAN KILL, HERS CAN!
THEN
DON'T LOOK-- DON'T LOOK--
OTHER ASHLEE'S GAZE: PIERCING
THEREEESA..!
THEREEESAAA...
I-I CAN'T SEE S[redacted]T, SPOOKY--!
I'M SORRY I'M SORRY I'M USELESS, LIKE YOU ALWAYS SAID--!

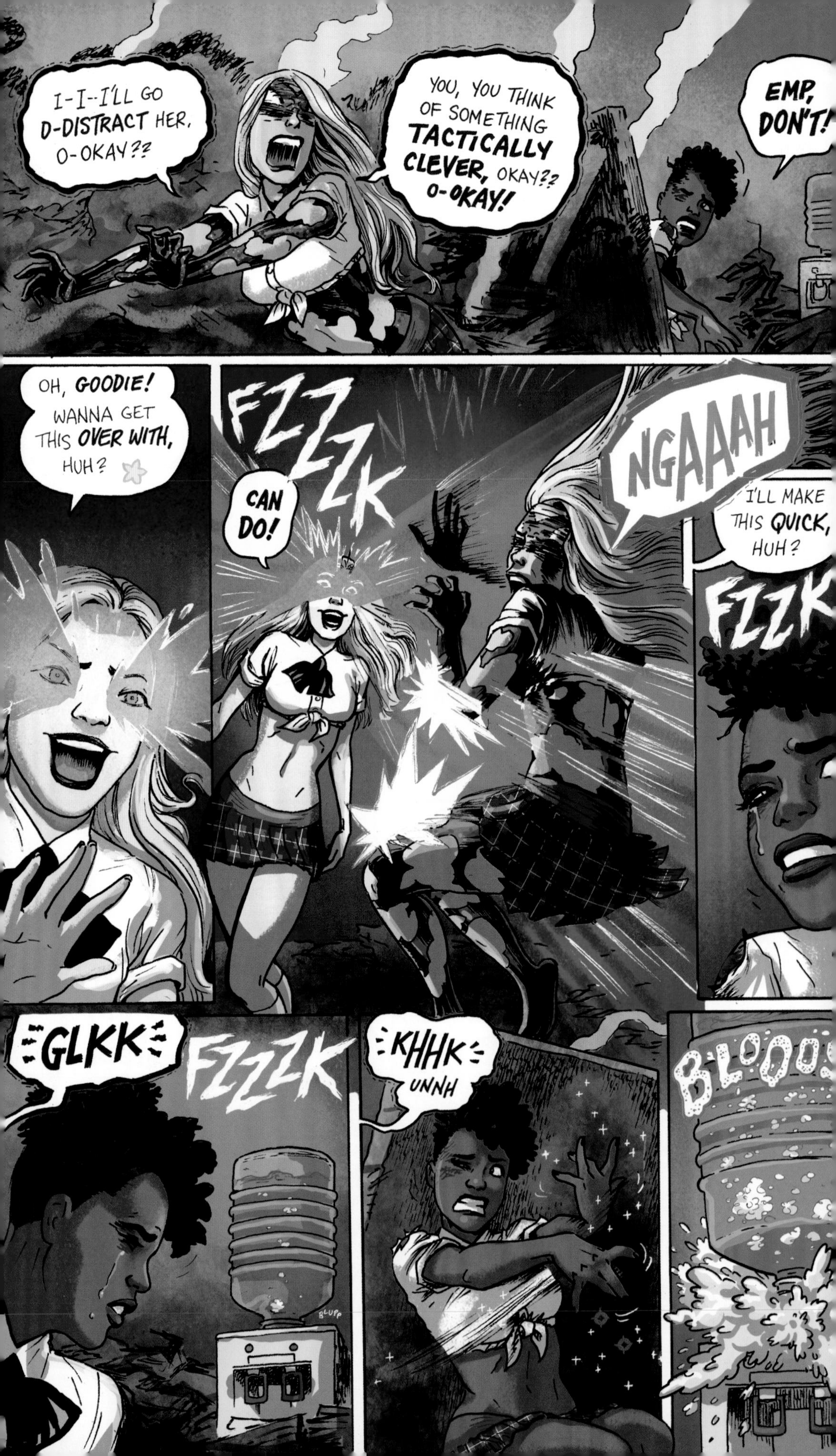
I-I--I'LL GO D-DISTRACT HER, O-OKAY??
YOU, YOU THINK OF SOMETHING TACTICALLY CLEVER, OKAY?? O-OKAY!
EMP, DON'T!
OH, GOODIE! WANNA GET THIS OVER WITH, HUH?
FZZZK
CAN DO!
NGAAAH
I'LL MAKE THIS QUICK, HUH?
FZZK
GLKK
FZZZK
BLUPP
KHHK UNNH
BLOOOS

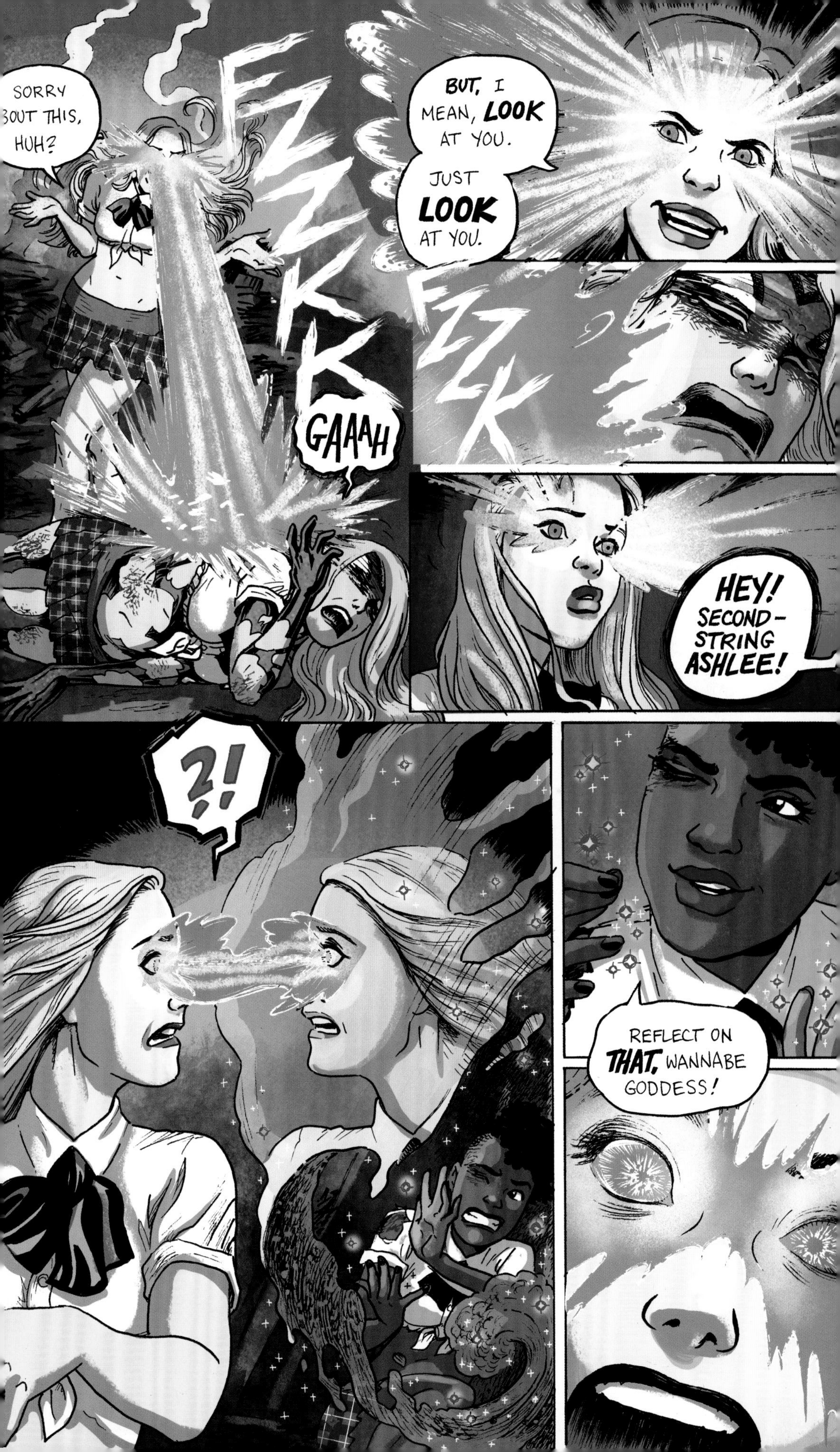
SORRY 'BOUT THIS, HUH?
FZZKKK
GAAAH
BUT, I MEAN, LOOK AT YOU.
JUST LOOK AT YOU.
FZZK
HEY! SECOND-STRING ASHLEE!
?!
REFLECT ON THAT, WANNABE GODDESS!

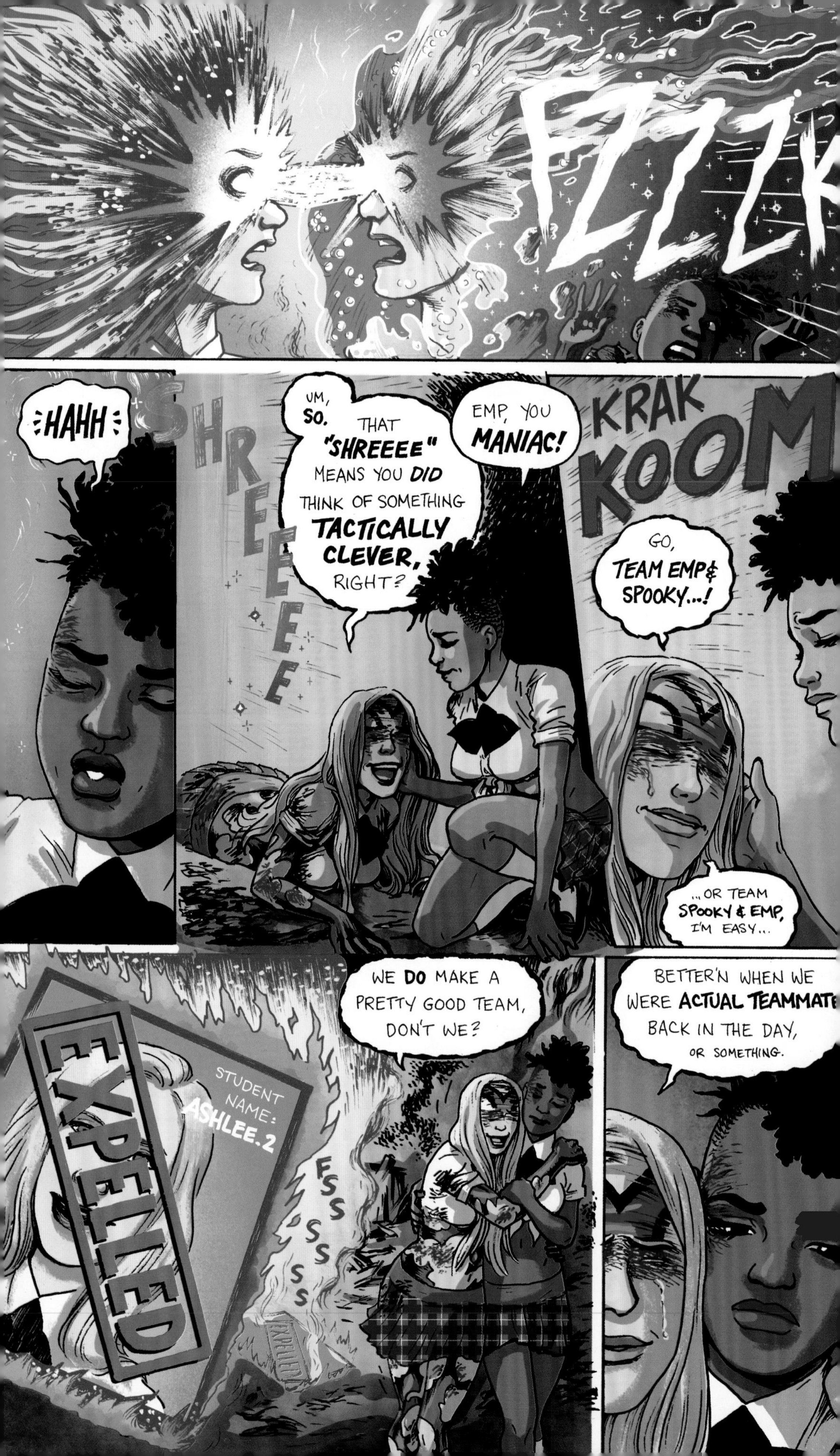
FZZZK
HAHH
SHREEEEE
UM, SO. THAT "SHREEEE" MEANS YOU DID THINK OF SOMETHING TACTICALLY CLEVER, RIGHT?
EMP, YOU MANIAC!
KRAK KOOM
GO, TEAM EMP & SPOOKY...!
...OR TEAM SPOOKY & EMP, I'M EASY...
EXPELLED
STUDENT NAME: ASHLEE.2
WE DO MAKE A PRETTY GOOD TEAM, DON'T WE?
FSSSSS
BETTER'N WHEN WE WERE ACTUAL TEAMMATE BACK IN THE DAY, OR SOMETHING.

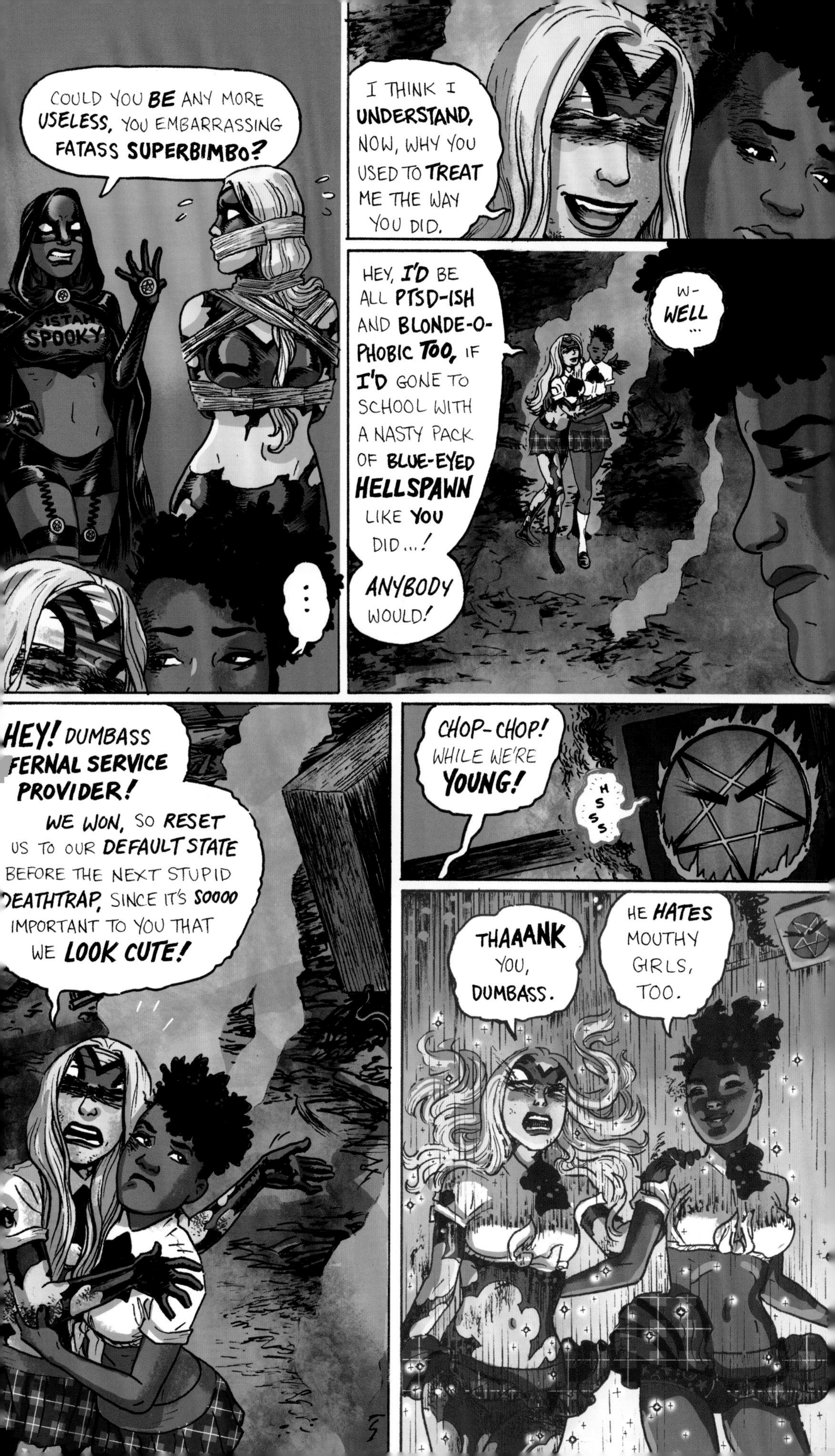
COULD YOU BE ANY MORE USELESS, YOU EMBARRASSING FATASS SUPERBIMBO?
SISTAH SPOOKY
...
I THINK I UNDERSTAND, NOW, WHY YOU USED TO TREAT ME THE WAY YOU DID.
HEY, I'D BE ALL PTSD-ISH AND BLONDE-O-PHOBIC TOO, IF I'D GONE TO SCHOOL WITH A NASTY PACK OF BLUE-EYED HELLSPAWN LIKE YOU DID...!
ANYBODY WOULD!
W-WELL...
HEY! DUMBASS FERNAL SERVICE PROVIDER!
WE WON, SO RESET US TO OUR DEFAULT STATE BEFORE THE NEXT STUPID DEATHTRAP, SINCE IT'S SOOOO IMPORTANT TO YOU THAT WE LOOK CUTE!
CHOP-CHOP! WHILE WE'RE YOUNG!
HSSS
THAAANK YOU, DUMBASS.
HE HATES MOUTHY GIRLS, TOO.

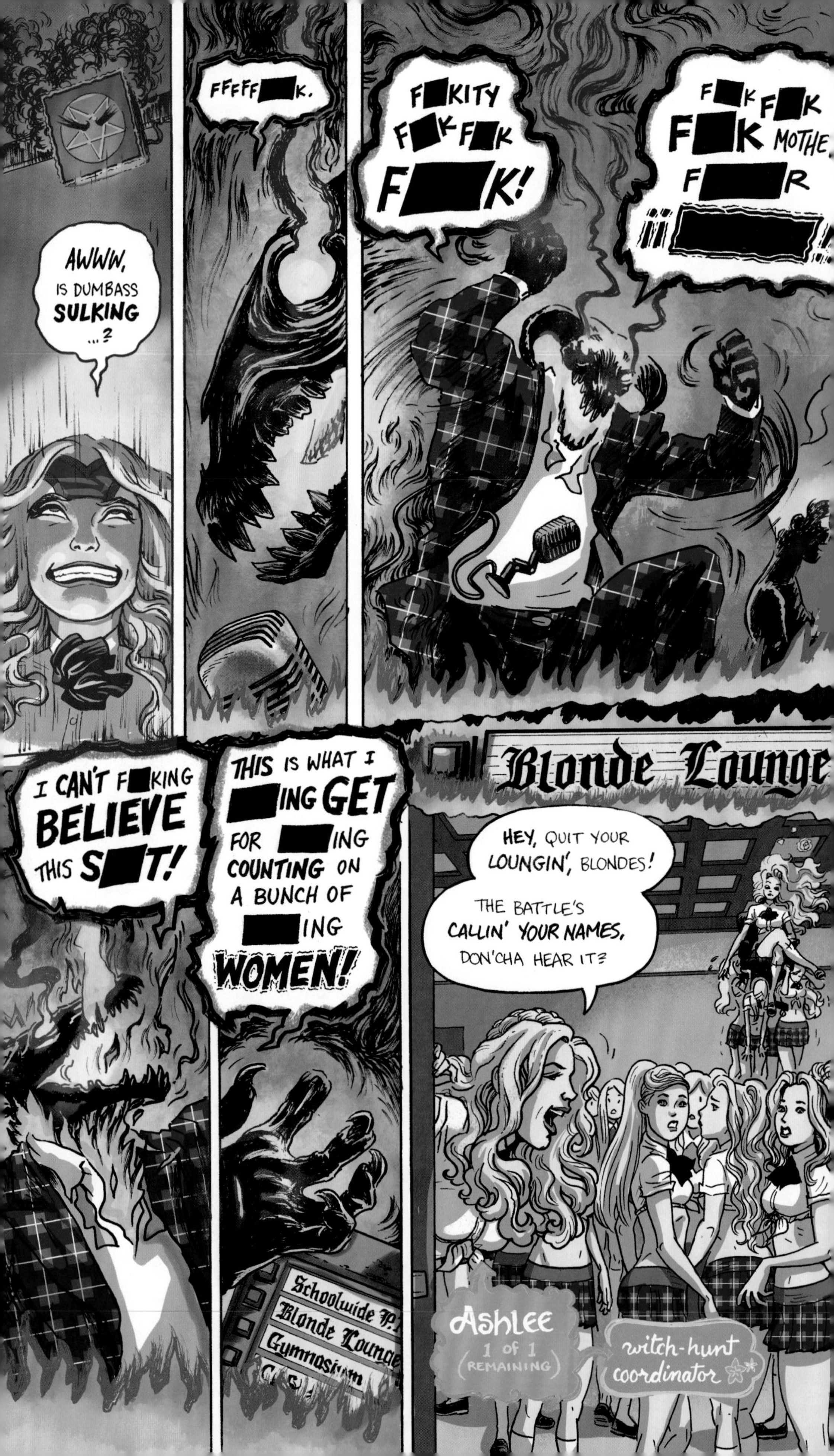
AWWW, IS DUMBASS SULKING ...?
FFFFF[redacted]K.
F[redacted]KITY F[redacted]K F[redacted]K F[redacted]K!
F[redacted]K F[redacted]K F[redacted]K MOTHE F[redacted]R [redacted]!
I CAN'T F[redacted]KING BELIEVE THIS S[redacted]T!
THIS IS WHAT I [redacted]ING GET FOR [redacted]ING COUNTING ON A BUNCH OF [redacted]ING WOMEN!
Schoolwide
Blonde Lounge
Gymnasium
Blonde Lounge
HEY, QUIT YOUR LOUNGIN', BLONDES!
THE BATTLE'S CALLIN' YOUR NAMES, DON'CHA HEAR IT?
Ashlee 1 of 1 (REMAINING)
witch-hunt coordinator

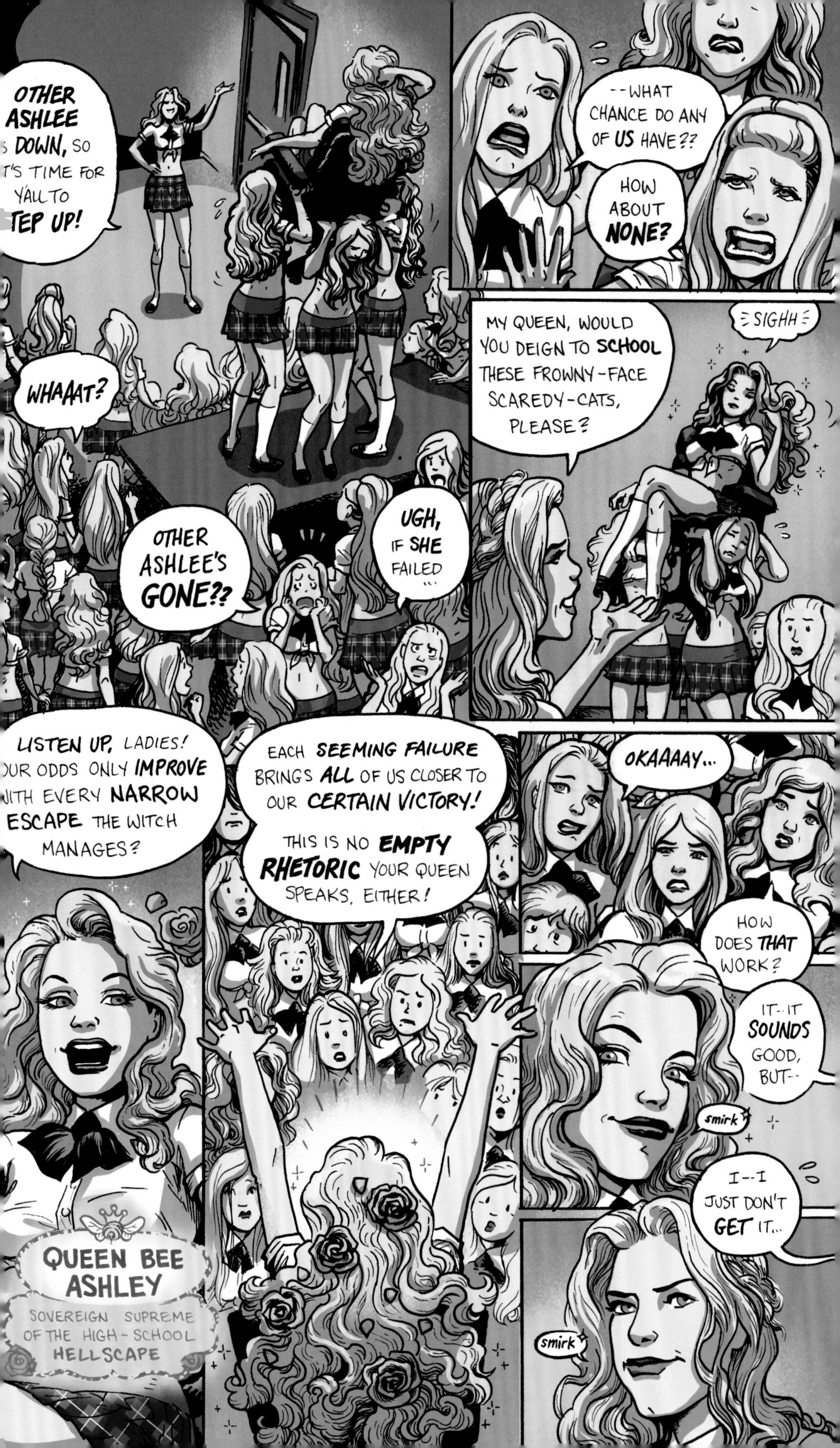

OTHER ASHLEE 'S DOWN, SO IT'S TIME FOR Y'ALL TO STEP UP!
--WHAT CHANCE DO ANY OF US HAVE??
HOW ABOUT NONE?
WHAAAT?
OTHER ASHLEE'S GONE??
UGH, IF SHE FAILED ...
MY QUEEN, WOULD YOU DEIGN TO SCHOOL THESE FROWNY-FACE SCAREDY-CATS, PLEASE?
SIGHH
LISTEN UP, LADIES! OUR ODDS ONLY IMPROVE WITH EVERY NARROW ESCAPE THE WITCH MANAGES!
EACH SEEMING FAILURE BRINGS ALL OF US CLOSER TO OUR CERTAIN VICTORY!
THIS IS NO EMPTY RHETORIC YOUR QUEEN SPEAKS, EITHER!
QUEEN BEE ASHLEY
SOVEREIGN SUPREME OF THE HIGH-SCHOOL HELLSCAPE
OKAAAAY...
HOW DOES THAT WORK?
IT--IT SOUNDS GOOD, BUT--
smirk
I--I JUST DON'T GET IT...
smirk

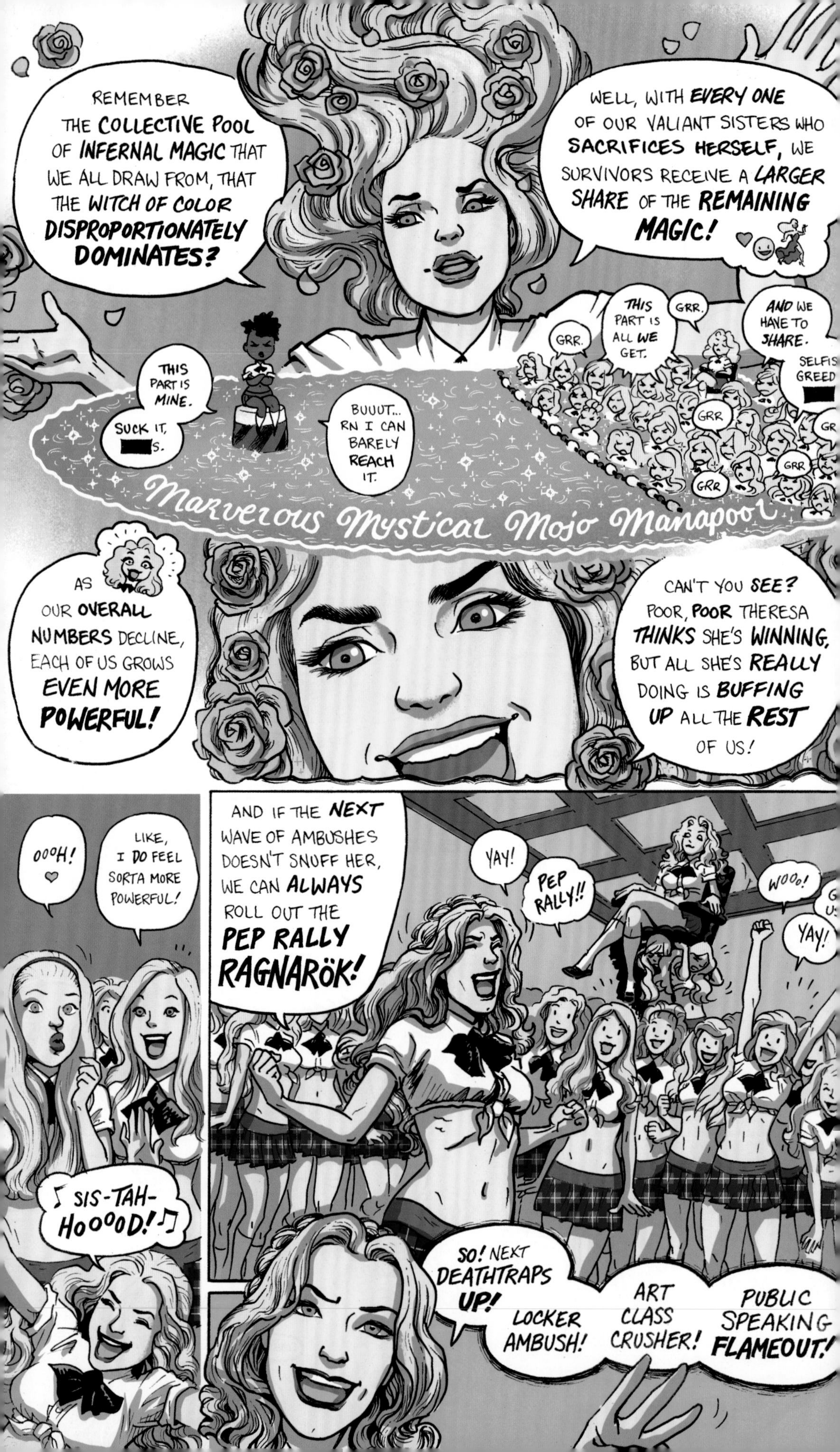
REMEMBER THE COLLECTIVE POOL OF INFERNAL MAGIC THAT WE ALL DRAW FROM, THAT THE WITCH OF COLOR DISPROPORTIONATELY DOMINATES?
WELL, WITH EVERY ONE OF OUR VALIANT SISTERS WHO SACRIFICES HERSELF, WE SURVIVORS RECEIVE A LARGER SHARE OF THE REMAINING MAGIC!
THIS PART IS MINE.
SUCK IT, [redacted]S.
BUUUT... RN I CAN BARELY REACH IT.
GRR.
THIS PART IS ALL WE GET.
GRR.
AND WE HAVE TO SHARE.
SELFIS GREED [redacted]
GRR
GRR
GRR
GRR
Marvelous Mystical Mojo Manapool
AS OUR OVERALL NUMBERS DECLINE, EACH OF US GROWS EVEN MORE POWERFUL!
CAN'T YOU SEE? POOR, POOR THERESA THINKS SHE'S WINNING, BUT ALL SHE'S REALLY DOING IS BUFFING UP ALL THE REST OF US!
OOOH! ♥
LIKE, I DO FEEL SORTA MORE POWERFUL!
♪ SIS-TAH-HOOOOD! ♫
AND IF THE NEXT WAVE OF AMBUSHES DOESN'T SNUFF HER, WE CAN ALWAYS ROLL OUT THE PEP RALLY RAGNARÖK!
YAY!
PEP RALLY!!
WOOO!
YAY!
SO! NEXT DEATHTRAPS UP!
LOCKER AMBUSH!
ART CLASS CRUSHER!
PUBLIC SPEAKING FLAMEOUT!

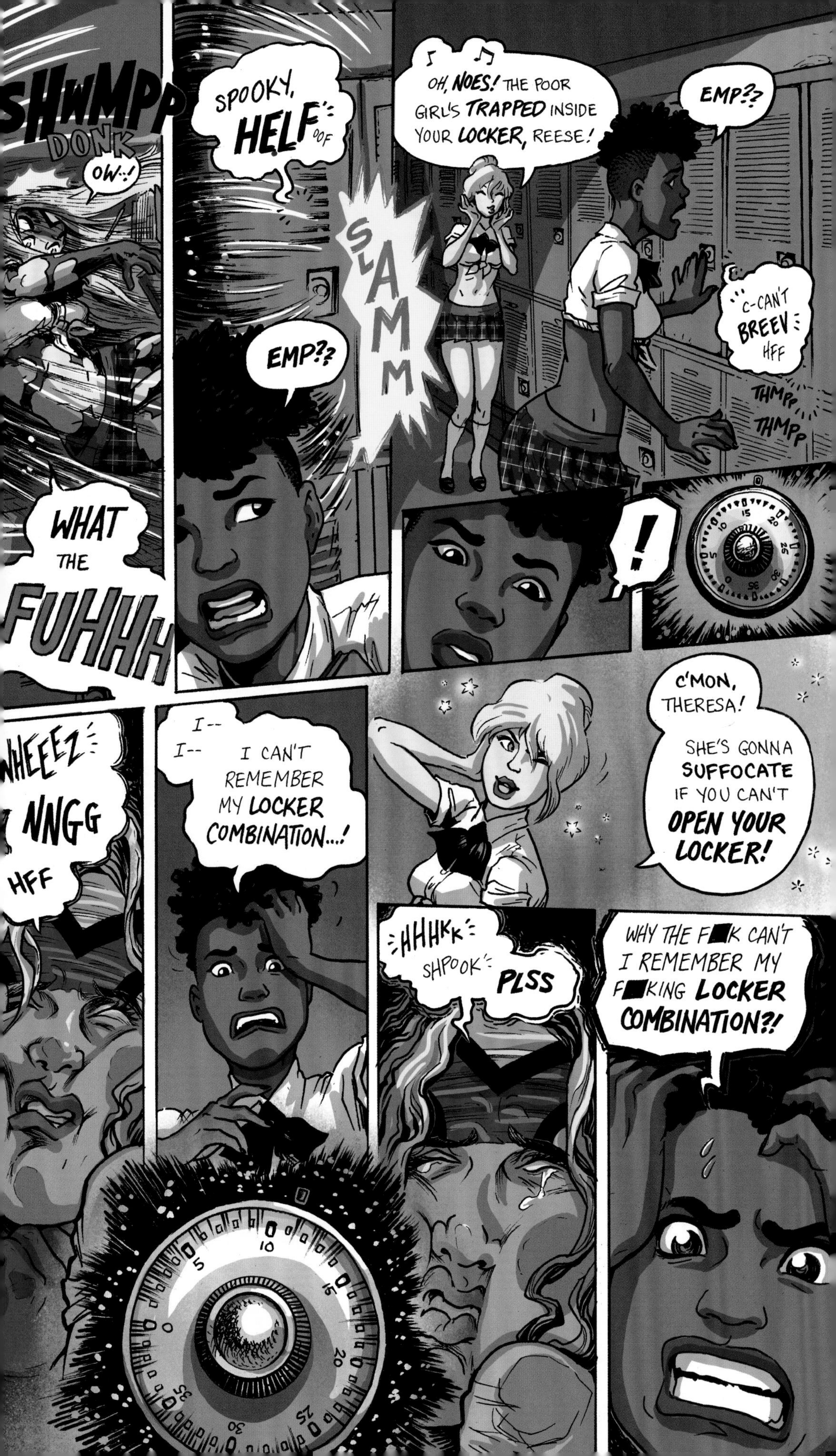
SHWMPP
DONK
OW..!
SPOOKY, HELF OOF
EMP??
SLAMM
OH, NOES! THE POOR GIRL'S TRAPPED INSIDE YOUR LOCKER, REESE!
EMP??
C-CAN'T BREEV HFF
THMPP
THMPP
WHAT THE FUHHH
!
WHEEEZ
NNGG
HFF
I-- I-- I CAN'T REMEMBER MY LOCKER COMBINATION...!
C'MON, THERESA!
SHE'S GONNA SUFFOCATE IF YOU CAN'T OPEN YOUR LOCKER!
HHHKK SHPOOK PLSS
WHY THE F[redacted]K CAN'T I REMEMBER MY F[redacted]KING LOCKER COMBINATION?!

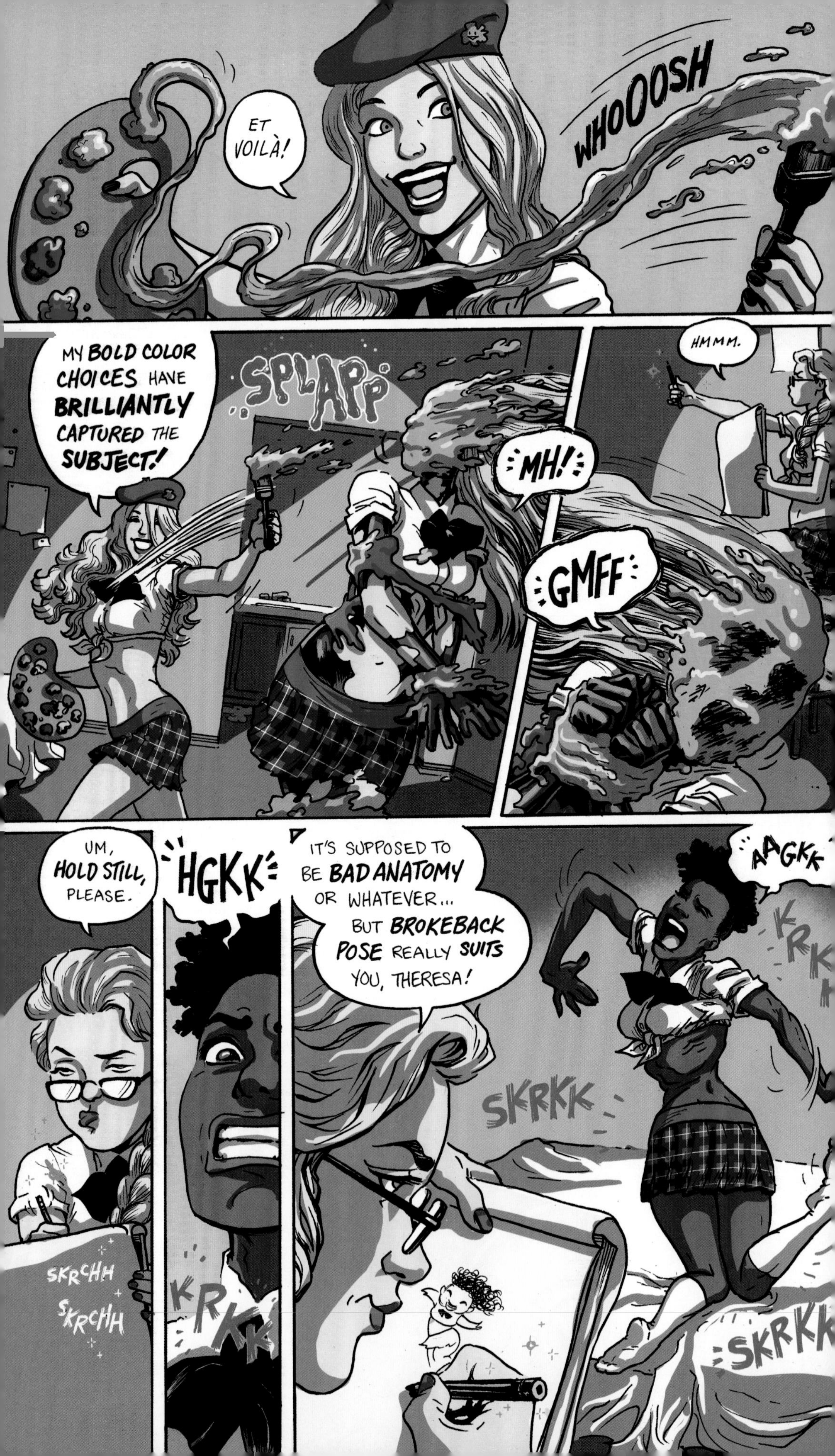

ET VOILÀ!
WHOOOOSH
MY BOLD COLOR CHOICES HAVE BRILLIANTLY CAPTURED THE SUBJECT!
SPLAPP
MH!
HMMM.
GMFF
UM, HOLD STILL, PLEASE.
HGKK
IT'S SUPPOSED TO BE BAD ANATOMY OR WHATEVER... BUT BROKEBACK POSE REALLY SUITS YOU, THERESA!
AAGKK
KRK
SKRKK
SKRCHH
SKRCHH
KRKK
SKRKK

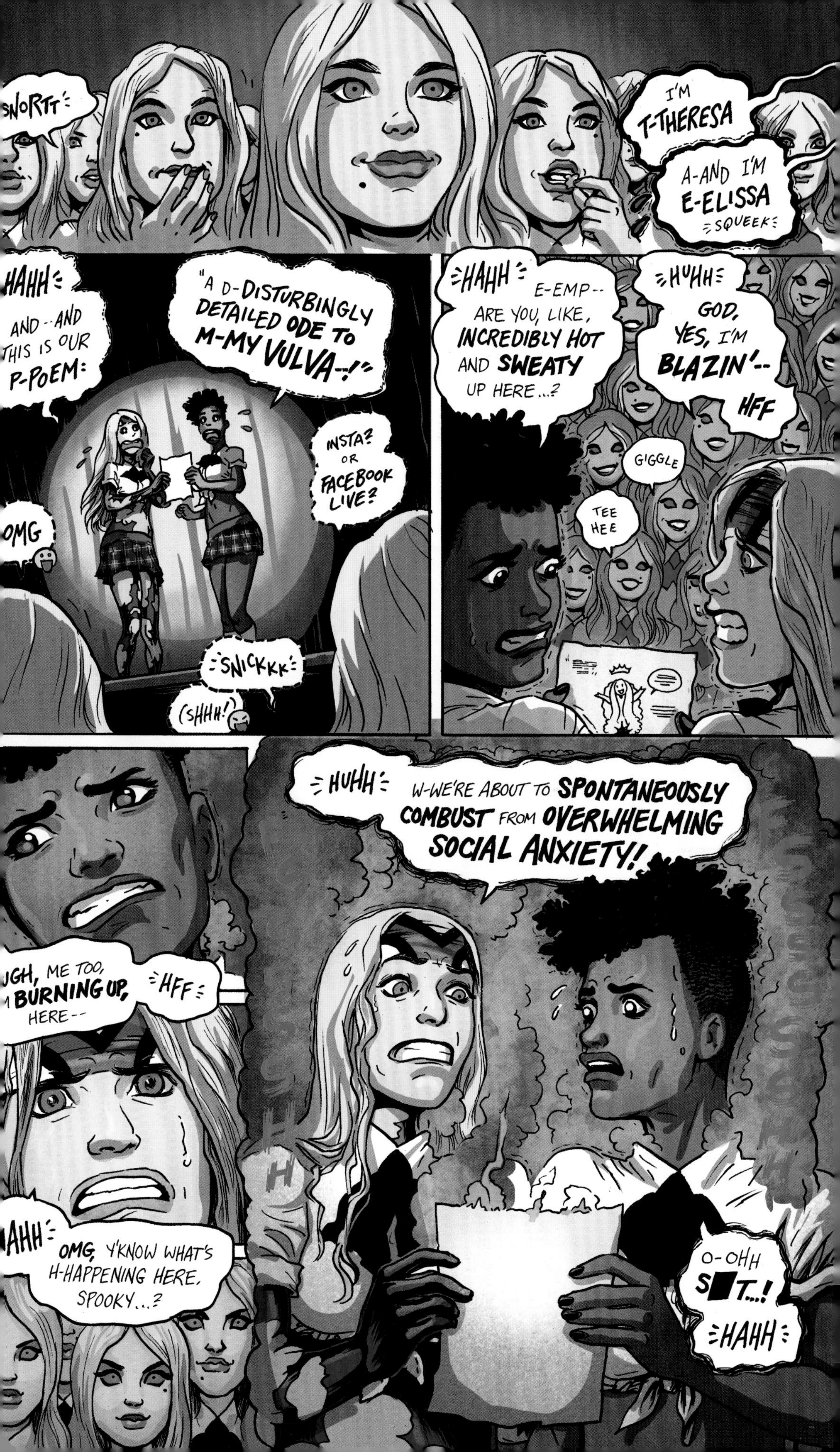

SNORTT
I'M T-THERESA
A-AND I'M E-ELISSA
SQUEEK
HAHH
AND--AND THIS IS OUR P-POEM:
"A D-DISTURBINGLY DETAILED ODE TO M-MY VULVA--!"
INSTA? OR FACEBOOK LIVE?
OMG
SNICKKK
(SHHH!)
HAHH
E-EMP-- ARE YOU, LIKE, INCREDIBLY HOT AND SWEATY UP HERE...?
HUHH
GOD, YES, I'M BLAZIN'--
HFF
GIGGLE
TEE HEE
HUHH
W-WE'RE ABOUT TO SPONTANEOUSLY COMBUST FROM OVERWHELMING SOCIAL ANXIETY!
GH, ME TOO, BURNING UP, HERE--
HFF
AHH
OMG, Y'KNOW WHAT'S H-HAPPENING HERE, SPOOKY...?
O-OHH S[redacted]T...!
HAHH

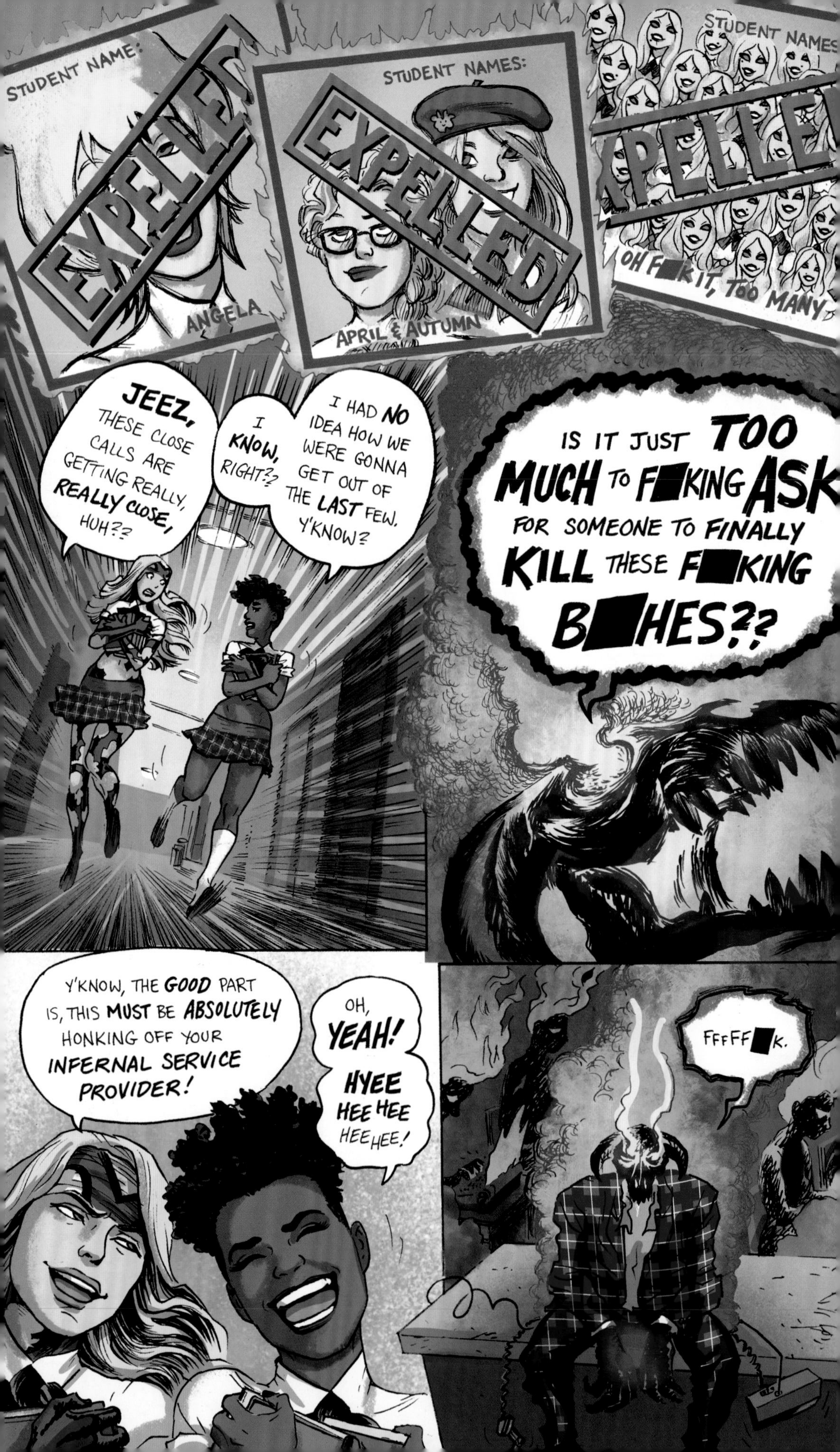

STUDENT NAME:
EXPELLED
ANGELA
STUDENT NAMES:
EXPELLED
APRIL & AUTUMN
STUDENT NAMES
EXPELLED
OH F[redacted]K IT, TOO MANY
JEEZ, THESE CLOSE CALLS ARE GETTING REALLY, REALLY CLOSE, HUH?!
I KNOW, RIGHT?!
I HAD NO IDEA HOW WE WERE GONNA GET OUT OF THE LAST FEW, Y'KNOW?
IS IT JUST TOO MUCH TO F[redacted]KING ASK FOR SOMEONE TO FINALLY KILL THESE F[redacted]KING B[redacted]HES?!
Y'KNOW, THE GOOD PART IS, THIS MUST BE ABSOLUTELY HONKING OFF YOUR INFERNAL SERVICE PROVIDER!
OH, YEAH!
HYEE HEE HEE HEE HEE!
FFFFF[redacted]K.

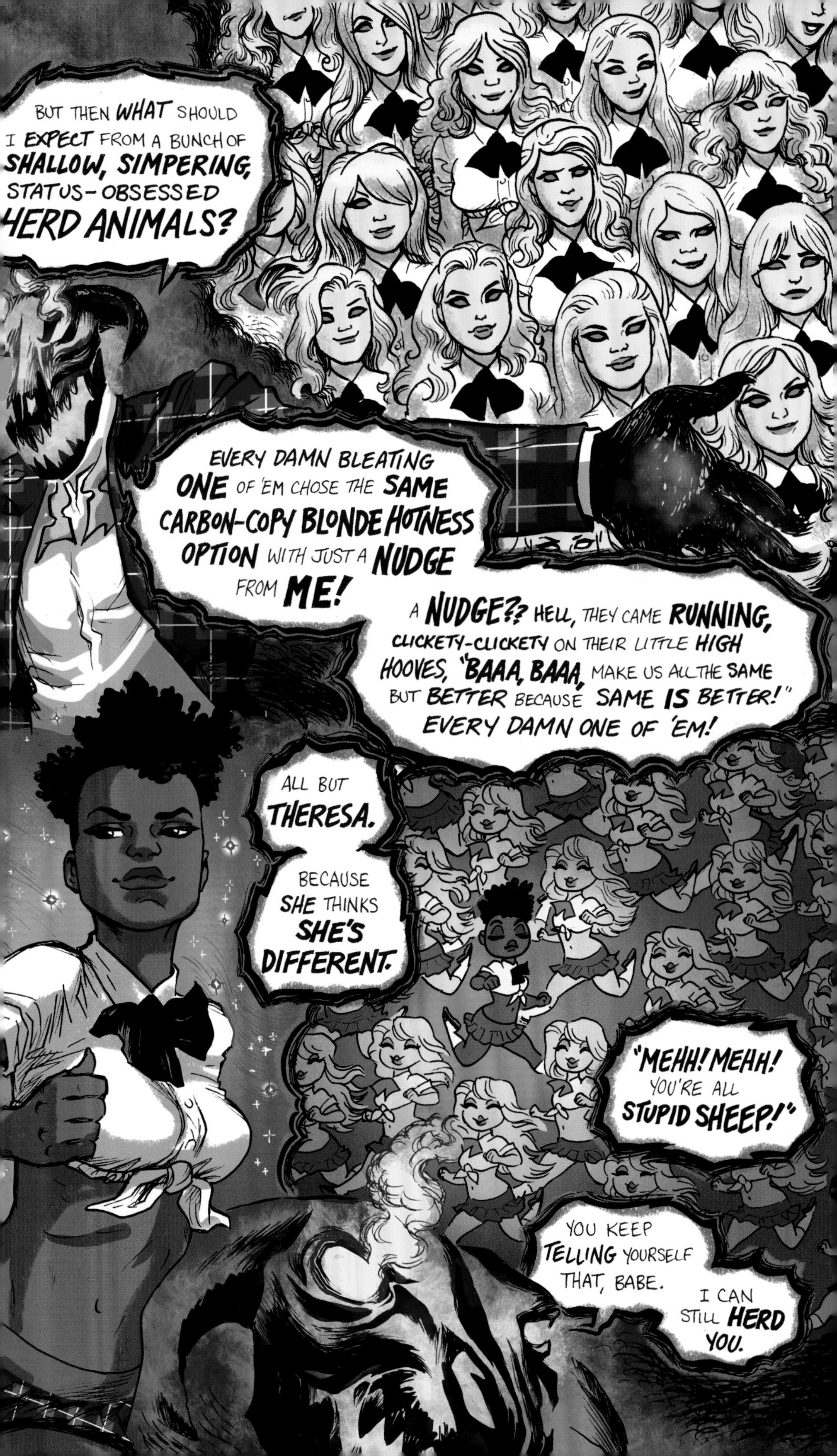
BUT THEN WHAT SHOULD I EXPECT FROM A BUNCH OF SHALLOW, SIMPERING, STATUS-OBSESSED HERD ANIMALS?
EVERY DAMN BLEATING ONE OF 'EM CHOSE THE SAME CARBON-COPY BLONDE HOTNESS OPTION WITH JUST A NUDGE FROM ME!
A NUDGE?? HELL, THEY CAME RUNNING, CLICKETY-CLICKETY ON THEIR LITTLE HIGH HOOVES, "BAAA, BAAA, MAKE US ALL THE SAME BUT BETTER BECAUSE SAME IS BETTER!" EVERY DAMN ONE OF 'EM!
ALL BUT THERESA.
BECAUSE SHE THINKS SHE'S DIFFERENT.
"MEHH! MEHH! YOU'RE ALL STUPID SHEEP!"
YOU KEEP TELLING YOURSELF THAT, BABE.
I CAN STILL HERD YOU.

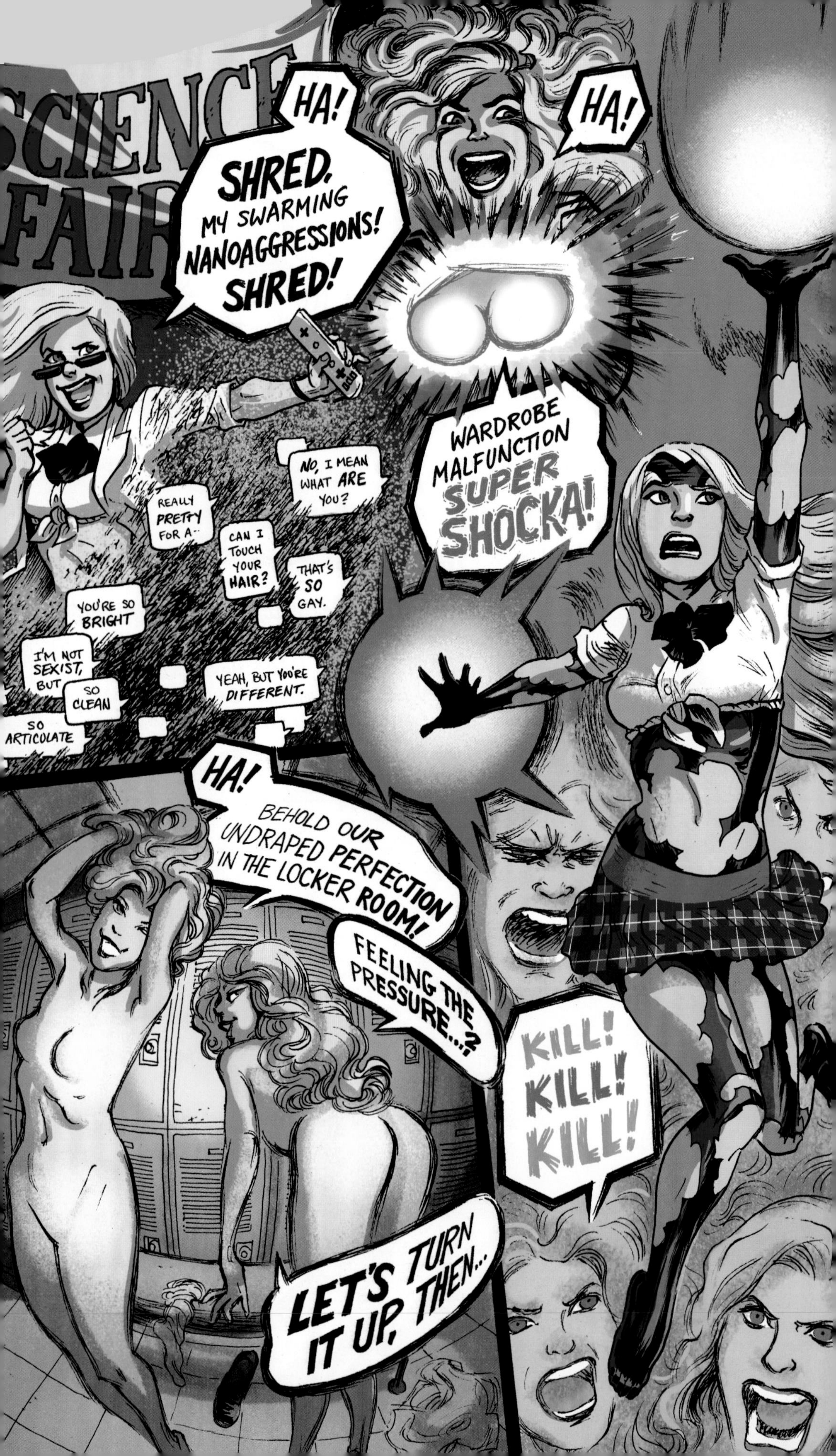
SCIENCE FAIR
HA!
HA!
SHRED. MY SWARMING NANOAGGRESSIONS! SHRED!
NO, I MEAN WHAT ARE YOU?
REALLY PRETTY FOR A...
CAN I TOUCH YOUR HAIR?
THAT'S SO GAY.
YOU'RE SO BRIGHT
I'M NOT SEXIST, BUT
SO CLEAN
YEAH, BUT YOU'RE DIFFERENT.
SO ARTICULATE
WARDROBE MALFUNCTION SUPER SHOCKA!
HA!
BEHOLD OUR UNDRAPED PERFECTION IN THE LOCKER ROOM!
FEELING THE PRESSURE...?
KILL! KILL! KILL!
LET'S TURN IT UP, THEN...

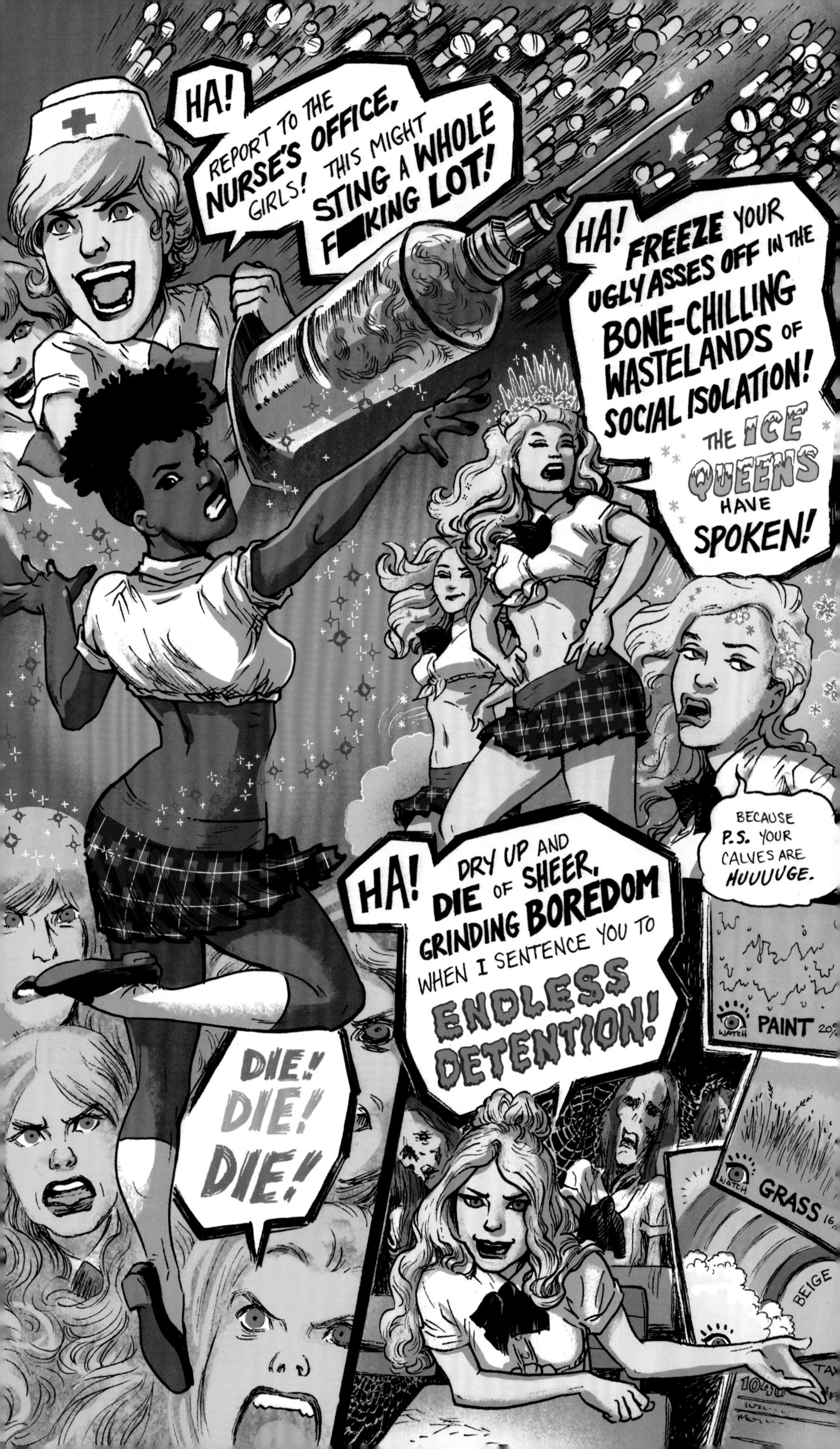
HA!
REPORT TO THE NURSE'S OFFICE, GIRLS! THIS MIGHT STING A WHOLE F[redacted]KING LOT!
HA! FREEZE YOUR UGLY ASSES OFF IN THE BONE-CHILLING WASTELANDS OF SOCIAL ISOLATION! THE ICE QUEENS HAVE SPOKEN!
BECAUSE P.S. YOUR CALVES ARE HUUUUGE.
HA! DRY UP AND DIE OF SHEER, GRINDING BOREDOM WHEN I SENTENCE YOU TO ENDLESS DETENTION!
DIE! DIE! DIE!
WATCH PAINT
WATCH GRASS
BEIGE

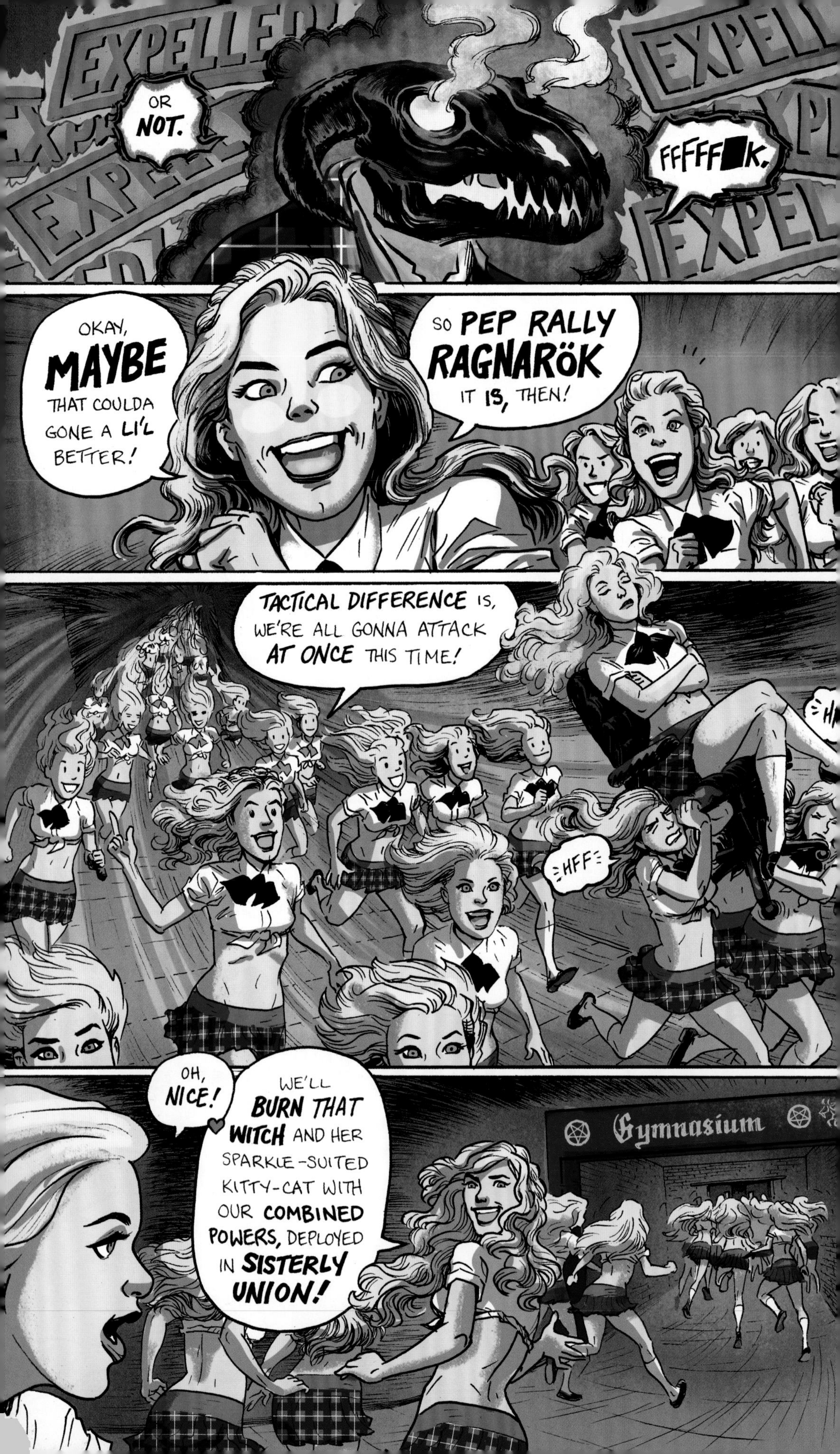

EXPELLED!
OR NOT.
FFFFF[redacted]K.
OKAY, MAYBE THAT COULDA GONE A LI'L BETTER!
SO PEP RALLY RAGNARÖK IT IS, THEN!
TACTICAL DIFFERENCE IS, WE'RE ALL GONNA ATTACK AT ONCE THIS TIME!
HFF
OH, NICE!
WE'LL BURN THAT WITCH AND HER SPARKLE-SUITED KITTY-CAT WITH OUR COMBINED POWERS, DEPLOYED IN SISTERLY UNION!
Gymnasium

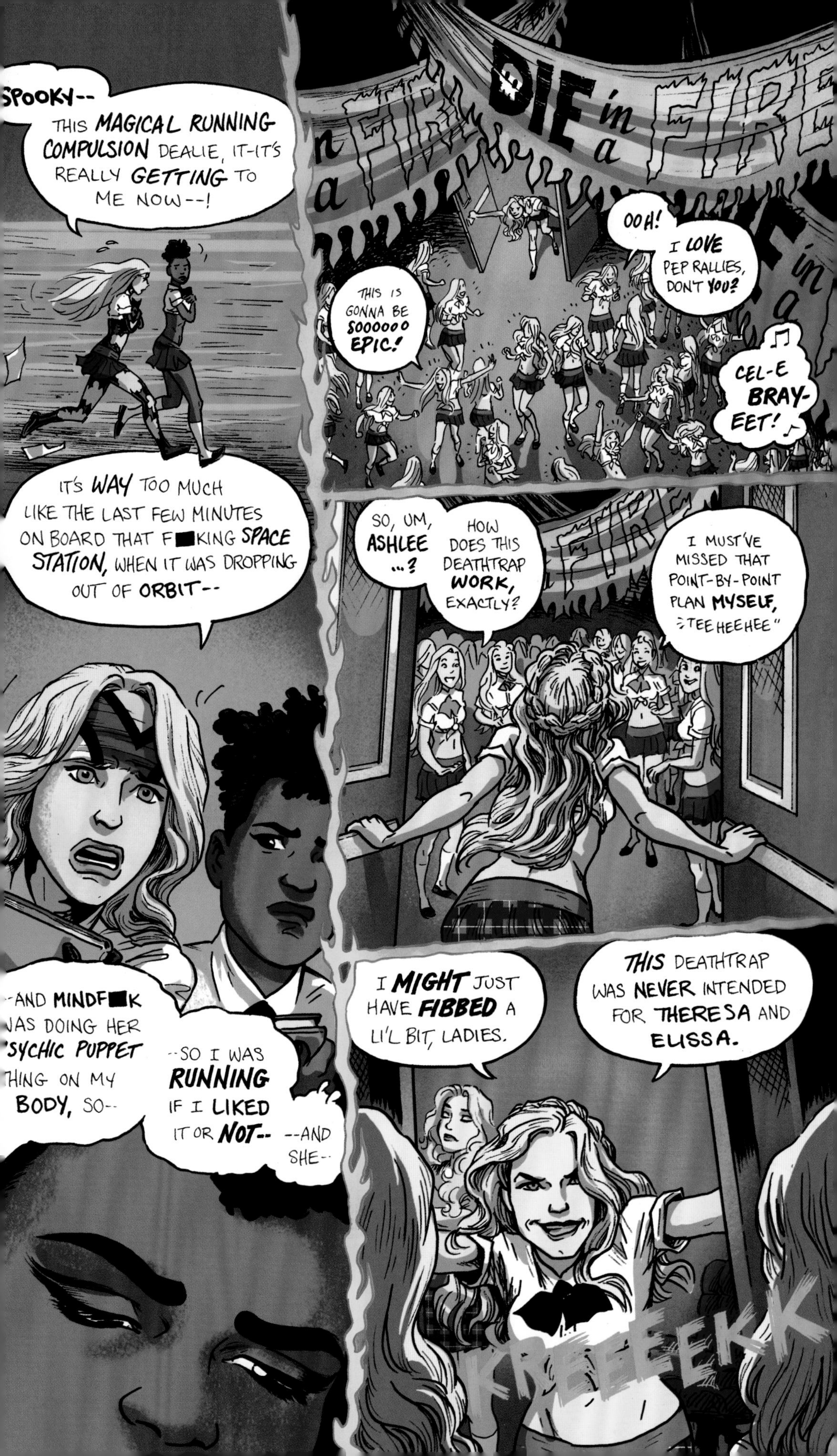
SPOOKY--
THIS MAGICAL RUNNING COMPULSION DEALIE, IT-IT'S REALLY GETTING TO ME NOW--!
DIE in a FIRE
THIS IS GONNA BE SOOOOOO EPIC!
OOH!
I LOVE PEP RALLIES, DON'T YOU?
CEL-E BRAY-EET!
IT'S WAY TOO MUCH LIKE THE LAST FEW MINUTES ON BOARD THAT F[redacted]KING SPACE STATION, WHEN IT WAS DROPPING OUT OF ORBIT--
SO, UM, ASHLEE ...?
HOW DOES THIS DEATHTRAP WORK, EXACTLY?
I MUST'VE MISSED THAT POINT-BY-POINT PLAN MYSELF, "TEE HEEHEE"
-AND MINDF[redacted]K JAS DOING HER 'SYCHIC PUPPET HING ON MY BODY, SO--
--SO I WAS RUNNING IF I LIKED IT OR NOT--
--AND SHE--
I MIGHT JUST HAVE FIBBED A LI'L BIT, LADIES.
THIS DEATHTRAP WAS NEVER INTENDED FOR THERESA AND ELISSA.
KREEEEKK

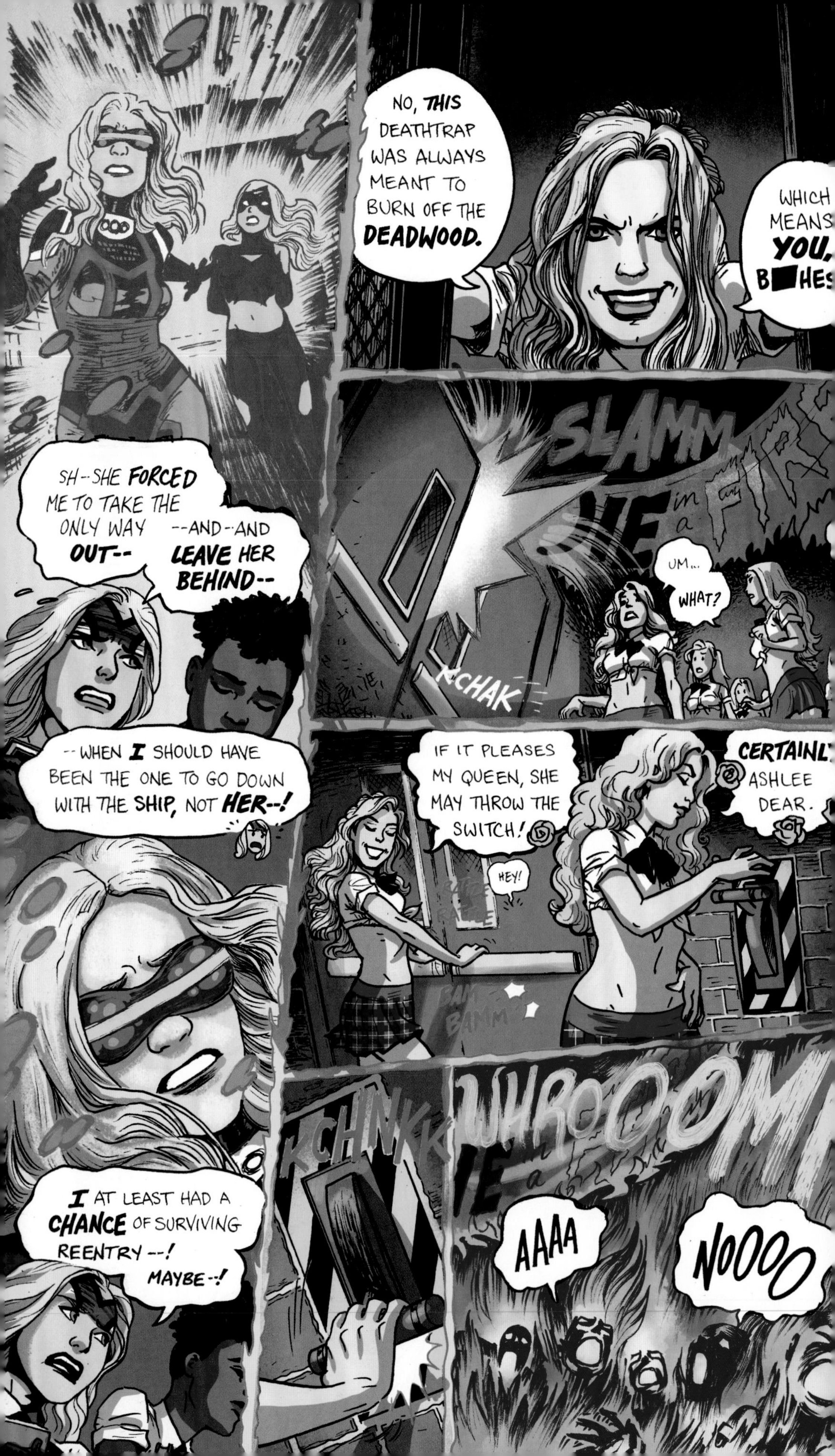

SH--SHE FORCED ME TO TAKE THE ONLY WAY OUT--
--AND--AND LEAVE HER BEHIND--
--WHEN I SHOULD HAVE BEEN THE ONE TO GO DOWN WITH THE SHIP, NOT HER--!
I AT LEAST HAD A CHANCE OF SURVIVING REENTRY--!
MAYBE--!
NO, THIS DEATHTRAP WAS ALWAYS MEANT TO BURN OFF THE DEADWOOD.
WHICH MEANS YOU, B[redacted]HES
SLAMM
UM...
WHAT?
KCHAK
IF IT PLEASES MY QUEEN, SHE MAY THROW THE SWITCH!
CERTAINLY, ASHLEE DEAR.
HEY!
BAM BAMM
KCHNKK
WHROOOOM
AAAA
NOOOO

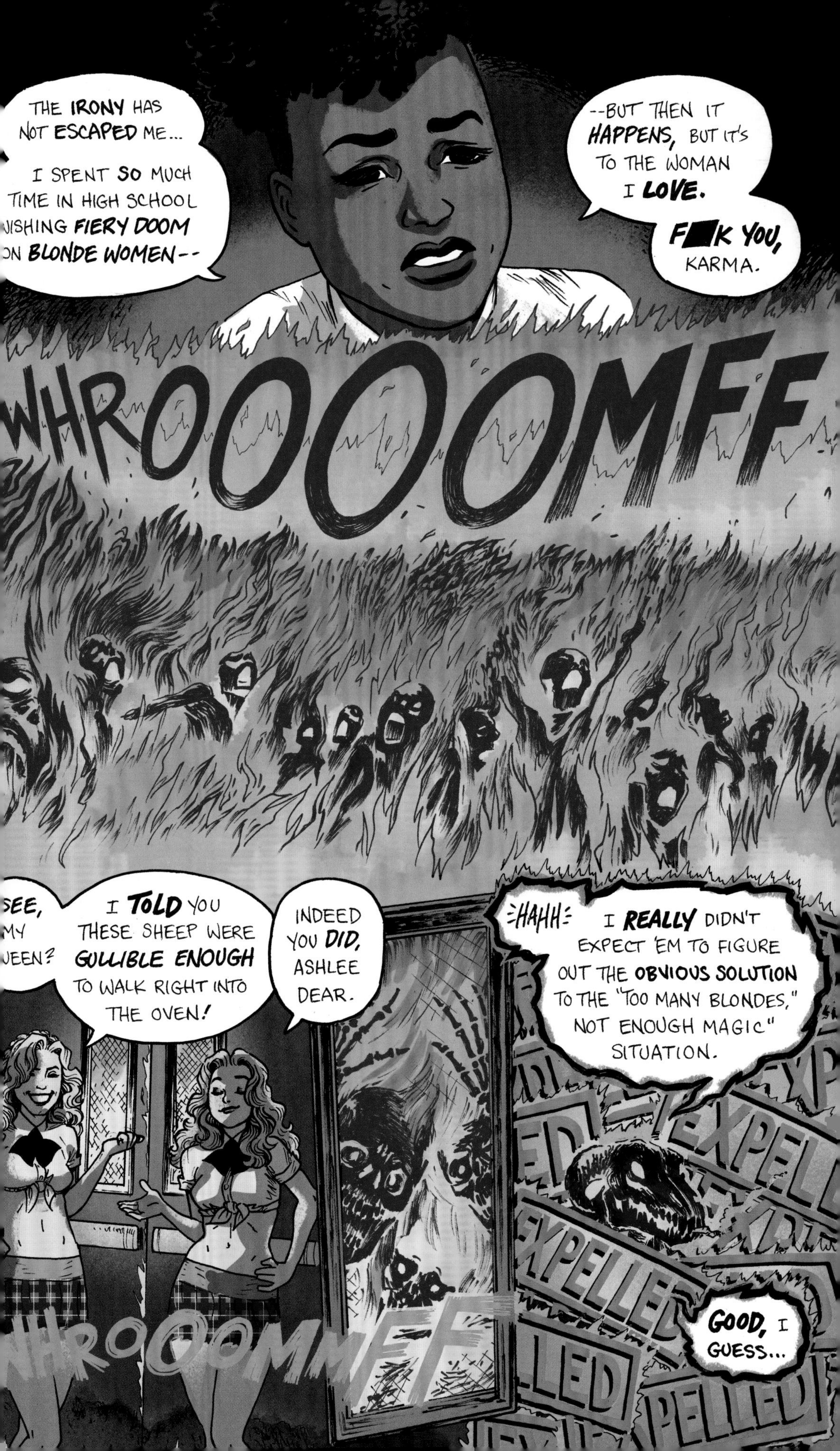

THE IRONY HAS NOT ESCAPED ME...
I SPENT SO MUCH TIME IN HIGH SCHOOL ISHING FIERY DOOM ON BLONDE WOMEN--
--BUT THEN IT HAPPENS, BUT IT'S TO THE WOMAN I LOVE.
F[redacted]K YOU, KARMA.
WHROOOOMFF
SEE, MY UEEN?
I TOLD YOU THESE SHEEP WERE GULLIBLE ENOUGH TO WALK RIGHT INTO THE OVEN!
INDEED YOU DID, ASHLEE DEAR.
HAHH
I REALLY DIDN'T EXPECT 'EM TO FIGURE OUT THE OBVIOUS SOLUTION TO THE "TOO MANY BLONDES," NOT ENOUGH MAGIC" SITUATION.
GOOD, I GUESS...
HROOOMMFF
EXPELLED

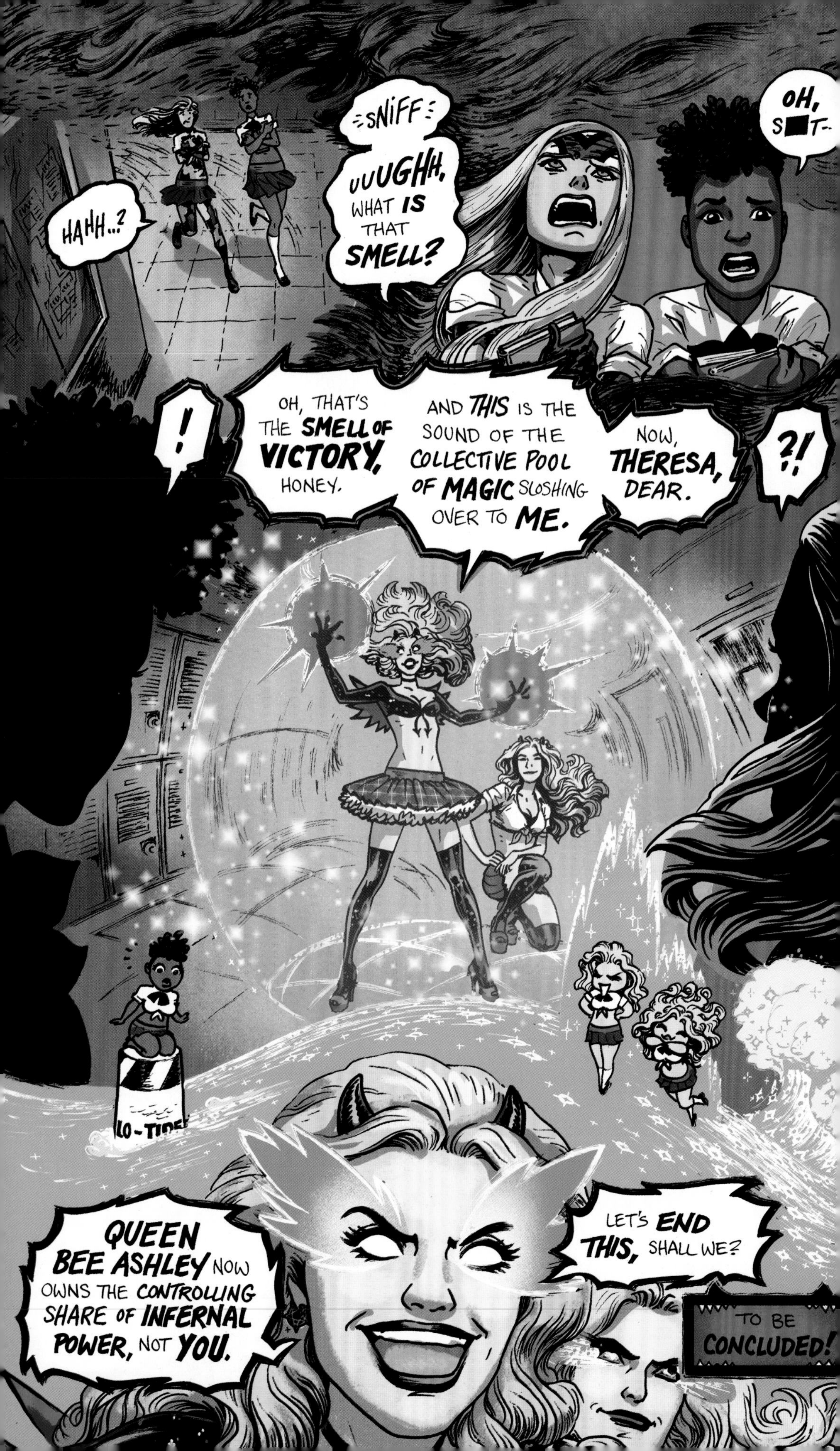
HAHH..?
SNIFF
UUUGHH, WHAT IS THAT SMELL?
OH, S[redacted]T-
!
OH, THAT'S THE SMELL OF VICTORY, HONEY.
AND THIS IS THE SOUND OF THE COLLECTIVE POOL OF MAGIC SLOSHING OVER TO ME.
NOW, THERESA, DEAR.
?!
LO-TIDE
QUEEN BEE ASHLEY NOW OWNS THE CONTROLLING SHARE OF INFERNAL POWER, NOT YOU.
LET'S END THIS, SHALL WE?
TO BE CONCLUDED!

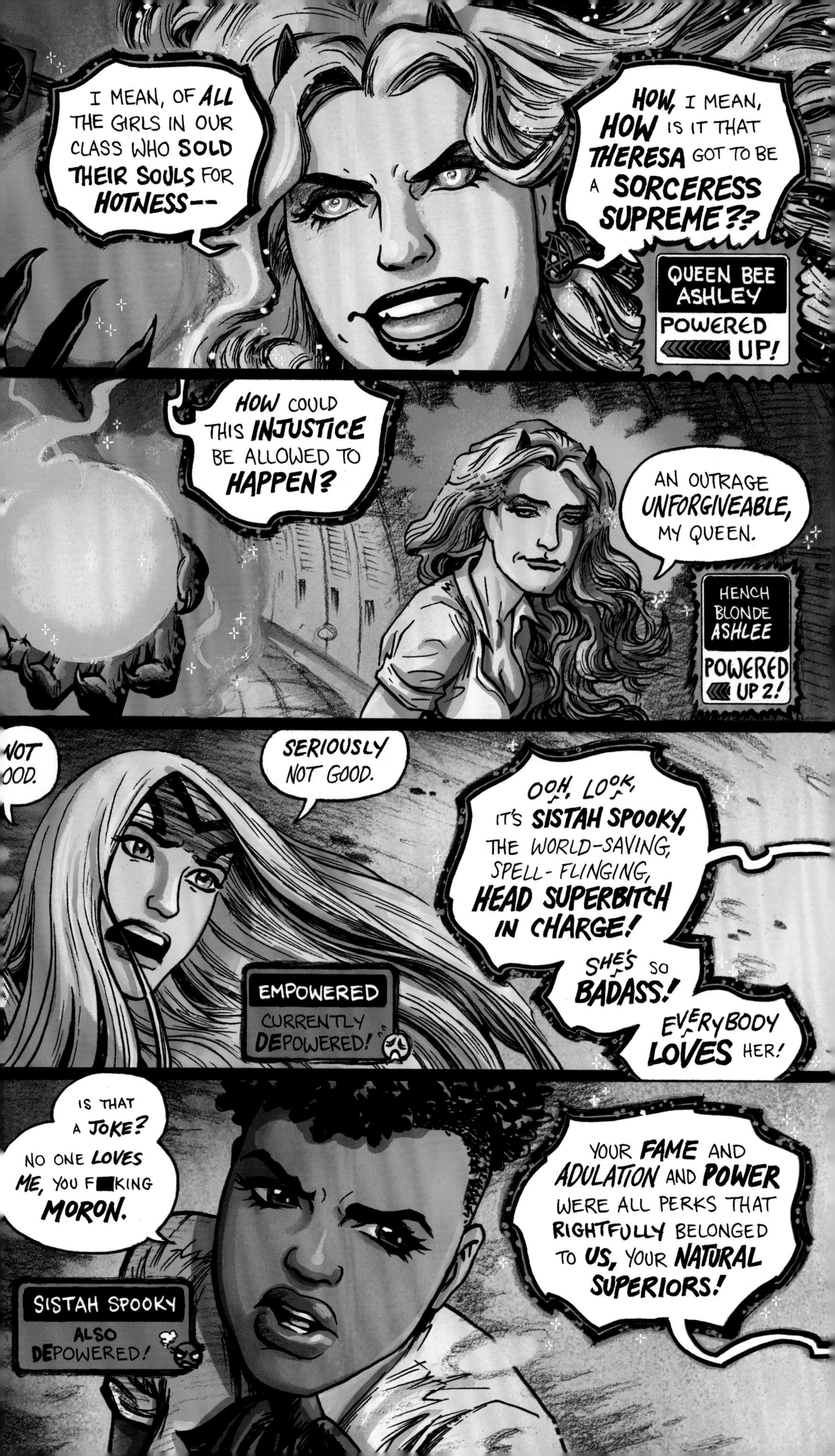

I MEAN, OF ALL THE GIRLS IN OUR CLASS WHO SOLD THEIR SOULS FOR HOTNESS--
HOW, I MEAN, HOW IS IT THAT THERESA GOT TO BE A SORCERESS SUPREME??
QUEEN BEE ASHLEY
POWERED UP!
HOW COULD THIS INJUSTICE BE ALLOWED TO HAPPEN?
AN OUTRAGE UNFORGIVEABLE, MY QUEEN.
HENCH BLONDE ASHLEE
POWERED UP 2!
NOT OOD.
SERIOUSLY NOT GOOD.
OOH, LOOK, IT'S SISTAH SPOOKY, THE WORLD-SAVING, SPELL-FLINGING, HEAD SUPERBITCH IN CHARGE!
SHE'S SO BADASS!
EVERYBODY LOVES HER!
EMPOWERED
CURRENTLY DEPOWERED!
IS THAT A JOKE? NO ONE LOVES ME, YOU F[redacted]KING MORON.
YOUR FAME AND ADULATION AND POWER WERE ALL PERKS THAT RIGHTFULLY BELONGED TO US, YOUR NATURAL SUPERIORS!
SISTAH SPOOKY
ALSO DEPOWERED!

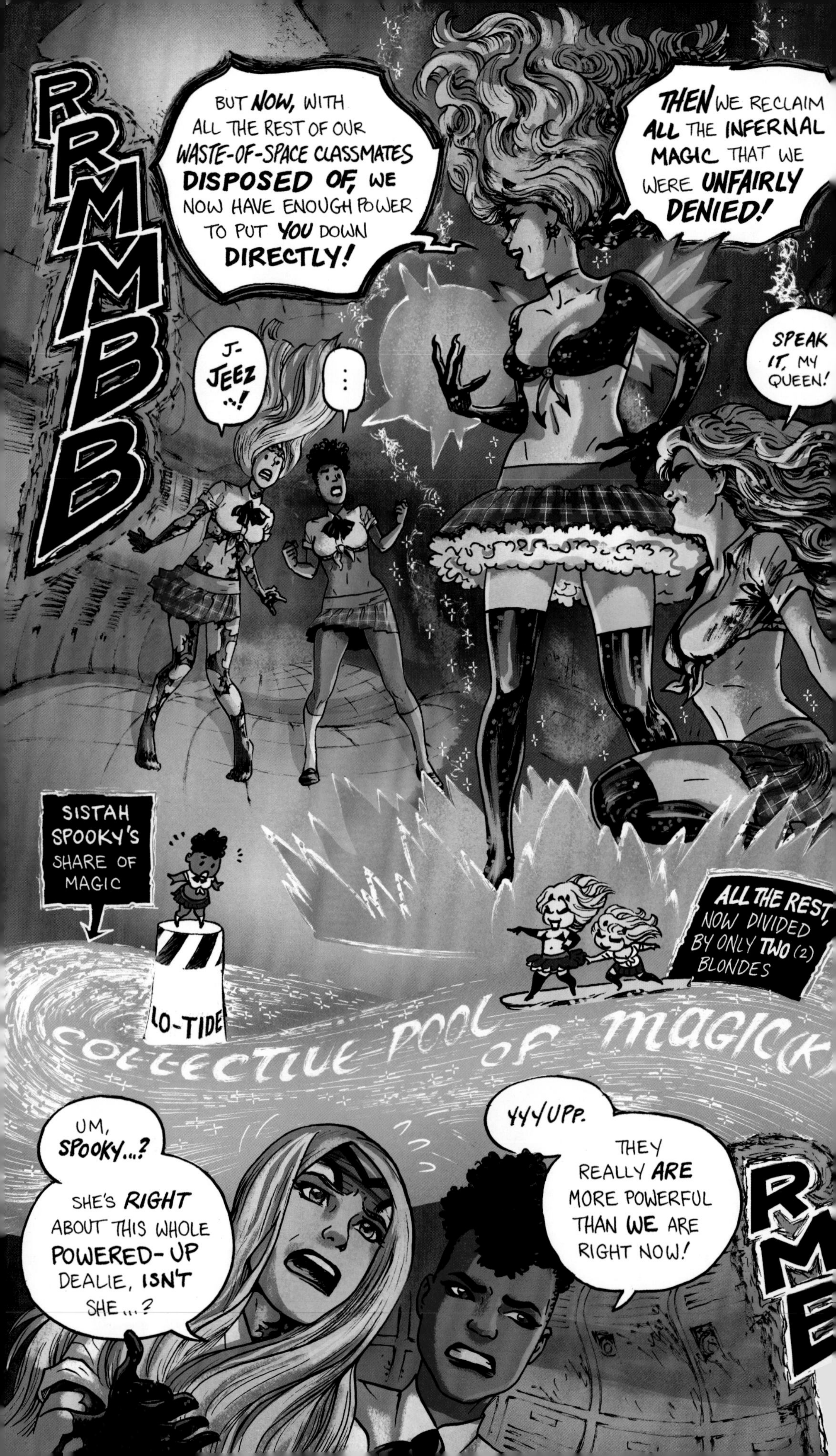
RRMMBB
BUT NOW, WITH ALL THE REST OF OUR WASTE-OF-SPACE CLASSMATES DISPOSED OF, WE NOW HAVE ENOUGH POWER TO PUT YOU DOWN DIRECTLY!
THEN WE RECLAIM ALL THE INFERNAL MAGIC THAT WE WERE UNFAIRLY DENIED!
J- JEEZ ..!
...
SPEAK IT, MY QUEEN!
SISTAH SPOOKY'S SHARE OF MAGIC
ALL THE REST, NOW DIVIDED BY ONLY TWO (2) BLONDES
LO-TIDE
COLLECTIVE POOL OF MAGIC(K)
UM, SPOOKY...?
SHE'S RIGHT ABOUT THIS WHOLE POWERED-UP DEALIE, ISN'T SHE...?
YYYUPP.
THEY REALLY ARE MORE POWERFUL THAN WE ARE RIGHT NOW!
RMB

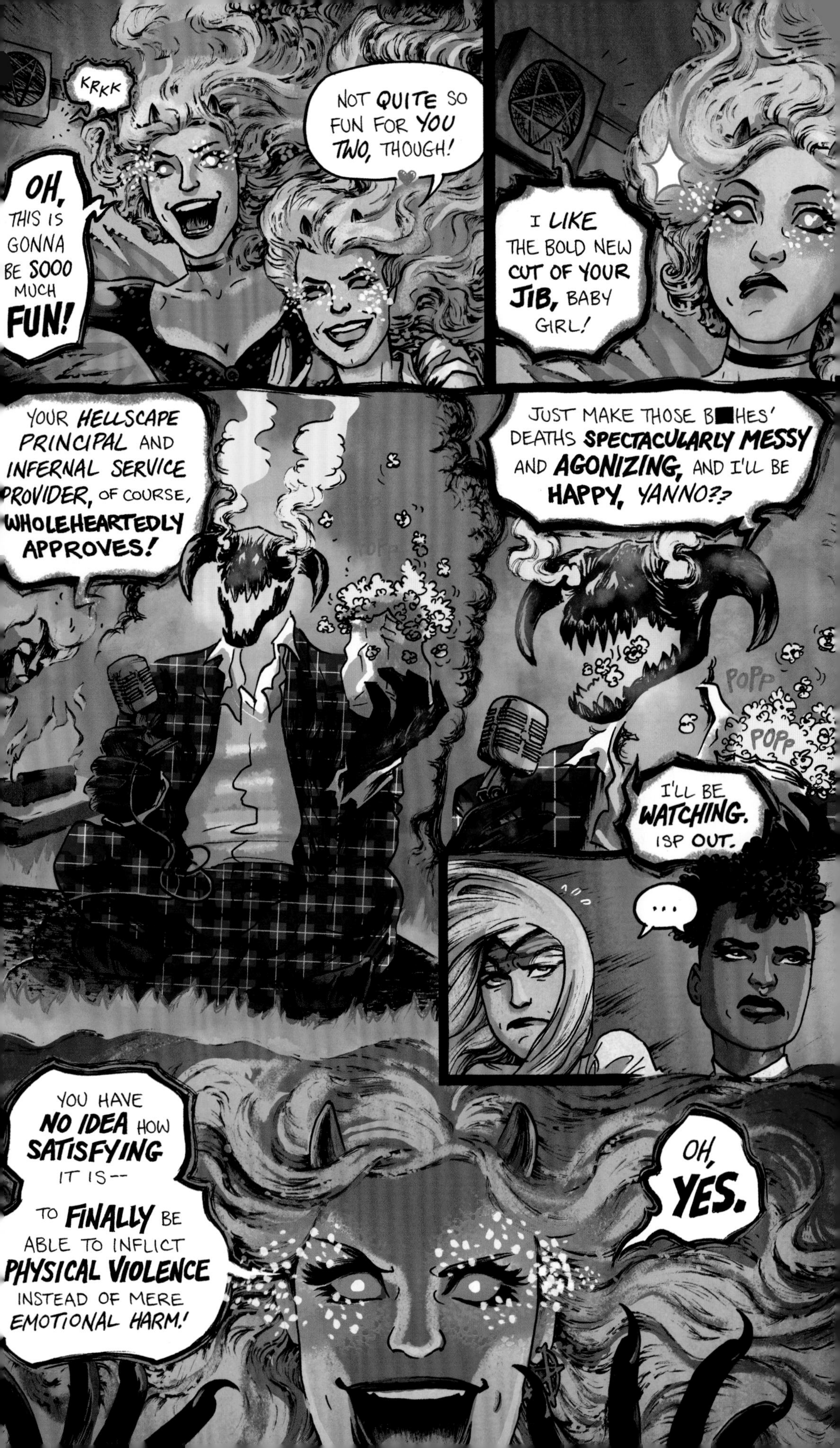
KRKK
OH, THIS IS GONNA BE SOOO MUCH FUN!
NOT QUITE SO FUN FOR YOU TWO, THOUGH!
I LIKE THE BOLD NEW CUT OF YOUR JIB, BABY GIRL!
YOUR HELLSCAPE PRINCIPAL AND INFERNAL SERVICE PROVIDER, OF COURSE, WHOLEHEARTEDLY APPROVES!
JUST MAKE THOSE B[redacted]HES' DEATHS SPECTACULARLY MESSY AND AGONIZING, AND I'LL BE HAPPY, YANNO??
POPP
POPP
I'LL BE WATCHING. ISP OUT.
...
YOU HAVE NO IDEA HOW SATISFYING IT IS--
TO FINALLY BE ABLE TO INFLICT PHYSICAL VIOLENCE INSTEAD OF MERE EMOTIONAL HARM!
OH, YES.

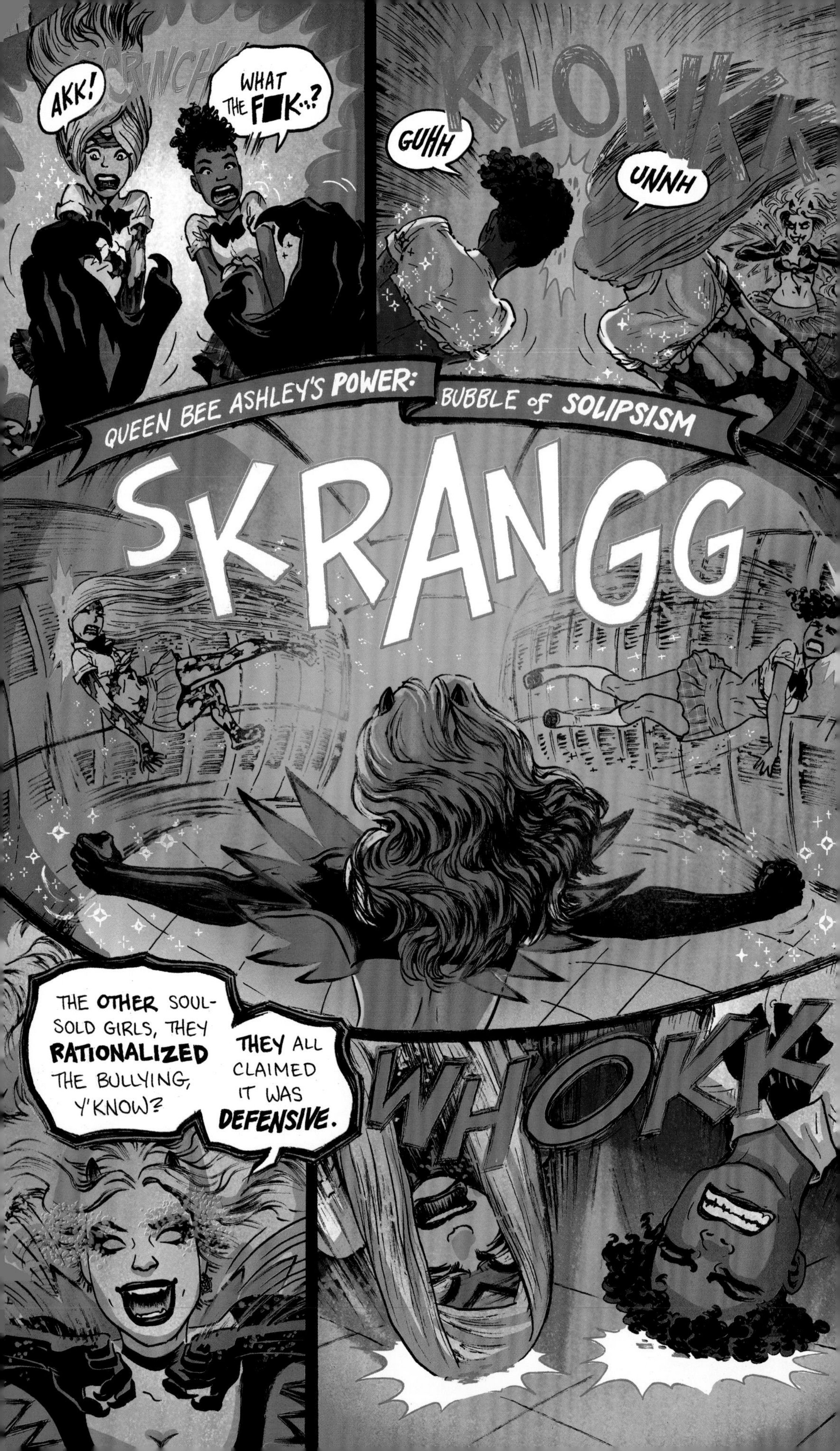
SCRUNCH
AKK!
WHAT THE F■K..?
KLONKK
GUHH
UNNH
QUEEN BEE ASHLEY'S POWER: BUBBLE of SOLIPSISM
SKRANGG
THE OTHER SOUL-SOLD GIRLS, THEY RATIONALIZED THE BULLYING, Y'KNOW?
THEY ALL CLAIMED IT WAS DEFENSIVE.
WHOKK

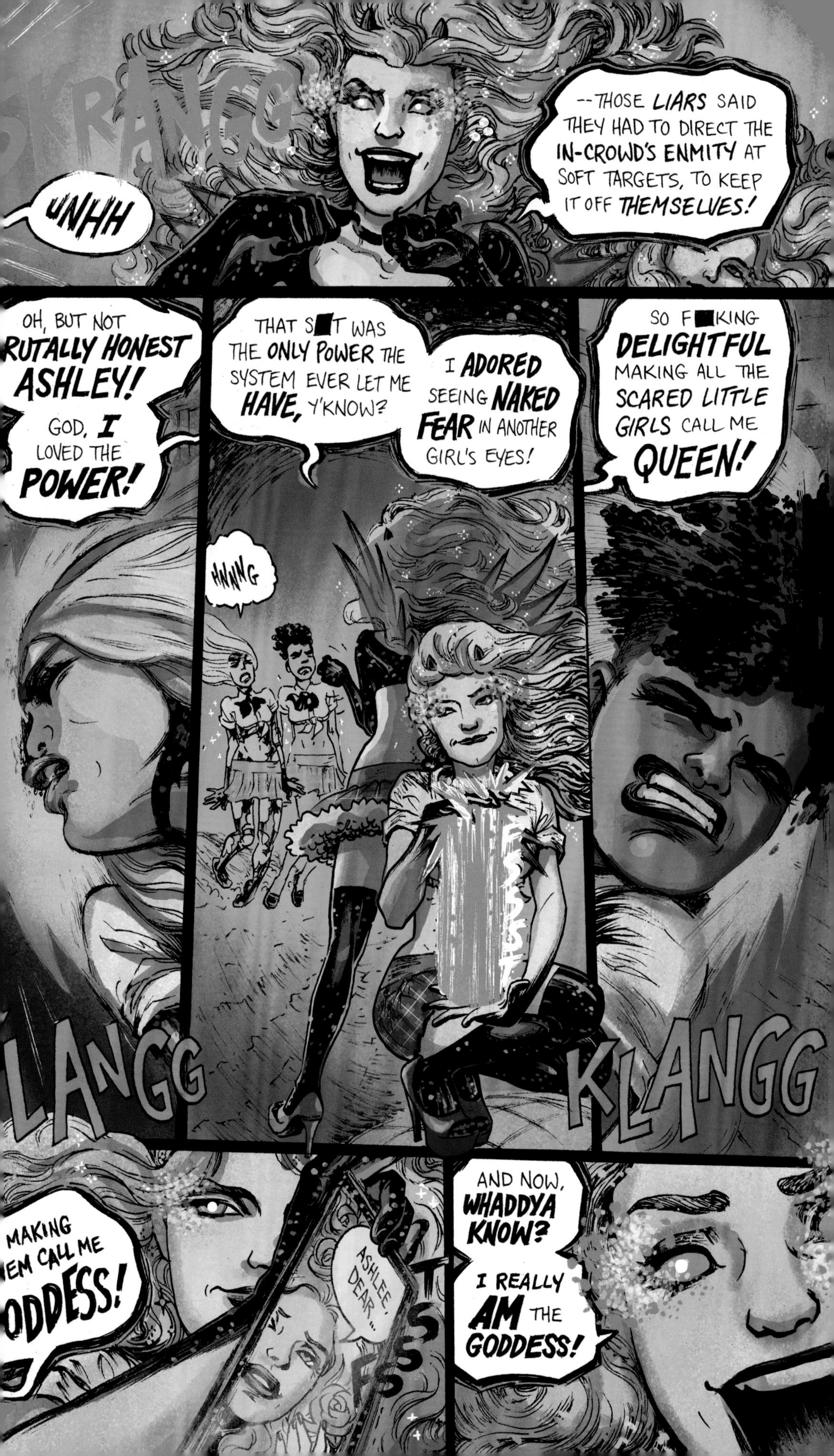
KRANGG
UNHH
--THOSE LIARS SAID THEY HAD TO DIRECT THE IN-CROWD'S ENMITY AT SOFT TARGETS, TO KEEP IT OFF THEMSELVES!
OH, BUT NOT RUTALLY HONEST ASHLEY!
GOD, I LOVED THE POWER!
THAT S[redacted]T WAS THE ONLY POWER THE SYSTEM EVER LET ME HAVE, Y'KNOW?
I ADORED SEEING NAKED FEAR IN ANOTHER GIRL'S EYES!
SO F[redacted]KING DELIGHTFUL MAKING ALL THE SCARED LITTLE GIRLS CALL ME QUEEN!
HNNNG
LANGG
KLANGG
MAKING
EM CALL ME
ODDESS!
ASHLEE, DEAR...
AND NOW, WHADDYA KNOW?
I REALLY AM THE GODDESS!

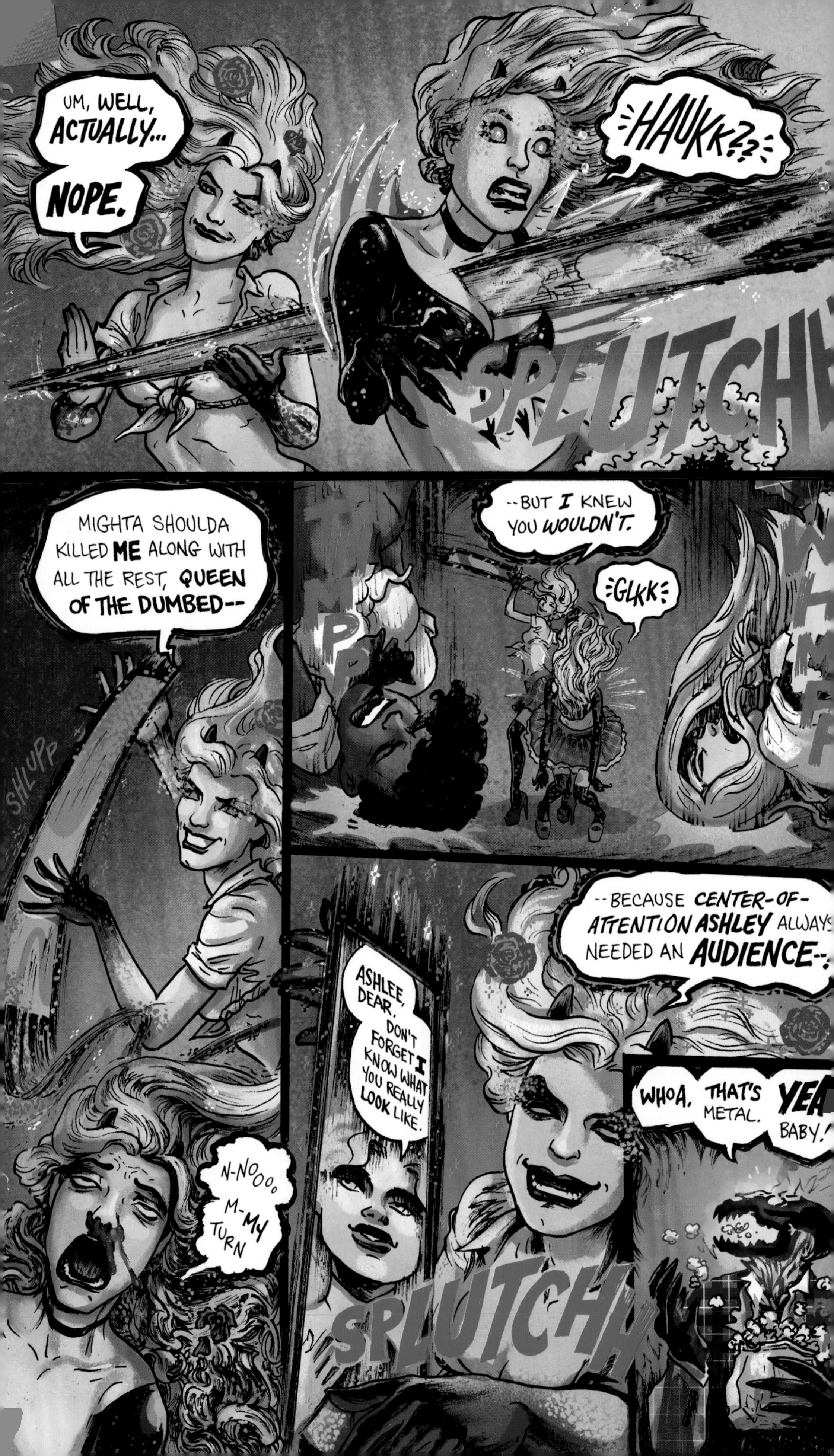
UM, WELL, ACTUALLY...
NOPE.
HAUKK???
SPLUTCH
MIGHTA SHOULDA KILLED ME ALONG WITH ALL THE REST, QUEEN OF THE DUMBED--
SHLUPP
N-NOooo M-MY TURN
THUMPP
--BUT I KNEW YOU WOULDN'T.
GLKK
WHUMPF
--BECAUSE CENTER-OF-ATTENTION ASHLEY ALWAYS NEEDED AN AUDIENCE--.
ASHLEE, DEAR, DON'T FORGET I KNOW WHAT YOU REALLY LOOK LIKE.
WHOA. THAT'S METAL.
YEA BABY!
SPLUTCH

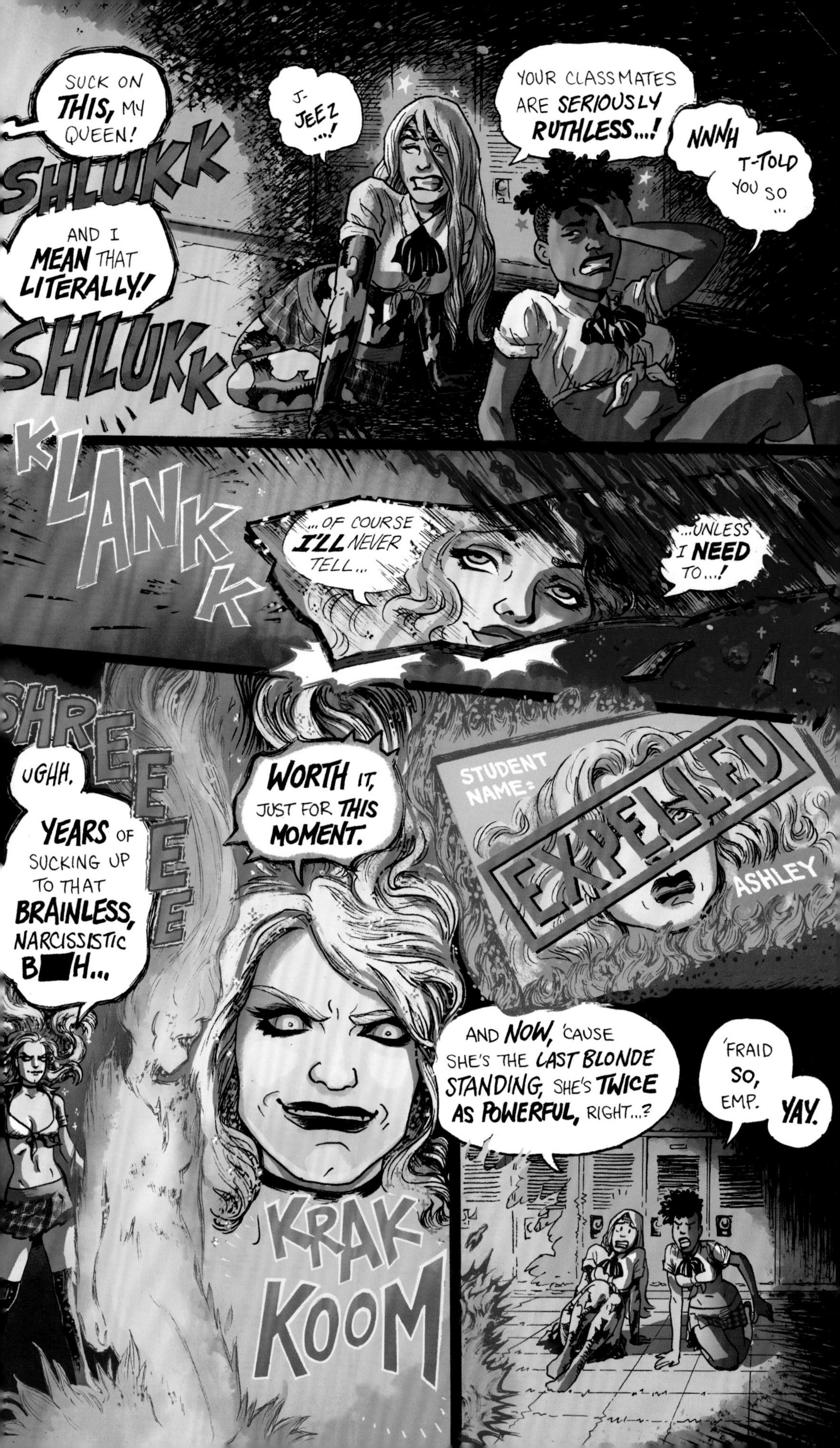
SUCK ON THIS, MY QUEEN!
SHLUKK
AND I MEAN THAT LITERALLY!
SHLUKK
J-JEEZ ...!
YOUR CLASSMATES ARE SERIOUSLY RUTHLESS...!
NNNH T-TOLD YOU SO ...
KLANKK
...OF COURSE I'LL NEVER TELL...
...UNLESS I NEED TO...!
SHREEEEE
UGHH.
YEARS OF SUCKING UP TO THAT BRAINLESS, NARCISSISTIC B[redacted]H...
WORTH IT, JUST FOR THIS MOMENT.
STUDENT NAME:
EXPELLED
ASHLEY
KRAK KOOM
AND NOW, 'CAUSE SHE'S THE LAST BLONDE STANDING, SHE'S TWICE AS POWERFUL, RIGHT...?
'FRAID SO, EMP.
YAY.

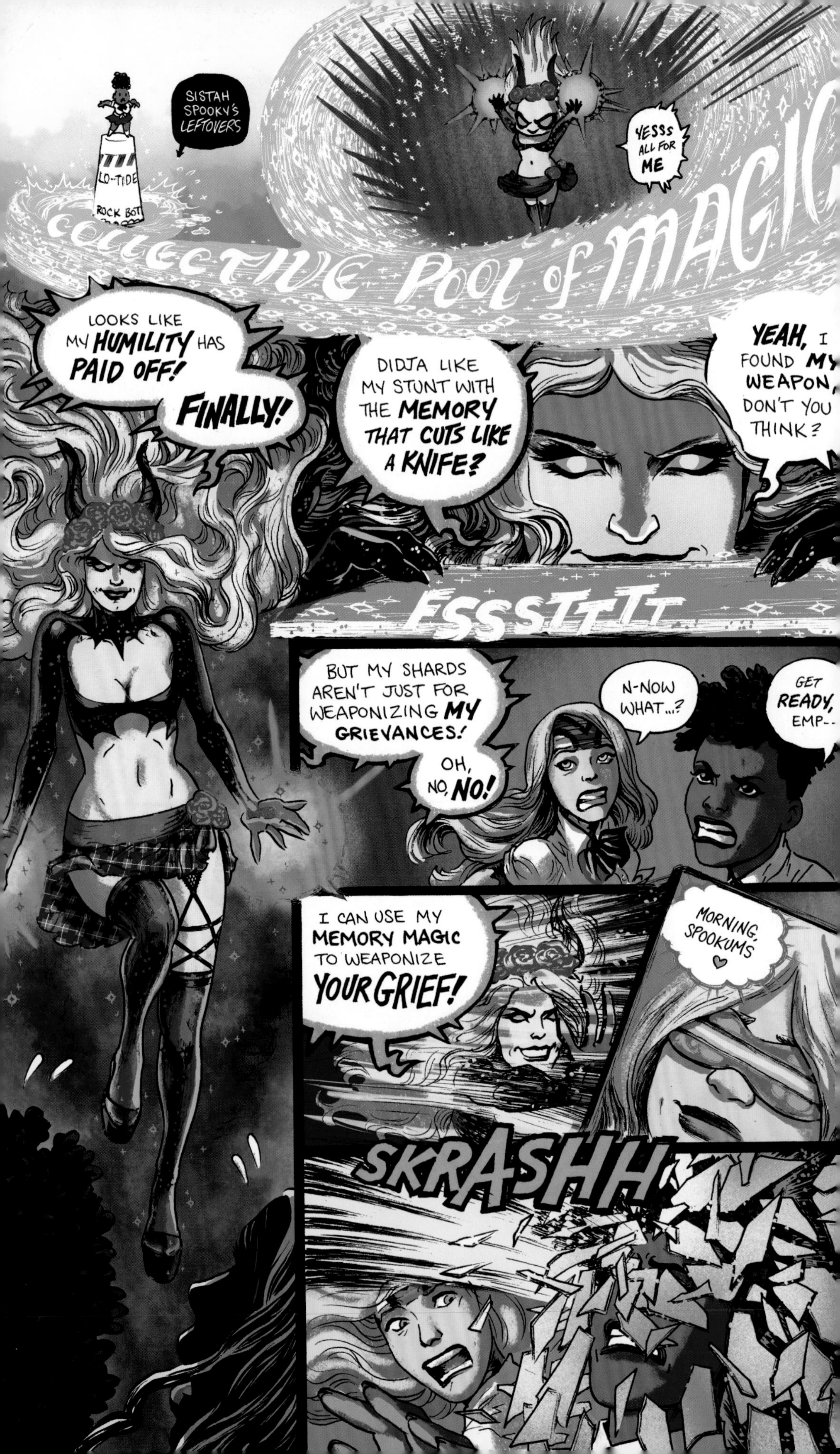
SISTAH SPOOKY'S LEFTOVERS
LO-TIDE
ROCK BOT
YESSS ALL FOR ME
COLLECTIVE POOL OF MAGIC
LOOKS LIKE MY HUMILITY HAS PAID OFF!
FINALLY!
DIDJA LIKE MY STUNT WITH THE MEMORY THAT CUTS LIKE A KNIFE?
YEAH, I FOUND MY WEAPON, DON'T YOU THINK?
FSSSTTTT
BUT MY SHARDS AREN'T JUST FOR WEAPONIZING MY GRIEVANCES!
OH, NO, NO!
N-NOW WHAT...?
GET READY, EMP--
I CAN USE MY MEMORY MAGIC TO WEAPONIZE YOUR GRIEF!
MORNING, SPOOKUMS
SKRASHH

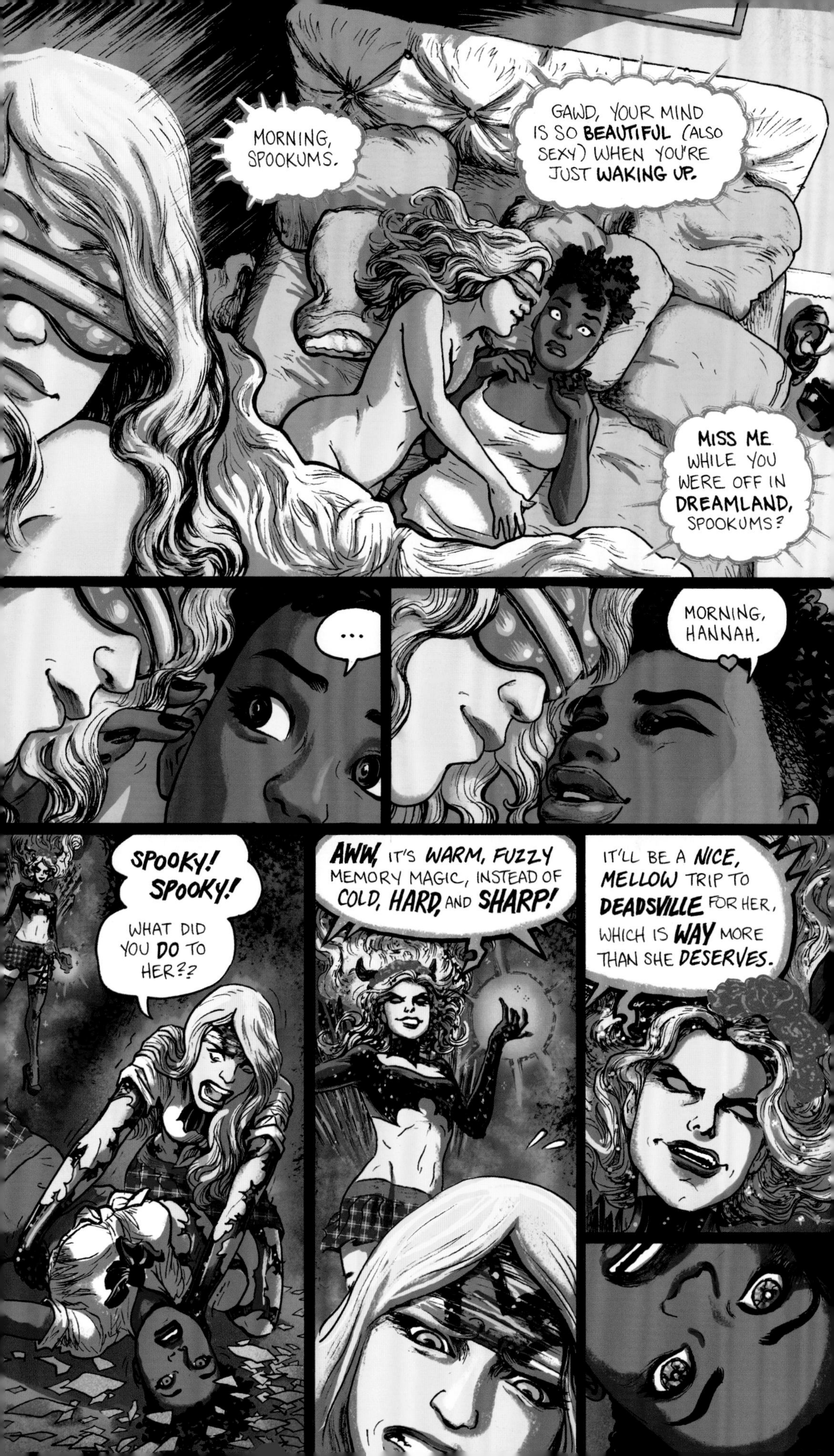
MORNING, SPOOKUMS.
GAWD, YOUR MIND IS SO BEAUTIFUL (ALSO SEXY) WHEN YOU'RE JUST WAKING UP.
MISS ME WHILE YOU WERE OFF IN DREAMLAND, SPOOKUMS?
...
MORNING, HANNAH.
SPOOKY! SPOOKY!
WHAT DID YOU DO TO HER?!?
AWW, IT'S WARM, FUZZY MEMORY MAGIC, INSTEAD OF COLD, HARD, AND SHARP!
IT'LL BE A NICE, MELLOW TRIP TO DEADSVILLE FOR HER, WHICH IS WAY MORE THAN SHE DESERVES.

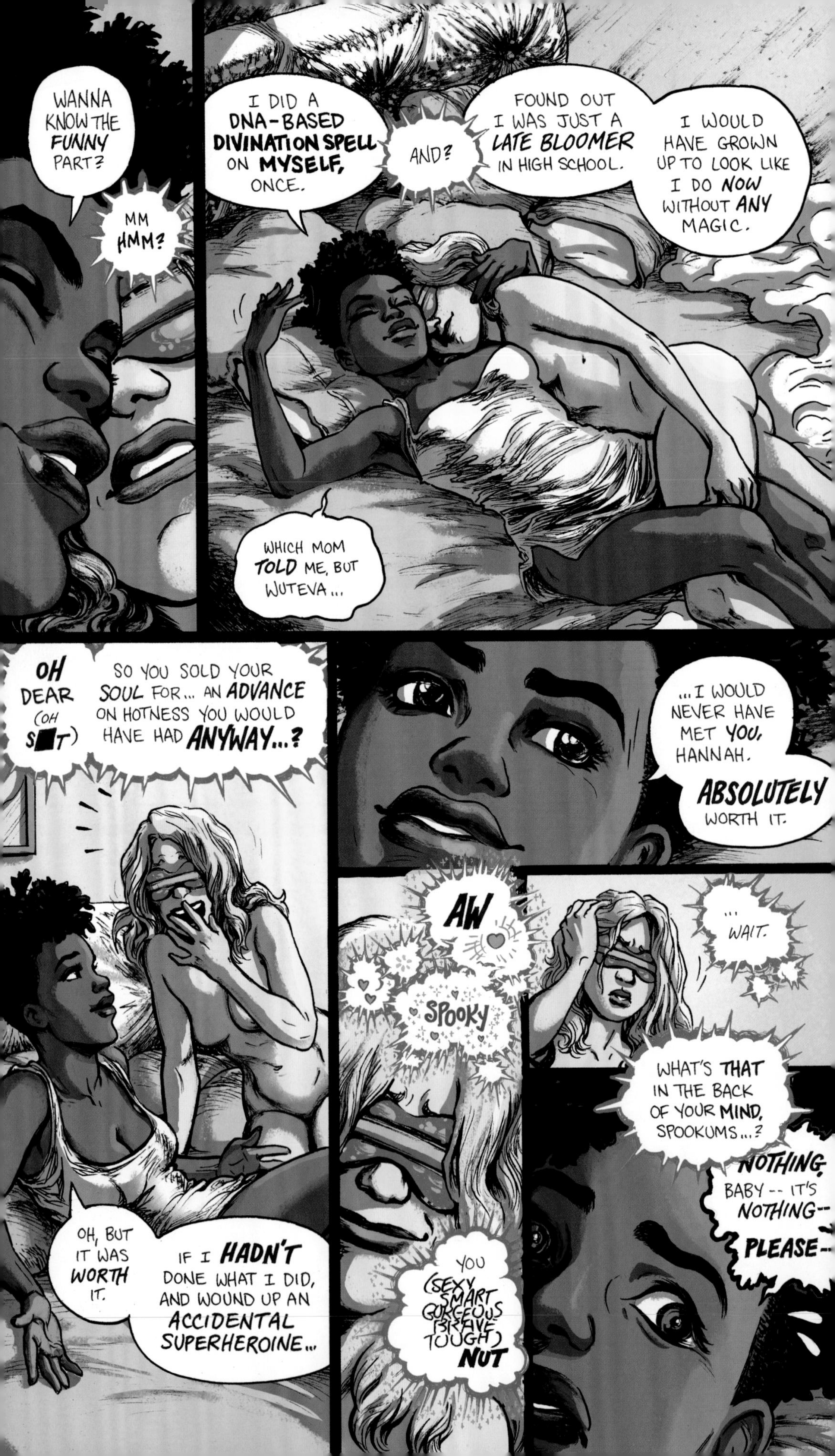
WANNA KNOW THE FUNNY PART?
MM HMM?
I DID A DNA-BASED DIVINATION SPELL ON MYSELF, ONCE.
AND?
FOUND OUT I WAS JUST A LATE BLOOMER IN HIGH SCHOOL.
I WOULD HAVE GROWN UP TO LOOK LIKE I DO NOW WITHOUT ANY MAGIC.
WHICH MOM TOLD ME, BUT WUTEVA...
OH DEAR (OH S[redacted]T)
SO YOU SOLD YOUR SOUL FOR... AN ADVANCE ON HOTNESS YOU WOULD HAVE HAD ANYWAY...?
OH, BUT IT WAS WORTH IT.
IF I HADN'T DONE WHAT I DID, AND WOUND UP AN ACCIDENTAL SUPERHEROINE...
...I WOULD NEVER HAVE MET YOU, HANNAH.
ABSOLUTELY WORTH IT.
AW
SPOOKY
YOU (SEXY SMART GORGEOUS BRAVE TOUGH) NUT
... WAIT.
WHAT'S THAT IN THE BACK OF YOUR MIND, SPOOKUMS...?
NOTHING, BABY -- IT'S NOTHING--
PLEASE--

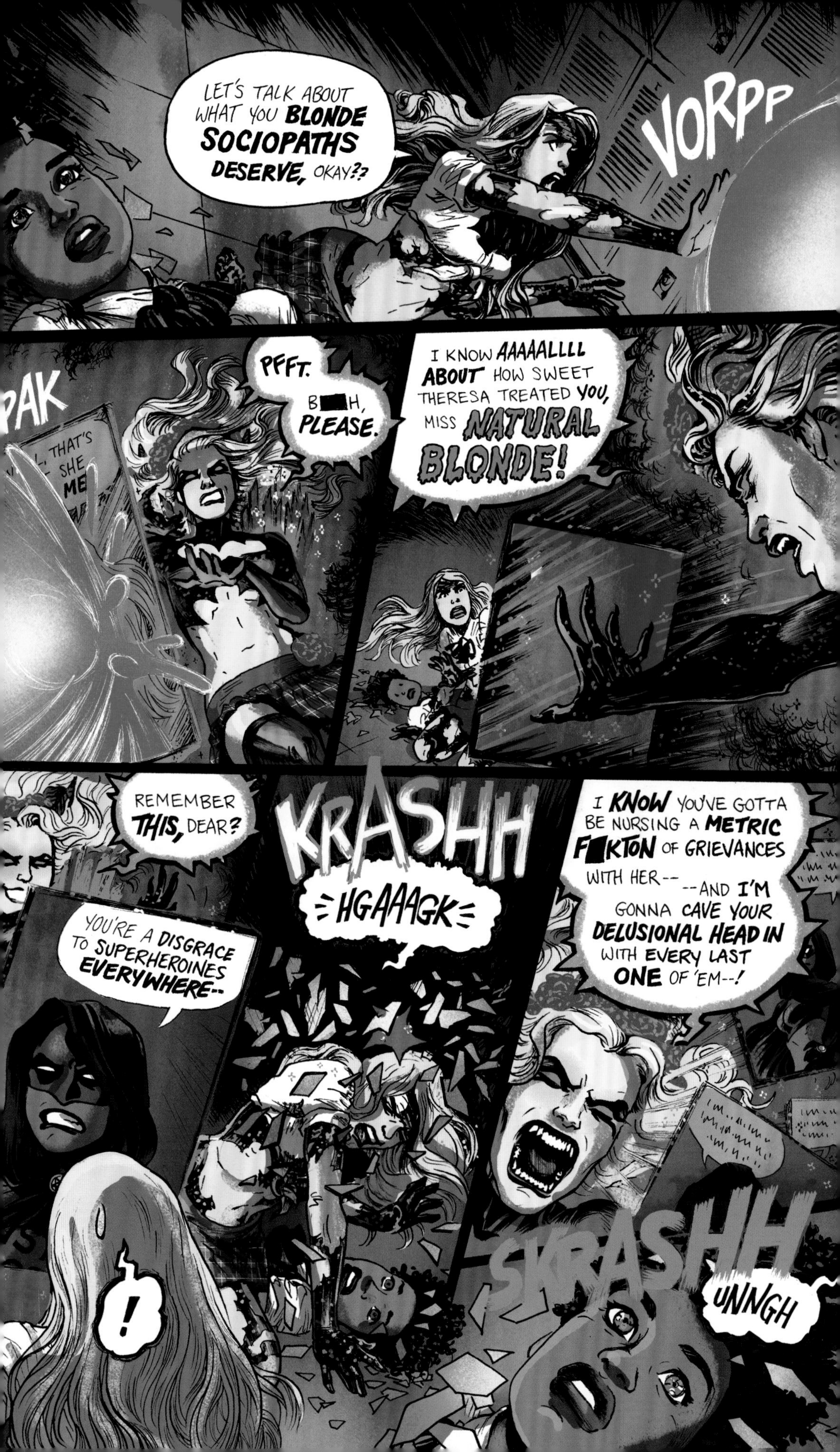
LET'S TALK ABOUT WHAT YOU BLONDE SOCIOPATHS DESERVE, OKAY??
VORPP
PAK
PFFT.
B[redacted]H, PLEASE.
I KNOW AAAAALLLL ABOUT HOW SWEET THERESA TREATED YOU, MISS NATURAL BLONDE!
REMEMBER THIS, DEAR?
YOU'RE A DISGRACE TO SUPERHEROINES EVERYWHERE--
KRASHH
HGAAAGK
!
I KNOW YOU'VE GOTTA BE NURSING A METRIC F[redacted]KTON OF GRIEVANCES WITH HER--
--AND I'M GONNA CAVE YOUR DELUSIONAL HEAD IN WITH EVERY LAST ONE OF 'EM--!
SKRASHH
UNNGH

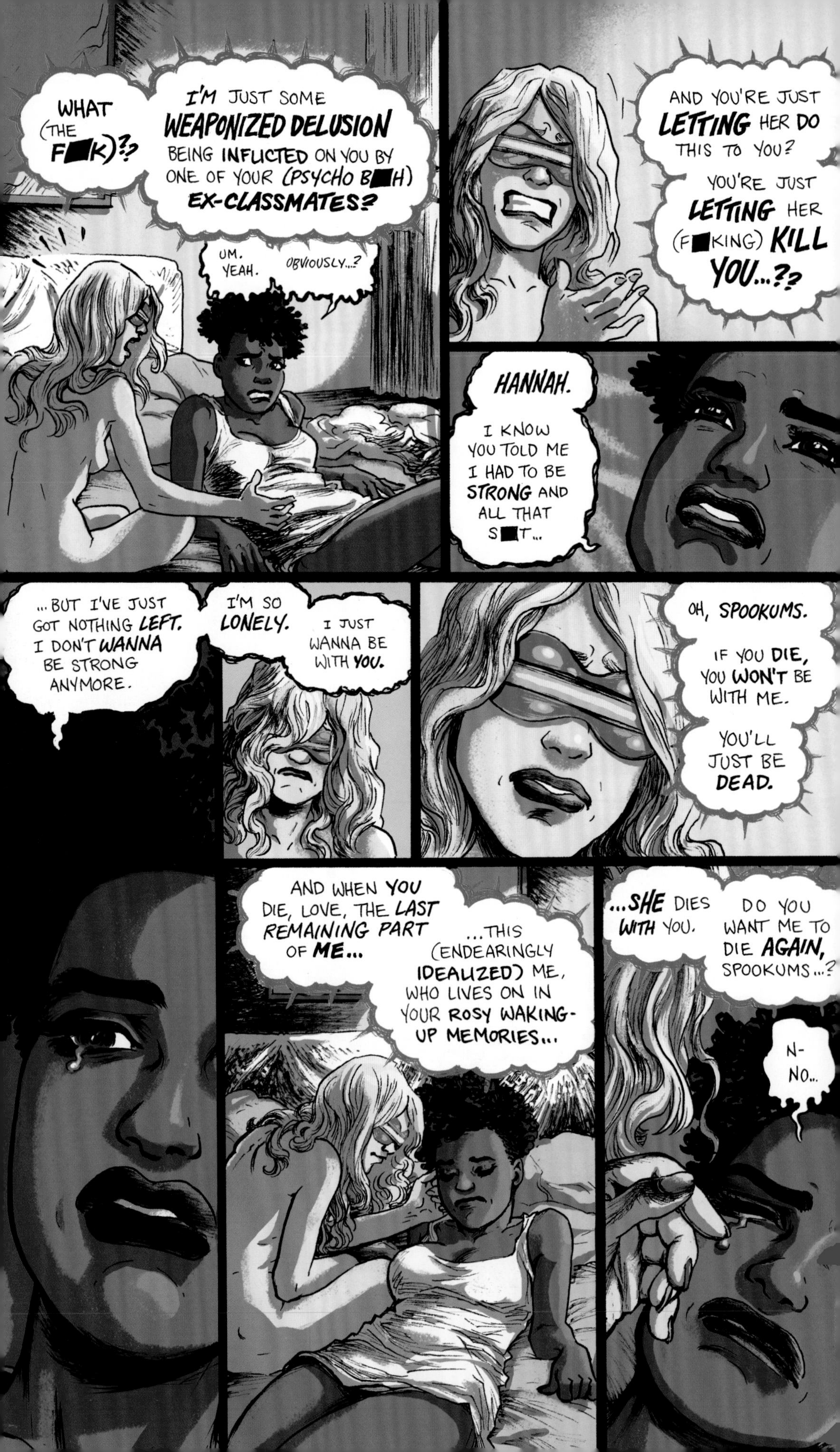

WHAT (THE F[redacted]K)??
I'M JUST SOME WEAPONIZED DELUSION BEING INFLICTED ON YOU BY ONE OF YOUR (PSYCHO B[redacted]H) EX-CLASSMATES?
UM. YEAH.
OBVIOUSLY...?
AND YOU'RE JUST LETTING HER DO THIS TO YOU?
YOU'RE JUST LETTING HER (F[redacted]KING) KILL YOU...??
HANNAH.
I KNOW YOU TOLD ME I HAD TO BE STRONG AND ALL THAT S[redacted]T...
...BUT I'VE JUST GOT NOTHING LEFT. I DON'T WANNA BE STRONG ANYMORE.
I'M SO LONELY.
I JUST WANNA BE WITH YOU.
OH, SPOOKUMS.
IF YOU DIE, YOU WON'T BE WITH ME.
YOU'LL JUST BE DEAD.
AND WHEN YOU DIE, LOVE, THE LAST REMAINING PART OF ME...
...THIS (ENDEARINGLY IDEALIZED) ME, WHO LIVES ON IN YOUR ROSY WAKING-UP MEMORIES...
...SHE DIES WITH YOU.
DO YOU WANT ME TO DIE AGAIN, SPOOKUMS...?
N- NO...

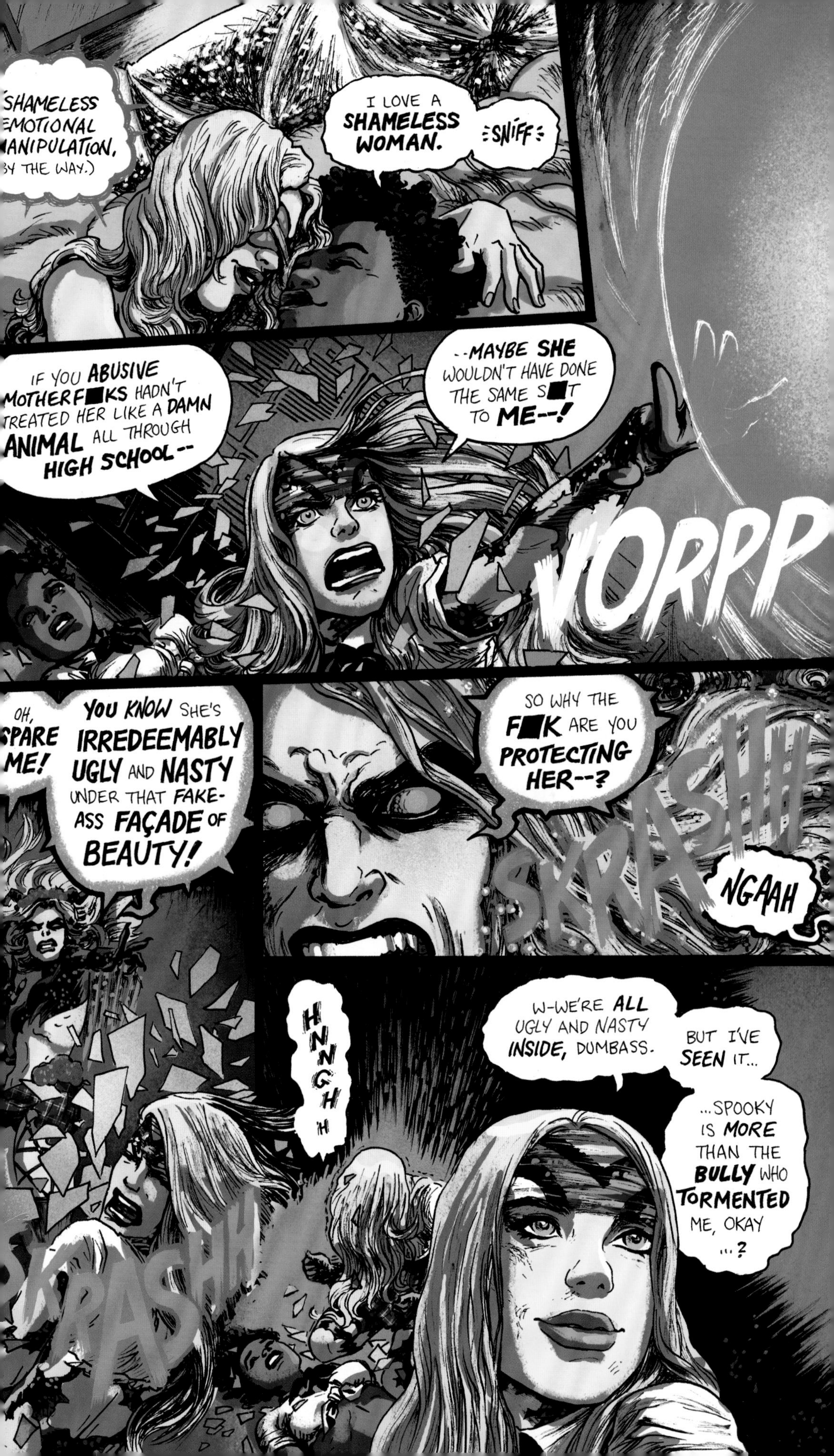

SHAMELESS EMOTIONAL ANIPULATION, Y THE WAY.)
I LOVE A SHAMELESS WOMAN.
SNIFF
IF YOU ABUSIVE MOTHERF[redacted]KS HADN'T TREATED HER LIKE A DAMN ANIMAL ALL THROUGH HIGH SCHOOL--
--MAYBE SHE WOULDN'T HAVE DONE THE SAME S[redacted]T TO ME--!
VORPP
OH, SPARE ME!
YOU KNOW SHE'S IRREDEEMABLY UGLY AND NASTY UNDER THAT FAKE-ASS FAÇADE OF BEAUTY!
SO WHY THE F[redacted]K ARE YOU PROTECTING HER--?
SKRASHH
NGAAH
HNNGHH
W-WE'RE ALL UGLY AND NASTY INSIDE, DUMBASS.
BUT I'VE SEEN IT...
...SPOOKY IS MORE THAN THE BULLY WHO TORMENTED ME, OKAY ...?
KRASHH

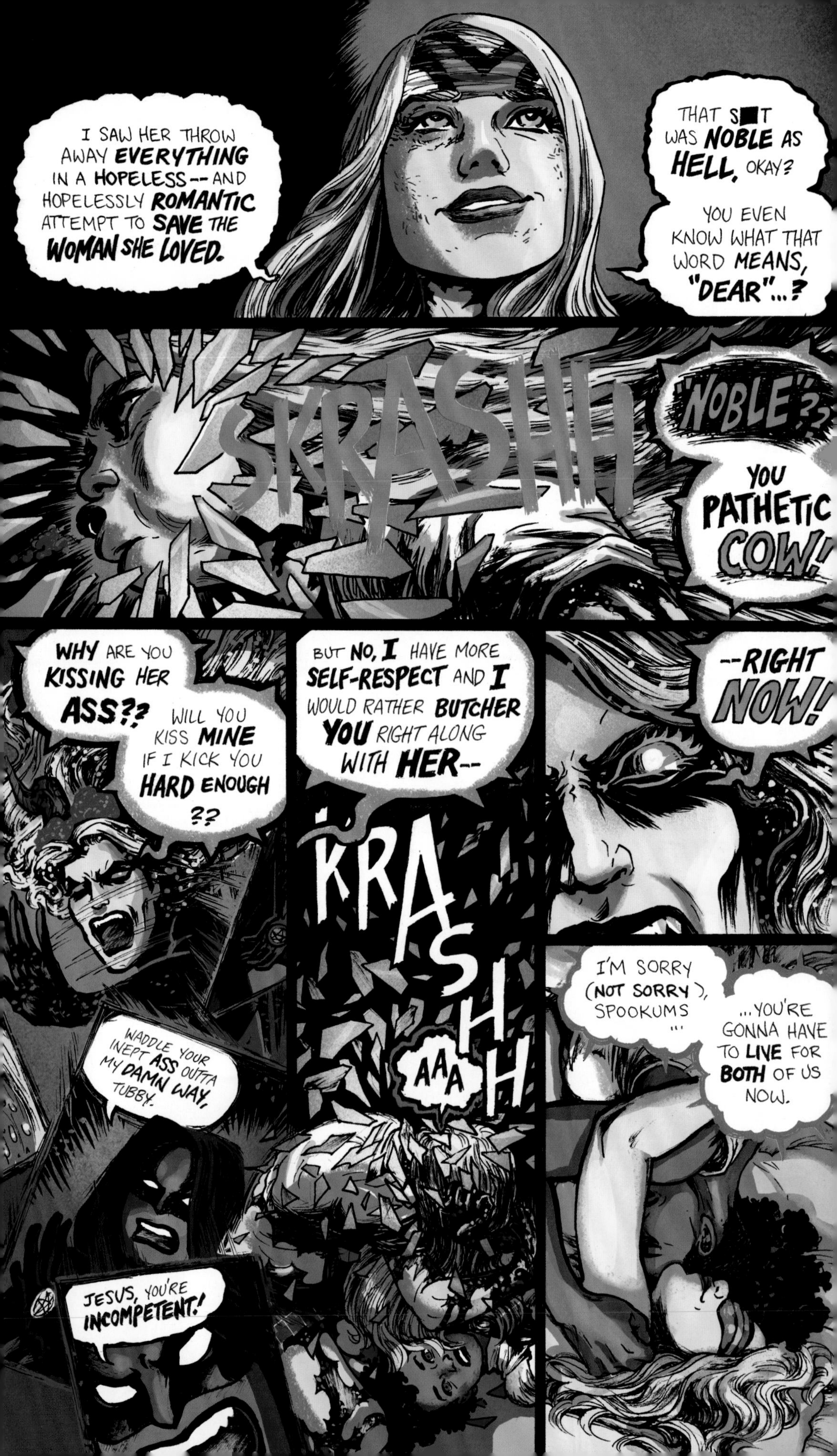
I SAW HER THROW AWAY EVERYTHING IN A HOPELESS -- AND HOPELESSLY ROMANTIC ATTEMPT TO SAVE THE WOMAN SHE LOVED.
THAT S[redacted]T WAS NOBLE AS HELL, OKAY?
YOU EVEN KNOW WHAT THAT WORD MEANS, "DEAR"...?
SKRASHH
"NOBLE"??
YOU PATHETIC COW!
WHY ARE YOU KISSING HER ASS??
WILL YOU KISS MINE IF I KICK YOU HARD ENOUGH ??
BUT NO, I HAVE MORE SELF-RESPECT AND I WOULD RATHER BUTCHER YOU RIGHT ALONG WITH HER--
--RIGHT NOW!
KRASHH
AAA
WADDLE YOUR INEPT ASS OUTTA MY DAMN WAY, TUBBY.
JESUS, YOU'RE INCOMPETENT!
I'M SORRY (NOT SORRY), SPOOKUMS ...
...YOU'RE GONNA HAVE TO LIVE FOR BOTH OF US NOW.

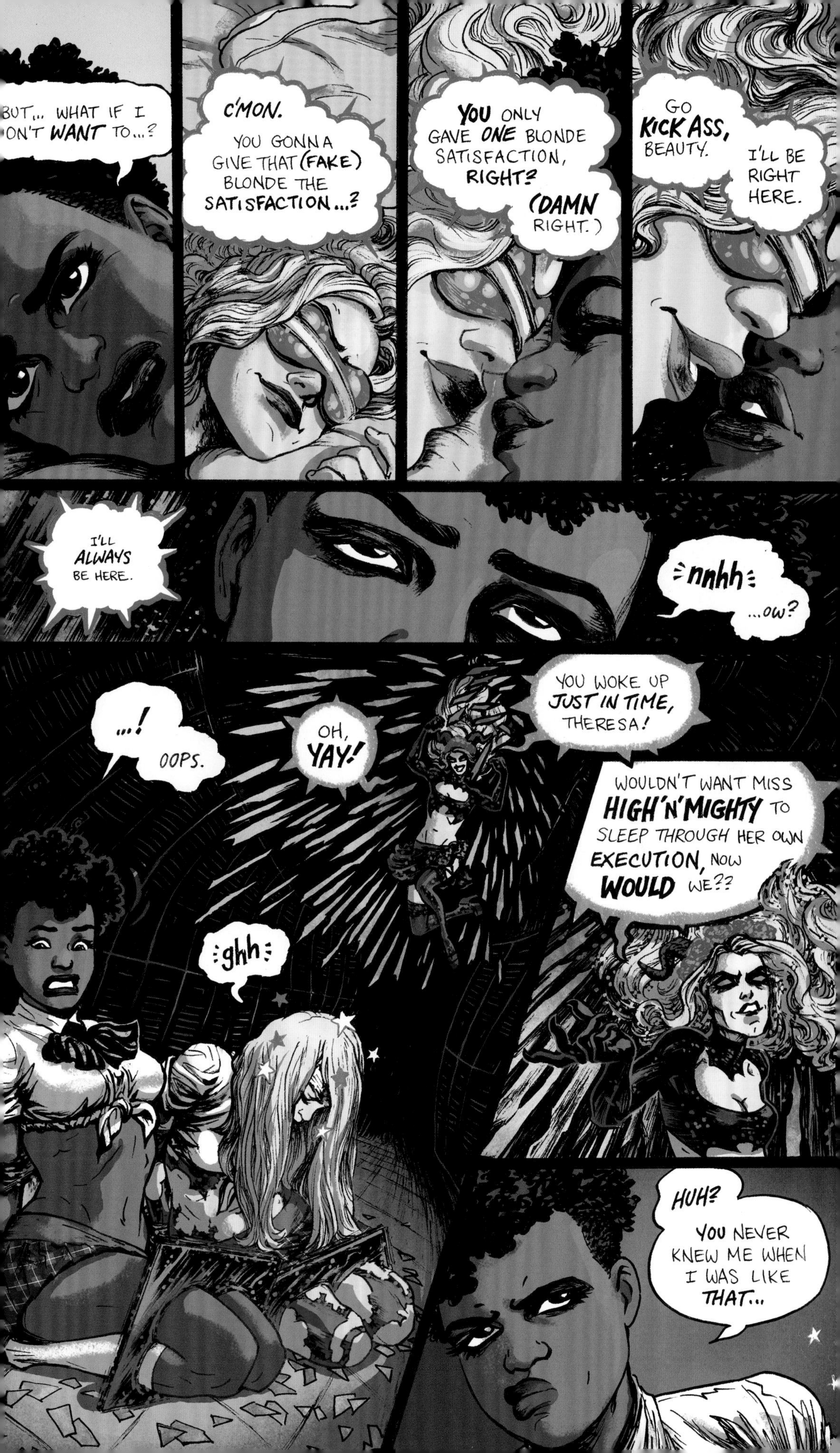
BUT... WHAT IF I ON'T WANT TO...?
C'MON.
YOU GONNA GIVE THAT (FAKE) BLONDE THE SATISFACTION...?
YOU ONLY GAVE ONE BLONDE SATISFACTION, RIGHT?
(DAMN RIGHT.)
GO KICK ASS, BEAUTY.
I'LL BE RIGHT HERE.
I'LL ALWAYS BE HERE.
nnhh
...ow?
...!
OOPS.
OH, YAY!
YOU WOKE UP JUST IN TIME, THERESA!
WOULDN'T WANT MISS HIGH'N'MIGHTY TO SLEEP THROUGH HER OWN EXECUTION, NOW WOULD WE??
ghh
HUH?
YOU NEVER KNEW ME WHEN I WAS LIKE THAT...

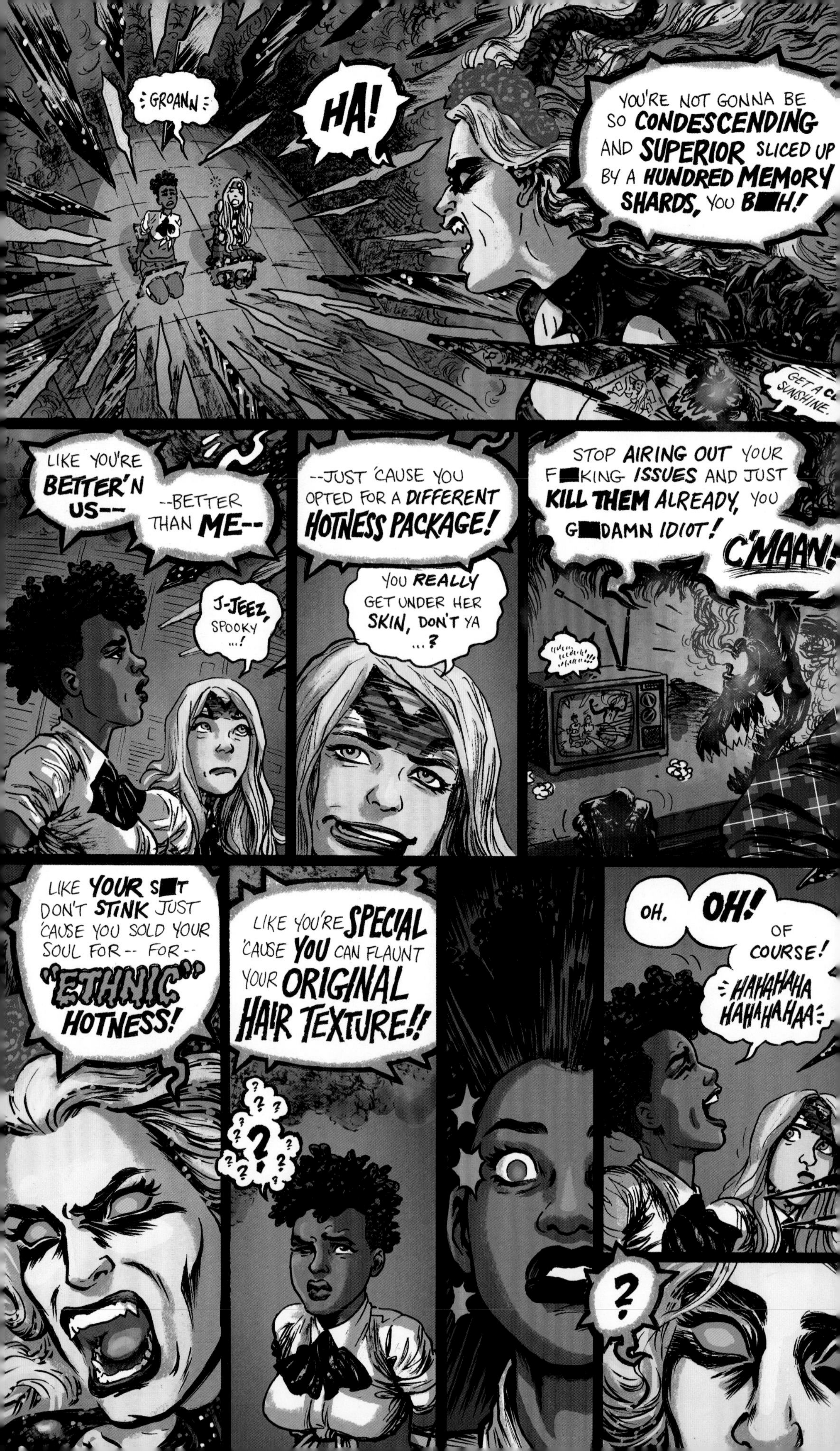
GROANN
HA!
YOU'RE NOT GONNA BE SO CONDESCENDING AND SUPERIOR SLICED UP BY A HUNDRED MEMORY SHARDS, YOU B[redacted]H!
SUNSHINE.
LIKE YOU'RE BETTER'N US--
--BETTER THAN ME--
J-JEEZ, SPOOKY ...!
--JUST 'CAUSE YOU OPTED FOR A DIFFERENT HOTNESS PACKAGE!
YOU REALLY GET UNDER HER SKIN, DON'T YA ...?
STOP AIRING OUT YOUR F[redacted]KING ISSUES AND JUST KILL THEM ALREADY, YOU G[redacted]DAMN IDIOT!
C'MAAN!
LIKE YOUR S[redacted]T DON'T STINK JUST 'CAUSE YOU SOLD YOUR SOUL FOR-- FOR--
"ETHNIC" HOTNESS!
LIKE YOU'RE SPECIAL 'CAUSE YOU CAN FLAUNT YOUR ORIGINAL HAIR TEXTURE!!
?
OH. OH!
OF COURSE!
HAHAHAHA HAHAHAHAA
?

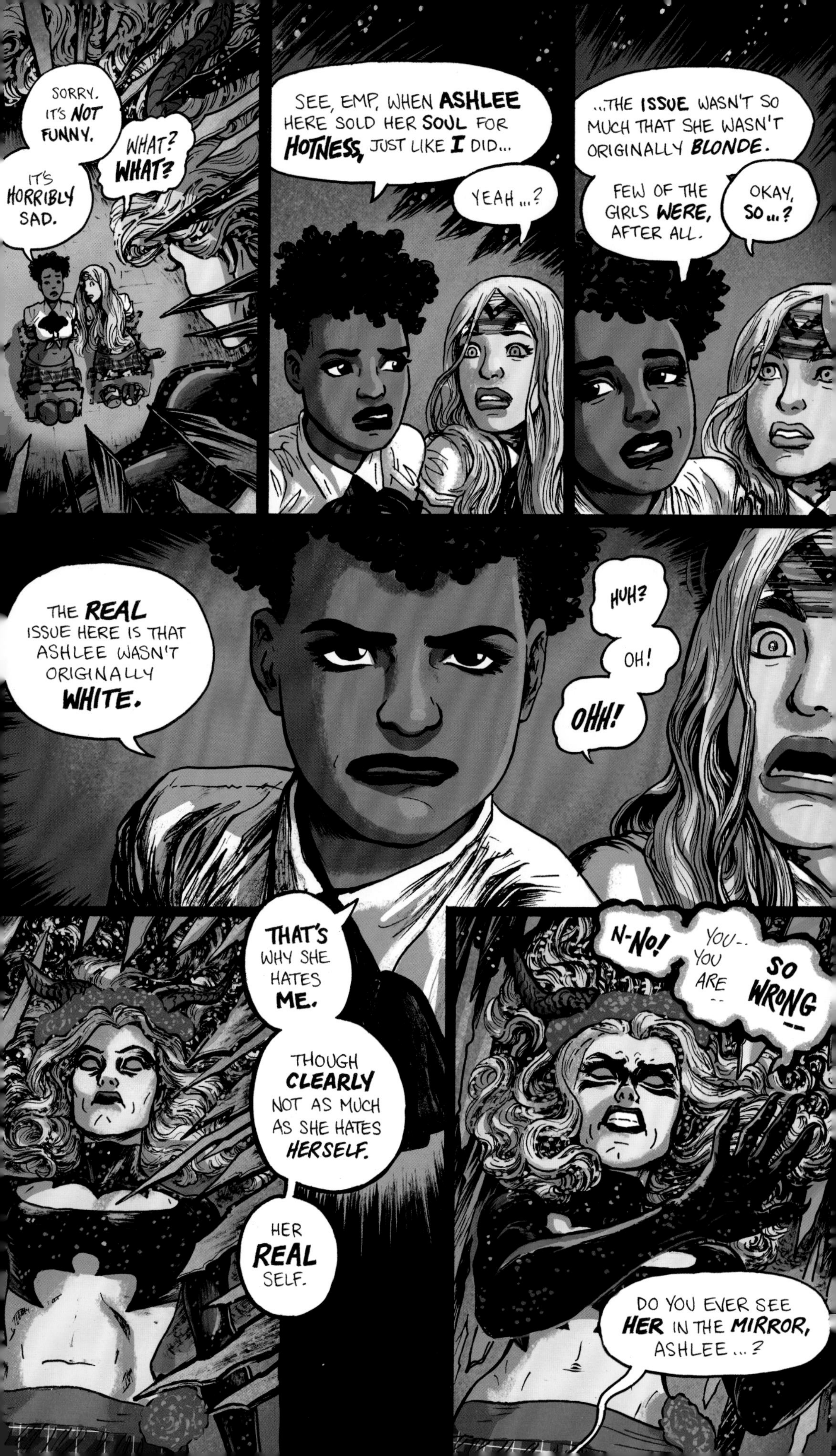

SORRY. IT'S NOT FUNNY.
IT'S HORRIBLY SAD.
WHAT? WHAT?
SEE, EMP, WHEN ASHLEE HERE SOLD HER SOUL FOR HOTNESS, JUST LIKE I DID...
YEAH...?
...THE ISSUE WASN'T SO MUCH THAT SHE WASN'T ORIGINALLY BLONDE.
FEW OF THE GIRLS WERE, AFTER ALL.
OKAY, SO...?
THE REAL ISSUE HERE IS THAT ASHLEE WASN'T ORIGINALLY WHITE.
HUH?
OH!
OHH!
THAT'S WHY SHE HATES ME.
THOUGH CLEARLY NOT AS MUCH AS SHE HATES HERSELF.
HER REAL SELF.
N-NO!
YOU-- YOU ARE --
SO WRONG --
DO YOU EVER SEE HER IN THE MIRROR, ASHLEE...?

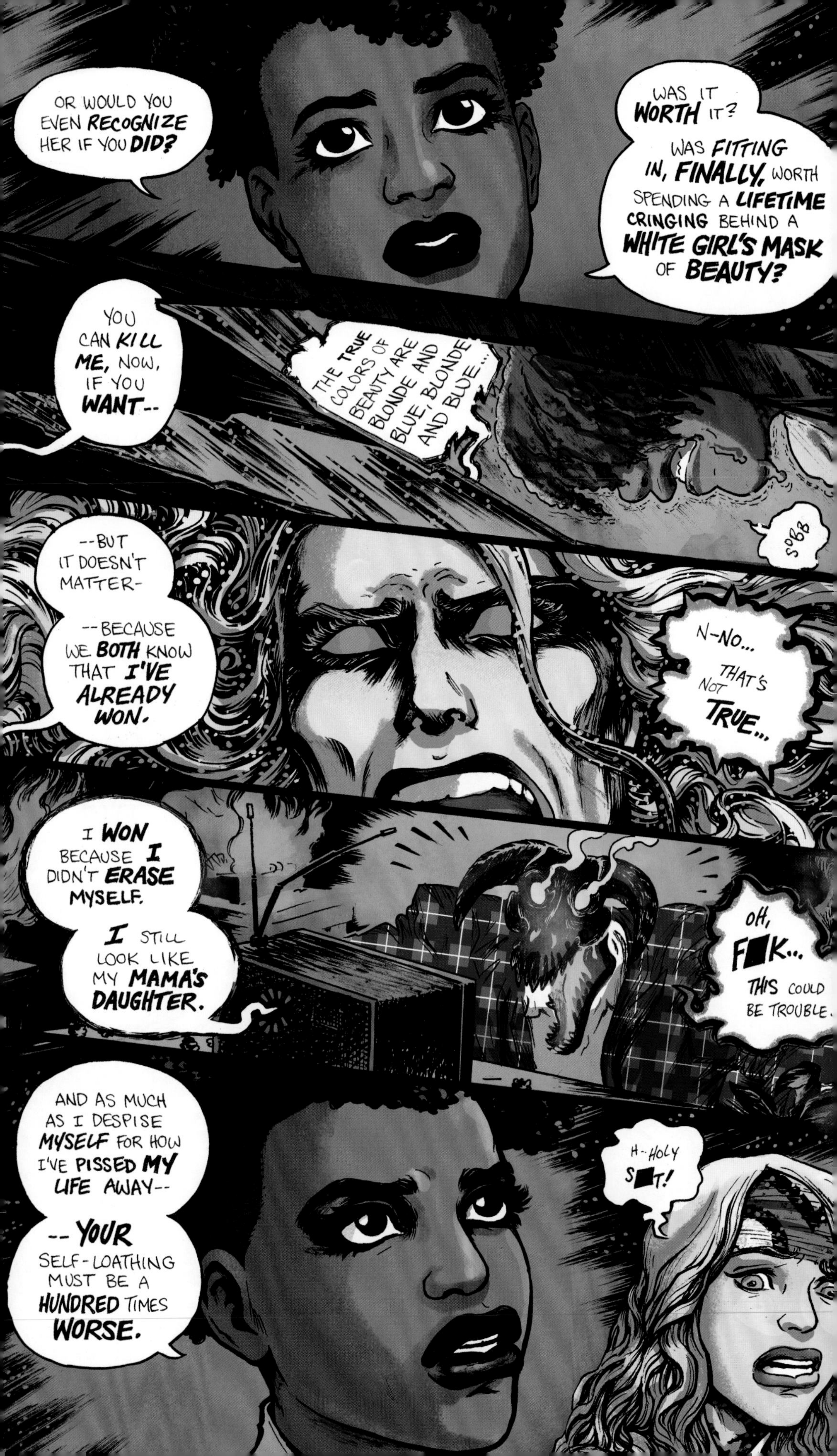
OR WOULD YOU EVEN RECOGNIZE HER IF YOU DID?
WAS IT WORTH IT?
WAS FITTING IN, FINALLY, WORTH SPENDING A LIFETIME CRINGING BEHIND A WHITE GIRL'S MASK OF BEAUTY?
YOU CAN KILL ME, NOW, IF YOU WANT--
THE TRUE COLORS OF BEAUTY ARE BLONDE AND BLUE, BLONDE AND BLUE...
SOBB
--BUT IT DOESN'T MATTER-
--BECAUSE WE BOTH KNOW THAT I'VE ALREADY WON.
N-NO... THAT'S NOT TRUE...
I WON BECAUSE I DIDN'T ERASE MYSELF.
I STILL LOOK LIKE MY MAMA'S DAUGHTER.
OH, F[redacted]K... THIS COULD BE TROUBLE.
AND AS MUCH AS I DESPISE MYSELF FOR HOW I'VE PISSED MY LIFE AWAY--
--YOUR SELF-LOATHING MUST BE A HUNDRED TIMES WORSE.
H-HOLY S[redacted]T!

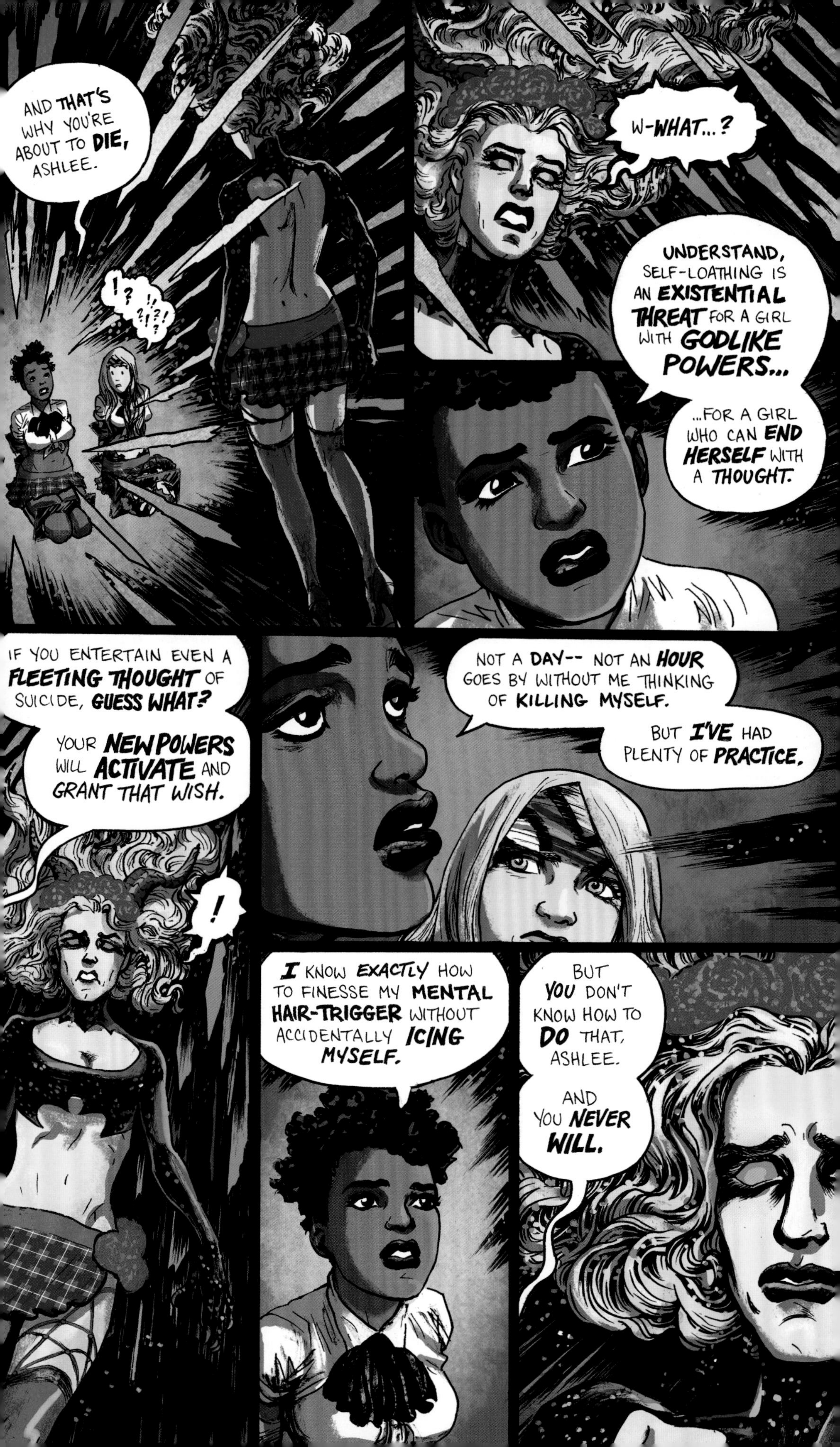
AND THAT'S WHY YOU'RE ABOUT TO DIE, ASHLEE.
!? !?!?!
W-WHAT...?
UNDERSTAND, SELF-LOATHING IS AN EXISTENTIAL THREAT FOR A GIRL WITH GODLIKE POWERS...
...FOR A GIRL WHO CAN END HERSELF WITH A THOUGHT.
IF YOU ENTERTAIN EVEN A FLEETING THOUGHT OF SUICIDE, GUESS WHAT?
YOUR NEW POWERS WILL ACTIVATE AND GRANT THAT WISH.
!
NOT A DAY-- NOT AN HOUR GOES BY WITHOUT ME THINKING OF KILLING MYSELF.
BUT I'VE HAD PLENTY OF PRACTICE.
I KNOW EXACTLY HOW TO FINESSE MY MENTAL HAIR-TRIGGER WITHOUT ACCIDENTALLY ICING MYSELF.
BUT YOU DON'T KNOW HOW TO DO THAT, ASHLEE.
AND YOU NEVER WILL.

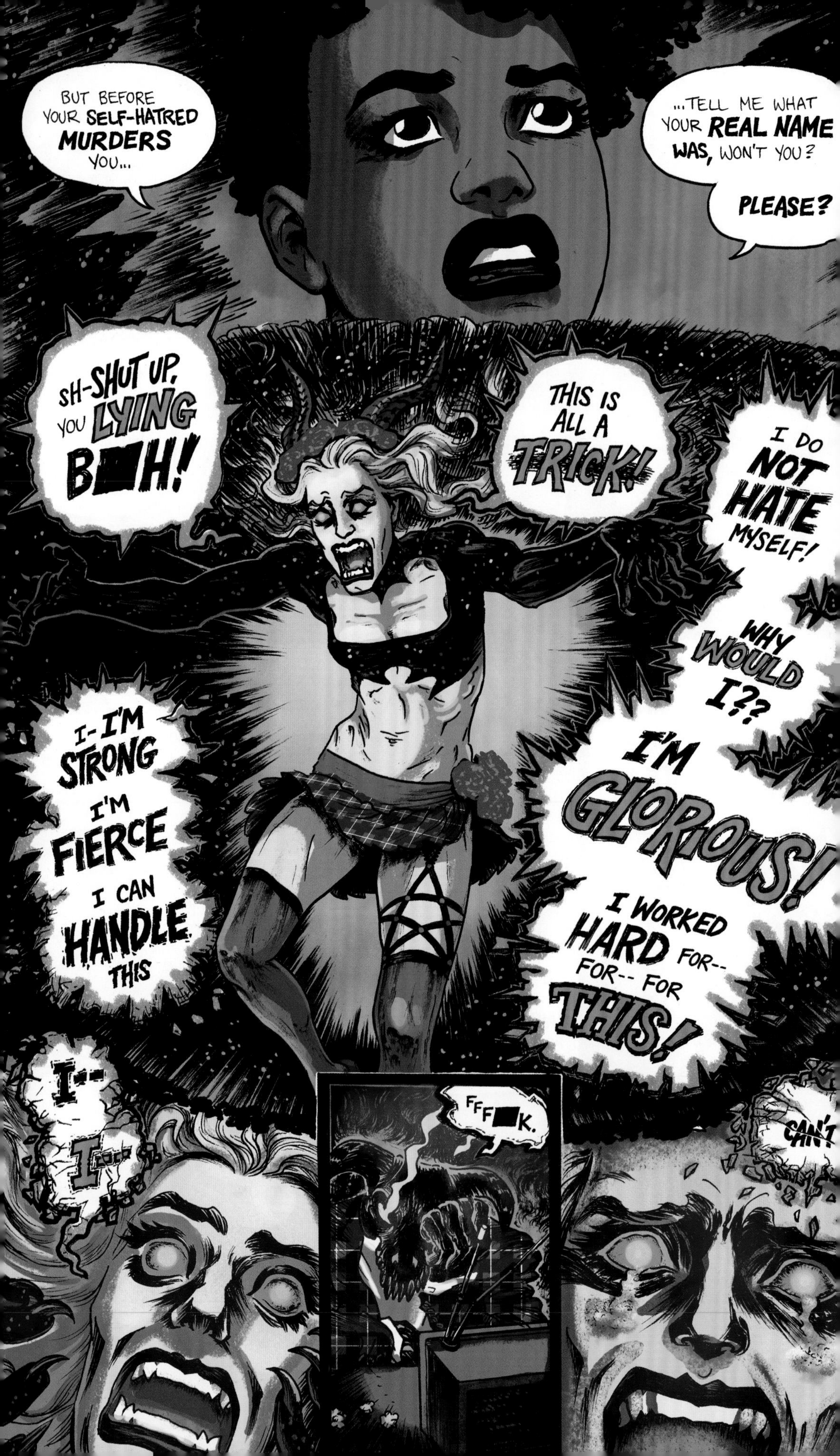
BUT BEFORE YOUR SELF-HATRED MURDERS YOU...
...TELL ME WHAT YOUR REAL NAME WAS, WON'T YOU?
PLEASE?
SH-SHUT UP, YOU LYING B[redacted]H!
THIS IS ALL A TRICK!
I DO NOT HATE MYSELF!
WHY WOULD I??
I-I'M STRONG
I'M FIERCE
I CAN HANDLE THIS
I'M GLORIOUS!
I WORKED HARD FOR-- FOR-- FOR THIS!
I--
I--
FFF[redacted]K.
CAN'T

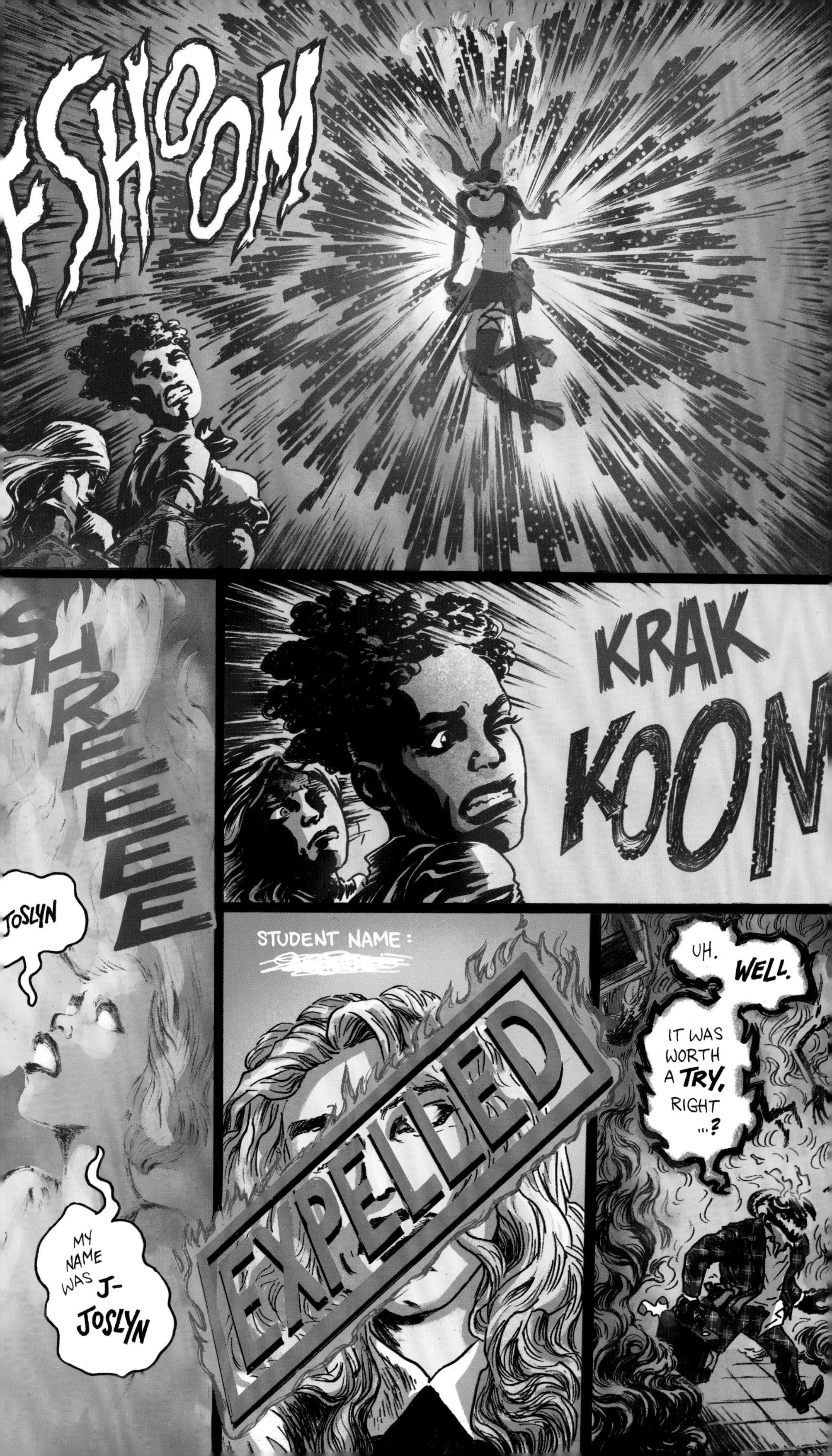
FSHOOM
SHREEEEE
KRAK
KOON
JOSLYN
MY NAME WAS J- JOSLYN
STUDENT NAME:
EXPELLED
UH. WELL.
IT WAS WORTH A TRY, RIGHT ...?

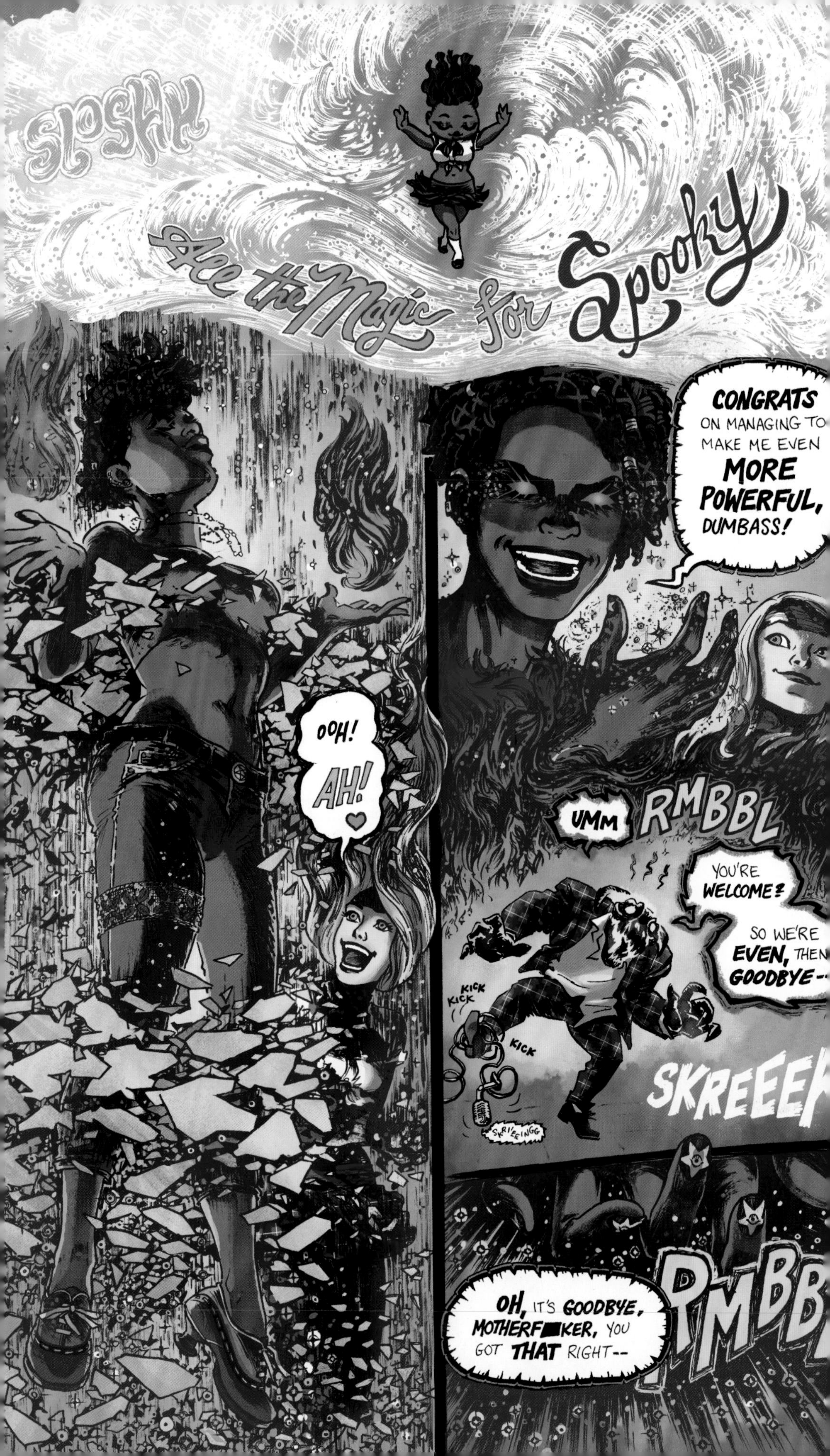
SLOSHH
All the Magic for Spooky
OOH!
AH! ♥
CONGRATS ON MANAGING TO MAKE ME EVEN MORE POWERFUL, DUMBASS!
UMM
RMBBL
YOU'RE WELCOME?
SO WE'RE EVEN, THEN GOODBYE--
KICK KICK
KICK
SKREEEE
SKRIEEINGG
OH, IT'S GOODBYE, MOTHERF■KER, YOU GOT THAT RIGHT--
RMBB

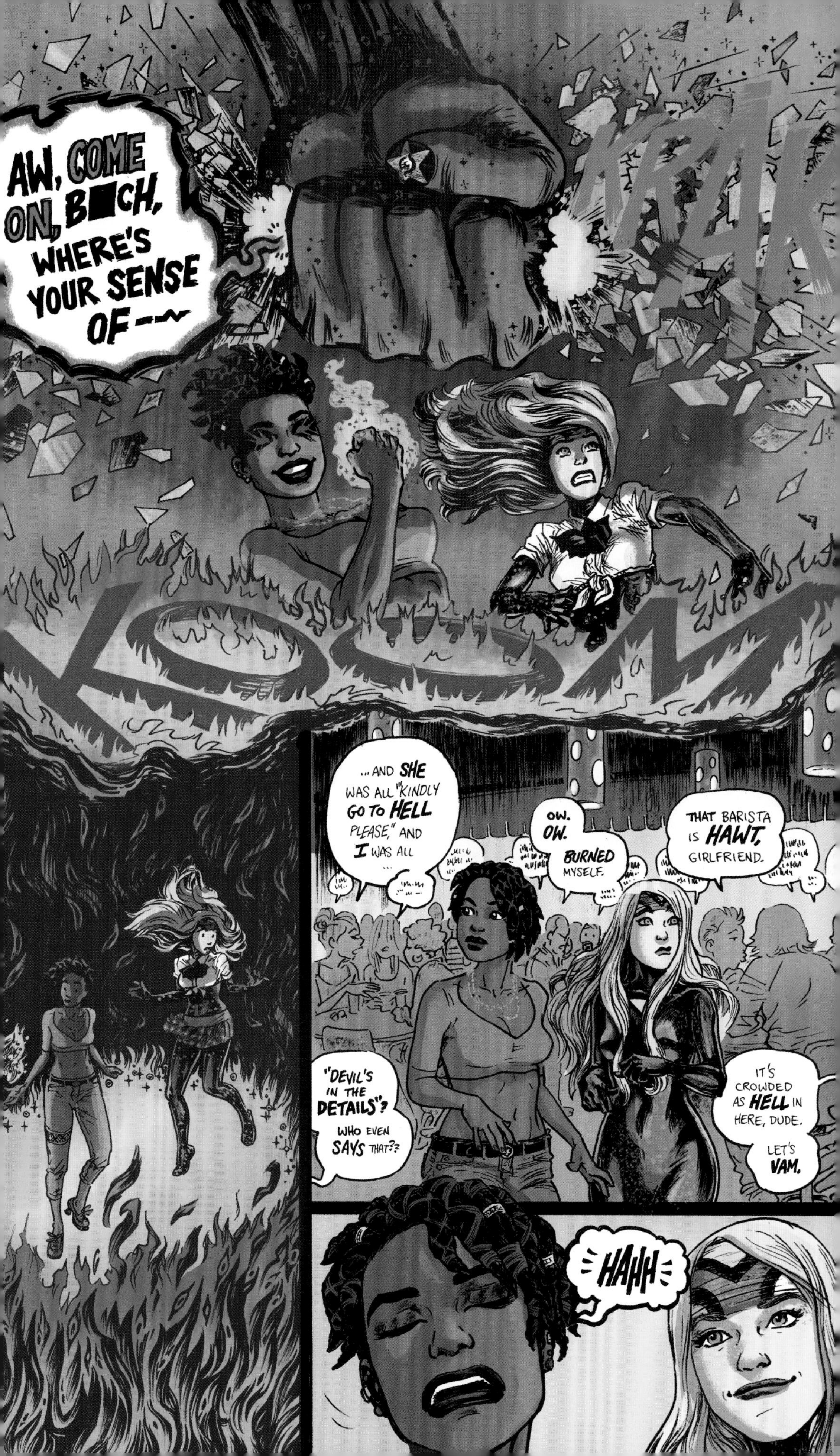
AW, COME ON, B[redacted]CH, WHERE'S YOUR SENSE OF--~
KRAK
KOOM
...AND SHE WAS ALL "KINDLY GO TO HELL PLEASE," AND I WAS ALL ...
OW. OW. BURNED MYSELF.
THAT BARISTA IS HAWT, GIRLFRIEND.
"DEVIL'S IN THE DETAILS"? WHO EVEN SAYS THAT?
IT'S CROWDED AS HELL IN HERE, DUDE.
LET'S VAM.
HAHH

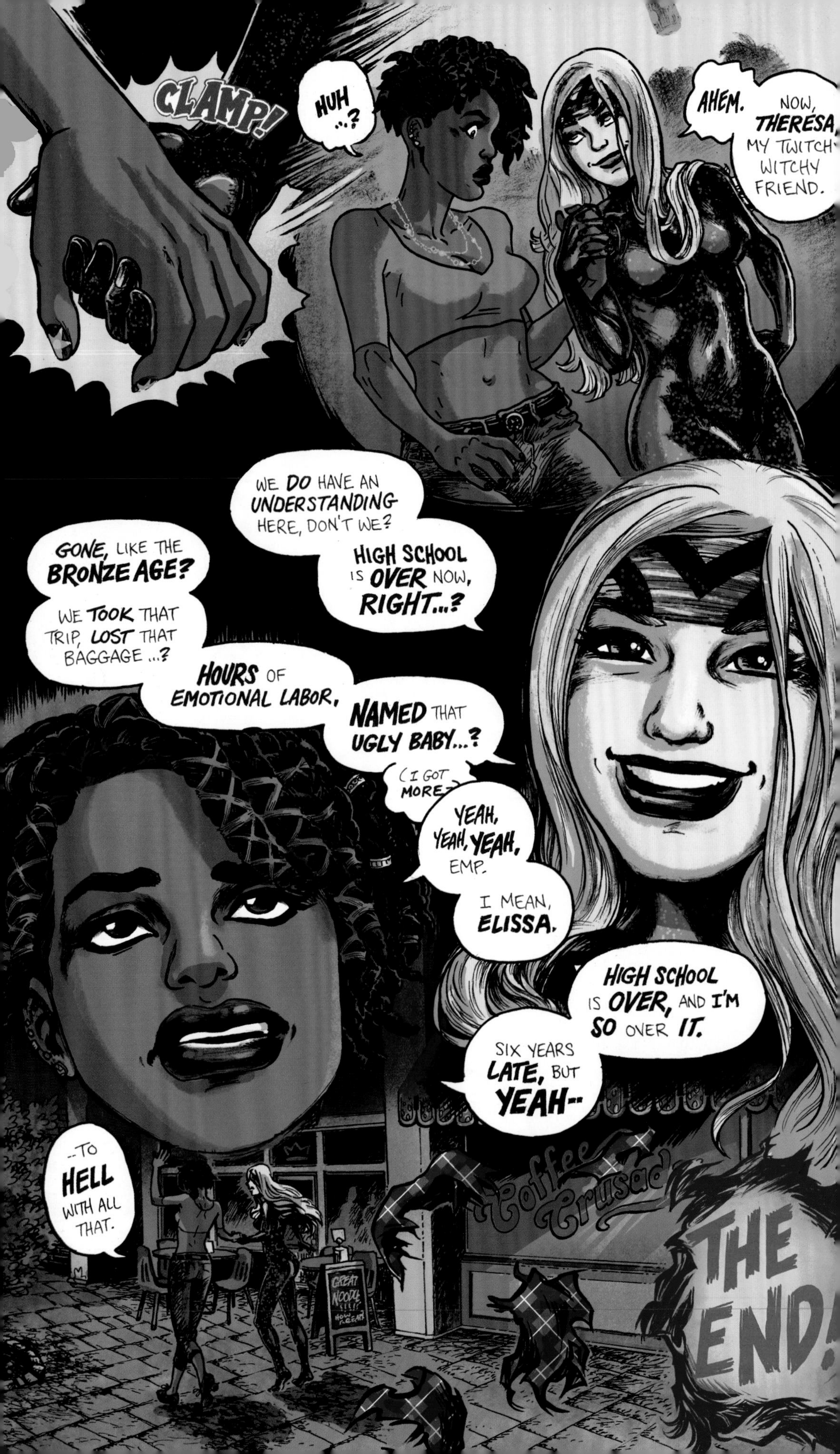
CLAMP!
HUH ...?
AHEM. NOW, THERESA MY TWITCH WITCHY FRIEND.
WE DO HAVE AN UNDERSTANDING HERE, DON'T WE?
HIGH SCHOOL IS OVER NOW, RIGHT...?
GONE, LIKE THE BRONZE AGE?
WE TOOK THAT TRIP, LOST THAT BAGGAGE ...?
HOURS OF EMOTIONAL LABOR,
NAMED THAT UGLY BABY...?
(I GOT MORE--)
YEAH, YEAH, YEAH, EMP.
I MEAN, ELISSA.
HIGH SCHOOL IS OVER, AND I'M SO OVER IT.
SIX YEARS LATE, BUT YEAH--
--TO HELL WITH ALL THAT.
Coffee Crusad
THE END!

GALLERY

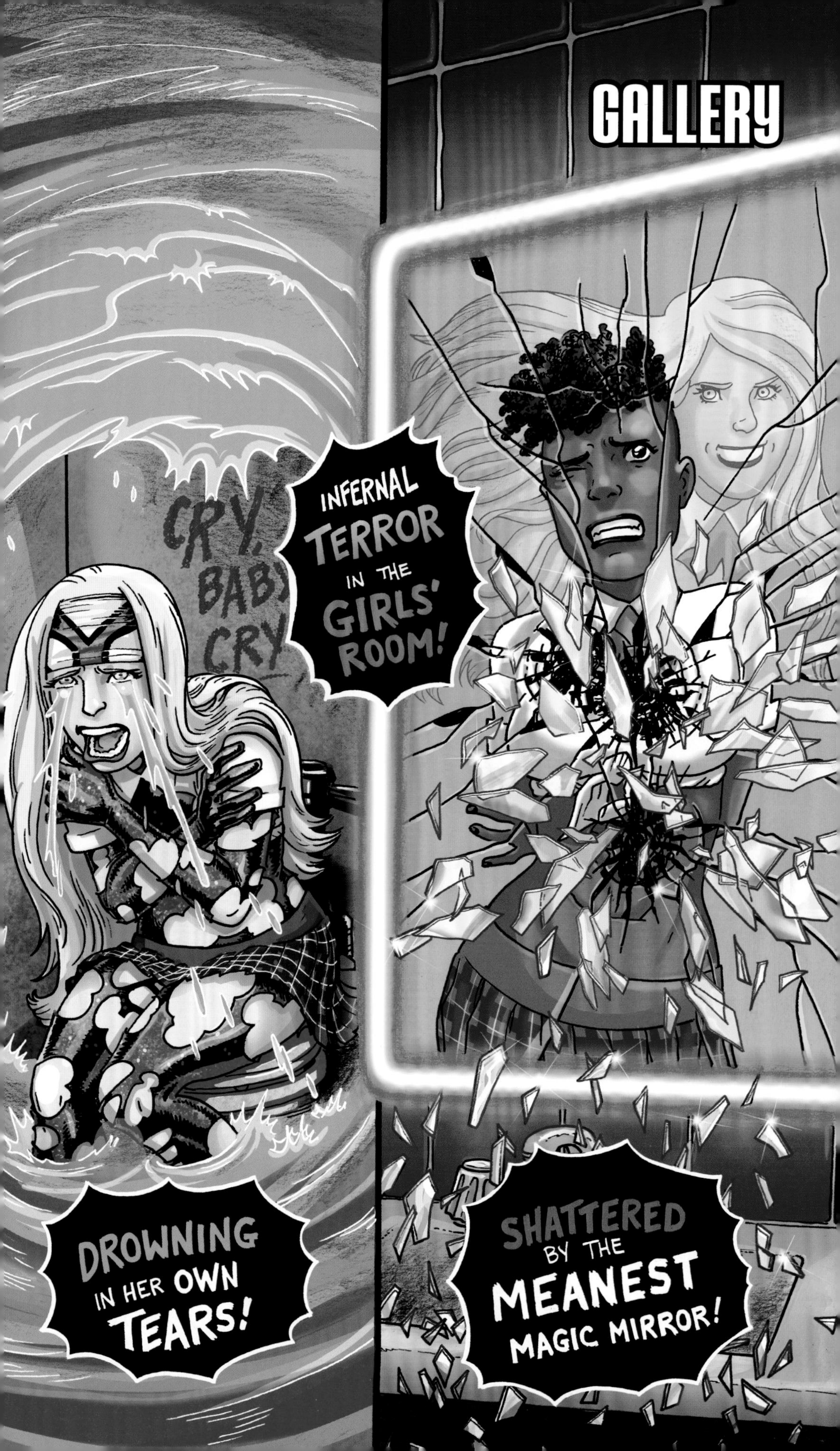
CRY, BABY CRY
INFERNAL TERROR IN THE GIRLS' ROOM!
DROWNING IN HER OWN TEARS!
SHATTERED BY THE MEANEST MAGIC MIRROR!

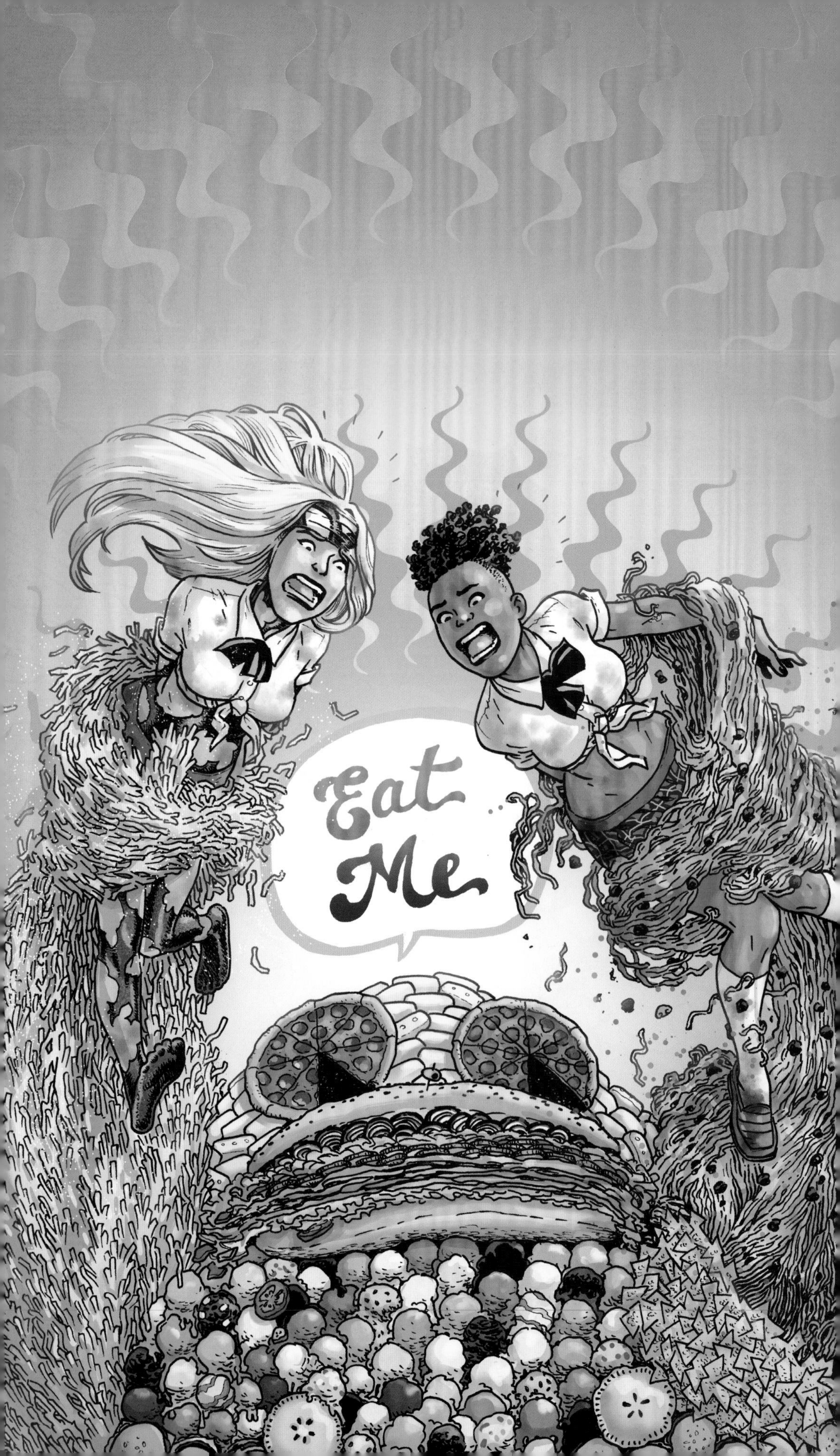
Eat Me

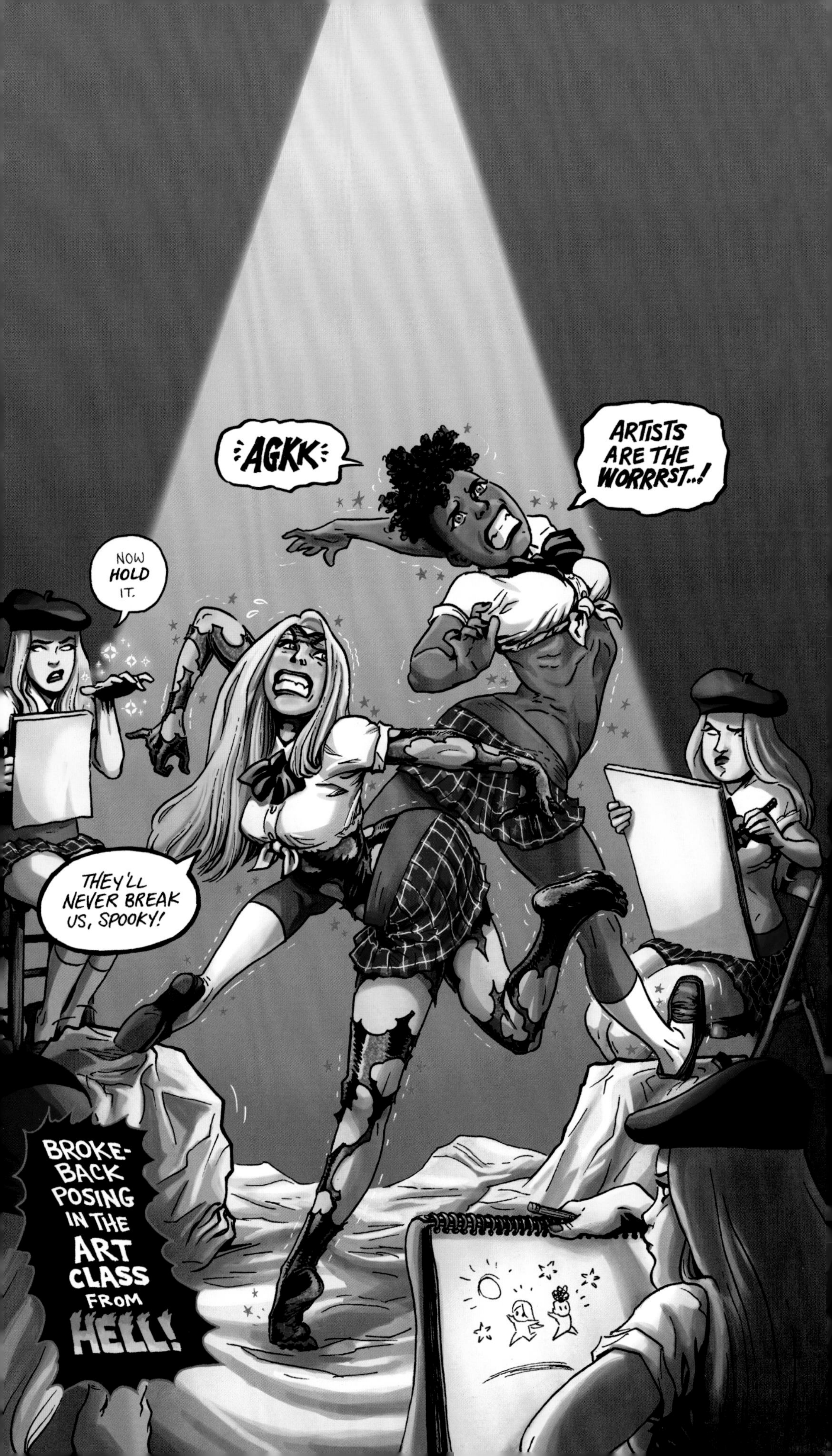
AGKK
ARTISTS ARE THE WORRRST..!
NOW HOLD IT.
THEY'LL NEVER BREAK US, SPOOKY!
BROKE-BACK POSING IN THE ART CLASS FROM HELL!

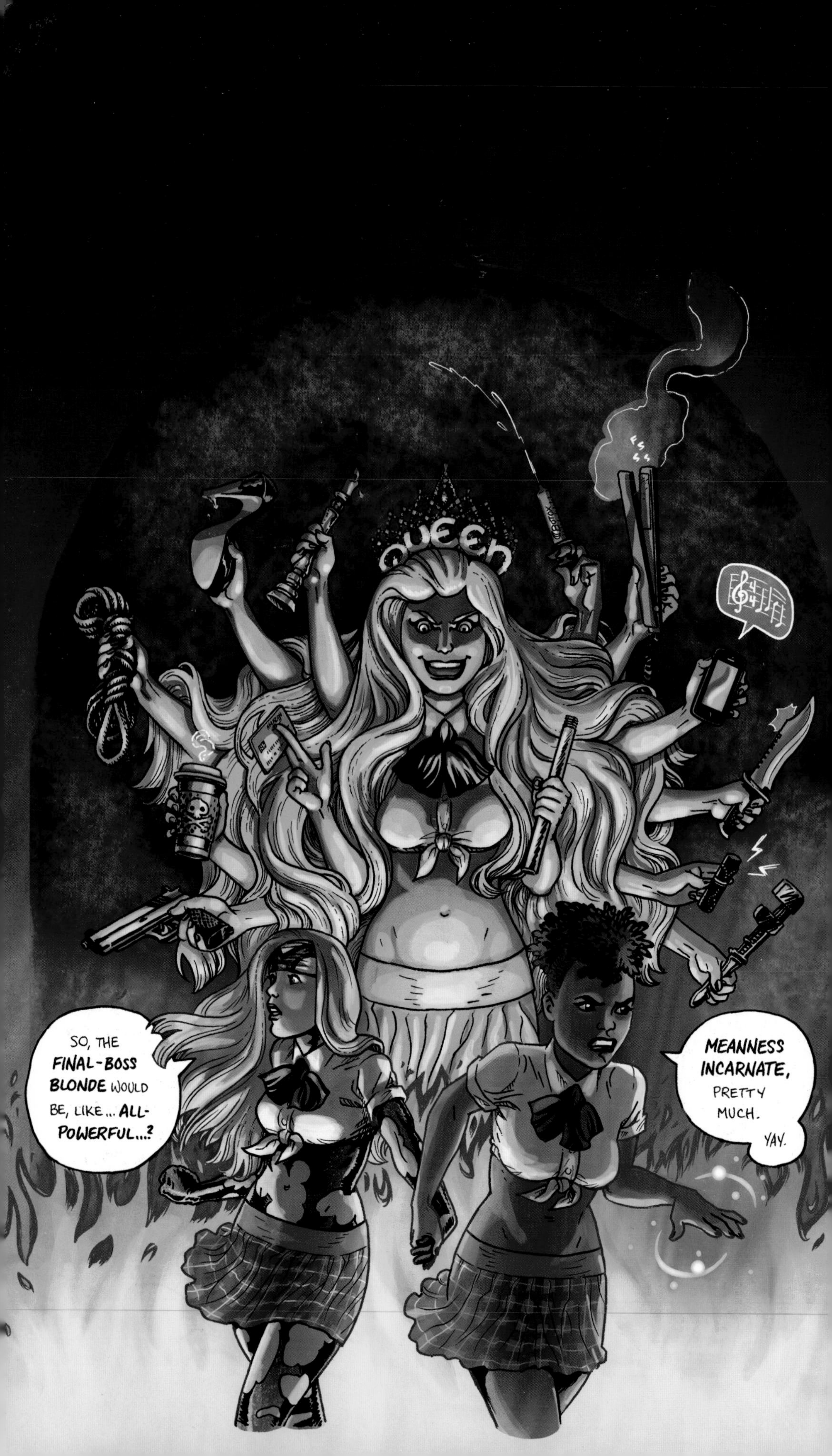
QUEEN
BOTOX
SO, THE FINAL-BOSS BLONDE WOULD BE, LIKE... ALL-POWERFUL...?
MEANNESS INCARNATE, PRETTY MUCH.
YAY.